Welcome to
WORLD FOOTBALL ANNUAL

When Brazil and Croatia kicked off the FIFA World Cup finals in Sao Paulo on 12 June 2014, not even the most optimistic football fan expected the engrossing totality of the drama ahead.

Nothing cautious, nothing negative. Instead, day after day, match after match, the 32 contenders generated excitement and entertainment beyond anything previously seen at the game's great showpiece.

The tournament produced a record 136 goals in the group stage and a record-equalling 171 across the entire 64 matches. These included 37 in the first four days, the most exciting start to the finals since 1958. Also the finals saw the lowest number of red cards (10) in 28 years and the fewest yellows (177) since 1990.

Not all the records were happy ones. Hosts Brazil suffered the worst defeat in their history by 7-1 in the semi-finals and it was small consolation that Germany, their conquerors, would become the first European winners of the FIFA World Cup in the Americas.

Yet the FIFA World Cup is merely the foreground of a great football landscape whose many aspects feature in the World Football Annual. Here are not only the FIFA World Cup finals but other major international football tournaments such as the UEFA European Championship and the Copa America.

Much of the fascination and attraction of football is how a framework of individual brilliance contributes to the overall construction of a team. Hence the achievements of a Germany, an Argentina, a Holland and a Brazil are built on the individual contributions of a Gotze, a Messi, a Robben and a Neymar.

The 2014 FIFA World Cup actually kicked off on 15 June 2011, at the Ato Boldon Stadium in Couva, Trinidad and Tobago. Belize beat Montserrat 5-2 in the first of 824 qualifying ties. Deon McCauley of Belize wrote his name into football history with the first goal of the entire tournament, in the 24th minute.

Not until seven minutes from the end of extra time in the very final match did Mario Gotze conjure up the magnificent winning strike. But an awful lot of football took place in between those two goals, as these pages illustrate.

WORLD FOOTBALL ANNUAL

Imagine Publishing Ltd
Richmond House
33 Richmond Hill
Bournemouth
Dorset BH2 6EZ
☎ +44 (0) 1202 586200
Website: www.imagine-publishing.co.uk
Twitter: @Books_Imagine
Facebook: www.facebook.com/ImagineBookazines

Publishing Director
Aaron Asadi

Head of Design
Ross Andrews

Production Editor
Mike Hine

Senior Art Editor
Greg Whitaker

Written by
Keir Radnedge

Photographer
James Sheppard

Printed by
William Gibbons, 26 Planetary Road, Willenhall, West Midlands, WV13 3XT

Distributed in the UK, Eire & the Rest of the World by
Marketforce, Blue Fin Building, 110 Southwark Street, London, SE1 0SU
Tel 0203 148 3300 www.marketforce.co.uk

Distributed in Australia by
Network Services (a division of Bauer Media Group), Level 21 Civic Tower, 66-68 Goulburn Street,
Sydney, New South Wales 2000, Australia Tel +61 2 8667 5288

IMAGINE
PUBLISHING

⚽ CONTENTS

PART 1: FIFA WORLD CUP
ALL-TIME RECORDS

GERMANY, IN BRAZIL, became the fourth country to win the FIFA World Cup at least four times, the same as Italy. However, Brazil remain the record-holders, with five victories, inspired by superstars from Pele and Garrincha to Ronaldo and Ronaldinho. Argentina and Uruguay (two each) are the other South American winners, with past champions from Europe being England, France and Spain (one apiece). Germany's 2014 glory in Brazil was their first FIFA World Cup as Germany, their first three coming as West Germany.

Four-star joy for Germany as their players show off the FIFA World Cup after winning the 2014 Final in Brazil and thus earning the right to have four stars on their shirts – one for each FIFA World Cup won by the nation.

FIFA WORLD CUP QUALIFIERS

BALLON D'ORIBE

Mexico booked the final spot at the 2014 FIFA World Cup by beating Oceania representatives New Zealand 9-3 on aggregate in a two-legged November 2013 play-off. Caretaker manager Miguel Herrera – Mexico's fourth boss of the year – earned himself the job permanently by masterminding wins by 5-1 at home and 4-2 away. His squad relied purely on domestic-based players, meaning there were no European-based stars such as Villarreal's Giovani dos Santos or Manchester United's Javier Hernandez. The goalscoring hero was **Oribe Peralta,** who scored five goals in the two games – including the first three of the 4-2 victory in Wellington's Westpac Stadium.

UAE IN A SQUEEZE

The **United Arab Emirates** reached the finals in 1990 by recording just one win and scoring only four goals in the Asian final round. They drew four of their five matches, but beat China 2-1 to qualify in second place behind South Korea.

T&T AT FULL STRETCH

Trinidad and Tobago share the record for the most games played to qualify for a FIFA World Cup finals. They played 20 in reaching the 2006 finals, beginning with 2-0 away and 4-0 home wins over the Dominican Republic in the preliminaries. T&T then finished second behind Mexico at the four-team first group stage to reach the six-team final group. After finishing fourth, they had to play off against Bahrain and won 2-1 on aggregate. Uruguay matched that figure in 2010, with 18 South America group matches and a two-legged play-off.

BIG BOS MAN

Bosnia and Herzegovina were the only first-time qualifiers among the 32 nations at the 2014 FIFA World Cup. After losing to Portugal in play-offs for both the 2010 FIFA World Cup and the 2012 UEFA European Championship, they secured a place at the 2014 tournament by topping their qualification group ahead of Greece on goal difference. Their coach since 2009 was Bosnian-born former Yugoslavia and Paris Saint-Germain midfielder Safet Susic.

FIFA OPENS WORLD CUP TO THE WORLD

FIFA has enlarged the World Cup finals twice since 1978, to take account of the rising football nations of Africa and Asia. The rise in interest is reflected in the massive number of sides entering the competition – 204 for the 2014 event. Brazilian **João Havelange**, FIFA president from 1974 to 1998, enlarged the organization both to take advantage of commercial opportunities and to give smaller nations a chance. The number of teams in the finals was first increased from 16 to 24 for the 1982 finals in Spain, with an extra place given for Africa and Asia and a chance for a nation from Oceania to reach the finals. The number of finalists was further increased to 32 for the 1998 tournament in France.

TAKING AIM

The 2014 World Cup culminated in a final staged in Rio's Maracana Stadium. Some 203 initially entered the qualifying competition – two fewer than the record 205 tilting at South Africa in 2010. The Bahamas and Mauritius subsequently later withdrew from the 2014 running, bringing the Brazil-bound contenders down to 201. Six more FIFA member states were missing, including the already-qualified hosts. New independent country South Sudan joined FIFA too late to compete, while four more nations opted not to take part this time: Bhutan, Brunei, Guam and Mauritania.

ALL-TIME QUALIFICATIONS BY REGIONAL CONFEDERATION

1	Europe	231
2	South America	80
3	Africa	39
=	North/Central America & Caribbean	39
5	Asia	32
6	Oceania	4

THE FIRST SHOOT-OUT

The first penalty shoot-out in qualifying history came on 9 January 1977 when Tunisia beat Morocco 4-2 on spot-kicks after a 1-1 draw in Tunis. The first game, in Casablanca, had also finished 1-1. Tunisia went on to qualify for the finals.

SPANISH INVINCIBLES

Several countries have qualified for a FIFA World Cup without losing or even drawing a single game. But the Spain side who cruised their way through to the 2010 tournament in South Africa were the first to do so while playing as many as 10 matches. Qualifying for the same finals from a smaller group, Holland won eight games out of eight. West Germany also went through eight matches without dropping a point in reaching the 1982 FIFA World Cup in Spain, and Brazil won six out of six in qualifying for the 1970 competition – at which Mario Zagallo's men won another six out of six on their way to lifting the trophy.

BAH HUMBUG

The Bahamas failed to qualify for Brazil despite winning all their matches – that is, both of them. The CONCACAF country beat Turks and Caicos Islands 4-0 and then 6-0 in their first-round tie, but then withdrew from the competition because rebuilding work on their Thomas A Robinson Stadium was not completed in time for their second-round group games.

THE GROWTH OF THE QUALIFYING COMPETITION

This charts the number of countries entering qualifiers for the FIFA World Cup finals. Some withdrew before playing.

World Cup	Teams entering
Uruguay 1930	–
Italy 1934	32
France 1938	37
Brazil 1950	34
Switzerland 1954	45
Sweden 1958	55
Chile 1962	56
England 1966	74
Mexico 1970	75
West Germany 1974	99
Argentina 1978	107
Spain 1982	109
Mexico 1986	121
Italy 1990	116
USA 1994	147
France 1998	174
Japan/South Korea 2002	199
Germany 2006	198
South Africa 2010	205
Brazil 2014	203

BYERS MARKS IT

Three players shared the title of 11-goal top scorer in qualifiers for the 2014 FIFA World Cup: Dutch striker Robin van Persie and Uruguay's Luis Suarez, whose sides both qualified for Brazil, and Belize's **Deon McCaulay**. Antigua and Barbuda's Peter Byers was the only man to score two separate hat-tricks during the campaign, both against the United States Virgin Islands.

THE FASTEST SUBSTITUTION

The quickest-ever substitution in the history of FIFA World Cup qualifiers came on 30 December 1980, when North Korea's Chon Byong Ju was substituted in the first minute of his country's home game against Japan.

KOSTADINOV STUNS FRANCE

On 17 November 1993, in the last game of the Group Six schedule, Bulgaria's Emil Kostadinov scored one of the most dramatic goals in qualifying history to deny France a place at the 1994 finals. France seemed to be cruising with the score at 1-1 in stoppage time, but Kostadinov earned Bulgaria a shock victory after David Ginola lost possession. The Bulgarians reached the semi-finals of the tournament in the United States, losing 2-1 to Italy.

PALMER BEATS THE WHISTLE

Carl Erik Palmer's second goal in Sweden's 3-1 win over the Republic of Ireland in November 1949 was one of the most bizarre in qualifying history. The Irish defenders stopped, having heard a whistle, while Palmer ran on and put the ball in the net. The goal stood, because the whistle had come from someone in the crowd, not the referee. The 19-year-old forward went on to complete a hat-trick.

BWALYA LEAVES IT LATE

Zambia's **Kalusha Bwalya** is the oldest player to have scored a match-winning goal in a FIFA World Cup qualifying match. The 41-year-old netted the only goal against Liberia on 4 September 2004 after coming on as a substitute. He had also scored in his first qualifier, 20 years previously, in Zambia's 3-0 win over Uganda.

AUSTRALIA'S INCREDIBLE GOAL SPREE

Australia set a FIFA World Cup qualifying record in 2001, one that is unlikely to be beaten, as the Socceroos scored 53 goals in the space of two days. The details:

9 April 2001, Sydney: Australia 22, Tonga 0
Australia scorers: Scott Chipperfield 3, 83 mins; Damian Mori 13, 23, 40; John Aloisi 14, 24, 37, 45, 52, 63; **Kevin Muscat** (No. 2, right) 18, 30, 54, 58, 82; Tony Popovic 67; Tony Vidmar 74; David Zdrilic 78, 90; Archie Thompson 80; Con Boutsiania 87

11 April 2001, Sydney: Australia 31, American Samoa 0
Australia scorers: Boutsiania 10, 50, 84 mins; Thompson 12, 23, 27, 29, 32, 37, 42, 45, 56, 60, 65, 68, 88; Zdrilic 13, 21, 25, 33, 58, 66, 78, 89; Vidmar 14, 80; Popovic 17, 19; Simon Colosimo 51, 81; Fausto De Amicis 55

THOMPSON SETS UNLIKELY MARK

Archie Thompson eased past Iran striker Karim Bagheri's record for the number of goals in a single qualifying match (seven) as Australia thrashed American Samoa 31-0 on 11 April 2001. He netted 13 goals. David Zdrilic also beat Bagheri's total with eight goals. Two days earlier, Australia had previously smashed Iran's scoring record after completing a 22-0 victory over Tonga.

THE FASTEST GOAL

Davide Gualtieri of minnows San Marino, scored the fastest goal in qualifying history. He netted after just nine seconds against England on 17 November 1993. England went on to win 7-1 but still failed to qualify.

CRIS IS IT

The UEFA play-off between Portugal and Sweden was widely billed as Cristiano Ronaldo versus Zlatan Ibrahimovic. Neither player disappointed and the pair were the only ones to hit the scoresheet, as Portugal won 1-0 at home and then 3-2 away. Ibrahamovic's second-leg double was not enough since two late goals from Ronaldo completed his second hat-trick of the campaign. His first international hat-trick had come in 15 minutes against Northern Ireland during the group stages, taking him above Eusebio in Portugal's list of all-time scorers – and his Sweden treble put him joint top with Pauleta.

REPEAT OFFENDERS

Three players were sent off twice during qualifiers for the 2014 FIFA World Cup: Bulgaria's Svetoslav Dyakov, Tanzania's Aggrey Morris and Montenegro's Savo Pavicevic. A total of 100 red cards and 2,916 yellow cards were shown throughout the campaign, while 2,286 goals were scored – an average of 2.8 per game. The highest-scoring teams were Germany and New Caledonia (36 apiece), Argentina (35), the Netherlands (34) and England (31).

RECORD HAT-TRICK

Abdel Hamid Bassiouny of Egypt scored the fastest-ever hat-trick in qualifying history in their 8-2 win over Namibia on 13 July 2001. He netted three times in just 177 seconds between the 39th and 42nd minutes.

YOUNGEST AND OLDEST

The youngest player to appear in the FIFA World Cup qualifiers is Souleymane Mamam of Togo, who was 13 years 310 days when he played against Zambia on 6 May 2001. The oldest was MacDonald Taylor, who was 46 years, 180 days when he played for the Virgin Islands against St Kitts Nevis on 18 February 2004.

DAEI TOPS THE SCORERS

Iran's **Ali Daei** is the all-time top scorer in FIFA World Cup qualifiers. His nine goals in the 2006 qualifying campaign took his total to 30, nine ahead of the previous joint record-holder, Japan's Kazu Miura. Daei also scored seven goals in the 1994 qualifiers, four in the 1998 preliminaries and ten in 2002.

HORST THE FIRST TO GIVE WAY

The first player to be substituted during a FIFA World Cup qualifier was West Germany's **Horst Eckel**, when he was replaced by Richard Gottinger in their 3-0 victory over the short-lived protectorate of Saarland in October 1953. Eckel would go on to play on the right side of midfield in the side that beat Hungary in the 1954 FIFA World Cup final, while Gottinger's delayed appearance against Saarland was his first and last for his country. By the time of the 1958 FIFA World Cup qualifiers, Saarland had been integrated within West Germany.

UNITED STATES LEAVE IT LATE

The latest of all qualifying play-offs took place in Rome on 24 May 1934, when the USA beat Mexico 4-2 to clinch the last slot in the FIFA World Cup finals. Three days later, the Americans were knocked out 7-1 by hosts Italy in the first round of the tournament.

ITALY FORCED TO QUALIFY

Italy are the only host country who have been required to qualify for their own tournament. The 1934 hosts beat Greece 4-0 to go through. FIFA decided that, for the 1938 finals, the holders and the hosts would qualify automatically. That decision was changed for the 2006 finals. Since then, only the hosts have been exempt from qualifying, though South Africa played in the second round of qualifying for 2010. This is because it doubled up as qualifiers for the 2010 Africa Cup of Nations.

TURKEY THROUGH ON LUCK OF THE DRAW

Turkey were the first team to qualify for the FIFA World Cup finals after the drawing of lots. Their play-off against Spain, in Rome on 17 March 1954, ended 2-2. Qualification was decided by a 14-year-old Roman boy, Luigi Franco Gemma. He was blindfolded to draw the lots – and pulled out Turkey, instead of much-fancied Spain.

FIRST-TIME QUALIFIERS

1930: Argentina, Belgium, Bolivia, Brazil, Chile, France, Mexico, Paraguay, Peru, Romania, USA, Uruguay, Yugoslavia

1934: Austria, Czechoslovakia, Egypt, Germany, Hungary, Italy, Netherlands, Spain, Sweden, Switzerland

1938: Cuba, Dutch East Indies, Norway, Poland

1950: England

1954: Scotland, South Korea, Turkey, West Germany

1958: Northern Ireland, Soviet Union, Wales

1962: Bulgaria, Colombia

1966: North Korea, Portugal

1970: El Salvador, Israel, Morocco

1974: Australia, East Germany, Haiti, Zaire

1978: Iran, Tunisia

1982: Algeria, Cameroon, Honduras, Kuwait, New Zealand

1986: Canada, Denmark, Iraq

1990: Costa Rica, Republic of Ireland, United Arab Emirates

1994: Greece, Nigeria, Russia, Saudi Arabia

1998: Croatia, Jamaica, Japan, South Africa, Yugoslavia

2002: China, Ecuador, Senegal, Slovenia

2006: Angola, Czech Republic, Ghana, Ivory Coast, Serbia and Montenegro, Togo, Trinidad and Tobago, Ukraine

2010: Serbia, Slovakia

2014: Bosnia and Herzegovina

THE "FOOTBALL WAR"

War broke out between El Salvador and Honduras after El Salvador beat Honduras 3-2 in a play-off on 26 June 1969 to qualify for the 1970 finals. Tension had been running high between the neighbours over a border dispute and there had been rioting at the match. On 14 July, the Salvador army invaded Honduras.

PLAY-OFF YOU GO

For the fourth FIFA World Cup in a row, Uruguay reached the 2014 tournament via a play-off, this one an easy aggregate win over Jordan. They won the away leg 5-0, the fifth scored by **Edinson Cavani** – the largest away win in the history of FIFA World Cup intercontinental play-offs – and eased through with a goalless draw on home soil. Jordan, aiming for their first FIFA World Cup finals, played 20 qualifying matches, including a 2-2 aggregate Asian play-off tie against Uzbekistan, which they won 9-8 on penalties.

THIERRY'S TRICKERY

France qualified for the 2010 FIFA World Cup finals thanks to one of the most controversial international goals of recent history. The second leg of their play-off against the Republic of Ireland in November 2009 was 14 minutes into extra-time when striker **Thierry Henry** clearly controlled the ball with his hand, before crossing to William Gallas who gave his side a decisive 2-1 aggregate lead. After Swedish referee Martin Hansson allowed the goal to stand, the Football Association of Ireland first called for the game to be replayed, then asked to be allowed into the finals as a 33rd country – but both requests proved in vain.

NICE ONE, SON

The latest goal of 2014 FIFA World Cup qualifiers was **Son Heung-Min**'s winner for South Korea, six minutes into stoppage-time of their crucial March 2013 match against Qatar. The strike not only secured a 2-1 win, but also South Korea's qualification for the finals in Brazil.

GOING UNDERCOVER

The Kingdome in Seattle, United States, hosted the first FIFA World Cup qualifier to be played indoors, when the US beat Canada 2-0 in October 1976 – just a few months after the same venue had staged its first rock concert, by Paul McCartney's post-Beatles band Wings, and a religious rally featuring evangelist Billy Graham and country singer Johnny Cash. Canada gained revenge by beating the US 3-0 in a play-off, hosted in Haiti, to reach the next stage of the CONCACAF qualifying round. But only Mexico would go on to represent the Confederation at the 1978 FIFA World Cup in Argentina.

MAMADOU CAN DO

No European team had ever come from two goals down to win a FIFA World Cup play-off until November 2013, when France lost 2-0 in Ukraine but then won 3-0 in Paris thanks to a goal by striker Karim Benzema and a surprise brace by centre-back Mamadou Sakho, including a 72nd-minute winner.

NOT SO FASO

Burkina Faso lost their final qualifying play-off in the Africa section on away goals to Algeria, following a 3-2 victory at home and a 1-0 defeat away. They then tried to have Algeria disqualified, claiming that crucial goalscorer **Madjid Bougherra** was ineligible. Burkina Faso officials, hoping to reach their first FIFA World Cup, claimed he should have been suspended following two yellow cards in previous matches but FIFA ruled he had been booked only the once.

FIFA WORLD CUP TEAM RECORDS

EXTRA SPECIAL GERMANS

Germany, in beating Argentina 1-0 in the Maracana stadium in 2014, became the fifth team to win the FIFA World Cup Final in extra time after Italy (1934), England (1966), Argentina (1978) and Spain (2010). In both 2010 and 2014, the Final had finished goalless after 90 minutes. Andres Iniesta, for Spain in 2010, and Mario Gozte, for Germany in Rio de Janeiro, both struck their lone winning goals in the second period of the additional 30 minutes. Extra time was not enough in 1994 and 2006, when Brazil and Italy, respectively, won on penalties.

SHARING THE GOALS

France in 1982 and winners Italy, in 2006, supplied the most individual goalscorers during a FIFA World Cup finals tournament – ten. Germany's 17 goals were shared among seven players on their way to ultimate success in Brazil in 2014: Thomas Muller (five), Andre Schurrle (three), Mats Hummels (two), Miroslav Klose (two), Toni Kroos (two), Mario Gotze (two) and Mesut Ozil (one).

BRAZIL COLOUR UP

Brazil's yellow shirts are famous around the world. But they wore **white shirts** at the first four FIFA World Cup finals. However, their 2-1 loss to Uruguay in the 1950 tournament's final match – when a draw would have given Brazil the Cup – was such a shock they switched to yellow. The Brazilian confederation insisted no further colour change would follow the shock of the 7-1 semi-final defeat by Germany and 3-0 third-place play-off loss to Holland in 2014.

COLOUR CODE CONNECTION

Germany sought to engage with Brazilian fans by incorporating the colours of one of the country's most popular clubs, Flamengo, when Die Nationalelf wore red-and-black hoops as their second kit in the 2014 FIFA World Cup.

ITALY KEEP IT TIGHT

Italy set the record for the longest run without conceding a goal at the FIFA World Cup finals. They went five games without conceding at the 1990 finals, starting with their 1-0 group win over Austria. Goalkeeper Walter Zenga was not beaten until Claudio Caniggia scored Argentina's equalizer in the semi-final. And a watertight defence did not bring Italy the glory it craved: Argentina reached the final by winning the penalty shoot-out 4-3.

TODAY EUROPE, TOMORROW THE WORLD

Spain's 2010 trophy-lifting coach **Vicente del Bosque** became only the second manager to have won both the FIFA World Cup and the UEFA Champions League or its previous incarnation, the European Champions' Cup. Marcello Lippi won the UEFA prize with Juventus in 1996, 10 years before his Italy team became world champions. Del Bosque won the UEFA Champions League twice with Real Madrid, in 2000 and 2002, though he was sacked in summer 2003 for "only" winning the Spanish league title the previous season.

SUPER EIGHT FOR 2014

The 2014 FIFA World Cup saw all eight group-winners win in the round-of-16 to reach the quarter-finals for the first time in the tournament's history. However there was an unwanted record, as well. Spain and 2010 Cup-winning skipper **Iker Casillas** exited in the first-round, meaning three of the last four FIFA World Cup winners have gone out in the following group stage (emulating France in 2002 and Italy in 2010). Only three countries have never exited at the first round group stage: Germany/West Germany, the Netherlands and the Republic of Ireland.

MOST APPEARANCES IN THE FIFA WORLD CUP FINAL

1	Germany/West Germany	8
2	Brazil	7
3	Italy	6
4	Argentina	5
5	Netherlands	3
6	Czechoslovakia	2
=	France	2
=	Hungary	2
=	Uruguay	2
10	England	1
=	Spain	1
=	Sweden	1

BRAZIL PROFIT FROM RIMET'S VISION

Jules Rimet, president of FIFA 1921–54, was the driving force behind the first FIFA World Cup, in 1930. The tournament, in Uruguay, was not high-profile, with only 13 nations taking part. The long sea journey kept most European teams away, and only Belgium, France, Romania and Yugoslavia made the trip. Rimet's dream has been realized and the FIFA World Cup has grown enormously in popularity. Brazil have been the competition's most successful team, winning five times. The only FIFA World Cup finals ever-presents, Brazil have more wins (70) than any other country, though Germany (66 wins) have played more matches: 106 to Brazil's 104. Germany and Italy are the most successful European nations with four World Cup wins apiece. The original finalists, Uruguay and Argentina, are both two-time champions, though Argentina have also lost two Finals. England (1966) and France (1998) both won once as hosts. Spain failed as hosts in 1982 but won in South Africa in 2010.

WHY THE BRITISH TEAMS STAYED OUT

England and Scotland are considered the homelands of football, but neither country entered the FIFA World Cup until the qualifiers for the 1950 finals. The four British associations – England, Scotland, Wales and Northern Ireland – quit FIFA in the 1920s over a row over broken-time (employment compensation) payments to amateurs. The British associations did not rejoin FIFA until 1946.

ONE-TIME WONDERS

Indonesia, then known as the Dutch East Indies, made one appearance in the finals, in the days when the tournament was a strictly knockout affair. On 5 June 1938, they lost 6-0 to Hungary in the first round, and have never qualified for the tournament since.

MOST APPEARANCES IN FIFA WORLD CUP FINALS TOURNAMENTS

1	Brazil	20
2	Germany/West Germany	18
=	Italy	18
4	Argentina	16
5	Mexico	15

FIFA WORLD CUP STOPS THE WORLD

The FIFA World Cup finals is the world's biggest single-sport event. Television was in its infancy when the first finals were held in 1930, and they have since become one of the most popular TV sporting events of all. The 2014 finals set ratings records around the world. In Germany, an all-time high of 41.89 million viewers (an 86.3 per cent share) watched the victory over Argentina in the final. The global audience for the match was expected to top the 909 million who watched Spain beat the Netherlands in 2010. A further 12 million German fans were estimated to have watched the final in a public space back home. All manner of online records were set. Germany's 7-1 thrashing of Brazil in the semi-final generated a world sports record of 35 million tweets.

GOLDEN NARROWS

Before 2010, no country had won five consecutive FIFA World Cup matches by a one-goal margin – but **Arjen Robben** and the Netherlands and became the first, thanks to their 3-2 semi-final victory over Uruguay. Before then, the record rested with Italy, who managed four single-goal wins in a row across the 1934 and 1938 FIFA World Cups. Spain's 1-0 defeat of the Dutch in the 2010 FIFA World Cup was also their fifth consecutive single-goal victory and fourth in the knockout stages.

BRAZIL'S GOALS GLOOM

The 14 goals conceded by Brazil in the 2014 FIFA World Cup finals are the most ever conceded by the host nation. The overall record was 16 goals shipped by South Korea in Switzerland in 1954. In those finals, West Germany let in 14 but still won the tournament for the first time. It included eight in a group match against beaten finalists Hungary.

THE FEWEST GOALS CONCEDED

FIFA World Cup winners France (1998), Italy (2006) and Spain (2010) hold the record for the fewest goals conceded on their way to victory. All three conceded just two. Spain also hold the record for fewest goals scored by FIFA World Cup winners. They netted just eight in 2010, below the 11 scored by Italy in 1938, England in 1966 or Brazil in 1994.

SPONSORS MAKE THE FINALS PAY

The Brazil 2014 FIFA World Cup was the most lucrative ever, with world football's governing body, FIFA, achieving a surplus of more than $2 billion. Two-thirds of FIFA World Cup revenues come from TV rights. This was the fifth finals played with 32 teams, the number going up from 24 for the France 1998 FIFA World Cup.

FEWEST GOALS CONCEDED IN ONE TOURNAMENT:
Switzerland: 0, 2006

MOST GOALS SCORED IN ONE TOURNAMENT
Hungary: 27, 1954

MOST WINS IN ONE TOURNAMENT
Brazil: 7, 2002

MOST GOALS SCORED IN ONE TOURNAMENT
Just Fontaine (France): 13, 1958

EVER RED

England's victory in 1966 was not just the only time they have won the FIFA World Cup – it also now remains the only time the prize has been clinched by a side wearing red shirts in the final. Spain might have emulated England's fashion sense in 2010 but had to wear blue to avoid clashing with the Netherlands' bright orange – they did, however, change back into their usual red to receive the trophy from FIFA president **Sepp Blatter**.

MOST CONSECUTIVE MATCHES SCORING A GOAL AT FIFA WORLD CUP FINALS

18	Brazil	1930–58
18	Germany	1934–58, 1986–98
17	Hungary	1934–62
16	Uruguay	1930–62
15	Brazil	1978–90
15	France	1978–86

PERFORMANCES BY HOST NATION AT FIFA WORLD CUP FINALS

1930	Uruguay	Champions
1934	Italy	Champions
1938	France	Quarter-finals
1950	Brazil	Runners-up
1954	Switzerland	Quarter-finals
1958	Sweden	Runners-up
1962	Chile	Third place
1966	England	Champions
1970	Mexico	Quarter-finals
1974	West Germany	Champions
1978	Argentina	Champions
1982	Spain	Second round
1986	Mexico	Quarter-finals
1990	Italy	Third place
1994	United States	Second round
1998	France	Champions
2002	South Korea	Fourth place
	Japan	Second round
2006	Germany	Third place
2010	South Africa	First round
2014	Brazil	Fourth place

SAFE EUROPEAN HOME

Germany's 1-0 victory over Argentina in the 2014 FIFA World Cup final meant they became the first European nation to win the FIFA World Cup in any of the eight tournaments staged in North, Central or South America, going back to 1930. Spain, winners of the 2010 FIFA World Cup in South Africa, were the first European victors to achieve it outside their home continent.

HOLDERS CRASH OUT

France produced the worst performance by a defending FIFA World Cup winner in Japan and South Korea in 2002: they lost their opening game 1-0 to Senegal, drew 0-0 against Uruguay and were eliminated after losing 1-0 to Denmark. They were the first defending champions to be knocked out without scoring a goal. In 2010 Italy emulated France by exiting at the first-round stage, and without winning a match – nor indeed ever taking the lead. At least Italy did achieve two draws – and scored four goals. They opened with a 1-1 draw against Paraguay, needed a penalty to force another 1-1 draw against minnows New Zealand, and they were on their way home after losing 3-2 to Slovakia.

THREE AND OUT

The Netherlands, coached by **Bert van Marwijk** in 2010, became the only country to have reached the final of three FIFA World Cups without managing to lift the trophy once. Their six victories en route to the 2010 final are also more than any other team has managed in one tournament without going on to claim the main prize.

BRAZIL LEAD THE WAY

Brazil scored the most victories in finals tournaments when they won all their seven games in 2002. They began with a 2-1 group win over Turkey and ended with a 2-0 final triumph over Germany. They scored 18 goals in their unbeaten run and conceded on only four occasions.

HOME DISCOMFORT

South Africa became the first host nation to fail to reach the second round of a FIFA World Cup, when staging the 2010 tournament – though their first-round record of one win, one draw and one defeat was only inferior on goal difference to the opening three games played by hosts Spain, in 1982, and the USA, in 1994, both of whom reached the second round. Uruguay's 3–0 victory over South Africa in Pretoria on 16 June 2010 equalled the highest losing margin suffered by a FIFA World Cup host, following Brazil's 5–2 win over Sweden in the 1958 final and Italy's 4–1 trouncing of Mexico in their 1970 quarter-final.

FIFA WORLD CUP GOALSCORING

HOST WITH THE MOST

Brazil have scored more goals (nine) in the opening matches of the FIFA World Cup than any other nation, though their status as double hosts in 1950 and 2014 certainly helped. Between 1974 and 2002 the holders, rather than the hosts, also had the honour of kicking off proceedings. Brazil beat Mexico easily by 4-0 in the 1950 opener in the Maracana stadium, with goals from Jair, Baltazar and Ademir (two). They defeated Scotland 2-1 in the Opening Match of France 1998 (Cesar Sampaio and Tom Boyd, own goal) and then Croatia, 3-1, in 2014, thanks to a double (one a penalty) from **Neymar** and a third from Oscar. A Brazilian also netted the very first goal of the 2014 finals, as left-back Marcelo gave Croatia the lead with an own goal. Italy's total of eight goals in the Opening Match was mainly thanks to a 7-1 beating of the United States in 1934 – they drew 1-1 with Bulgaria in 1986.

HIGHEST SCORES

The highest-scoring game in the FIFA World Cup finals was the quarter-final between Austria and Switzerland on 26 June 1954. Austria staged a remarkable comeback to win 7-5, with centre-forward **Theodor Wagner** scoring a hat-trick, after trailing 3-0 in the 19th minute. Three other games have produced 11 goals – Brazil's 6-5 win over Poland in the 1938 first round, Hungary's 8-3 win over West Germany in their 1954 group game and the Hungarians' 10-1 rout of El Salvador at the group stage in 1982.

LOW-SCORING SPAIN

Spain won the 2010 FIFA World Cup despite scoring just eight goals in seven games on their way to the title – fewer than any world champions in history, including 11-goal Italy in 1934, England in 1966 and Brazil in 1994. Vicente del Bosque's Spain were also the first team to win 1-0 in all four of their knockout matches. David Villa scored the decisive goal in two of those matches.

GENEROUS OPPONENTS

Chile was the first team to benefit from an opponent's own goal at the FIFA World Cup. Mexico's Manuel Rosas put the ball into his own net during the Chileans' 3-0 win at the inaugural 1930 finals in Uruguay. France, Germany and Italy share the record for receiving the most FIFA World Cup finals own goals, with four each. At the 2014 World Cup, France profited from two own goals, the first courtesy of Honduras goalkeeper Noel Valladares in a 3-0 group stage win; the second was by Nigeria's Joseph Yobo, to make it 2-0 in the second-round. Valladares's own goal – the ball struck him off a goal-post and thus denied Karim Benzema a hat-trick – was ratified by goal-line technology, in operation in the finals in Brazil for the first time.

ZERO TOLERANCE

Four is the most number of penalty shootouts in the knockout phases of the FIFA World Cup since the first One in 1982. A further 25 have been needed in the eight finals thereafter. The record of four came at Italy 1990, Germany 2006 and Brazil 2014, where 26 of 36 kicks succeeded. The most crucial failures came after the goalless **Argentina** v Netherlands semi-final, and Dutchmen Ron Vlaar and Wesley Sneijder both were denied by keeper Sergio Romero.

THE FASTEST GOAL

Turkey's **Hakan Sukur** holds the record for the quickest goal scored in the FIFA World Cup finals. He netted after 11 seconds against South Korea in the 2002 third-place play-off. Turkey went on to win 3-2. The previous record was held by Vaclav Masek of Czechoslovakia, who struck after 15 seconds against Mexico in 1962.

BIGGEST FIFA WORLD CUP FINALS WINS

Hungary 10, El Salvador 1 (15 June 1982)
Hungary 9, South Korea 0 (17 June 1954)
Yugoslavia 9, Zaire 0 (18 June 1974)
Sweden 8, Cuba 0 (12 June 1938)
Uruguay 8, Bolivia 0 (2 July 1950)
Germany 8, Saudi Arabia 0 (1 June 2002)

MOST GOALS IN ONE FIFA WORLD CUP

Goals	Country	Year
27	**Hungary**	1954
25	**West Germany**	1954
23	**France**	1958
22	**Brazil**	1950
19	**Brazil**	1970

MOST GOALS IN FIFA WORLD CUP FINALS (MINIMUM 100)

1	**Germany/W Germany**	224
2	**Brazil**	221
3	**Argentina**	131
4	**Italy**	128
5	**France**	103

MOST AND LEAST

Mario Gotze's winner for Germany in the 2014 FIFA World Cup Final meant the tournament matched the record aggregate of 171 goals at the 1998 finals in France, the first expanded to 32 teams and 64 games. The two finals shared a goals average of 2.67 per game. The record goals per match average is 5.38, set at the 1954 finals, when there were 140 goals in 26 matches in Switzerland. The lowest average came at the 1990 FIFA World Cup in Italy, when the 52 matches generated only 115 goals, an average of only 2.21.

YOUNGEST AND OLDEST

The youngest-ever scorer of a goal in FIFA World Cup finals history is **Pele.** He was 17 years and 239 days old when he notched Brazil's winner against Wales in the 1958 quarter-finals. Cameroon's **Roger Milla** – aged 42 years and 39 days – became the oldest scorer when he netted his country's only goal in a 6-1 defeat by Russia in 1994.

COLOMBIAN GOLD

James Rodriguez claimed the adidas Golden Boot prize as leading scorer at the 2014 FIFA World Cup in Brazil, the first Colombian winner. The AS Monaco forward's explosion was all the more of a surprise since Colombia had expected their goals to come from his club-mate Radamel Falcao, who missed the finals after a knee injury. Rodriguez scored in all five of his country's matches, including a penalty in the 2-1 quarter-final loss to Brazil and a volley in the second-round against Uruguay which was a contender for goal of the tournament. His six goals were one more than Germany's Thomas Muller and two more than Brazil's Neymar, Argentina's Lionel Messi and the Netherlands' Robin Van Persie.

KLOSE ENCOUNTERS

Eight players have scored at FIFA World Cups 12 years apart. The most notable was Miroslav Klose. The Polish-born centre-forward opened with a hat-trick when Germany beat Saudi Arabia 8-0 in Japan in 2002 and scored a 16th goal in the 7-1 destruction of hosts Brazil in the 2014 semi-finals. That established Klose as the finals' all-time record marksman with one more goal than Brazil's Ronaldo. The other seven men to have scored in FIFA World Cups 12 years apart are: Pele (Brazil), Uwe Seeler (West Germany), Diego Maradona (Argentina), Michael Laudrup (Denmark), Henrik Larsson (Sweden), Sami Al-Jaber (S Arabia) and Cuauhtemoc Blanco (Mexico).

HEAD FOR FIGURES

When **Jermaine Jones** thundered home from 30 metres for the United States in their 2-2 draw with Portugal in a Group G clash at the 2014 FIFA World Cup, he registered the 2,300th goal of the finals. Mario Gotze's winning goal for Germany in the Final against Argentina lifted the overall tally to 2,379.

EUSEBIO THE STRIKE FORCE

Portugal's **Eusebio** was the striking star of the 1966 FIFA World Cup finals. Ironically, he would not be eligible to play for Portugal now. He was born in Mozambique, then a Portuguese colony, but now an independent country. He finished top scorer with nine goals, including two as Portugal eliminated champions Brazil and four as they beat North Korea 5-3 in the quarter-finals after trailing 3-0.

FIFA WORLD CUP FINALS TOP SCORERS

Maximum 16 teams in finals

Year	Venue	Top Scorer	Country	Goals
1930	Uruguay	Guillermo Stabile	Argentina	8
1934	Italy	Oldrich Nejedly	Czechoslovakia	5
1938	France	Leonidas	Brazil	7
1950	Brazil	Ademir	Brazil	9
1954	Switzerland	Sandor Kocsis	Hungary	11
1958	Sweden	Just Fontaine	France	13
1962	Chile	Garrincha	Brazil	4
		Vava	Brazil	
		Leonel Sanchez	Chile	
		Florian Albert	Hungary	
		Valentin Ivanov	Soviet Union	
		Drazen Jerkovic	Yugoslavia	
1966	England	Eusebio	Portugal	9
1970	Mexico	Gerd Muller	West Germany	10
1974	West Germany	Grzegorz Lato	Poland	7
1978	Argentina	Mario Kempes	Argentina	6

24 teams in finals

Year	Venue	Top Scorer	Country	Goals
1982	Spain	Paolo Rossi	Italy	6
1986	Mexico	Gary Lineker	England	6
1990	Italy	Salvatore Schillaci	Italy	6
1994	United States	Oleg Salenko	Russia	6
		Hristo Stoichkov	Bulgaria	6

32 teams in finals

Year	Venue	Top Scorer	Country	Goals
1998	France	Davor Suker	Croatia	6
2002	Korea/Japan	Ronaldo	Brazil	8
2006	Germany	Miroslav Klose	Germany	5
2010	South Africa	Thomas Muller*	Germany	5
		Diego Forlan	Uruguay	5
		Wesley Sneijder	Netherlands	5
		David Villa	Spain	5
2014	Brazil	James Rodriguez	Colombia	6

* = Won Golden Boot (had most assists)

KEMPES MAKES HIS MARK

Mario Kempes was Argentina's only foreign-based player in the hosts' squad at the 1978 finals. Twice top scorer in the Spanish league, Valencia's Kempes was crucial to Argentina's success. Coach Cesar Luis Menotti told him to shave off his moustache after he failed to score in the group games. Kempes then netted two against Peru, two more against Poland, and two decisive goals in the final against the Netherlands.

NO GUARANTEES FOR TOP SCORERS

Topping the FIFA World Cup finals scoring chart is a great honour for all strikers, but few have gained the ultimate prize and been leading scorer. Argentina's Guillermo Stabile started the luckless trend in 1930, topping the scoring charts but finishing up on the losing side in the final. The list of top scorers who have played in the winning side is small: Garrincha and Vava (joint top scorers in 1962), Mario Kempes (top scorer in 1978), Paolo Rossi (1982) and Ronaldo (2002). Gerd Muller, top scorer in 1970, gained his reward as West Germany's trophy winner four years later. Other top scorers, such as Sandor Kocsis, 1954, Just Fontaine, 1958, and Gary Lineker, 1986, have been disappointed in the final stages. Kocsis was the only one to reach the final – and Hungary were defeated. Four players finished tied on five goals at the 2010 FIFA World Cup and one – David Villa – collected a winner's medal, but the Golden Boot went to Germany's Thomas Muller.

STABILE MAKES AN IMPACT

Guillermo Stabile, top scorer in the 1930 FIFA World Cup finals, had never played for Argentina before the tournament. He made his debut – as a 25-year-old – against Mexico because first-choice Roberto Cherro had suffered a panic attack. He netted a hat-trick then scored twice against both Chile and the United States as Argentina reached the final. He struck one of his side's goals in the 4-2 defeat by Uruguay in the final.

SUPER SUBS

Germany's winner in the 2014 FIFA World Cup Final was scored by **Mario Gotze** and created by a pass from Andre Schurrle. This was the first time both the assist and goal itself in a FIFA World Cup Final had come from two substitutes. It was also the first winning goal scored by a substitute.

HURST MAKES HISTORY

England's **Geoff Hurst** became the first and to date only player to score a hat-trick in a FIFA World Cup final when he netted three in the hosts' 4-2 victory over West Germany in 1966. Hurst headed England level after the Germans took an early lead, then scored the decisive third goal with a shot that bounced down off the crossbar and just over the line, according to the Soviet linesman. Hurst hit his third in the last minute. The British TV commentator Kenneth Wolstenholme described Hurst's strike famously with the words: "Some people are on the pitch ... They think it's all over ... It is now!"

⚽ THREE OUT OF 10

Only three players wearing the iconic No.10 shirt have won the FIFA World Cup finals Golden Boot: Argentina's Mario Kempes in 1978, England's Gary Lineker in 1986 and Colombia's six-goal James Rodriguez at Brazil 2014. Lionel Messi and Neymar, Argentina's and Brazil's No.10s, both scored four goals, one behind Germany's No.13, Thomas Muller.

⚽ ANDRES THE GIANT

Spain's hero in the 2010 FIFA World Cup final was **Andres Iniesta** (right), whose 116th-minute goal was also the latest trophy-winning strike in the tournament's history – not counting penalty shoot-outs, that is.

⚽ FIFA WORLD CUP FINALS ALL-TIME LEADING GOALSCORERS

	Name	Country	Tournaments	Goals
1	Miroslav Klose	Germany	2002, 2006, 2010, 2014	16
2	Ronaldo	Brazil	1998, 2002, 2006	15
3	Gerd Muller	West Germany	1970, 1974	14
4	Just Fontaine	France	1958	13
5	Pele	Brazil	1958, 1962, 1966, 1970	12
6	Jurgen Klinsmann	Germany	1990, 1994, 1998	11
=	Sandor Kocsis	Hungary	1954	11
8	Gabriel Batistuta	Argentina	1994, 1998, 2002	10
=	Teofilo Cubillas	Peru	1970, 1978	10
=	Grzegorz Lato	Poland	1974, 1978, 1982	10
=	Gary Lineker	England	1986, 1990	10
=	Thomas Muller	Germany	2010, 2014	10
=	Helmut Rahn	West Germany	1954, 1958	10

⚽ THE BRADLEY BUNCH

Michael Bradley's late equalizer for the United States, in their Group C 2-2 draw with Slovenia in June 2010, made him the first person to score a FIFA World Cup goal for a team coached by his own father – in this case, Bob Bradley.

⚽ MESSI MISSING OUT

Argentina's captain **Lionel Messi** left the 2014 FIFA World Cup with a runners-up medal and the Golden Ball, awarded to the finals' best player. The winner, once chosen by a poll of journalists, was judged in Brazil by the technical study group. This comprises present and former coaches appointed by FIFA to monitor football trends. The last player to win both the award and the FIFA World Cup was Romario, back in 1994.

PELE SO UNLUCKY

Pele would surely have been the all-time FIFA World Cup top scorer but for injuries. He was sidelined early in the 1962 finals, and again four years later. He scored six goals in Brazil's 1958 triumph, including two in the 5-2 final victory over Sweden. He also netted Brazil's 100th FIFA World Cup goal as they beat Italy 4-1 in the 1970 final.

MULLER'S SCORING HABIT

West Germany's **Gerd Muller** had the knack of scoring in important games. He struck the winner against England in the 1970 quarter-final and his two goals in extra-time against Italy almost carried his side to the final. Four years later, Muller's goal against Poland ensured that West Germany reached the final on home soil. Then he scored the winning goal against the Netherlands in the FIFA World Cup final. He also had a goal disallowed for offside – wrongly, as TV replays proved.

RONALDO SO CONSISTENT

Ronaldo was a consistent scorer in the three FIFA World Cup finals tournaments he played in. He netted four times in 1998, when they were runners-up to France, eight as Brazil won the 2002 tournament – including both goals in the final – and three more in 2006. He became the all-time top scorer when netting Brazil's opener in a 3-0 win over Ghana in the last-16 round at Dortmund on 27 June 2006. As a teenager, Ronaldo had been a member of Brazil's FIFA World Cup winning squad in the United States in 1994, but did not play.

WHO SCORED THE FIRST HAT-TRICK?

For many years, Argentina's Guillermo Stabile was considered the first hat-trick scorer in the FIFA World Cup finals. He netted three in Argentina's 6-3 win over Mexico on 19 July 1930, but has since been superseded by Bert Patenaude of the United States. FIFA changed its records in November 2006, to acknowledge that Patenaude's treble two days earlier, in the Americans' 3-0 win over Paraguay, had been the tournament's first hat-trick.

KLINSMANN'S CONTRIBUTION

Jurgen Klinsmann has been one of the most influential personalities at the modern FIFA World Cup. He scored three goals when West Germany won the FIFA World Cup in 1990 and a further eight in 1994 and 1998. As team coach he then led Germany to third place in 2006, and the United States to the second round in 2014.

HIGH FIVES

Germany forwards **Thomas Muller** (in 2010 and 2014) and Miroslav Klose (2002 and 2006) are the only men to have scored five or more goals at successive FIFA World Cup finals. Muller's 10 goals have come in only 13 matches and he will be only 28 years old when the Russia 2018 FIFA World Cup kicks-off.

FIFA WORLD CUP APPEARANCES

Goalkeeper Gianluigi Buffon was in Italy's squad for his fifth FIFA World Cup in Brazil in 2014 and, after missing the victory over England, he captained the Azzurri in losses to Costa Rica and Uruguay. Buffon actually played in only four tournaments, however, having been an unused substitute in 1998. Two players have appeared in matches in five FIFA World Cups: Mexico's Antonio Carbajal (1950–66) and West Germany/Germany's Lothar Matthaus (1982–98).

YOUNGEST AND OLDEST

Northern Ireland's Norman Whiteside is the youngest player in FIFA World Cup finals history, being just 17 years and 41 days when he started against Yugoslavia in 1982. The oldest player to feature is Colombia goalkeeper Faryd Mondragon as a late substitute in a 4-1 win over Japan in 2014. Aged 43 years and three days, he outdid the 42 years 39 days of Cameroon's Roger Milla.

THIS IS ENGLAND

England captain **Steven Gerrard** led the 110 players from the top-represented English Premier League at the 2014 FIFA World Cup. This was down seven on 2010. Celtic goalkeeper Fraser Forster was the England squad's only non-Premier League player. Belgium had 12 Premier League players and France 10. Chelsea sent 17 players, Manchester United 14, Liverpool 12 and champions Manchester City 10.

MOST APPEARANCES IN FIFA WORLD CUP FINALS

25	**Lothar Matthaus** (West Germany/Germany)
24	**Miroslav Klose** (Germany)
23	**Paolo Maldini** (Italy)
21	**Diego Maradona** (Argentina)
	Uwe Seeler (West Germany)
	Wladyslaw Zmuda (Poland)
20	**Cafu** (Brazil)
	Philipp Lahm (Germany)
	Grzegorz Lato (Poland)
	Bastian Schweinsteiger (Germany)

DOUBLE WINNERS

Players who have played on the winning side in two FIFA World Cup finals:

Giovanni Ferrari (Italy), 1934, 1938
Giuseppe Meazza (Italy), 1934, 1938
Pele (Brazil), 1958, 1970
Didi (Brazil), 1958, 1962
Djalma Santos (Brazil), 1958, 1962
Garrincha (Brazil), 1958, 1962
Gilmar (Brazil), 1958, 1962
Nilton Santos (Brazil), 1958, 1962
Vava (Brazil), 1958, 1962
Zagallo (Brazil), 1958, 1962
Zito (Brazil), 1958, 1962
Cafu (Brazil), 1994, 2002

THE "DOUBLE" CHAMPIONS

Franz Beckenbauer and Mario Zagallo are a unique duo. They have both won the FIFA World Cup as a player and a coach. Beckenbauer also had the distinction of captaining West Germany to victory on home soil in 1974. As coach, he steered them to the final in Mexico in 1986 and to victory over Argentina in Italy four years later. He was nicknamed "Der Kaiser" (The Emperor) both for his style and his achievements. Zagallo gained two winners' medals as a player. He was the left-winger in Brazil's triumphant march to the 1958 championship, before playing a deeper role in their 1962 victory. He took over from the controversial Joao Saldanha as Brazil coach three months before the 1970 finals and guided the side to victory in all six of its games, scoring 19 goals and routing Italy 4-1 in the final. Zagallo later filled the role of the team's technical director when Brazil won the FIFA World Cup for a fourth time in 1994.

MOST FIFA WORLD CUP FINALS TOURNAMENTS

The following all played in at least four FIFA World Cup finals.

5 **Antonio Carbajal** (Mexico) 1950, 1954, 1958, 1962, 1966
   Lothar Matthaus (W Germany/Germany) 1982, 1986, 1990, 1994, 1998
4 **Sami Al-Jaber** (Saudi Arabia) 1994, 1998, 2002, 2006
   DaMarcus Beasley (United States) 2002, 2006, 2010, 2014
   Giuseppe Bergomi (Italy) 1982, 1986, 1990, 1998
   Gianluigi Buffon (Italy) 2002, 2006, 2010, 2014
   Cafu (Brazil) 1994, 1998, 2002, 2006
   Denis Caniza (Paraguay) 1998, 2002, 2006, 2010
   Fabio Cannavaro (Italy) 1998, 2002, 2006, 2010
   Iker Casillas (Spain) 2002, 2006, 2010, 2014
   Samuel Eto'o (Cameroon) 1998, 2002, 2010, 2014
   Thierry Henry (France) 1998, 2002, 2006, 2010
   Miroslav Klose (Germany) 2002, 2006, 2010, 2014
   Paolo Maldini (Italy) 1990, 1994, 1998, 2002
   Diego Maradona (Argentina) 1982, 1986, 1990, 1994
   Rafael Marquez (Mexico) 2002, 2006, 2010, 2014
   Hong Myung-Bo (South Korea) 1990, 1994, 1998, 2002
   Pele (Brazil) 1958, 1962, 1966, 1970
   Gianni Rivera (Italy) 1962, 1966, 1970, 1974
   Pedro Rocha (Uruguay) 1962, 1966, 1970, 1974
   Djalma Santos (Brazil) 1954, 1958, 1962, 1966
   Karl-Heinz Schnellinger (W. Germany) 1958, 1962, 1966, 1970
   Enzo Scifo (Belgium) 1986, 1990, 1994, 1998
   Uwe Seeler (West Germany) 1958, 1962, 1966, 1970
   Rigobert Song (Cameroon) 1994, 1998, 2002, 2010
   Franky van der Elst (Belgium) 1986, 1990, 1994, 1998
   Xavi (Spain) 2002, 2006, 2010, 2014
   Wladyslaw Zmuda (Poland) 1974, 1978, 1982, 1986
   Andoni Zubizarreta (Spain) 1986, 1990, 1994, 1998

BAYERN BEAT

Seven of Germany's 2014 FIFA World Cup-winning squad came from champions Bayern Munich: Manuel Neuer, Philipp Lahm, Jerome Boateng, Bastian Schweinsteiger, Toni Kroos, Thomas Muller and Mario Gotze. All started the final against Argentina – except match-winner Gotze. Immediately after the final the Bayern contingent was reduced when Kroos joined Real Madrid.

KHEDIRA'S DOUBLE PAIN

Sami Khedira was in a world of his own in Brazil in 2014 as he ended the season with a winner's medal from both the FIFA World Cup and the UEFA Champions League. First Khedira lined up in midfield as Spanish club Real Madrid scored a 4-1 extra-time win over neighbours Atletico in Europe's club season climax. He then joined up with Germany's World Cup squad in Brazil. Here he won a second medal, despite withdrawing from the final just before kick-off after aggravating a muscle injury in the warm-up. Khedira was the 10th player to clinch the World Cup/European Cup double.

SONG FAMILY GOES OFF KEY

In playing 17 minutes at the 2010 FIFA World Cup, Cameroon defender **Rigobert Song** became the first African to play in four finals tournaments – nine matches, across 16 years and nine days. He featured in 1994, 1998, 2002 and 2010 – Cameroon failed to qualify in 2006. He, and Colombia's Faryd Mondragon, share the fourth-longest FIFA World Cup career-spans, bettered only by Mexicans Antonio Carbajal (spanning 16 years, 25 days) and Hugo Sanchez (16 years, 17 days) and West Germany/Germany's Lothar Matthaus (16 years, 14 days). On the down side, Song was sent off twice at World Cups and cousin Alex Song was dismissed at the 2014 finals for elbowing Mario Mandzukic in a 4-0 loss to Croatia. Thus, the Song family is responsible for three of Cameroon's eight FIFA World Cup finals red cards.

MOST FIFA WORLD CUP FINALS MATCHES (BY POSITION)

Goalkeeper: Sepp Maier (West Germany, 18 matches) and Claudio Taffarel (Brazil, 18 matches)
Defence: Paolo Maldini (Italy, 23); Wladyslaw Zmuda (Poland, 21); Cafu (Brazil, 20); Philipp Lahm (Germany, 20)
Midfielders: Lothar Matthaus (W. Germany/Germany, 25); Bastian Schweinsteiger (Germany, 20)
Forwards: Miroslav Klose (Germany, 24); Diego Maradona (Argentina, 21); Uwe Seeler (West Germany, 21); Grzegorz Lato (Poland, 20)

PROSINECKI'S SCORING RECORD

Robert Prosinecki is the only player to have scored for different countries in FIFA World Cup finals tournaments. He netted for Yugoslavia in their 4-1 win over the United Arab Emirates in the 1990 tournament. Eight years later, following the break-up of the old Yugoslavia, he scored for Croatia in their 3-0 group-game win over Jamaica, and then netted the first goal in his side's 2-1 third-place play-off victory over the Netherlands.

QUICKEST SUBSTITUTIONS

The three fastest substitutions in the history of the FIFA World Cup finals have all come in the fourth minute. In each case the player substituted was so seriously injured that he took no further part in the tournament: Steve Hodge came on for Bryan Robson in England's 0-0 draw with Morocco in 1986; Giuseppe Bergomi replaced Alessandro Nesta in Italy's 2-1 win over Austria in 1998; and Peter Crouch subbed for Michael Owen in England's 2-2 draw with Sweden in 2006.

PRIZE PROBLEM

Winning the FIFA World Player of the Year award, or Ballon d'Or, has not proved a lucky omen for its proud bearers. The winner has never gone on to win the next World Cup. The 2014 FIFA World Cup was no different as **Cristiano Ronaldo**, 2013 FIFA World Player of the Year, and his Portugal team-mates went out in the group stage. His predecessor as Ballon d'Or-holder, Lionel Messi of Argentina, was on the losing side in the 2014 Final. Messi was also the incumbent going into the 2010 FIFA World Cup, but lost in the quarter-finals.

SIMUNIC'S THREE-CARD MATCH

Croatia's Josip Simunic shares (with Ray Richards of Australia in 1974) the record for collecting the most yellow cards in one match at the FIFA World Cup finals – three. He received three yellows against Australia in 2006 before he was sent off by English referee Graham Poll. When Poll showed Simunic his second yellow, he forgot he had already booked him.

LEADING CAPTAINS

Three players have each captained their teams in two FIFA World Cup finals – Diego Maradona of Argentina, Dunga of Brazil and West Germany's Karl-Heinz Rummenigge. Maradona lifted the trophy in 1986, but was a loser four years later. Dunga was the winning skipper in 1994, but was on the losing side in 1998. Rummenigge was a loser on both occasions, in 1982 and 1986. Maradona has made the most appearances as captain at the FIFA World Cup finals, leading out Argentina 16 times between 1986 and 1994.

FASTEST RED CARDS IN THE FIFA WORLD CUP FINALS

1 min Jose Batista (Uruguay) v Scotland, 1986
8 min Giorgio Ferrini (Italy) v Chile, 1962
14 min Zeze Procopio
 (Brazil) v Czechoslovakia, 1938
19 min Mohammed Al Khlaiwi
 (Saudi Arabia) v France, 1998
 Miguel Bossio (Uruguay) v Denmark, 1986
21 min Gianluca Pagliuca
 (Italy) v Rep of Ireland, 1994

FASTEST YELLOW CARDS IN THE FIFA WORLD CUP FINALS

1 min Sergei Gorlukovich (Russia) v Sweden, 1994
 Giampiero Marini (Italy) v Poland, 1982
2 min Jesus Arellano (Mexico) v Italy, 2002
 Henri Camara (Senegal) v Uruguay, 2002
 Michael Emenalo (Nigeria) v Italy, 1994
 Humberto Suazo (Chile) v Switzerland, 2010
 Mark van Bommel (Netherlands) v Port., 2006

SUPER SUBS IMPOSE THEIR WILL

Substitutes scored more goals in the Brazil 2014 FIFA World Cup than in any previous finals. Mario Gotze's goal in the final was the 32nd by a substitute, extending the record from the previous mark of 24 set in 2006 in Germany. Substitutes, two of them, were first permitted for the 1970 finals in Mexico, and it went up to three from 1998. The 1998 FIFA World Cup finals also saw the fastest goal by a substitute. Denmark's **Ebbe Sand** scored 16 seconds after coming on against Nigeria.

FIRST ELEVEN

In an age of squad numbers, **Brazil** may have pleased some traditionalists when fielding players wearing shirt numbers one to 11 in the starting line-ups for their first two games of the 2010 FIFA World Cup, against North Korea and the Ivory Coast. Kicking off for coach Dunga on each occasion were: 1 Julio Cesar, 2 Maicon, 3 Lucio, 4 Juan, 5 Felipe Melo, 6 Michel Bastos, 7 Elano, 8 Gilberto Silva, 9 Luis Fabiano, 10 Kaka and 11 Robinho. **The Netherlands** managed a similar starting structure for not only their second-round tie against Slovakia, but the final against Spain: 1 Maarten Stekelenburg, 2 Gregory van der Wiel, 3 Johnny Heitinga, 4 Joris Mathijsen, 5 Giovanni van Bronckhorst, 6 Mark van Bommel, 7 Dirk Kuyt, 8 Nigel de Jong, 9 Robin van Persie, 10 Wesley Sneijder and 11 Arjen Robben. Both Brazil and the Netherlands came close to the same feat when they met in the quarter-finals, though both featured a number 13 – Brazil's Dani Alves, in place of 7 Elano, and the Netherlands' Andre Ooijer instead of 4 Joris Mathijsen (Elano and Mathijsen were unavailable through injury).

YOUNGEST PLAYERS IN FIFA WORLD CUP FINAL
Pele (Brazil) – 17 years, 249 days, in 1958
Giuseppe Bergomi (Italy) – 18 years, 201 days, in 1982
Ruben Moran (Uruguay) – 19 years, 344 days, in 1950

OLDEST PLAYERS IN FIFA WORLD CUP FINAL
Dino Zoff (Italy) – 40 years, 133 days, in 1982
Gunnar Gren (Sweden) – 37 years, 241 days, in 1958
Jan Jongbloed (Netherlands) – 37 years, 212 days, in 1978
Nilton Santos (Brazil) – 37 years, 32 days, in 1962

PUZACH THE FIRST SUB
The first substitute in FIFA World Cup finals history was Anatoli Puzach of the Soviet Union. He replaced Viktor Serebrianikov at half-time of the Soviets' 0-0 draw with hosts Mexico on 31 May 1970. The 1970 tournament was the first in which substitutes were allowed, with two permitted for each side. FIFA increased this to three per team for the 1998 finals.

FOUR AND OUT
The most players sent off in one FIFA World Cup finals game is four. Costinha and Deco of Portugal and Khalid Boulahrouz and Gio van Bronckhorst of the Netherlands were sent off by Russian referee Valentin Ivanov in their second-round match in Germany in 2006.

CANIGGIA – SENT OFF, WHILE ON THE BENCH…
Claudio Caniggia of Argentina became the first player to be sent off from the substitutes' bench, during the match against Sweden in 2002. Caniggia was dismissed in first-half stoppage time for dissent towards UAE referee Ali Bujsaim. Caniggia carried on protesting after the referee warned him to keep quiet, so Bujsaim showed him a red card.

MALDINI'S MINUTES RECORD
Lothar Matthaus of West Germany/Germany has started the most FIFA World Cup finals matches – 25. But Italy defender Paolo Maldini (left) has stayed on the field for longer, despite starting two games fewer. Maldini played for 2,220 minutes, Matthaus for 2,052. According to the stopwatch, the top four are completed by Uwe Seeler of West Germany, who played for 1,980 minutes, and Argentina's Diego Maradona, who played for 1,938.

GERMANY UNITED
Germany and West Germany are counted together in World Cup records because the Deutscher Fussball-Bund, founded in 1900, was the original governing body and the DFB was in charge of the national game before World War 2, during the East–West split and post-reunification. German sides have won the World Cup four times and appeared in the Final a record eight times. In 2014, match-deciding substitutes Andre Schurrle and Mario Gotze were the first players born in Germany since reunification to win the World Cup, while team-mate Toni Kroos was the only 2014 squad-member to have been born in what was East Germany. Kroos was also the first player from the former East Germany to win the World Cup.

UNBEATEN GOALKEEPERS IN THE FIFA WORLD CUP FINALS*

Walter Zenga (Italy)	517 minutes without conceding a goal, 1990
Peter Shilton (England)	502 minutes, 1986–90
Iker Casillas (Spain)	476 minutes, 2010–14
Sepp Maier (W Germany)	475 minutes, 1974–78
Gianluigi Buffon (Italy)	460 minutes, 2006
Emerson Leao (Brazil)	458 minutes, 1978
Gordon Banks (England)	442 minutes, 1966

* Pascal Zuberbuhler did not concede a goal in all 390 minutes played by Switzerland in the 2006 FIFA World Cup.

FIFA WORLD CUP GOALKEEPING

HAIL CESAR!

Brazil goalkeeper **Julio Cesar** wept with relief and joy after his penalty shoot-out defiance helped the 2014 FIFA World Cup hosts beat Chile in a round-of-16 tie in Belo Horizonte. Coach Luiz Felipe Scolari had kept faith with the 34-year-old, even though he had barely played for his English club Queens Park Rangers and gone on loan to FC Toronto of the MLS. Cesar was blamed by many Brazilians for a mistake which led to defeat by Netherlands in the 2010 quarter-finals. In 2014, however, he saved Chile's first two kicks and rocketed from scapegoat to national hero.

NOT THINKING OUTSIDE THE BOX

Italy's Gianluca Pagliuca was the first goalkeeper to be sent off at a FIFA World Cup match – for handball outside his penalty area – against Norway in 1994. Despite sacrificing playmaker Roberto Baggio for goalkeeper Luca Marchegiani, Italy still won 1-0.

ITALY'S ELDER STATESMEN

Dino Zoff became both the oldest player and oldest captain to win the FIFA World Cup when Italy lifted the trophy in Spain in 1982. He was 40 years 133 days old. A predecessor as goalkeeper and captain of both Italy and Juventus, Gianpiero Combi, had led Italy to World Cup glory in 1934.

FIVE-STAR CARBAJAL

Antonio Carbajal, of Mexico, is one of only two men to have appeared at five FIFA World Cup finals – the other was Germany's versatile Lothar Matthaus. Carbajal, who played in 1950, 1954, 1958, 1962 and 1966, conceded a record 25 goals in his 11 FIFA World Cup finals appearances – the same number let in by Saudi Arabia's Mohamed Al-Deayea across ten games in 1994, 1998 and 2002. Al-Deayea was a member of the Saudi squad for the 2006 tournament but did not play.

ZERO TO HERO

One of the unlikeliest stars of the 2014 FIFA World Cup finals was Mexico goalkeeper **Guillermo Ochoa**. He had spent the previous three years in the European shadows at modest French Corsican club Ajaccio. He feared for his World Cup place when Ajaccio were relegated, but Mexico coach Miguel Herrera was unconcerned and Ochoa repaid him with a string of outstanding performances. Best of all was his brilliant defiance of hosts Brazil in a goalless draw in the group phase. Ochoa, who ended the finals with 61 caps for Mexico, conceded just three times in four games as Mexico lost 2-1 to two late Netherlands goals in the round-of-16.

NUMBER ONE NUMBER ONES

The Lev Yashin Award was introduced in 1994 for the man voted best goalkeeper of the FIFA World Cup – though a goalkeeper was selected subsequently for an all-star team at the end of every tournament dating back 1930. The all-star team was expanded from 11 to 23 players in 1998, allowing room for more than one goalkeeper, but returned to 11 players in 2010. Players who were picked for the all-star teams but missed out on the Lev Yashin Award were Paraguay's Jose Luis Chilavert in 1998, Turkey's Rustu Recber in 2002, and Germany's Jens Lehmann and Portugal's Ricardo in 2006. The first Lev Yashin Award was presented to Belgium's Michel Preud'homme, even though he only played four games, conceding four goals, at the 1994 competition – his side were edged out 3-2 by Germany in the second round. Legendary Soviet goalkeeper Lev Yashin, after whom the trophy was named, played in the 1958, 1962 and 1966 FIFA World Cups and was a member of his country's 1970 squad as third-choice keeper and assistant coach – although he was never chosen for a FIFA World Cup team of the tournament. From 2010 commercial priorities led to Yashin's name being dropped from the award and it was renamed the Golden Glove award.

OLIVER'S ARMS

Germany's **Oliver Kahn** is the only goalkeeper to have been voted FIFA's Player of the Tournament, winning the award at the 2002 FIFA World Cup – despite taking a share of the blame for Brazil's winning goals in the final.

RIGHT WAY FOR RICARDO

Spain's Ricardo Zamora became the first man to save a penalty in a FIFA World Cup finals match, stopping Valdemar de Brito's spot-kick for Brazil in 1934. Spain went on to win 3-1.

HOWARD'S WAY

Tim Howard wrote his name into the FIFA World Cup history books with his amazing performance in the United States' second round clash with Belgium in 2014. Howard registered 16 superb saves in defying wave upon wave of Belgian attacks. This was the most saves ever recorded in a FIFA World Cup tie since the statistic was first introduced in 1966. It was not enough, however: the United States lost a thriller of a match 2-1 after extra time.

LEADING FROM THE BACK

Iker Casillas became the third goalkeeper to captain his country to FIFA World Cup glory, when Spain became champions in South Africa in 2010. He emulated Italians Gianpiero Combi (in 1934) and Dino Zoff (1982). Casillas was also the first man to lift the trophy after his side had lost their opening match of the tournament.

UNLUCKY BREAK

Goalkeeper Frantisek Planicka broke his arm during Czechoslovakia's 1938 second-round clash against Brazil, but played on, even though the game went to extra-time before ending in a 1-1 draw. Not surprisingly, given the extent of his injury, Planicka missed the replay two days later, which the Czechs lost 2-1, and the goalkeeper of the 1938 FIFA World Cup never added to his tally of 73 caps.

PLAYERS VOTED BEST GOALKEEPER OF THE TOURNAMENT

1930	Enrique Ballestrero (Uruguay)	1978	Ubaldo Fillol (Argentina)
1934	Ricardo Zamora (Spain)	1982	Dino Zoff (Italy)
1938	Frantisek Planicka (Czechoslovakia)	1986	Harald Schumacher (West Germany)
1950	Roque Maspoli (Uruguay)	1990	Sergio Goycoechea (Argentina)
1954	Gyula Grosics (Hungary)	1994	Michel Preud'homme (Belgium)
1958	Harry Gregg (Northern Ireland)	1998	Fabien Barthez (France)
1962	Viliam Schrojf (Czechoslovakia)	2002	Oliver Kahn (Germany)
1966	Gordon Banks (England)	2006	Gianluigi Buffon (Italy)
1970	Ladislao Mazurkiewicz (Uruguay)	2010	Iker Casillas (Spain)
1974	Jan Tomaszewski (Poland)	2014	Manuel Neuer (Germany)

BATTERING RAMON

Argentina's 6-0 win over Peru at the 1978 FIFA World Cup aroused suspicion because the hosts needed to win by four goals to reach the final at the expense of arch-rivals Brazil – and Peruvian goalkeeper Ramon Quiroga had been born in Argentina. He insisted, though, that his saves prevented the defeat from being even more embarrassingly emphatic. Earlier in the same tournament, Quiroga had been booked for a foul on Grzegorz Lato after running into the Polish half of the field.

END TO END STUFF

When Miroslav Klose raced on to a long ball from German team-mate **Manuel Neuer** to score against England in their 2010 FIFA World Cup second round tie, it made Neuer the first goalkeeper to directly set up a finals goal for 44 years. The last before then had been the Soviet Union's Anzor Kavazashvili, providing an assist for Valery Porkuyan's late winner against Chile in the 1966 group stage.

MORE AND MORA

Luis Ricardo Guevara Mora holds the unenviable record for most goals conceded in just one FIFA World Cup finals match. The 20-year-old had to pick the ball out of the net ten times in El Salvador's thrashing by Hungary in 1982 – and his team-mates managed only one goal of their own in reply. In this game he also set the record for being the youngest goalkeeper to participate in the FIFA World Cup finals.

TONY AWARD

United States goalkeeper **Tony Meola** left the national team after the 1994 FIFA World Cup because he wanted to switch sports and take up American football instead. He failed to make it in gridiron and returned to soccer, but did not play for his country again until 1999. He retired for a second time after reaching a century of international appearances and still holds the record for being the youngest FIFA World Cup captain, having worn the armband for the US's 5-1 defeat to Czechoslovakia in 1990, aged 21 years 316 days.

SWEDISH STALEMATE

Gilmar and Colin McDonald were the goalkeepers who made history at the 1958 FIFA World Cup in Sweden when first round group rivals Brazil and England fought out the first goalless draw in the history of the finals.

KEEPING THE FAITH

Switzerland's **Diego Benaglio** was the only goalkeeper to register a shot at the 2014 FIFA World Cup in Brazil. With the Swiss losing their second-round tie 1-0 to Argentina in Sao Paulo, he charged upfield at a corner. The ball fell loose to him in the penalty area, but his effort on goal was blocked. Benaglio's Swiss predecessor, at the 2006 finals, was equally unlucky. Pascal Zuberbuhler kept a clean sheet in all four of their matches, three in the group stage and a goalless draw with Ukraine in the second round. However the Swiss lost the resulting penalty shoot-out 3-0, despite Zuberbuhler saving Ukraine's first kick by Andriy Shevchenko.

TOP GOALS

Year	Goals	Per match
1930	70	(3.89 per match)
1934	70	(4.12 per match)
1938	84	(4.67 per match)
1950	88	(4 per match)
1954	140	(5.38 per match)
1958	126	(3.6 per match)
1962	89	(2.78 per match)
1966	89	(2.78 per match)
1970	95	(2.97 per match)
1974	97	(2.55 per match)
1978	102	(2.68 per match)
1982	146	(2.81 per match)
1986	132	(2.54 per match)
1990	115	(2.21 per match)
1994	141	(2.71 per match)
1998	171	(2.67 per match)
2002	161	(2.52 per match)
2006	147	(2.3 per match)
2010	145	(2.27 per match)
2014	171	(2.67 per match)
Total	**2,379**	(2.85 per match)

THE PETER PRINCIPLE

Peter Shilton became the oldest FIFA World Cup captain when he led England for their 1990 third-place play-off against hosts Italy. He was 40 years and 292 days old as he made his 125th and final appearance for his country – though his day was spoiled by a 2-1 defeat, including a goalkeeping error that gifted Roberto Baggio Italy's opener. Shilton, born in Leicester on 18 September 1949, also played for England at the 1982 and 1986 tournaments. He became captain in Mexico in 1986 after Bryan Robson was ruled out of the tournament by injury and Ray Wilkins by suspension, and featured in one of the FIFA World Cup's all-time memorable moments, when he was out-jumped by Argentina's Diego Maradona for the infamous "Hand of God" goal. Shilton jointly holds the record for most FIFA World Cup clean sheets, with ten – along with France's Fabien Barthez, who played at the 1998, 2002 and 2006 tournaments. Both men made 17 FIFA World Cup finals appearances apiece.

TRADING PLACES

The first goalkeeper to be substituted at a FIFA World Cup was Romania's Stere Adamache, who was replaced by Rica Raducanu 27 minutes into a 3-2 defeat to Brazil in 1970. Romania were 2-0 down at the time.

PLAYING THROUGH THE PAIN BARRIER

The first FIFA World Cup clean sheet was kept by Jimmy Douglas of the United States in a 3-0 win over Belgium in 1930. He followed that up with another, as Paraguay were beaten by the same scoreline – but Argentina proved too good, winning 6-1 in the semi-final. Douglas injured his knee after only four minutes, but had to play on as this occurred in the days before substitutes were allowed.

HOW GOING DUTCH PAYS OFF

Argentina's **Sergio Romero** will never be forgotten in the Netherlands – for using the experience he gained there to put the Dutchmen out of the 2014 FIFA World Cup. Romero had been brought to Europe in 2007 by Louis Van Gaal when the Dutch master coach was boss of AZ Alkmaar. In 2011 Romero moved to Italy to play for Sampdoria. Then he fell out of favour with the Genoese club and was loaned to French club AS Monaco in August 2013. Romero was hardly a regular in Ligue 1 either, indeed he played only three league matches in the season leading up to the FIFA World Cup. However, he did remain the first-choice with Argentina coach Alejandro Sabella. Argentina won all their group matches and then Romero kept clean sheets in initial knockout victories over Switzerland and Belgium. When the semi-final went to penalties, Romero became a national hero, with match-winning saves from the Netherlands' Ron Vlaar and Wesley Sneijder. Romero said later he owed Van Gaal special thanks … "for teaching me how to save penalties."

FIFA WORLD CUP MANAGERS

MANAGING SUCCESS

Germany provided the largest single contingent of coaches at the 2014 FIFA World Cup in Brazil. Most successful was Die Nationalelf's boss, **Joachim Low**, who became, following the 1-0 final victory over Argentina, the fourth German coach to win the trophy after Sepp Herberger (1954), Helmut Schon (1974) and Franz Beckenbauer (1990). Low was appointed in 2006 after having been assistant for two years. **Jurgen Klinsmann** (United States) and Ottmar Hitzfeld (Switzerland) both reached the second round, but the group stage was the end of the line for Volker Finke (Cameroon) and Berlin-born Nico Kovac (Croatia).

YOUNG JUAN

Juan Jose Tramutola remains the youngest-ever FIFA World Cup coach, leading Argentina in the 1930 tournament at the age of 27 years and 267 days. Italian Cesare Maldini became the oldest in 2002, taking charge of Paraguay when aged 70 years and 131 days.

DREAM TO NIGHTMARE

Luiz Felipe Scolari quit as Brazil coach after the 2014 FIFA World Cup brought the worst defeat in their history, by 7-1 against Germany in the semi-finals, and then a 3-0 defeat to Holland in the third-place play-off. However, he had won the FIFA World Cup with Brazil in 2002 and went on, with Portugal in 2006, to set an individual record of 11 successive wins at the finals.

PUFF DADDIES

The coaches of the two sides appearing at the 1978 FIFA World Cup final were such prolific smokers that an oversized ashtray was produced for Argentina's Cesar Luis Menotti and the Netherlands's Ernst Happel so they could share it on the touchline.

SOCCER SIX

Only one man has gone to six FIFA World Cups as coach: Brazilian **Carlos Alberto Parreira**, whose greatest moment came when he guided Brazil to the trophy for the fourth time in 1994. His second stint as Brazil coach was less successful – they fell in the quarter-finals in 2006. Parreira also led Kuwait (1982), the United Arab Emirates (1990), Saudi Arabia (1998) and hosts South Africa (2010) at the finals. He had stepped down as South Africa coach in April 2008, for family reasons, but returned late the following year. Parreira was once sacked midway through a FIFA World Cup. In 1998 he led Saudi Arabia for the first two of their three games – losing 1-0 to Denmark and 4-0 to France – before receiving his marching orders.

ELDEST STATESMAN OTTO

Otto Rehhagel became the oldest coach in FIFA World Cup history in South Africa in 2010. He was 71 years and 317 days old when his Greece team lost 2-0 to Argentina in their final group game. German Rehhagel had led Greece to their UEFA European Championship victory in 2004.

CRASHING BORA

Only one tournament behind record-holder Carlos Alberto Parreira, **Bora Milutinovic** has coached at five different FIFA World Cups – with a different country each time, two of them being the hosts. As well as Mexico in 1986 and the United States in 1994, he led Costa Rica in 1990, Nigeria in 1998 and China in 2002. He reached the knockout stages with every country except China – who failed to score a single goal.

DIVIDED LOYALTIES

No coach has won the FIFA World Cup in charge of a foreign team, but several have faced their homeland. These include Jurgen Klinsmann, who played for Germany when they won the Cup in 1990 and then managed them to third-place in 2006. Klinsmann, who was German boss 2004–06, having already made his home in California, was appointed United States coach in 2011. In the 2014 FIFA World Cup, "Klinsi" and the US lost 1-0 in a group match to Germany, now led by his former assistant Joachim Low, whom he had appointed in 2004. Other managers to face their native land include Brazilian Didi (with Peru in 1970), Frenchman Bruno Metsu (with Senegal in 2002) and Swede Sven-Goran Eriksson (with England in 2002 and 2006).

FIFA WORLD CUP– WINNING COACHES

1930	Alberto Suppici
1934	Vittorio Pozzo
1938	Vittorio Pozzo
1950	Juan Lopez
1954	Sepp Herberger
1958	Vicente Feola
1962	Aymore Moreira
1966	Alf Ramsey
1970	Mario Zagallo
1974	Helmut Schon
1978	Cesar Luis Menotti
1982	Enzo Bearzot
1986	Carlos Bilardo
1990	Franz Beckenbauer
1994	Carlos Alberto Parreira
1998	Aime Jacquet
2002	Luiz Felipe Scolari
2006	Marcello Lippi
2010	Vicente del Bosque
2014	Joachim Low

SCHON SHINES

West Germany's **Helmut Schon** was coach for more FIFA World Cup matches than any other man – 25, across the 1966, 1970, 1974 and 1978 tournaments. He has also won the most games as a coach, 16 in all – including the 1974 final against the Netherlands. The 1974 tournament was third time lucky for Schon. He he had taken West Germany to second place in 1966 and to third in 1970. Before taking charge of the national side, Schon had worked as an assistant to Sepp Herberger, coach of West Germany's 1954 FIFA World Cup-winning team – Schon was coach of the then-independent Saarland regional side at the time. Dog-lover Schon, born in Dresden on 15 September 1915, scored 17 goals in 16 internationals for Germany between 1937 and 1941. He succeeded Herberger in 1964 and spent 14 years in charge of his country. He was the first coach to win both the FIFA World Cup (1974) and the European Championship (1972).

FIFA WORLD CUP DISCIPLINE

⚽ FIFA BITES BACK

Uruguay's **Luis Suarez** incurred a record instant FIFA sanction after biting Italy's Giorgio Chiellini during Uruguay's 1-0 win in the 2014 World Cup, a result that put them, and not the Azzurri, into the second round. Suarez missed the subsequent 2-0 defeat by Colombia because he had been banned from all football for four months, from international competition for nine games and fined 100,000 Swiss francs. It was not the first time Suarez had been in trouble at the FIFA World Cup finals, having been banned for one match at the 2010 finals after being dismissed for handball on the goal-line in a quarter-final against Ghana.

⚽ REPEAT OFFENDERS

France's **Zinedine Zidane** and Brazil's **Cafu** are both FIFA World Cup winners – and both notched up a record six FIFA World Cup cards, though Cafu escaped any reds, while Zidane was sent off twice. Most famously, Zidane was dismissed for headbutting Italy's Marco Materazzi in extra-time of the 2006 final in Berlin – the final match of the Frenchman's career. He had also been sent off during a first-round match against Saudi Arabia in 1998, but returned from suspension in time to help France win the trophy with a sensational two-goal performance in the final. The only other man to have been sent off twice at two different FIFA World Cups is Cameroon's Rigobert Song. When dismissed against Brazil in 1994, he became the FIFA World Cup's youngest red card offender – aged just 17 years and 358 days. He saw red for the second time against Chile in 1998.

⚽ NOT LEADING BY EXAMPLE

The first man to be sent off at a FIFA World Cup was Peru's Placido Galindo, at the first tournament in 1930 during a 3-1 defeat to Romania. Chilean referee Alberto Warnken dismissed the Peruvian captain for fighting.

⚽ ARGIE BARGEY

Argentina defender Pedro Monzon became the first player sent off in a World Cup final when he was dismissed in 1990 for a foul on West Germany's Jurgen Klinsmann. Monzon had been on the pitch only 20 minutes after coming on as a half-time substitute. Three minutes from full-time Mexican referee Edgardo Codesal reduced Argentina to nine men by dismissing Gustavo Dezotti after a skirmish with Jurgen Kohler. Marcel Desailly, of France in 1998, is the only member of a winning team to have been sent off in a World Cup final.

⚽ CARDS CLOSE TO CHEST

Only one group in FIFA World Cup finals history has featured no bookings at all – Group 4 in 1970, featuring West Germany, Peru, Bulgaria and Morocco. In contrast, the 2006 FIFA World Cup in Germany was the worst for both red and yellow cards, with 28 dismissals and 345 bookings in 64 matches.

FIFA WORLD CUP RED CARDS, BY TOURNAMENT

Year	Red Cards
1930	1
1934	1
1938	4
1950	0
1954	3
1958	3
1962	6
1966	5
1970	0
1974	5
1978	3
1982	5
1986	8
1990	16
1994	15
1998	22
2002	17
2006	28
2010	17
2014	10

FINAL COUNT

England's Howard Webb set a record with one red card and 14 yellows in the 2010 FIFA World Cup final between Spain and Netherlands. The previous 18 finals had featured 40 bookings and three dismissals between them. Webb's card total of 15 was nine more than the six shown by Brazil's Romualdo Arppi Filho in the 1986 final between Argentina (four) and Germany (two). Italy's Nicola Rizzoli showed four yellow cards (two each) when the same teams met in the 2014 FIFA World Cup final.

SOLE CHANCE OF GLORY

India withdrew from the 1950 FIFA World Cup because some of their players wanted to play barefoot but FIFA insisted all players must wear football boots. India have not qualified for the tournament since.

BREAKING COVER

Zaire defender Mwepu Llunga was booked for running out of the wall and kicking the ball away as Brazil prepared to take a free-kick, at the 1974 FIFA World Cup. Romanian referee Nicolae Rainea ignored Llunga's pleas of innocence.

ALL'S FAIR

FIFA World Cup organizers hailed a vast improvement in fair play at the 2014 finals in Brazil. The total of 10 red cards was the lowest since eight in Mexico in 1986 and the tally of 177 yellow cards the fewest since 165 in Italy in 1990 (both finals contained 24 teams and 52 matches). The first dismissal in the group stage was Uruguay's Maxi Pereira against Costa Rica, but the earliest in a game was Portugal defender **Pepe** for a headbutt on Germany's Thomas Muller in the 37th minute of their clash in Salvador. FIFA referee's chief Massimo Busacca also put a sharp reduction in injuries down to greater discipline among players.

GOOD SON, BAD SON

Cameroon's Andre Kana-Biyik served two suspensions during the 1990 FIFA World Cup. The first came after he was sent off in the opening match against Argentina – six minutes before his brother Francois Omam-Biyik scored the only goal. His second ban came after yellow cards in the final group game against Russia and in the second-round defeat of Colombia.

YELLOW MELO'S RED MIST

Felipe Melo's red card for stamping on Arjen Robben, in Brazil's 2010 FIFA World Cup quarter-final defeat to the Netherlands, meant Brazil have had more players sent off in FIFA World Cup history than any other team – one more than Argentina. Melo was Brazil's 11th dismissal, after Kaka had become the 10th in a first-round victory over the Ivory Coast. Melo could also have gone down as the first player ever to score an own goal and be sent off in the same FIFA World Cup match, but the first Dutch goal was later officially awarded to their own playmaker Wesley Sneijder.

THREE LIONS' THREE REDS

Ray Wilkins, David Beckham and Wayne Rooney are the only three England players to have been sent off at the FIFA World Cup. Wilkins was dismissed for a second yellow card in a group game against Morocco in 1986; Beckham incurred a straight red in the second round against Argentina in 1998; and Rooney also received a straight red against Portugal in the 2006 quarter-finals. All three matches ended in draws, but England lost penalty shoot-outs to Argentina and Portugal.

FIFA WORLD CUP REFEREEING

YEARS OF EXPERIENCE

Spain's Juan Gardeazabal Garay remains the youngest man to referee at a FIFA World Cup, being just 24 years 193 days old when he took charge at the 1958 tournament in Sweden. He also officiated in 1962 and 1966. Englishman **George Reader** is not only the oldest man to have refereed a FIFA World Cup final – 56 years 236 days old when he ran the effective climax between Brazil and Uruguay in 1950 – but also the oldest referee at any FIFA World Cup. He died on 13 July 1978, exactly 48 years to the day since the first FIFA World Cup fixture.

THE ITALIAN JOB

Nicola Rizzoli had designs on refereeing the FIFA World Cup final ever since he was promoted to the FIFA international list in 2007. Rizzoli, an architect away from the pitches of the world, had made such high-speed progress that he was refereeing in Italy's Serie A at the age of 30. He was named in FIFA's world elite group in the spring of 2013 and, two months later, refereed the UEFA Champions League final. He was in the middle for four matches at the 2014 FIFA World Cup and became the third Italian to referee the final.

BAKU OF THE NET

The official who signalled that Geoff Hurst's controversial extra-time goal for England in the 1966 FIFA World Cup final had crossed the line is often wrongly described as a Russian linesman. In fact, Tofik Bakhramov was from Azerbaijan, so he was officially a Soviet Union linesman. The Azeri national football stadium in the capital Baku, is now named after him.

DOUBLE DUTY

Only two men have refereed a FIFA World Cup final and a European Championship final. Italian Sergio Gonella officiated at the 1978 World Cup final between Argentina and the Netherlands, two years after overseeing the European Championship final between West Germany and Czechoslovakia. Swiss official Gottfried Dienst took control of the 1966 FIFA World Cup final, between England and West Germany, and the drawn 1968 European Championship final between Italy and Yugoslavia – Spain's Jose Maria Ortiz de Mendibil was awarded the replay.

FRENCH CONNECTION

Frenchman **Georges Capdeville**, in charge for Italy's win over Hungary in 1938, is the only man to referee the final in a FIFA World Cup hosted by his own country.

FIFA WORLD CUP FINAL REFEREES

Year	Referee
1930	Jean Langenus (Belgium)
1934	Ivan Eklind (Sweden)
1938	Georges Capdeville (France)
1950	George Reader (England)
1954	William Ling (England)
1958	Maurice Guigue (France)
1962	Nikolay Latyshev (USSR)
1966	Gottfried Dienst (Switzerland)
1970	Rudi Glockner (West Germany)
1974	Jack Taylor (England)
1978	Sergio Gonella (Italy)
1982	Arnaldo Cezar Coelho (Brazil)
1986	Romualdo Arppi Filho (Brazil)
1990	Edgardo Codesal (Mexico)
1994	Sandor Puhl (Hungary)
1998	Said Belqola (Morocco)
2002	Pierluigi Collina (Italy)
2006	Horacio Elizondo (Argentina)
2010	Howard Webb (England)
2014	Nicola Rizzoli (Italy)

COUPE DU MONDE 1938

WORLDWIDE WEBB

Former Yorkshire policeman **Howard Webb** became the fourth Englishman to referee a FIFA World Cup final when he was chosen for the 2010 showdown between Spain and the Netherlands. He had earlier controlled two group games and a second-round tie between Spain and Chile. The honour came less than two months after he refereed the UEFA Champions League final between Inter Milan and Bayern Munich, making him the first man in charge of both World Cup and European Cup final matches in the same summer. Webb also became the first FIFA World Cup debutant ref to be given the final. At just three days short of his 39th birthday, Webb was also the youngest FIFA World Cup final referee since Frenchman Georges Capdeville, who took charge of the 1938 final aged 38 years and 232 days. Webb also refereed two matches at the 2014 FIFA World Cup finals in Brazil.

PROLIFIC OFFICIALS

Ravshan Irmatov, from Uzbekistan, became the most experienced FIFA World Cup referee of all time at the 2014 finals. He totalled a record nine matches after controlling five in 2010 and four in Brazil. Irmatov, whose father had also been a top referee in the former Soviet Union, became a FIFA official when only 26 in 2003. Four times he was voted best referee in Asia and he controlled the final of the FIFA Club World Cup in both 2008 and 2011. His FIFA World Cup debut was in South Africa in 2010 when, despite being the youngest official present, he was awarded the Opening Match between the hosts and Mexico. In Brazil, Irmatov was the subject of controversy after he took no action against Netherlands goalkeeper Tim Krul as he confronted all of Costa Rica's penalty takers during the penalty shootout to decide the quarter-final – which the Dutchmen won, thanks to Krul's two saves. Irmatov's multi-match campaign saw him surpass the eight-match mark of Frenchman Joel Quiniou, Mexico's Benito Archundia and Uruguay's Jorge Larrionda.

TIME, GENTLEMEN

Welsh referee Clive Thomas disallowed what would have potentially been a winning goal by Brazil against Sweden in the 1978 FIFA World Cup. Thomas said he had blown the final whistle seconds before Zico headed in from a corner, and the game ended in a 1-1 draw. In contrast, Israeli referee Abraham Klein tried to blow the final whistle several times when England played Brazil at the 1970 FIFA World Cup in Guadalajara, but none of the players appeared to hear him.

NOW YOU SEE IT …

Referees were given two supporting aids at the 2014 FIFA World Cup. One was goal-line technology, approved two years earlier by the law-making International Board. The other was a vanishing spray used by refs to "fix" defensive walls in their place at free-kicks. The spray, which faded after half a minute, had been developed by Brazilian inventor Heine Allemagne. Already used widely in Latin America and FIFA junior tournaments, it impressed European referees by helping quell dissent at free-kicks.

RED CARD CARTER

Mexican referee **Arturo Brizio Carter** has sent off more players at FIFA World Cups than any other official. He showed seven red cards in his six games at the 1994 and 1998 finals. 'Victims' included Italy's Gianfranco Zola, Argentina's Ariel Ortega and France's Zinedine Zidane.

FIFA WORLD CUP ATTENDANCES

CAPACITY PLANNING

If current plans are realised and every seat is occupied, the attendances at the final of each of the next two FIFA World Cups will exceed significantly the 74,738 who attended the Maracana in Rio de Janeiro for the 2014 climax. Projected capacity for the redeveloped Luzhniki in Moscow, which will stage the 2018 FIFA World Cup final, is 81,000 while 86,250 is the maximum estimated for the **Lusail** Iconic Stadium in Qatar in 2022. The smallest proposed capacities at the next two World Cups are 43,702 at the Rostov-on-Don stadium in 2018 and then 43,520 at the Qatar University Stadium in Doha in 2022. FIFA regulations insist on a minimum capacity for a finals venue of 40,000.

TWO'S COMPANY, 300'S A CROWD

The 300 people who were recorded as watching Romania beat Peru 3-1 in 1930 formed the FIFA World Cup finals' smallest attendance, with plenty of room for manoeuvre inside the Estadio Pocitos in Montevideo. A day earlier, ten times as many people are thought to have been there to watch France's 4-1 win over Mexico.

BONANZA IN BRAZIL

The 2014 FIFA World Cup in Brazil was watched by a total of 3,429,873 spectators, across the 64 matches in 12 different stadia – the second highest aggregate attendance in the tournament's history, behind only the United States in 1994. The average attendance was 53,592 which meant a 98.4 per cent capacity. That was a marked improvement on South Africa in 2010 when the attendance average was 49,670 with "only" 92.9 per cent of the seats being filled.

CITY SLICKER

The capacity of **Soccer City**, venue for the first FIFA World Cup Final in Africa, was 84,490. This followed a total redevelopment of the original Johannesburg stadium, which had held a maximum 78,000. The design of the new stadium was based on traditional African pottery and nicknamed The Calabash. Soccer City hosted the opening match, final, four group games, and one each in the second round quarter-finals.

GENDER EQUALITY

Only two stadiums have hosted the finals of the FIFA World Cup for both men and women. The **Rose Bowl**, in Pasadena, California, was the venue for the men's final in 1994 – when Brazil beat Italy – and the women's showdown between the victorious US and China five years later, which was watched by 90,185 people. But Sweden's Rasunda Stadium, near Stockholm, just about got there first – though it endured a long wait between the men's final in 1958 and the women's in 1995. Both sets of American spectators got their money's worth, watching games that went into extra-time and which were settled on penalties.

FIFA WORLD CUP FINAL ATTENDANCES

Year	Attendance	Stadium	City
1930	93,000	Estadio Centenario	Montevideo
1934	45,000	Stadio Nazionale del PNF	Rome
1938	60,000	Stade Olympique de Colombes	Paris
1950	173,850	Estadio do Maracana	Rio de Janeiro
1954	60,000	Wankdorfstadion	Berne
1958	51,800	Rasunda Fotbollstadion	Solna
1962	68,679	Estadio Nacional	Santiago
1966	98,000	Wembley Stadium	London
1970	107,412	Estadio Azteca	Mexico City
1974	75,200	Olympiastadion	Munich
1978	71,483	Estadio Monumental	Buenos Aires
1982	90,000	Estadio Santiago Bernabeu	Madrid
1986	114,600	Estadio Azteca	Mexico City
1990	73,603	Stadio Olimpico	Rome
1994	94,194	Rose Bowl	Pasadena
1998	80,000	Stade de France	Paris
2002	69,029	International Stadium	Yokohama
2006	69,000	Olympiastadion	Berlin
2010	84,490	Soccer City	Johannesburg
2014	74,738	Maracana	Rio de Janeiro

TOURNAMENT ATTENDANCES

Year	Total	Average
1930	434,500	24,139
1934	358,000	21,059
1938	376,000	20,889
1950	1,043,500	47,432
1954	889,500	34,212
1958	919,580	26,274
1962	899,074	28,096
1966	1,635,000	51,094
1970	1,603,975	50,124
1974	1,768,152	46,530
1978	1,546,151	40,688
1982	2,109,723	40,572
1986	2,393,331	46,026
1990	2,516,348	48,391
1994	3,587,538	68,991
1998	2,785,100	43,517
2002	2,705,197	42,269
2006	3,359,439	52,491
2010	3,178,856	49,670
2014	3,429,873	53,592
TOTAL	34,538,837	44,903

FAN FESTS FIND FAVOUR

City centre "**Fan Fests**", including giant television screens, food service and entertainment provision, proved more popular than ever at the 2014 FIFA World Cup in Brazil. Several of the 12 city authorities had been reluctant, initially, to put in the work. But their efforts were rewarded with more than five million fans visiting the sites across Brazil. This was a major improvement on the total of 2.6 million across South Africa in 2010 and the initial fan fests in Germany in 2006. Not surprising, the liveliest party venue in 2014 was the fan fest on **Copacabana** beach in Rio de Janeiro.

ABSENT FRIENDS

Only 2,823 spectators turned up at the Rasunda Stadium in Stockholm to see Wales play Hungary in a first-round play-off match during the 1958 FIFA World Cup. More than 15,000 had attended the first game between the two sides, but boycotted the replay in tribute to executed Hungarian uprising leader Imre Nagy.

MORBID MARACANA

The largest attendance for a FIFA World Cup match was at Rio de Janeiro's Maracana for the last clash of the 1950 tournament – though no one is quite sure how many were there. The final tally was officially given as 173,850, though some estimates suggest as many as 210,000 witnessed the host country's traumatic defeat. Tensions were so high at the final whistle, winning Uruguay captain Obdulio Varela was not awarded the trophy in a traditional manner, but had it surreptitiously nudged into his hands. FIFA president Jules Rimet described the crowd's overwhelming silence as "morbid, almost too difficult to bear". Uruguay's triumphant players barricaded themselves inside their dressing room for several hours before they judged it safe enough to emerge. However, at least Brazil did make it to Maracana in 1950. In the 2014 FIFA World Cup, as hosts again, Brazil played in Sao Paulo, Fortaleza, Brasilia and Belo Horizonte but, after losing in the semi-finals, ended up back in Brasilia for the third-place play-off instead of Maracana for the Final.

BERLIN CALL

Despite later becoming the capital of a united Germany, then-divided Berlin only hosted three group games at the 1974 FIFA World Cup in West Germany – the host country's surprise loss to East Germany took place in Hamburg. An unexploded World War Two bomb was discovered beneath the seats at Berlin's Olympiastadion in 2002, by workers preparing the ground for the 2006 tournament. Germany, along with Brazil, had applied to host the tournament in 1942, before it was cancelled due to the outbreak of World War Two.

TWIN PEAKS

Five stadiums hold the distinction of having staged both the final of a FIFA World Cup and the summer Olympics athletics: Berlin's Olympiastadion (1936 Olympics, 2006 World Cup), Paris's Stade Colombes (1924 Olympics, 1938 World Cup), London's Wembley (1948 Olympics, 1966 World Cup), Rome's Stadio Olimpico (1960 Olympics, 1990 World Cup) and Munich's Olympiastadion (1972 Olympics, 1974 World Cup). The Estadio Azteca (Mexico City) and Rose Bowl (Pasadena) have both hosted World Cup finals as well as Olympic football finals.

OLYMPIC NAMES

The stadium hosting the opening match of the 1930 FIFA World Cup had stands named after great Uruguayan footballing triumphs: Colombes, in honour of the 1924 Paris Olympics venue; Amsterdam, after the site where that title was retained four years later; and Montevideo, even though it would be another fortnight before the home team clinched the first FIFA World Cup in their own capital city.

RIO'S MARIO

Most people know Brazil's largest stadium as the Maracana, named after the Rio neighbourhood and a small nearby river. But, since the mid-1960s, the official title has been "Estadio Mario Filho" after the influential sports journalist and editor who campaigned for the stadium's construction on that site.

TERRITORIAL GAINS

History was made twice over when **FIFA** decided in December 2010 which countries would stage the 2018 and 2022 FIFA World Cups. The 2018 vote went in favour of Russia – ahead of Spain/Portugal, Belgium/Netherlands and England – meaning the first FIFA World Cup to be held in Eastern Europe. The tournament will then go to the Middle East for the first time in 2022, after Qatar emerged ahead of rival bids from the USA, Japan, South Korea and Australia.

MEXICAN SAVE

Mexico was not the original choice to host the 1986 FIFA World Cup, but stepped in when Colombia withdrew in 1982 due to financial problems. Mexico held on to the staging rights despite suffering from an earthquake in September 1985 that left approximately 10,000 people dead, but which left the stadiums unscathed. FIFA kept faith in the country, and the **Azteca Stadium** went on to become the first venue to host two FIFA World Cup final matches – and Mexico the first country to stage two FIFA World Cups. The Azteca – formally named the "Estadio Guillermo Canedo", after a Mexican football official – was built in 1960 using 100,000 tonnes of concrete, four times as much as was needed for the old Wembley.

⚽ ARCHITECTS' PREROGATIVE

Distinctive and creative elements were added to the stadiums built especially for the 2010 FIFA World Cup in South Africa, including the giraffe-shaped towers at **Nelspruit's Mbombela stadium**, the 350-metre-long arch with its mobile viewing platform soaring above **Durban's main arena**, and the white "petals" shrouding the Nelson Mandela Bay stadium in Port Elizabeth.

⚽ UNSUCCESSFUL HOSTING BIDS

Year	Bids
1930	Hungary, Italy, Netherlands, Spain, Sweden
1934	Sweden
1938	Argentina, Germany
1950	None
1954	None
1958	None
1962	Argentina, West Germany
1966	Spain, West Germany
1970	Argentina
1974	Spain
1978	Mexico
1982	West Germany
1986	Colombia*, Canada, USA
1990	England, Greece, USSR
1994	Brazil, Morocco
1998	Morocco, Switzerland
2002	Mexico
2006	Brazil, England, Morocco, South Africa
2010	Egypt, Libya/Tunisia, Morocco
2014	None
2018	England, Netherlands/Belgium, Spain/Portugal
2022	Australia, Japan, South Korea, USA

* Colombia won hosting rights for 1986 but later withdrew.

⚽ MORE MARACANA

No other stadium than the **Maracana** in Rio de Janeiro was considered for even a moment when it came to choosing the host venue for the 2014 FIFA World Cup in Brazil. On 13 July it duly became the second venue, after the Estadio Azteca in Mexico City, to host the FIFA World Cup final for the second time. Although the official attendance is now given as 173,850, it is thought that anything up to 210,000 may have jammed the Maracana for the 1950 final group match between Brazil and Uruguay. Several redevelopments saw capacity reduced to an all-seater capacity of around 75,000 by the time of the 2014 showpiece between Germany and Argentina. The latest facelift for Maracana, which is owned by the Rio de Janeiro state government, cost an estimated $500m. As one of the first stadiums to be ready, it hosted the final of the 2013 Confederations Cup "rehearsal" tournament. The Maracana will also stage the Opening and Closing Ceremonies of the Rio de Janeiro 2016 Olympic Games.

⚽ RATIONAL IN RUSSIA

Organizers of the 2018 FIFA World Cup in Russia plan to return to the "clusters" system of adjacent city venues to ease travel, accommodation and logistical problems, thus reducing the costs for fans. Unlike Brazil 2014, one city – Moscow – will have two venues: the **Luzhniki** Olympic Stadium and Spartak Moscow's new home. The "clusters" concept was last used in the United States in 1994. Michel Platini, president of the France 1998 organizing committee, scrapped the idea to spread the top teams all around the country. FIFA wanted to reinstate the system for the 2014 finals in Brazil but local organizers refused.

⚽ HOSTS WITH THE MOST

No other single-hosted FIFA World Cup has used as many venues as the 14 spread across Spain in 1982. The 2002 tournament was played at 20 different venues, but ten of these were in Japan and ten in co-host country South Korea.

FIFA WORLD CUP PENALTIES

FIFA WORLD CUP PENALTY SHOOT-OUTS

Year	Round	120-minute Score	Winners	Shoot-out Score
1982	Semi-final	West Germany 3 France 3	West Germany	5-4
1986	Quarter-final	West Germany 0 Mexico 0	West Germany	4-1
1986	Quarter-final	France 1 Brazil 1	France	4-3
1986	Quarter-final	Belgium 1 Spain 1	Belgium	5-4
1990	Second round	Republic of Ireland 0 Romania 0	Republic of Ireland	5-4
1990	Quarter-final	Argentina 0 Yugoslavia 0	Argentina	3-2
1990	Semi-final	Argentina 1 Italy 1	Argentina	4-3
1990	Semi-final	West Germany 1 England 1	West Germany	4-3
1994	Second round	Bulgaria 1 Mexico 1	Bulgaria	3-1
1994	Quarter-final	Sweden 2 Romania 2	Sweden	5-4
1994	Final	Brazil 0 Italy 0	Brazil	3-2
1998	Second round	Argentina 2 England 2	Argentina	4-3
1998	Quarter-final	France 0 Italy 0	France	4-3
1998	Semi-final	Brazil 1 Netherlands 1	Brazil	4-2
2002	Second round	Spain 1 Republic of Ireland 1	Spain	3-2
2002	Quarter-final	South Korea 0 Spain 0	South Korea	5-3
2006	Second round	Ukraine 0 Switzerland 0	Ukraine	3-0
2006	Quarter-final	Germany 1 Argentina 1	Germany	4-2
2006	Quarter-final	Portugal 0 England 0	Portugal	3-1
2006	Final	Italy 1 France 1	Italy	5-3
2010	Second round	Paraguay 0 Japan 0	Paraguay	5-3
2010	Quarter-final	Uruguay 1 Ghana 1	Uruguay	4-2
2014	Second round	Brazil 1 Chile 1	Brazil	3-2
2014	Second round	Costa Rica 1 Greece 1	Costa Rica	5-3
2014	Quarter-final	Netherlands 0 Costa Rica 0	Netherlands	4-3
2014	Semi-final	Argentina 0 Netherlands 0	Argentina	4-2

BAGGIO OF DISHONOUR

Pity poor **Roberto Baggio**: the Italian maestro stepped up in three FIFA World Cup penalty shoot-outs, more than any other player – and has been a loser in every one. Most painfully, it was his shot over the bar that gifted Brazil the trophy at the end of the 1994 Final. But he had also ended on the losing side against Argentina in a 1990 semi-final and would do so again, against France in a 1998 quarter-final. At least, in 1990 and 1998, his own attempts were successful.

FIRST IS BETTER

Nine penalty shoot-outs in a row were won by the team taking the first kick. The run started with South Korea's quarter-final defeat of Spain in the 2002 FIFA World Cup and ended after Costa Rica's second round win over Greece in 2014. The Netherlands went second and still beat Costa Rica in the 2014 quarter-finals and then went first when losing the semi-final to Argentina.

WOE FOR ASAMOAH

Ghana striker **Asamoah Gyan** is the only player to have missed two penalties during match-time at FIFA World Cups. He hit the post with a spot-kick against the Czech Republic during a group game at the 2006 tournament, then struck a shot against the bar with the final kick of extra-time in Ghana's 2010 quarter-final versus Uruguay. Had he scored then, Gyan would have given Ghana a 2–1 win – following Luis Suarez's goal-stopping handball on the goal-line – and a first African place in a FIFA World Cup semi-final. Despite such a traumatic miss, Gyan did then step up to take Ghana's first penalty in the shoot-out, again striking it high – but this time into the back of the net. His team still lost, though, 4–2 on penalties.

FRENCH KICKS

The first penalty shoot-out at a FIFA World Cup finals came in the 1982 semi-final in Seville between West Germany and France, when French takers Didier Six and **Maxime Bossis** were the unfortunate players to miss. The same two countries met in the semi-finals four years later – and West Germany again won, though in normal time, 2-0. The record for most shoot-outs is shared by the 1990 and 2006 tournaments, with four apiece. Both semi-finals in 1990 went to penalties, while the 2006 final was the second to be settled that manner – Italy beating France 5-3 after David Trezeguet struck the crossbar.

PENALTY SHOOT-OUTS BY COUNTRY

5	Argentina (4 wins, 1 defeat)	1	Belgium (1 win)
4	Germany/West Germany (4 wins)	1	Bulgaria (1 win)
4	Brazil (3 wins, 1 defeat)	1	Paraguay (1 win)
4	France (2 wins, 2 defeats)	1	Portugal (1 win)
4	Italy (1 win, 3 defeats)	1	South Korea (1 win)
3	Netherlands (1 win, 2 defeats)	1	Sweden (1 win)
3	Spain (1 win, 2 defeats)	1	Ukraine (1 win)
3	England (3 defeats)	1	Uruguay (1 win)
2	Costa Rica (1 win, 1 defeat)	1	Yugoslavia (1 win)
2	Republic of Ireland (1 win, 1 defeat)	1	Chile (1 defeat)
2	Mexico (2 defeats)	1	Ghana (1 defeat)
2	Romania (2 defeats)	1	Greece (1 defeat)
		1	Japan (1 defeat)
		1	Switzerland (1 defeat)

COSTA RICA'S KRUL FATE

Costa Rica enjoyed a thrilling ride at the 2014 FIFA World Cup. Los Ticos started by topping a first round "Group of Death", featuring three former world champions in Uruguay, Italy and England. Coach Jorge Luis Pinto then saw his men draw 1-1 with Greece in the second round and win the shoot-out 5-3 to reach the quarter-finals for the first time ever. Heroes were goalkeeper Keylor Navas, in saving from Teo Gekas, and last-shot defender Michael Umana. History appeared to be repeating itself when Costa Rica held Netherlands goalless to earn another shoot-out. But this time they were foiled by Dutch coach Louis Van Gaal. He sent on reserve goalkeeper **Tim Krul** as substitute for Jasper Cillessen in the last minute of extra time, as Van Gaal explained, "because he has a longer reach." Krul duly saved kicks from Bryan Ruiz and Umana and the Dutch won the shoot-out 4-3. Costa Rica were still welcomed home as heroes.

THREE IN ONE

Argentina's stand-in goalkeeper Sergio Goycochea set a tournament record by saving four shoot-out penalties in 1990 – though West Germany's Harald Schumacher managed as many, across the 1982 and 1986 tournaments. Portugal's Ricardo achieved an unprecedented feat by keeping out three attempts in a single shoot-out, becoming an instant hero in his side's quarter-final win over England in 2006.

GERMAN EFFICIENCY

Germany, or West Germany, have won all four of their FIFA World Cup penalty shoot-outs, more than any other team. Argentina also have four wins, but they have lost one – to Germany in the 2006 quarter-final. The German run began with a semi-final victory over France in 1982, when goalkeeper Harald Schumacher was the matchwinner, despite being lucky to stay on the pitch for a vicious extra-time foul on France's Patrick Battiston. West Germany also reached the 1990 final thanks to their shoot-out expertise, this time proving superior to England – as they similarly did in the 1996 European Championships semi-final. In that 2006 quarter-final, Germany's goalkeeper Jens Lehmann consulted a note predicting the direction the Argentine players were likely to shoot towards. The vital information was scribbled on a scrap of hotel notepaper by Germany's chief scout Urs Siegenthaler. The only German national team to lose a major tournament penalty shoot-out were the West Germans, who contested the 1976 UEFA European Championships final against Czechoslovakia – their first shoot-out experience, and clearly an effective lesson, because they have not lost a shoot-out since.

THE PLAYERS WHO MISSED IN SHOOT-OUTS

Argentina: Diego Maradona (1990), Pedro Troglio (1990), Hernan Crespo (1998), Roberto Ayala (2006), Esteban Cambiasso (2006)
Brazil: Socrates (1986), Julio Cesar (1986), Marcio Santos (1994), Willian (2014), Hulk (2014)
Bulgaria: Krassimir Balakov (1994)
Chile: Mauricio Pinilla (2014), Alexis Sanchez (2014), Gonzalo Jara (2014)
Costa Rica: Bryan Ruiz (2014), Michael Umana (2014)
England: Stuart Pearce (1990), Chris Waddle (1990), Paul Ince (1998), David Batty (1998), Frank Lampard (2006), Steven Gerrard (2006), Jamie Carragher (2006)
France: Didier Six (1982), Maxime Bossis (1982), Michel Platini (1986), Bixente Lizarazu (1998), David Trezeguet (2006)
Germany/West Germany: Uli Stielike (1982)
Ghana: John Mensah (2010), Dominic Adiyiah (2010)
Greece: Theofanis Gekas (2014)
Italy: Roberto Donadoni (1990), Aldo Serena (1990), Franco Baresi (1994), Daniele Massaro (1994), Roberto Baggio (1994), Demetrio Albertini (1998), Luigi Di Biagio (1998)

Japan: Yuichi Komano (2010)
Mexico: Fernando Quirarte (1986), Raul Servin (1986), Alberto Garcia Aspe (1994), Marcelino Bernal (1994), Jorge Rodriguez (1994)
Netherlands: Phillip Cocu (1998), Ronald de Boer (1998), Ron Vlaar (2014), Wesley Sneijder (2014)
Portugal: Hugo Viana (2006), Petit (2006)
Republic of Ireland: Matt Holland (2002), David Connolly (2002), Kevin Kilbane (2002)
Romania: Daniel Timofte (1990), Dan Petrescu (1994), Miodrag Belodedici (1994)
Spain: Eloy (1986), Juanfran (2002), Juan Carlos Valeron (2002), Joaquin (2002)
Sweden: Hakan Mild (1994)
Switzerland: Marco Streller (2006), Tranquillo Barnetta (2006), Ricardo Cabanas (2006)
Ukraine: Andriy Shevchenko (2006)
Uruguay: Maximiliano Pereira (2010)
Yugoslavia: Dragan Stojkovic (1990), Dragoljub Brnovic (1990), Faruk Hadzibegic (1990)

PART 2: THE COUNTRIES

SOME CALL IT soccer, others say futbol or calcio or futebol – but go to virtually any country on earth and someone will be speaking about this game by whatever label. Association football knows no boundaries of race or politics or religion.

The structure is simple, helping ensure the sport's international success. At the head of the world football pyramid is FIFA, the world federation. Supporting FIFA's work are the six regional geographical confederations representing Africa, Asia, Europe, Oceania, South America, plus the Caribbean, Central and North America. Backing up the regions in turn are the national associations of 209 countries – and thus FIFA can boast more member countries than even the United Nations or the Olympic movement.

The countries are pivotal. They field the national teams who have built sporting history through their many and varied achievements in world-focused competitions such as the FIFA World Cup. But they also oversee the growth of football in their nation – from professional leagues to the game at grass-roots level.

Representative teams from England and Scotland played out the first formal internationals in the late 19th century, thus laying the foundation for the four British home nations' unique independent status within a world football family otherwise comprised of nation states. The original British Home Championships was the first competition for national teams but its demise, as a result of a congested fixture list, has left the Copa America in South America as the oldest survivor – apart from the Olympic Games.

The trend-setting example of the Olympic Games in the 1920s led directly to the creation of the FIFA World Cup and its launch in 1930. Already South America had its own national team championship and all the other five FIFA regions followed in due course. The winners meet once every four years in the FIFA Confederations Cup which is the rehearsal event for the extravaganza, one year later, which is the FIFA World Cup itself – the ultimate celebration of the planet's favourite sport.

Jennifer Lopez, Pitbull and Claudia Leitte raise the excitement levels in Sao Paulo in a colourful Opening Ceremony for the 2014 FIFA World Cup ahead of Brazil's 3-1 win over Croatia.

EUROPE

As soon as modern association football's rules were written in England the game's growth was rapid – enthusiasm spreading swiftly across Europe, the cradle of the game. UEFA, the European football confederation, now boasts 54 member states, from tiny Andorra and Gibraltar to world giants, Spain, Germany, Italy, England, the Netherlands and France. The game is played and followed with a fervent passion across the continent, not only at club but also at national levels. Germany's 2014 FIFA World Cup glory made it a record three straight wins for Europe.

German fans, in Brazil in 2014, celebrating their heroes' fourth FIFA World Cup victory – making history as Europe's first winners in eight stagings of the finals in the Americas.

ENGLAND

England is where football began: the [...] game was first developed, which [...] the game's first [football association] [...] organized league [...] the richest [...] England h[...] the intern[...] solid [...] as l[...] hav[...] [...]

IF THE CAP FITS

England's players in the historic first game against Scotland all wore **cricket-style caps** while the Scots wore hoods. England's "fashion statement" prompted the use of the term "cap" to refer to any international appearance. The tradition of awarding a cap to British international footballers still survives today.

HAVE A BASH, ASH

Left-back **Ashley Cole** is one of only eight England footballers to win 100 caps but is the only outfield player to reach the mark without ever having scored a goal – next on the list is Gary Neville (85 caps). He overtook Kenny Sansom as England's most-capped full-back when he represented his country for the 87th time, against Denmark in February 2011, and made his 100th appearance against Brazil at Wembley in February 2013. Cole's 98th international, against Italy in the Euro 2012 quarter-final, ended unhappily, as he missed England's final penalty in the shoot-out. But Cole did set another record that day: his 22nd finals match is the most by an England player. After 107 apperances, Cole announced his retirement from international football after being omitted from England's 2014 FIFA World Cup squad. In the club game he boasts more FA Cup winner's medals than any other player, three with Arsenal and four with Chelsea.

RUNAWAY SUCCESS

England have hit double figures five times: beating Ireland 13-0 and 13-2 in 1882 and 1899, thrashing Austria 11-1 in 1908, crushing Portugal 10-0 in Lisbon in 1947 and then the United States 10-0 in 1964 in New York. The ten goals were scored by Roger Hunt (four), Fred Pickering (three), Terry Paine (two) and **Bobby Charlton**.

IN THE BEGINNING

The day it all began ... 30 November 1872, when England played their first official international match, against Scotland, at Hamilton Crescent, Partick. The result was a 0-0 draw in front of a then massive crowd of 4,000, who each paid an admission fee of one shilling (5p). In fact, teams representing England and Scotland had played five times before, but most of the Scottish players had been based in England and the matches are considered unofficial. England's team for the first official game was selected by Charles Alcock, the secretary of the Football Association. His one regret was that, because of injury, he could not pick himself to play. In contrast, the first rugby union international between England and Scotland had been played in 1871, but England's first Test cricket match was not played until March 1877, against Australia in Melbourne.

FIRST DEFEAT

Hungary's 6-3 win at Wembley in 1953 was the first time England had lost at home to continental opposition. Their first home defeat by non-British opposition came against the Republic of Ireland, who beat them 2-0 at Goodison Park, Liverpool, in 1949.

STEVIE G FORCE

Steven Gerrard won his 100th cap in a 4-2 friendly defeat to Sweden in November 2012 and could have secured more but injury. He scored at the 2006 and 2010 FIFA World Cups and was the only Englishman named in the Euro 2012 "team of the tournament". His next international brought an unwanted record: his red card against Ukraine in September 2012 saw him become the oldest player ever sent off for England.

ENGLAND'S BIGGEST WINS

1882	Ireland 0 England 13	
1899	England 13 Ireland 2	
1908	Austria 1 England 11	
1964	United States 0 England 10	
1947	Portugal 0 England 10	
1982	England 9 Luxembourg 0	
1960	Luxembourg 0 England 9	
1895	England 9 Ireland 0	
1927	Belgium 1 England 9	
1896	Wales 1 England 9	
1890	Ireland 1 England 9	

ENGLAND'S BIGGEST DEFEATS

1954	Hungary 7 England 1	
1878	Scotland 7 England 2	
1881	England 1 Scotland 6	
1958	Yugoslavia 5 England 0	
1964	Brazil 5 England 1	
1928	England 1 Scotland 5	
1882	Scotland 5 England 1	
1953	England 3 Hungary 6	
1963	France 5 England 2	
1931	France 5 England 2	

NAUGHTY BOYS

Raheem Sterling's red card against Ecuador in June 2014 was the 15th for an England player in a full international, but only the second in a friendly, after Trevor Cherry against Argentina in June 1977. Alan Mullery was England's first player to be dismissed, against Yugoslavia in June 1968 in the UEFA European Championship. David Beckham and Wayne Rooney have both been sent off twice, while Rob Green is the only England goalkeeper to be red-carded – in a FIFA World Cup qualifier against Ukraine in October 2009. **Paul Scholes** was the only England player to be sent off at the old Wembley Stadium, against Sweden in June 1999, before it was refurbished in the 2000s.

SENIOR MOMENT

Goalkeeper David James became the oldest player ever to make his FIFA World Cup finals debut, aged 39 years and 321 days, when he appeared for England at the 2010 competition in South Africa. He kept a clean sheet in a goalless Group C draw against Algeria.

HEAD FOR GOAL

Robust and commanding centre-backs had the honour of scoring both the last England goal at the old Wembley stadium, closed down in 2000, and the first in the new version, which was finally opened in 2007. Tony Adams scored England's second in a 2-0 win over Ukraine in May 2000 – Germany's Dietmar Hamann hit the only goal of the final international at the old Wembley, four months later – and captain John Terry headed his side ahead in the new stadium's showpiece June 2007 friendly against Brazil, which ended 1-1. Terry shares the honour of scoring the most England goals (six) by a defender with 1966 FIFA World Cup winner **Jack Charlton**.

BLANKS OF ENGLAND

A goalless draw against Algeria in Cape Town in June 2010 made England the first country to finish 10 different FIFA World Cup matches 0-0. Their first was against Brazil in 1958, while the tally also includes both second-round group games in 1982 against eventual runners-up West Germany and hosts Spain. An 11th goalless draw followed against Costa Rica at Belo Horizonte in 2014.

WORST OF ALL WORLDS

England recorded their worst-ever performance at a FIFA World Cup finals in Brazil in 2014, when they finished bottom of Group D and were eliminated in the first round. It was the country's first exit at the first-round stage since Sweden 1958 and only the third time overall – the first occasion had been in 1950, the first time the finals had been in Brazil. Roy Hodgson's men managed just one point from their three group games – losing 2-1 to both Italy and Uruguay before playing out a goalless draw with surprise group-winners Costa Rica. Back in 1950 they did at least win one and lose two, while in 1958 they drew all three group games before losing a play-off to the Soviet Union. To add injury to insult in 2014, veteran physio Gary Lewin was stretchered off with a dislocated ankle and had to be flown home early after slipping on a water bottle while celebrating **Daniel Sturridge's** equaliser against Italy.

THE LONG AND THE SHORT OF IT

At 6ft 7in, centre-forward Peter Crouch is the tallest player ever to stretch above opposing defences for England – while Fanny Walden, the Tottenham winger who won two caps in 1914 and 1922, was the shortest at 5ft 2in. Sheffield United goalkeeper Billy "Fatty" Foulke became the heaviest England player at 18st when he played against Wales on 29 March 1897.

TEENAGE PROMISE

England left-back Luke Shaw was the youngest player to appear at the 2014 FIFA World Cup, at 18 years and 347 days, when starting against Costa Rica on 24 June. He was 36 days younger than USA forward Julian Green. The youngest squad member at the tournament was Cameroon striker Fabrice Olinga, ten months Shaw's junior, but he did not play. England's youngest debutant is **Theo Walcott**, 17 years and 75 days old, against Hungary in May 2006. Michael Owen – at 18 years and 183 days – set the national record for a FIFA World Cup when a substitute against Tunisia at the 1998 FIFA World Cup.

WAITING FOR THE CALL

Four England internationals played at the 1966 FIFA World Cup yet missed out on the triumphant final against West Germany – Ian Callaghan, John Connelly, Jimmy Greaves and Terry Paine. Liverpool winger Callaghan would then endure the longest wait between England appearances, when he went 11 years and 49 days between his showing in a 2-0 win over France at that 1966 tournament and his return to international action in a goalless draw with Switzerland in September 1977. The game against the Swiss was his third – and penultimate – outing for England.

FRANK'S A LOT

Frank Lampard has scored more penalties for England than any other player, successfully striking nine since his debut in October 2005 – despite missing another two. The prolific ex-West Ham United and Chelsea midfielder should have had another goal to add to his international tally, but his potential equalizer against Germany during the two countries' 2010 FIFA World Cup second-round match was wrongly deemed not to have crossed the line – prompting the eventual introduction of goal-line technology. Lampard became then-reigning European champions Chelsea's all-time leading scorer in May 2013 with his 203rd goal for the West London club, despite being a midfielder.

BECKHAM'S RECORD

David Beckham played for England for the 109th time when he appeared as a second-half substitute in the 4-0 win over Slovakia in a friendly international on 28 March 2009. That overtook the record number of England games for an outfield player, which had been set by Bobby Moore, England's 1966 FIFA World Cup-winning captain. Beckham, born on 2 May 1975, in Leytonstone, London, made his first appearance for his country on 1 September 1996, in a FIFA World Cup qualifying match against Moldova. He was appointed full-time England captain in 2001 by the then manager Sven-Goran Eriksson – stepping down after England's quarter-final defeat by Portugal at the 2006 FIFA World Cup. He ended his England career on 115 caps and hung up his boots in May 2013, at the age of 38, having just won the league in a fourth different country with French club Paris Saint-Germain. His 68 competitive matches for England are also a national record. Also retiring from the game in summer 2013 was England's fourth highest scorer **Michael Owen**, who netted a stunning solo goal against Argentina at the 1998 FIFA World Cup – only for Beckham to be sent off in a 2-2 draw before England lost on penalties.

ALEXANDER THE LATE

The oldest player to make his debut for England remains Alexander Morten, who was 41 years and 114 days old when facing Scotland on 8 March 1873 in England's first home game, at The Oval in Kennington, London. He was also captain that day and is still the country's oldest-ever skipper.

THE GOOD SONS

Eighteen-year-old winger Alex Oxlade-Chamberlain became the fifth son of a former England international to earn a cap for his country when he made his debut against Norway in May 2012 – 28 years after the last of his father Mark Chamberlain's eight appearances. Oxlade-Chamberlain became England's youngest scorer in a FIFA World Cup qualifier with his strike against San Marino in October 2013. The earlier pairings were George Eastham Snr (one cap, 1935) and George Eastham Jnr (19, 1963–66); Brian Clough (two, 1959) and Nigel Clough (14, 1989–93); Frank Lampard Snr (two, 1972–80) and **Frank Lampard Jnr** (106, 1999–2014); and Ian Wright (33, 1991–98) and his adopted son Shaun Wright-Phillips (36, 2004–10). The only grandfather and grandson to play for England are Bill Jones, who won two caps in 1950, and Rob Jones, who won eight between 1992 and 1995.

GRAND OLD MAN

Stanley Matthews became England's oldest-ever player when he lined up at outside-right against Denmark on 15 May 1957 at the age of 42 years 104 days. That was 22 years and 229 days after his first appearance. Matthews was also England's oldest marksman. He was 41 years eight months old when he scored against Northern Ireland on 10 October 1956.

TOP SCORERS

1	Bobby Charlton	49
2	Gary Lineker	48
3	Jimmy Greaves	44
4	Michael Owen	40
=	Wayne Rooney	40
6	Tom Finney	30
=	Nat Lofthouse	30
=	Alan Shearer	30
9	Frank Lampard	29
=	Vivian Woodward	29

CAPTAIN SOLO

Claude Ashton, the Corinthians centre-forward, set a record when he captained England on his only international appearance. This was a 0-0 draw against Northern Ireland in Belfast on 24 October 1925.

TOP CAPS

1	Peter Shilton	125
2	David Beckham	115
3	Steven Gerrard	114
4	Bobby Moore	108
5	Ashley Cole	107
6	Bobby Charlton	106
=	Frank Lampard	106
8	Billy Wright	105
9	Wayne Rooney	95
10	Bryan Robson	90

CAPTAINS COURAGEOUS

The international careers of Billy Wright and **Bobby Moore**, who both captained England a record 90 times, very nearly overlapped. Wright, from Wolves, played for England between 1946 and 1959 and Moore, from West Ham, between 1962 and 1973, including England's FIFA World Cup win in 1966.

SHARED RESPONSIBILITY

Substitutions meant the captain's armband passed between four different players during England's 2-1 friendly win over Serbia and Montenegro on 3 June 2003. Regular captain David Beckham was missing, so Michael Owen led the team out, but was substituted at half-time. England's second-half skippers were Owen's then-Liverpool team-mates Emile Heskey and Jamie Carragher and Manchester United's Philip Neville. The first time three different players have captained England in one FIFA World Cup finals match was against Morocco in 1986, when first-choice skipper Bryan Robson went off injured, his vice-captain Ray Wilkins was then sent off and goalkeeper Peter Shilton took over leadership duties.

CAMEO ROLE

Tottenham Hotspur striker **Jermain Defoe** has come on as substitute for England more often than any other player in history, 34 times since his debut in March 2004 – and his initial 17 starting appearances all ended in him being replaced before the end of 90 minutes.

SEVEN UP

Roy Hodgson's England equalled a national record when they trounced San Marino 8-0 in a March 2013 FIFA World Cup qualifier: the seven different goalscorers were as many who found the net when England defeated Luxembourg 9-0 in December 1982. This time, though, thanks to the opening own goal by Alessandro Della Valle, only six of the scorers were Englishmen. Adding to the tally were a Jermain Defoe brace and single strikes by **Alex Oxlade-Chamberlain**, Ashley Young, Frank Lampard, Wayne Rooney and Daniel Sturridge.

WAITING WAYNE

The 2-1 defeats to Italy and Uruguay in 2014 made it only the second time England had lost consecutive matches at a FIFA World Cup – having previously done so against the USA and Spain in 1950. The Uruguay game did at least give **Wayne Rooney** his first FIFA World Cup goal, having failed to find the net at the 2006 and 2010 tournaments. The strike took him to 40 international goals, level with former England and Manchester United team-mate Michael Owen.

COMING OVER HERE

Argentina were the first non-UK side to play at Wembley – England won 2-1 on 9 May 1951 – while Ferenc Puskas and the "Magical Magyars" of Hungary were the first "foreign", or "continental", side to beat England at home, with their famous 6-3 victory at Wembley in 1953. This humiliation marked Alf Ramsey's last game as an England player. England first tasted defeat to a "foreign" side when they lost 4-3 to Spain in Madrid on 15 May 1929. Two years later England gained their revenge with a 7-1 win at Highbury.

WRONG WAY!

Though the goal is sometimes credited to Scottish striker John Smith, it is believed that Edgar Field was the first England player to score an "own goal", which was his fate as Scotland crushed England 6-1 at The Oval on 12 March 1881. By the time Field put the ball in his own net, Scotland were already 4-1 up. The full-back, who was an FA Cup winner and loser with Clapham Rovers, is in good company. Manchester United's Gary Neville has scored two own goals "against" England.

ROLL UP, ROLL UP

The highest attendance for an England game came at Hampden Park on 17 April 1937, when 149,547 spectators crushed in to see Scotland's 3-1 victory in the British Home Championships. Only 2,378 turned up in Bologna, Italy, to see San Marino stun England after nine seconds in Graham Taylor's side's 7-1 victory that was not enough to secure qualification to the 1994 FIFA World Cup.

FIRST AND FOREMOST

England's first official international was a 0-0 draw against Scotland in Glasgow on 30 November 1872, though England and Scotland had already played a number of unofficial representative matches against each other prior to that. Given that England's only opponents for four decades were the home nations – and only Scotland for the first seven years, it is not surprising that England's first draw, win and defeat were all against their northern neighbours. After the goalless first game, the second fixture – played at The Oval on 8 March 1873 – proved a more exciting affair: England won 4-2 in a six-goal thriller. In their third game, back in Glasgow almost exactly a year later, Scotland evened things up with a 2-1 win. These fixtures completed the trio of first wins, defeats and draws for the oldest participants in international football. The Football Association's 150-year anniversary celebrations in 2013 included a 2013 Wembley friendly against Scotland, the first time the two sides were scheduled to meet since a two-leg play-off to qualify for Euro 2000 in October 1999. England won that tie 2-1 on aggregate, after a 2-0 victory at Hampden Park and a 1-0 defeat at home.

ROY'S BOYS

After Fabio Capello faced criticism for his struggles with the English language, his successor **Roy Hodgson** could claim fluency in not only his mother tongue but also Swedish, Norwegian, Italian and German. Much-travelled Hodgson – a former Switzerland, Finland and Inter Milan manager – was appointed England boss just six weeks before the 2012 UEFA European Championship, but his side topped their group before losing to Italy in the quarter-finals on penalties. First-round victories came against Sweden – England's first competitive victory over them at the eighth attempt – and co-hosts Ukraine, the first time England had beaten the hosts at a major tournament since Switzerland in 1954.

YOUR COUNTRY NEEDS YOU

The first England teams were selected from open trials of Englishmen who responded to the FA's adverts for players. It was only when these proved too popular and unwieldy that, in 1887, the FA decided that it would be better to manage the process through an International Selection Committee, which continued to pick the team until Sir Alf Ramsey's appointment in 1962.

MANAGERIAL ROLL OF HONOUR

Walter Winterbottom	(1946–62)
Sir Alf Ramsey	(1962–74)
Joe Mercer	(1974)
Don Revie	(1974–77)
Ron Greenwood	(1977–82)
Bobby Robson	(1982–90)
Graham Taylor	(1990–93)
Terry Venables	(1994–96)
Glenn Hoddle	(1996–98)
Howard Wilkinson	(1999–2000)
Kevin Keegan	(1999–2000)
Peter Taylor	(November 2000)
Sven-Goran Eriksson	(2001–06)
Steve McClaren	(2006–07)
Fabio Capello	(2008–2012)
Stuart Pearce	(March 2012)
Roy Hodgson	(2012–)

THE ITALIAN JOB

Italian Fabio Capello became England's second foreign coach when he took over from Steve McClaren in January 2008 and led the country to the 2010 FIFA World Cup in South Africa. Capello already had happy memories of national stadium Wembley from his playing days – he scored the only goal for Italy there on 14 November 1973, giving them their first-ever away win against England. He steered England through qualifiers for the 2012 UEFA European Championship, but suddenly resigned in February 2012, in protest at the Football Association stripping John Terry of the captaincy.

WONDERFUL WALTER

Walter Winterbottom was the England national team's first full-time manager – and remains both the longest-serving (with 138 games in charge) and the youngest-ever England manager, aged just 33 when he took the job in 1946 (initially as a coach and then, from 1947, as manager). The former teacher and Manchester United player led England to four FIFA World Cups.

FRANCE

France – nicknamed "Les Bleus" – are one of the most successful teams in the history of international football. They are one of only three countries to be World and European champions at the same time. They won the FIFA World Cup in 1998 as tournament hosts, routing Brazil 3-0 in the final. Two years later, they staged a sensational, last-gasp recovery to overhaul Italy in the Euro 2000 final. The French equalized in the fifth minute of stoppage time, then went on to win 2-1 on a golden goal. France had previously won the UEFA European Championship in 1984, beating Spain 2-0 in the final in Paris. They reached the 2006 FIFA World Cup final too, but lost to Italy in a penalty shoot-out. France also won the 2001 and 2003 FIFA Confederations Cup and took the Olympic football gold medal in 1984.

KOPA – FRANCE'S FIRST SUPERSTAR

Raymond Kopa (born on 13 October 1931) was France's first international superstar. Born into a family of Polish immigrants (the family name was Kopaszewski), he was instrumental in Reims's championship successes of the mid-1950s. He later joined Real Madrid and became the first French player to win a European Cup winner's medal. He was the playmaker of the France team that finished third in the 1958 FIFA World Cup finals. His performances for his country that year earned him the European Footballer of the Year award.

PLATINI'S GLITTERING CAREER

Michel Platini (born in Joeuf on 21 June 1955) has enjoyed a glittering career, rising from a youngster at Nancy to become one of France's greatest-ever players, a hero in Italy, and now the president of UEFA. He was also joint organizing president (along with Fernand Sastre) of the 1998 FIFA World Cup finals in France. Platini was the grandson of an Italian immigrant who ran a café in Joeuf, Lorraine. He began with the local club, Nancy, before starring for Saint-Etienne, Juventus and France. He was instrumental in France's progress to the 1982 FIFA World Cup semi-finals and was the undisputed star of the UEFA European Championship two years later, when France won the tournament on home soil.

BENZ MAKES AMENDS

Karim Benzema was the first French player to miss a penalty during a FIFA World Cup match – excluding shoot-outs. His effort, saved by Diego Benaglio, came in a Group E match against Switzerland at the 2014 tournament – the tenth FIFA World Cup spot-kick awarded to France. He did atone for the failure by scoring France's fourth in their 5-2 victory. Benzema had struck twice in France's first game, a 3-0 defeat of Honduras, and was denied a hat-trick after his shot struck the far post and trickled over the goal-line, but it crossed the line only after rebounding off goalkeeper Noel Valladares, so was ruled an own goal. This was the first time in FIFA World Cup history that a goal was given thanks to goal-line technology, introduced for the 2014 finals. And Benzema was denied another goal in the Swiss game when Dutch referee Bjorn Kuipers blew the final whistle as he was in the act of smashing a long-range shot which ended up in the Swiss net. Benzema's three goals at the 2014 finals lifted him up to ninth place in France's all-time scoring table, above Jean Vincent, who had died at the age of 82 the previous October.

TO BE FRANCK

Franck Ribery has become one of modern-day France's most important and influential footballers. His displays off both wings helped them reach the 2006 FIFA World Cup final as well as helping lift Bayern Munich to success in the 2013 UEFA Champions League. He is the first man to have been named Footballer of the Year in both France and Germany. Yet he was rejected as a teenager by French club Lille, with 1.7m-tall Ribery later claming they deemed him too short. Ribery was severely injured in a car crash as a two year old, leaving him with lifelong scars across the right side of his face. He finished third behind Cristiano Ronaldo and Lionel Messi for FIFA's annual Ballon d'Or award in December 2013, yet his luck turned the following summer when a back injury ruled him out of the 2014 FIFA World Cup.

KISSING COLLEAGUES

Marseille colleagues centre-back **Laurent Blanc** and goalkeeper **Fabien Barthez** had a special ritual during France's run to the 1998 FIFA World Cup crown. Before the game, Blanc would always kiss Barthez's shaven head, even when the veteran defender was suspended for the final. Blanc was on the winning side when France won the 2000 UEFA European Championship final, after which he announced his retirement from international football. He said at the time: "The French team has been my life and has led me to do things I shouldn't have. It has been my mistress – a beautiful mistress."

IT'S A SHAME ABOUT RAY

France's failure to win a match at the 2010 FIFA World Cup meant coach Raymond Domenech equalled but failed to exceed Michel Hidalgo's record of 41 victories in charge of the national side. Domenech did at least end his six-year reign having surpassed Euro 84-winning Hidalgo's tally of matches in the job. Domenech's final game, against South Africa, was his 79th as coach, four more than Hidalgo achieved. Domenech, a tough-tackling defender who was picked for France by Hidalgo, proved eccentric as national coach. He admitted partly judging players by their star signs and responded to being knocked out of the 2008 UEFA European Championship by proposing to his girlfriend on live television.

MICHEL PLATINI (league and national career)

Duration	Team	Appearances	Goals
1972–79	Nancy	181	98
1979–82	Saint-Etienne	104	58
1982–87	Juventus	147	68
1976–87	France	72	41

WRONG KIND OF STRIKERS

During France's disastrous 2010 FIFA World Cup campaign, the players went on strike, refusing to train two days before their final Group A match, in protest at striker Nicolas Anelka being sent home early for insulting coach Raymond Domenech. France finished bottom of the group after a goalless draw with Uruguay and defeats to Mexico and hosts South Africa. The country's president Nicolas Sarkozy ordered an investigation into all that had gone wrong, while former French international defender Lilian Thuram called for captain **Patrice Evra** to be banned from playing for the team ever again. Despite serving a five-match international ban for his role in the unrest, Evra returned to the fold in 2011 – albeit no longer as skipper – and was a starter for France at both the 2012 UEFA European Championship and the 2014 FIFA World Cup.

FRANCE AND FIFA

France were one of FIFA's founding members in 1904. Frenchman Robert Guerin became the first president of the governing body. Another Frenchman, Jules Rimet, was president from 1921 to 1954. He was the driving force behind the creation of the FIFA World Cup and the first version of football's most coveted trophy was named in his honour.

HENRY BENCHED

France's record scorer Thierry Henry missed out on an appearance in the 1998 FIFA World Cup final because of Marcel Desailly's red card. Henry was France's leading scorer in the competition with three goals and coach Aime Jacquet planned to use him as a substitute in the final. But Desailly's sending-off forced a re-think: Jacquet decided to reinforce the midfield, with Arsenal team-mate Patrick Vieira going on instead, so Henry spent the full 90 minutes of the final on the bench. But Henry does have the distinction of being the only Frenchman to play at four different FIFA World Cups (1998, 2002, 2006 and 2010). He passed Michel Platini's all-time goal-scoring record for France with a late brace against Lithuania in October 2007.

TOP SCORERS

1	Thierry Henry	51
2	Michel Platini	41
3	David Trezeguet	34
4	Zinedine Zidane	31
5	Just Fontaine	30
=	Jean-Pierre Papin	30
7	Youri Djorkaeff	28
8	Sylvain Wiltord	26
9	Karim Benzema	24
10	Jean Vincent	22

UNITED FOR ABIDAL

Defender Eric Abidal, a key member of the French teams at the 2006 and 2010 FIFA World Cups, was enjoying his best form for Spanish club Barcelona when he was diagnosed with liver cancer in March 2011 – but managed to recover in time for a surprise return to action by the season's end. Club rivalries were put aside when players from rivals Real Madrid wore T-shirts bearing the supportive message "Animo Abidal" after their UEFA Champions League tie against Abidal's former club Olympique Lyonnais a few days later. Barcelona fans then clapped throughout the 22nd minute of their La Liga game against Getafe, in recognition of Abidal's shirt number. Remarkably, he was fit enough to return to action, as a substitute, in Barcelona's UEFA Champions League semi-final victory over Madrid in May 2011. Abidal started in the final and, although not the captain, was given the armband to lift the cup after their 3-1 win over Manchester United. Abidal came through further trauma in March 2012, when he was told he needed a liver transplant. Yet again Abidal would return to action with Barcelona, taking the field again towards the end of the 2012-13 season.

TOP CAPS

1	Lilian Thuram	142
2	Thierry Henry	123
3	Marcel Desailly	116
4	Zinedine Zidane	108
5	Patrick Vieira	107
6	Didier Deschamps	103
7	Laurent Blanc	97
=	Bixente Lizarazu	97
9	Sylvain Wiltord	92
10	Fabien Barthez	87

DESCHAMPS THE LEADER

Compatriot Eric Cantona contemptuously dismissed him as a mere "water-carrier" in central midfield but **Didier Deschamps** provided his infamous critic with the perfect riposte in becoming the most successful captain in French football history. He lifted both the 1998 FIFA World Cup and 2000 UEFA European Championship trophies as skipper and wore the captain's armband a record 55 times during his 103 internationals before retiring in July 2000. Deschamps succeeded Laurent Blanc as national coach after the 2012 UEFA European Championship. Deschamps' ten-match unbeaten run at FIFA World Cups, as a player and manager, came to an end in the 2014 quarter-finals as his side lost 1-0 to Germany. Until then he had enjoyed five victories and one draw on the pitch, and three victories and one draw in the dug-out.

BITTERSWEET FOR TREZEGUET

Striker David Trezeguet has bittersweet memories of France's clashes with Italy in major finals. He scored the "golden goal" that beat the Italians in extra-time in the Euro 2000 final but, six years later, he was the man who missed as France lost the FIFA World Cup final on penalties. Trezeguet's shot bounced off the bar and failed to cross the line.

PRESIDENTIAL PARDON

Imperious centre-back Laurent Blanc was known as "Le President" during his playing days and went on to become national coach when he succeeded Raymond Domenech after the 2010 FIFA World Cup. He was unlucky to miss the 1998 FIFA World Cup final after being sent off in the semi-final for pushing Slaven Bilic in the face, though replays showed Bilic had over-reacted. Blanc did enjoy some redemption by being part of the French team that won the UEFA European Championship two years later. He became national coach 12 months after leading Bordeaux to the 2008–09 domestic championship, ending Olympique Lyonnais's run of seven league titles in a row.

ARMBAND FINALLY IN SAFE HANDS

After Patrick Evra lost the French captaincy for his role in their 2010 FIFA World Cup fiasco, new coach Laurent Blanc tried three captains before turning to goalkeeper **Hugo Lloris,** who was finally named as permanent skipper ahead of Euro 2012. He was the only man to play every single minute of France's qualifying campaign, and was an ever-present in the finals too. Overall, he kept seven clean sheets in France's 14 matches. Lloris remained captain throughout qualifying for the 2014 FIFA World Cup and at the tournament itself, in which he kept three clean sheets and conceded three goals in five games.

THE FULL SET

Five France stars have a full set of top international medals as FIFA World Cup, UEFA European Championship and UEFA Champions League winners. Didier Deschamps, Marcel Desailly, Christian Karembeu, Bixente Lizarazu and Zinedine Zidane all played for France's winning teams in 1998 and 2000. Desailly won the European Cup with Marseille in 1993 and AC Milan the following year. Deschamps won with Marseille in 1993 and Juventus in 1996; Lizarazu did so with Bayern Munich in 2001, Karembeu with Real Madrid in 1998 and 2000, and Zidane with Real Madrid in 2002. While Karembeu ended the 1999–2000 season with UEFA Champions League and UEFA European Championship winners' medals, he was an unused substitute in both finals – making him the only player to have achieved that particular bittersweet double.

LILIAN IN THE PINK

Defender **Lilian Thuram** made his 142nd and final appearance for France in their defeat by Italy at Euro 2008. His international career had spanned nearly 14 years, since his debut against the Czech Republic on 17 August 1994. Thuram was born in Pointe a Pitre, Guadeloupe, on 1 January 1972. He played club football for Monaco, Parma, Juventus and Barcelona before retiring in the summer of 2008 because of a heart problem. He was one of the stars of France's 1998 FIFA World Cup-winning side and scored both goals in their semi-final victory over Croatia – the only international goals of his career. He gained another winner's medal at Euro 2000. He first retired from international football after Euro 2004, but was persuaded by coach Raymond Domenech to return for the 2006 FIFA World Cup campaign and made his second appearance in a FIFA World Cup final. He broke Marcel Desailly's record of 116 caps in the group game against Togo.

ALBERT THE FIRST

Albert Batteux (1919–2003) was France's first national manager. Before his appointment in 1955, a selection committee had picked the team. Batteux was also the most successful coach in the history of French football. He combined managing France with his club job at Reims. His biggest achievement was guiding the national team to third place at the 1958 FIFA World Cup finals. The team's two big stars, Raymond Kopa and Just Fontaine, had both played under his charge at Reims.

REVEILLERE REMAINS

Anthony Reveillere is the only player to be picked by all of the last four France managers: Jacques Santini, Raymond Domenech, Laurent Blanc and Didier Deschamps. Yet in a decade the full-back has only made 19 appearances since his debut against Israel in October 2003.

OVAL BALL

The father of France's most capped goalkeeper Fabien Barthez was also a French international. Alain Barthez was a fine rugby union player who won one cap for France.

JACQUET'S TRIUMPH

Aime Jacquet, who guided France to FIFA World Cup glory in 1998, was one of their most controversial national coaches. He had been attacked for alleged defensive tactics despite France's run to the semi-finals of Euro 96 and a record of only three defeats in four years. A month before the 1998 finals, the sports daily *L'Equipe* claimed he was not capable of building a successful team!

NO TIME FOR FONTAINE

Former striker **Just Fontaine** spent the shortest-ever spell in charge of the France team. He took over on 22 March 1967 and left on 3 June after two defeats in friendlies. More happily, he still holds the record for most goals at a single FIFA World Cup – 13 across all six games he played at the 1958 tournament, including four in France's 6-3 victory over West Germany to finish third.

FRANCE MANAGERS

Albert Batteux	1955–62
Henri Guerin	1962–66
Jose Arribas/Jean Snella	1966
Just Fontaine	1967
Louis Dugauguez	1967–68
Georges Boulogne	1969–73
Stefan Kovacs	1973–75
Michel Hidalgo	1976–84
Henri Michel	1984–88
Michel Platini	1988–92
Gerard Houllier	1992–93
Aime Jacquet	1993–98
Roger Lemerre	1998–2002
Jacques Santini	2002–04
Raymond Domenech	2004–10
Laurent Blanc	2010–12
Didier Deschamps	2012–

JOLLY OLI DAY

France became the fifth country to reach 100 FIFA World Cup goals, when **Olivier Giroud** scored the 17th-minute opener during their 5-2 victory over Switzerland at Salvador in their 2014 first-round clash. The French thus joined Brazil, Germany (including West Germany), Argentina and Italy on three-figure tallies. By the end of the 2014 FIFA World Cup, France, with 106 in total, were more than 20 goals behind fourth-placed Italy – who had slipped behind Argentina after a second poor showing in a row – but a dozen clear of the sixth most prolific nation, Spain.

WINNING WITH YOUTH

In the early 1990s, France became the first European country to institute a national youth development programme. The best young players were picked to attend the national youth academy at Clairefontaine. Then they went on to the top clubs' academies throughout the nation. The scheme has produced a rich harvest of stars. FIFA World Cup winners Didier Deschamps, Marcel Desailly and Christian Karembeu started at Nantes. Lilian Thuram, Thierry Henry, Manu Petit and David Trezeguet began with Monaco and **Zinedine Zidane** and Patrick Vieira were graduates from Cannes.

BLINK AND YOU'LL MISS HIM

Unfortunate defender Franck Jurietti's international debut proved bittersweet – it lasted just five seconds and he never won another cap. The Bordeaux full-back came on just before the final whistle of France's match against Cyprus in October 2005, amounting to an international career even shorter than fellow defender Bernard Boissier's two minutes against Portugal in April 1975.

PACKING THEM IN

A record home crowd of 80,051 people were inside the Stade de France, in Saint-Denis, to see France take a major step towards qualifying for the 2008 UEFA European Championship with a 2-0 defeat of Ukraine in June 2007. The goals were scored by Franck Ribery and Nicolas Anelka.

EARNING THEIR STRIPES

France are the only country to play at a FIFA World Cup wearing another team's kit. In the 1978 tournament in Argentina, for a first-round match at Mar del Plata, *Les Bleus* were forced to wear the green and white stripes of a local club side, Atletico Kimberley, when they met Hungary. France brought their second, white, kit instead of their normal blue, while Hungary turned up in their second strip, white, too. The quick-change did not seem to affect France, who won the match 3-1.

WHAM BAM THANK YOU SAM

Samir Nasri scored the winner to give France a 2-1 victory over Spain in the final of the UEFA European U-17 Championship on home soil in 2004, the only time France have lifted that trophy. They have also won the UEFA European U-19 Championship seven times, most recently in 2010 with another final triumph over Spain, and the UEFA European U-21 Championship once, in 1988, when Laurent Blanc was named player of the tournament. Midfielder Nasri is one of the successful graduates from that acclaimed "Generation '87" team that won in 2004, also featuring Jeremy Menez, Hatem Ben Arfa and Karim Benzema. After behaving badly with the senior side at the 2010 FIFA World Cup and 2012 UEFA European Championship, Nasri was left out of Didier Deschamps' 2014 FIFA World Cup squad – despite having just played a key role in Manchester City winning the English league title. Nasri's girlfriend, Anara Atanes, loyally if divisively responded to his omission by posting a series of Twitter messages abusing Deschamps.

GERMANY

German footballers are almost ever-presents in the closing stages of major tournaments, but their well-deserved 2014 FIFA World Cup triumph provided much joy and relief back home as it ended an 18-year trophy drought. It was also the first FIFA World Cup triumph for the united Germany, having been West Germany when becoming champions in 1954, 1974 and 1990. The Germans are also three-time UEFA European champions (1972, 1980 and 1996) and in 1974 became the first country to hold the world and European titles simultaneously. Further glory is likely.

SHOOT-OUT SURE-SHOTS

Germany are renowned as penalty specialists, but they needed no shoot-outs when winning the 2014 FIFA World Cup, unlike their previous two titles, the 1990 FIFA World Cup and the 1996 UEFA European Championship. These both involved semi-final victories on penalties against England.

BELITTLE ITALY

Germany may have become England's bogey-team, but their misfortune against Italy goes on. They have never managed to beat the Italians in an international tournament, a sequence that reached eight games when Germany, with stars such as midfielder **Bastian Schweinsteiger** and goalkeeper Manuel Neuer, lost 2-1 in their 2012 UEFA European Championship semi-final. Perhaps the most dramatic clash was Italy's 4-3 victory, after extra-time, in the semi-finals of the 1970 FIFA World Cup. Italy also reigned triumphant in the 2006 FIFA World Cup semi-finals and the 1982 FIFA World Cup final. Germany can at least celebrate one recent success over their Italian rivals – albeit at club level. Since 2011–12, Germany's Bundesliga has had four clubs eligible for each year's UEFA Champions League, gaining their extra space at the expense of Italy's Serie A. And first-round departees Italy watched enviously as Germany clinched the 2014 FIFA World Cup.

NO LOSS

Germany maintained their record of never losing their opening game at a UEFA European Championship by beating Portugal 1-0 at Euro 2012, thanks to a header by **Mario Gomez**. Their 4-2 quarter-final victory over Greece that same summer set a new world record of 15 consecutive wins in competitive matches, one more than the best tallies set by both Spain and the Netherlands.

BOTH SIDES NOW

Eight players appeared for both the old East Germany and then Germany after reunification in October 1990.

Player	East Germany	Germany
Ulf Kirsten	49	51
Matthias Sammer	23	51
Andreas Thom	51	10
Thomas Doll	29	18
Dariusz Wosz	7	17
Olaf Marschall	4	13
Heiko Scholz	7	1
Dirk Schuster	4	3

⚽ EAST GERMANY –
TOP APPEARANCES AND GOALS

Appearances
1	**Joachim Streich**	98
2	Hans-Jurgen Dorner	96
3	Jurgen Croy	86
4	Konrad Weise	78
5	Eberhard Vogel	69

Goals
1	Joachim Streich	53
2	Eberhard Vogel	24
3	Hans-Jurgen Kreische	22
4	Rainer Ernst	20
5	Henning Frenzel	19

⚽ SAMBA SILENCED

Germany's 1-0 win over Argentina in 2014 came in their record eighth FIFA World Cup Final, this coming after they were the first side to reach four consecutive semi-finals. But the 7-1 semi-final humiliation of Brazil may live longest in the memory – and the record books. Germany led 5-0 at half-time in what became the biggest FIFA World Cup semi-final win and the hosts' heaviest defeat. Other FIFA World Cup finals records include: Toni Kroos's two goals in 69 seconds were the fastest brace and Germany were the first team to score four goals in six minutes. Also Thomas Muller's opening goal was Germany's 2,000th.

⚽ BERLIN ALL

Berlin will host the 2015 UEFA Champions League final, making it the second German city, after Munich, to have hosted the Olympic Games, FIFA World Cup final and UEFA European Cup final. Berlin hosted the Olympics in 1936 and the FIFA World Cup in 2006, while Munich staged the Olympics in 1972, the FIFA World Cup in 1974 and four European Cup finals.

⚽ HOTTEST SHOTS

Germany's 7-1 defeat of Brazil in the 2014 FIFA World Cup semi-finals not only stunned the hosts, but also toppled them as the tournament's all-time top scorers. Germany's FIFA World Cup goals total is now 224, three more than Brazil. Stanislaus Kobierski scored Germany's first-ever FIFA World Cup goal, in a 5-2 victory over Belgium in 1934. Germany became the first team to enjoy three four-goal sprees at one tournament, beating Australia 4-0, England 4-1 and Argentina 4-0 in 2010. The 2014 vintage got off to a flying start by crushing Portugal 4-0 in their opening match.

⚽ HISTORY MAN

East and West Germany met only once at senior national team level. That was on 22 June 1974, in the FIFA World Cup finals. Drawn in the same group, East Germany produced a shock 1-0 win in Hamburg, but both teams advanced. Jurgen Sparwasser, scorer of East Germany's winning goal, defected to West Germany in 1988 – two years before the two countries reunited.

⚽ SCHNELL, SCHNELL

Lukas Podolski scored one of the fastest goals in international football history when he gave Germany the lead after just nine seconds in their May 2013 friendly away to Ecuador. When Lars Bender added another shortly afterwards, it was the first time ever that Germany had scored twice in the opening four minutes of a match. Both Podolski and Bender scored again by the time 24 minutes were on the clock and Germany ultimately went on to win the match 4-2.

⚽ GOLDEN WONDER

Germany became the first team to win a major title thanks to the now-discarded golden goal system when they beat the Czech Republic in the UEFA Euro 96 final at Wembley. **Oliver Bierhoff**'s equalizer forced extra-time after Patrik Berger scored a penalty for the Czechs. Bierhoff grabbed Germany's winner five minutes into extra-time to end the game and the championship.

MEIN BENDERS

You could have thought you were seeing double when manager Joachim Low made a double substitution with 12 minutes remaining during Germany's 5-3 defeat to Switzerland in May 2012. His two midfield substitutes were twin brothers **Lars** and **Sven Bender**. Born on 27 April 1989, they both began their careers with 1860 Munich before Lars (the elder by 12 minutes) moved to Bayer Leverkusen and Sven to Borussia Dortmund. Both were members of Germany's 2008 UEFA U-19 European Championship-winning side, but only Lars was selected for Euro 2012. They were were the second twins to play for Germany after Erwin and Helmut Kramers. Striker Erwin scored three goals in 15 games between 1972 and 1974, while full-back Helmut played eight times without scoring. Erwin was part of the 1972 UEFA European Championship-winning squad, but was overlooked for the triumphant 1974 FIFA World Cup-winning squad, a set-up that included Helmut.

"DER BOMBER"

Gerd Muller was the most prolific scorer of the modern era. Neither tall nor graceful, he was quick, strong and had a predator's eye for the net. He also had the temperament to score decisive goals in big games, including the winner in the 1974 FIFA World Cup final, the winner in the semi-final against Poland and two goals in West Germany's 1972 UEFA European Championship final victory over the USSR. He netted 68 goals in 62 appearances for West Germany and remains the leading scorer in the Bundesliga and all-time record scorer for his club, Bayern Munich.

KING OTTO

Thomas Muller was the last man to score a hat-trick for Germany, in his country's opening game of the 2014 FIFA World Cup finals, a 4-0 victory over Portugal. Gerd Muller has more hat-tricks than any other German international – eight in all, four of which were four-goal hauls. But Otto Siffling remains the only player to score five in one match for Germany, during an 8-0 triumph over Denmark on 16 May 1937, in the Polish city of Wroclaw – then a German territory known as Breslau.

A LAHM CALL

Philipp Lahm surprised many when retiring from international football after the 2014 FIFA World Cup, at the age of only 30. He went out on a high, having just lifted the trophy as German captain at the end of his 113th appearance. Lahm had already made a mark in his two previous finals. He scored the opening goal of the 2006 FIFA World Cup, and played every minute of that tournament. Four years later, he became the youngest man to captain Germany at a FIFA World Cup – and the only action he missed was when given a well-earnest rest for the third-place play-off against Uruguay. In his youth, Lahm was a ballboy at Bayern Munich and he later captained them to 2013 UEFA Champions League glory.

DER KAISER

Franz Beckenbauer is widely regarded as the greatest player in German football history. He has also made a huge mark as a FIFA World Cup-winning coach, administrator and organizer. Beckenbauer (born on 11 September 1945) was a 20-year-old attacking wing-half when West Germany reached the 1966 FIFA World Cup final. He later defined the role of attacking sweeper, first in the 1970 FIFA World Cup finals, and then as West Germany won the 1972 UEFA European Championship and the 1974 FIFA World Cup. When West Germany needed a coach in the mid-1980s, they turned to Beckenbauer, despite his lack of experience. He delivered a FIFA World Cup final appearance in 1986, a Euro 88 semi-final and 1990 FIFA World Cup triumph in his final game in charge. He later became president of Bayern Munich, the club he captained to three consecutive European Cup victories between 1974 and 1976. He also led Germany's successful bid for the 2006 FIFA World Cup finals and headed the organizing committee. No wonder he is known as "Der Kaiser" ("the Emperor") for his enormous influence on German football.

MAGICAL MATTHAUS

Lothar Matthaus is Germany's most-capped player. He appeared in five FIFA World Cup finals – 1982, 1986, 1990, 1994 and 1998 – a record for an outfield player. Versatile Matthaus could operate as a defensive midfielder, an attacking midfielder, or as a sweeper. He was a FIFA World Cup winner in 1990, a finalist in 1982 and 1986 and a UEFA European Championship winner in 1980. His record 150 appearances – spread over a 20-year international career – were split 87 for West Germany and 63 for Germany. He also scored 23 goals and was voted top player at the 1990 FIFA World Cup.

TOP CAPS
(West Germany & Germany)

1	Lothar Matthaus	150
2	Miroslav Klose	137
3	Lukas Podolski	116
4	Philipp Lahm	113
5	Jurgen Klinsmann	108
=	Bastian Schweinsteiger	108
7	Jurgen Kohler	105
8	Per Mertesacker	104
9	Franz Beckenbauer	103
10	Thomas Hassler	101

TOP SCORERS
(West Germany & Germany)

1	Miroslav Klose	71
2	Gerd Muller	68
3	Jurgen Klinsmann	47
=	Lukas Podolski	47
=	Rudi Voller	47
6	Karl-Heinz Rummenigge	45
7	Uwe Seeler	43
8	Michael Ballack	42
9	Oliver Bierhoff	37
10	Fritz Walter	33

KLOSE ENCOUNTERS

Miroslav Klose became the third player, after Uwe Seeler and Pele to score in four FIFA World Cup finals. His first goal in Brazil, an equalizer against Ghana, put him alongside Ronaldo at the top of the all-time FIFA World Cup scoring charts. And it was against Ronaldo's Brazil that Klose pushed ahead on his own, his 16th finals goal being a typically-opportunistic finish to give Germany a 2-0 semi-final lead. All 16 of Klose's FIFA World Cup goals have come from inside the penalty area. He ended the 2014 FIFA World Cup not only with the scoring record and a winners' medal, but also on 24 appearances – behind only Italy's Paolo Maldini (25) – and 17 wins, one ahead of previous record-holder Cafu, of Brazil. Klose is also now Germany's all-time leading scorer, with 71 goals in 137 matches – and his team-mates have never lost an international in which he found the net.

GOLDEN GLOVES

Sepp Maier was at the heart of West Germany's triumphs of the early 1970s, including the 1972 UEFA European Championship and the 1974 FIFA World Cup. He remains West Germany's most-capped goalkeeper, winning 95 caps in an international career lasting from 1965 to 1979. He played his whole club career for Bayern Munich and helped them win the European Cup three times. A car crash in 1979, in which he received life-threatening injuries, ended his playing days, but he went on to become a goalkeeping coach for both Germany and his old club.

YOUNGEST CENTURION LUKAS

Lukas Podolski became the youngest European footballer to reach 100 caps when, aged 27 years and 13 days old, he appeared in Germany's third first-round game of the 2012 UEFA European Championship, against Denmark. He marked the occasion by scoring the opener in a 2-1 win – his 44th goal for his country. Podolski was born in Gliwice in Poland, but opted to play for Germany – his family having emigrated there when he was two years old. He was voted best young player of the tournament when Germany hosted and finished third at the 2006 FIFA World Cup.

KHEDIRA CROCKED

Midfielder **Sami Khedira** was an injury doubt ahead of the 2014 FIFA World Cup but was among Germany's scorers and best players in their 7-1 semi-final rout of Brazil. His luck changed, though, moments before the Final – as he was injured in the warm-up and replaced by Christoph Kramer. Sadly, Kramer lasted only 31 minutes before a concussion forced him off. He later admitted he could not remember any of the first half. Germany's triumph made Khedira the tenth player to win the FIFA World Cup and UEFA Champions League in the same season, having been part of Real Madrid's successful side a few weeks earlier.

KEEPING A LOW PROFILE

Joachim Low was, in 2014, the 19th coach to win the FIFA World Cup, but the first German coach to do so without having played for his country. After a respectable career as a midfielder for a number of clubs, including Freiburg, and coaching spells in Germany, Austria and Turkey, Low was appointed as Jurgen Klinsmann's assistant in 2004, before taking the top job after the 2006 FIFA World Cup. He led Germany to the 2008 UEFA European Championship Final and the semi-finals of Euro 2012, as well as third-place at the 2010 FIFA World Cup. West Germany's 1954 FIFA World Cup-winning manager Sepp Herberger had won three caps as a player, 1974 boss Helmut Schon made 16 appearances and 1990 coach Franz Beckenbauer won 103 caps and lifted the trophy as captain in 1974.

THE WORST OF STARTS

Goalkeeper Marc-Andre ter Stegen had an international debut to forget when Switzerland beat Germany 5-3 in a May 2012 friendly. He became the first German goalkeeper to concede more than three goals on debut for 58 years. The last to do so was Heinrich Kwiatowski, who was in goal when Hungary won 8-3 in West Germany's opening game of the 1954 FIFA World Cup – it was Kwiatowki's only appearance of the tournament (and he would make only three further appearances), but he still ended up with a winners' medal when they beat the same opponents 3-2 in the final. Despite ter Stegen's promise, Germany's current undisputed number one is Manuel Neuer.

GERMANY'S MANAGERS

Otto Nerz	1928–36
Sepp Herberger	1936–64
Helmut Schon	1964–78
Jupp Derwall	1978–84
Franz Beckenbauer	1984–90
Berti Vogts	1990–98
Erich Ribbeck	1998–2000
Rudi Voller	2000–04
Jurgen Klinsmann	2004–06
Joachim Low	2006–

GOAL RUSH

Germany's biggest win was 16-0 against Russia in the 1912 Olympic Games in Stockholm. Karlsruhe's Gottfried Fuchs scored ten of the goals, still a national team record.

BONUS BATTLE

Helmut Schon's 1974 FIFA World Cup winners came close to walking out before the finals started. Schon was prepared to send his squad home in a row over bonuses. A last-minute deal was brokered between Franz Beckenbauer and federation vice-president Hermann Neuberger. The vote among the squad went 11-11, but Beckenbauer persuaded the players to accept the DFB's offer. It was a great decision: they beat Holland 2-1 in the final.

NEW BOYS REUNION

Bayern Munich's **Mario Gotze** was the hero when Germany finally overcame Argentina's resistance in the 2014 FIFA World Cup final. His 113th-minute volley was the first winner hit by a substitute. It seemed apt that Germany's first FIFA World Cup triumph since the reunification of East and West Germany in 1990 was secured by Gotze, set up by Andre Schurrle. They had jointly become the first German football internationals born post-reunification, when making their debuts as 79th-minute substitutes against Sweden in November 2010.

SCHON IN SAARLAND

Helmut Schon is remembered as one of Germany's most successful managers. He started his international coaching career with Saarland, now part of Germany, but which had been made a separate state (with a population of 970,000) after the country's post-war division. Saarland's greatest moment came in the 1954 FIFA World Cup qualifiers, when they beat Norway 3-2 in Oslo to top their qualifying group. They were eventually eliminated by Sepp Herberger's West Germany.

GERMANY'S BRONZE AGES

The 2010 FIFA World Cup third-place play-off between Germany and Uruguay was a rematch of the same tie at the 1970 tournament, when West Germany won 1-0. The German side again took third place 40 years later, thanks to a dramatic 3-2 victory in Port Elizabeth's Nelson Mandela Bay stadium. The result, secured by Sami Khedira's late goal, meant Germany had a record four third-place finishes at FIFA World Cups, having also come third in 1934 and 2006.

PRESSURE ON JULIAN

Julian Draxler became Germany's fifth-youngest player when he made his debut against Switzerland in May 2012, aged 18 years 248 days old. Team-mate Mario Gotze is third on that list, having been 18 years and 166 days old when he made his first appearance, against Sweden in November 2010, at the age of 18 years and 166 days. Germany's youngest-ever player remains Oskar Ritter, who was 17 years and 254 days old when he made his debut, also against Sweden, in June 1925. Uwe Seeler was 90 days older when he debuted against France in October 1954. Olaf Thon was 63 days older than Gotze when he made his first international appearance, against Malta, in December 1984.

SEPP'S SURPRISE

Sepp Herberger (1897–1977) was one of the most influential figures in Germany's football history. He was their longest-serving coach (28 years at the helm) and his legendary status was assured after West Germany surprised odds-on favourites Hungary to win the 1954 FIFA World Cup final – a result credited with dragging the country out of a post-war slump. Herberger took charge in 1936 and led the team into the 1938 FIFA World Cup finals. During the war years he used his influence to try to keep his best players away from the heavy fighting. When organized football resumed in 1949, the federation decided to advertise for a national coach, but Herberger persuaded DFB chief Peco Bauwens to give him back his old job. He had a clause in his contract guaranteeing him a totally free hand in organization and selection policy. Among Herberger's favourite sayings was: "The ball is round and the match lasts 90 minutes. Everything else is just theory."

ITALY

Only Brazil (with five victories) can claim to have won the FIFA World Cup more times than Italy. The *Azzurri* became the first nation to retain the trophy (through back-to-back successes in 1934 and 1938), snatched a surprise win in Spain in 1982, and collected football's most coveted trophy for a fourth time in 2006 following a dramatic penalty shoot-out win over France. Add the 1968 UEFA European Championship success to the mix and few nations can boast a better record. The success story does not end there. Italian clubs have won the European Cup on 11 occasions and the country's domestic league, Serie A, is considered among the strongest in the game. Italy are a true powerhouse of world football.

ROTTEN RETURN

Italy were knocked out of the FIFA World Cup in the first round in both 2010 and 2014 – the first time they had done so in consecutive tournaments since 1962 and 1966. At least the modern players did not suffer the fate of those arriving home from England in 1966: they were pelted with rotten fruit after a dismal showing most notable for a 1-0 defeat to minnows North Korea.

OFF THE SPOT

Only England have lost as many FIFA World Cup penalty shoot-outs as Italy – three apiece. **Roberto Baggio**, nicknamed "The Divine Ponytail", was involved in all three of Italy's spot-kick defeats, in 1990, 1994 and 1998. Left-back Antonio Cabrini is the only man to have missed a penalty during normal time in a FIFA World Cup final – the score was 0-0 at the time but, fortunately for him, Italy still beat West Germany 3-1 in 1982.

THE IDES OF MARCH

Juventus midfielder Claudio Marchisio went from hero to villain at the 2014 FIFA World Cup. He opened Italy's account at the tournament with a fizzing long-range drive against England in Manaus, in what proved to be a 2-1 Italy win. This was his second goal in consecutive internationals – having managed just two goals in his previous 43 appearances for his country. But his tournament turned sour not only with a 1-0 defeat to Costa Rica in their second match, but another 1-0 defeat and a straight red card in their decisive final first-round fixture against Uruguay.

IN SAFE KEEPING

During World War Two, the Jules Rimet Trophy, the FIFA World Cup – won by Italy in 1938 – was hidden in a shoebox under the bed of football official Ottorino Barassi. He preferred to keep it there, rather than at its previous home – a bank in Rome. The trophy was handed back to FIFA, safe and untouched, only when the FIFA World Cup resumed in 1950.

BLUE BOYS

Internazionale full-back Davide Santon became Italy's second-youngest international of the post-war era when he played against Northern Ireland in a June 2009 friendly, aged just 18 years and 155 days and following just 20 first-team appearances for his club. Another Internazionale defender, the richly moustachioed Giuseppe Bergomi, was 42 days younger when he made his debut against East Germany in April 1982, just three months before helping Italy win the FIFA World Cup. Even more junior were Casale midfielder Luigi Barbesino, 18 years and 61 days old against Sweden in July 1912, and record-holder Renzo De Vecchi, an AC Milan defender who was aged just 16 years and 112 days when he lined up against Hungary in May 1910.

GLOVE CONQUERS ALL

Walter Zenga went 517 minutes without conceding a goal at the 1990 FIFA World Cup, an all-time tournament record only brought to an end by Argentina's Claudio Caniggia in the semi-finals.

BOSSI DE ROSSI

Combative central midfielder **Daniele de Rossi** was roundly condemned when he was sent off for elbowing the United States' Brian McBride during Italy's second match of the 2006 FIFA World Cup. He returned from suspension in time to come on as a substitute in the final, which Italy won against France. Yet earlier that year, in March, he had won widespread praise for his honesty during a Serie A match for AS Roma against Messina. Roma were awarded a goal when he diverted the ball into the net using his hand, but De Rossi persuaded the referee to disallow his strike – Roma went on to win 2-1. His international honours for Italy include a bronze medal at the 2004 Summer Olympics – not long before he made his international debut.

TOP DRAW

No team has drawn more FIFA World Cup matches than Italy, who took their tally to 21 with 1-1 draws against both Paraguay and New Zealand in Group F at the 2010 competition in South Africa. Their first draw had also been 1-1, against Spain in a 1934 quarter-final tie. Italy's Giuseppe Meazza scored the only goal of a replay the following day, and Italy went on to lift the trophy for the first time that year.

TOURNAMENT SPECIALISTS

FIFA WORLD CUP: 18 appearances – winners 1934, 1938, 1982, 2006
UEFA EUROPEAN CHAMPIONSHIP: 8 appearances – winners 1968
FIRST INTERNATIONAL: Italy 6 France 2 (Milan, 15 May 1910)
BIGGEST WIN: Italy 9 USA 0 (Brentford, London, 17 August 1948 – Olympic Games)
BIGGEST DEFEAT: Hungary 7 Italy 1 (Budapest, 6 April 1924)

FLYING HIGH

Vittorio Pozzo is the only man to have won the FIFA World Cup twice as manager – both times with Italy, in 1934 and 1938 (only two players, Giuseppe Meazza and Giovanni Ferrari, were selected in both finals). Pozzo also led Italy to the 1936 Olympics title. Born in Turin on 2 March 1886, Pozzo learned to love football as a student in England, watching Manchester United. He returned home reluctantly when his family bought him a return ticket for his sister's wedding and then refused to let him leave Italy again. Pozzo fired up his Italian team ahead of their 1938 semi-final against Brazil by revealing their opponents had already booked their plane to Paris for the final – Italy won 2-1.

CHAMPS TO CHUMPS

Italy's dismal 2010 FIFA World Cup campaign was the worst in their history, despite going into the tournament as defending world champions. Their two draws and 3-2 defeat to Slovakia meant they ended a FIFA World Cup without a win for the first time ever. Finishing bottom of their first-round group was also unprecedented. The poor showing must have left 2006 World Cup-winning coach **Marcello Lippi** regretting his decision to resume control in 2008. Immediately after the Slovakia match, which ended the defending champions' run, Lippi insisted the players should not be faulted and he should take all the blame. He had already announced his intention to resign after the finals.

ITALY'S NATIONAL COACHES

Vittorio Pozzo	1912, 1924
Augusto Rangone	1925–28
Carlo Carcano	1928–29
Vittorio Pozzo	1929–48
Ferruccio Novo	1949–50
Carlino Beretta	1952–53
Giuseppe Viani	1960
Giovanni Ferrari	1960–61
Giovanni Ferrari/Paolo Mazza	1962
Edmondo Fabbri	1962–66
Helenio Herrera/ Ferruccio Valcareggi	1966–67
Ferruccio Valcareggi	1967–74
Fulvio Bernardini	1974–75
Enzo Bearzot	1975–86
Azeglio Vicini	1986–91
Arrigo Sacchi	1991–96
Cesare Maldini	1997–98
Dino Zoff	1998–2000
Giovanni Trapattoni	2000–04
Marcello Lippi	2004–06
Roberto Donadoni	2006–08
Marcello Lippi	2008–10
Cesare Prandelli	2010–14

COMEBACK KID

Paolo Rossi was the unlikely hero of Italy's 1982 FIFA World Cup triumph, winning the Golden Boot with six goals – including a memorable hat-trick against Brazil in the second round, and the first of Italy's three goals in their final win over West Germany. But he only just made it to the tournament at all, having completed a two-year ban for his alleged involvement in a betting scandal only six weeks before the start of the tournament.

HELPING HANDS

Goalkeeper Angelo Peruzzi was a 14-year-old ballboy at the 1984 European Cup final between Roma and Liverpool. He made 16 appearances for Roma before playing for Juventus, Internazionale and Lazio as well as 31 times for Italy between 1995 and 2006.

ONCE BITTEN, TWICE SHY

Italy crashed out of the 2014 FIFA World Cup in Brazil in the first round, just as they had done in South Africa four years earlier. After beating England in Manaus, they lost 1-0 to surprise group winners Costa Rica – their first FIFA World Cup defeat to a Central American nation in eight meetings. They then lost a decisive final game against Uruguay by the same scoreline, thanks to a late goal by Diego Godin – although the Italians were incensed opposing striker Luis Suarez was not sent off earlier for biting **Giorgio Chiellini** on the shoulder. The Italy vice-captain pulled down his shirt to show Mexican referee Marco Rodriguez the toothmarks left in his skin, but to no avail.

TOP CAPS

1	Gianluigi Buffon	142
2	Fabio Cannavaro	136
3	Paolo Maldini	126
4	Andrea Pirlo	112
=	Dino Zoff	112
6	Gianluca Zambrotta	98
7	Daniele De Rossi	97
8	Giacinto Facchetti	94
9	Alessandro Del Piero	91
10	Franco Baresi	82

TOP SCORERS

1	Luigi Riva	35
2	Giuseppe Meazza	33
3	Silvio Piola	30
4	Roberto Baggio	27
=	Alessandro Del Piero	27
6	Alessandro Altobelli	25
=	Adolfo Baloncieri	25
=	Filippo Inzaghi	25
9	Francesco Graziani	23
=	Christian Vieri	23

MISTER INTER, GIACINTO

No Internazionale footballer will ever wear the No.3 shirt after it was retired in tribute to the legendary full-back **Giacinto Facchetti**, following his death in 2006 at the age of 64. He spent his entire senior career at Inter, between 1960 and 1978, and later served as the club's technical director and president. In his playing days he helped pioneer the role of a full-back as a stampeding, attacking presence – though favoured his right foot despite advancing on the left. He captained Italy 70 times, during his 94-cap international career and lifted the UEFA European Championship trophy in 1968.

ZOFF THE SCALE

Goalkeeper **Dino Zoff** set an international record by going 1,142 minutes without conceding a goal between September 1972 and June 1974. Zoff was Italy's captain when they won the 1982 FIFA World Cup – emulating the feat of another Juventus goalkeeper, Gianpiero Combi, who had been the victorious skipper in 1934. Zoff coached Italy to the final of the 2000 UEFA European Championship, which they lost 2-1 to France thanks to an extra-time "golden goal" – then quit a few days later, unhappy following the criticism levelled at him by Italy's then prime minister, Silvio Berlusconi.

SOMETIMES SUPER MARIO

Mario Balotelli is one of football's most explosive footballers – and not only because the fire brigade had to be called when fireworks were set off from the bathroom of his home the night before he scored in his club Manchester City's 6-1 trouncing of local rivals United. He marked his opening goal by revealing a T-shirt under his club kit bearing the question: "WHY ALWAYS ME?" His turbulent time in Manchester included a Premier League title but also a training-ground fight with manager Roberto Mancini and a reported £100,000 in parking fines. He was born in Palermo to Ghanaian parents, but health problems as a child prompted him to be adopted by an Italian couple when he was three, changing his name from Mario Barwuah to Mario Balotelli. He was given clearance to play for Italy when given citizenship at the age of 18 and was one of the country's star players at the 2012 UEFA European Championship, when he scored his first three international goals – including a decisive double against Germany in the semi-finals. But his volatile nature brought him a red card in a 2014 FIFA World Cup qualifier against the Czech Republic in June 2013 – and he lashed out at water bottles and then a brick wall after making his way off the pitch.

RIGHT CALL

Italy captain Giacinto Facchetti called correctly when their 1968 UEFA European Championship semi-final against the Soviet Union ended in a draw after extra-time (in the days before penalties) and had to be settled by the toss of a coin. The attacking left-back had luck on his side that time, then lifted the trophy after a 2-0 replay victory in the final against Yugoslavia. Facchetti, who also won the European Cup with Internazionale in 1964 and 1965, had an impressive scoring record for a defender, ending his career with 59 goals in 476 league appearances. He played on the left flank, even though he was a naturally right-footed player.

ROLLING RIVA

Italy's all-time top scorer is **Luigi "Gigi" Riva**, who scored 35 goals in 42 appearances for his country. One of his most important strikes was the opening goal in the 1968 UEFA European Championship final win over Yugoslavia. Despite his prolific form after having switched from left-winger to striker, he never played for one of Italy's traditional club giants. Instead, Riva – born in Leggiuno on 7 November 1944 – spent his entire league career with unfashionable Sardinian club Cagliari, and at one point turned down a move to the mighty Juventus. His goals (21 of them) fired the club to their one and only league championship in 1970. Riva suffered his fair share of bad luck with injuries, breaking his left leg while playing for Italy in 1966, then his right leg in 1970, again when he was away on international duty.

HAPPY CENTENARY

After captaining Italy to the 2006 FIFA World Cup title, **Fabio Cannavaro** was named FIFA World Player of the Year – at 33, the oldest winner of the prize, as well as the first defender. Cannavaro, born in Naples in 1973, played every minute of the 2006 tournament and the final triumph against France was the ideal way to celebrate his 100th international appearance.

WHEN THE GOING GETS BUFF

Italy goalkeeper **Gianluigi Buffon** has not only been one of the finest modern-day goalkeepers in the world but has also even surpassed some of the achievements of legendary Italian predecessor Dino Zoff. Buffon emulated 1982 world champion Dino Zoff by being part of Italy's 2006 FIFA World Cup-winning side – only conceding two goals during the tournament, one an own goal and the other a penalty. Italy's progress to the 2012 UEFA European Championship final allowed him to play his 25th game at a finals for Italy, one more than Zoff – and behind only defenders Paolo Maldini (36) and Fabio Cannavaro (26). Italy's dismal first-round exit at the 2010 FIFA World Cup could be blamed at least more than a little on Buffon's back injury in the first half of their first match that ruled him out of the rest of the tournament. Unlike fellow veterans Cannavaro and Gennaro Gattuso, who retired from internationals after the finals, Buffon insisted he would go on and was rewarded with the captaincy by incoming coach Cesare Prandelli. Buffon became only the third footballer selected for five different FIFA World Cups when he made two appearances in Brazil in 2014, only missing the opening match against England due to a late ankle injury.

CLEAN SWEEP

Italian clubs won all three UEFA trophies in the 1989–90 season, a unique treble. AC Milan took the European Cup (beating Benfica 1-0 in the final), Juventus the UEFA Cup (beating Fiorentina 3-1) and Sampdoria the Cup-Winners' Cup (beating Anderlecht 2-0).

KEEPING IT IN THE FAMILY

Cesare and **Paolo Maldini** are the only father and son to have hoisted the European Cup as winning captains – both with AC Milan and both for the first time in England. Cesare lifted the trophy after his team beat Benfica at Wembley, London, in 1963. Paolo repeated the feat 40 years later, when Milan defeated Juventus at Old Trafford, Manchester. Cesare was Italy coach and Paolo Italy captain at the 1998 FIFA World Cup, and they both featured at the 2002 tournament – though by now Cesare was in charge of Paraguay. The Maldini dynasty may not end there – Paolo's son, Christian, is emerging through the youth ranks at Milan. If he makes it into the first team, Christian will be the only player allowed to wear Paolo's famous No. 3 jersey. Although retired as Italy's second most-capped player, Paolo never managed to win an international tournament – he played for Italy sides that finished third and runners-up at the FIFA World Cup and runners-up in the UEFA European Championship.

ITALY'S GREATEST PLAYERS
(as chosen by the Italian football association)

1 Giuseppe Meazza	**5** Giacinto Facchetti
2 Luigi Riva	**6** Sandro Mazzola
3 Roberto Baggio	**7** Giuseppe Bergomi
4 Paolo Maldini	**8** Valentino Mazzola

TRAVELLING TRAPATTONI

Italian **Giovanni Trapattoni** has won domestic league titles as a coach in Italy, Germany, Portugal and Austria – with Juventus, Bayern Munich, Benfica and Salzburg. Only Portugal's Jose Mourinho has also coached teams in four different top countries to league title success. Trapattoni is the only manager to have won all three UEFA club competitions as well as the World Club Cup, all with the great Juventus sides of the 1980s.

PEERLESS PIRLO

Deep-lying playmaker **Andrea Pirlo** is one of the finest passers of a football in the modern era. He was one of the stand-out performers when Italy won the 2006 FIFA World Cup and the only player to win three man-of-the-match prizes at the 2012 UEFA European Championship. Perhaps his finest moment of Euro 2012 was the "Panenka" penalty he audaciously chipped down the centre of the goal in Italy's quarter-final shoot-out victory over England. Pirlo came to the tournament having gone through the Italian league season unbeaten, helping Juventus lift the Serie A title after joining them in 2011 from AC Milan on a free transfer.

MEDAL COLLECTORS

Giovanni Ferrari not only enjoys the status of having won both the 1934 and 1938 FIFA World Cups with Italy, he also shares the record for most Serie A titles, with eight triumphs. Five were with Juventus, two with Internazionale and one with Bologna. He shares the record of eight league championship medals with Virginio Rosetta, twice with Pro Vercelli and six times with Juventus, and Giuseppe Furino, all with Juventus.

ITALIAN LEAGUE TITLES

Juventus	30	Lazio	2
Internazionale	18	Napoli	2
AC Milan	18	Cagliari	1
Genoa	9	Casale	1
Bologna	7	Hellas Verona	1
Pro Vercelli	7	Novese	1
Torino	7	Sampdoria	1
Roma	3	Spezia	1
Fiorentina	2		

GRAND OLD TEAM TO PLAY FOR

Every Italian FIFA World Cup squad has featured at least one Juventus player. The Turin team, known as the "Grand Old Lady" of Italian club football, were relegated a division in 2006 after being found guilty of match-fixing – and, as a result, were forced to endure their first season outside the top division since the club's foundation in 1897. Their 55 trophies are an Italian club record, following the three consecutive league title triumphs of 2012–14 – and, in 1985, they became the first team to have won the European, UEFA and Cup Winners' Cups.

PRANDELLI'S PLEDGE

Cesare Prandelli was in Africa during the 2010 FIFA World Cup tournament, before he succeeded Marcello Lippi as Italy coach. But the ex-Fiorentina boss went there not only to watch football; he and his daughter went to Zanzibar, Tanzania, to open a school in memory of his wife Manuela, who had died of cancer three years earlier. Prandelli's first competitive home match in charge of Italy was in Florence, and his new team crushed the Faroe Islands 5-0. The coach exceeded most expectations by leading Italy to the 2012 UEFA European Championship final. The defeat that day to Spain was Prandelli's first in 16 competitive matches in charge. Prandelli's son Nicolo, a fitness coach, became part of the national team's back-up staff in the build-up to Euro 2012.

BEEFING UP

The stadium shared by AC Milan and Internazionale is popularly known as the San Siro, after the district in which it is located. Its official title, however, is Stadio Giuseppe Meazza, named after the star inside-forward on the pitch and dance enthusiast off it who played for both clubs as well as Italy's 1934 and 1938 FIFA World Cup-winning sides. Meazza, born in Milan on 23 August 1910, was first spotted by an Inter scout while playing keepy-uppy in the street with a ball made of rags – but he was so thin he had to be fattened up with plenty of steaks. His last goal for Italy was a penalty in the 1938 World Cup semi-final against Brazil – taken while trying to pull up his shorts, whose elastic had broken.

TRAGIC TORINO

Torino were Italy's most successful club side when their first-team squad was wiped out in an air crash at Superga, above Turin, on 4 May 1949. The club has only won the Serie A title once since then, in the 1976–77 season. Among the victims was star forward Valentino Mazzola, who had gone along on the trip despite being ill. His son **Sandro Mazzola**, only six at the time of the disaster, went on to star in the Italy teams that won the 1968 UEFA European Championship and finished as FIFA World Cup runners-up two years later.

NETHERLANDS

The walled banks of orange-shirted Netherlands fans may have become a regular feature at the world's major football tournaments, but that has not always been the case. It wasn't until the 1970s, with Johan Cruyff and his team's spectacular brand of Total Football, that the country possessed a side worthy of the modern legend. They won the UEFA European Championship in 1988 and have regularly challenged for the game's major honours.

NETHERLANDS MANAGERS (SINCE 1980)

Jan Zwartkruis	1978–81
Rob Baan	1981
Kees Rijvers	1981–84
Rinus Michels	1984–85
Leo Beenhakker	1985–86
Rinus Michels	1986–88
Thijs Libregts	1988–90
Nol de Ruiter	1990
Leo Beenhakker	1990
Rinus Michels	1990–92
Dick Advocaat	1992–95
Guus Hiddink	1995–98
Frank Rijkaard	1998–2000
Louis van Gaal	2000–02
Dick Advocaat	2002–04
Marco van Basten	2004–08
Bert van Marwijk	2008–12
Louis van Gaal	2012–14
Guus Hiddink	2014–

MICHELS THE MASTER

Rinus Michels (1928–2005) was named FIFA's Coach of the Century in 1999 for his achievements with the Netherlands and Ajax. The former Ajax and Netherlands striker took over the manager's job at his old club in 1965 and began creating the side that would dominate European football in the early 1970s. Michels built the team around Johan Cruyff – as he later did with the national side – and introduced the concept known as "Total Football". He moved to Barcelona after Ajax's 1971 European Cup victory, but he was called back to mastermind the Netherlands' 1974 FIFA World Cup bid. Nicknamed "The General", he was known as a disciplinarian who could impose order on the many different factions within the Dutch dressing room. Michels used that skill to great effect after taking over the national team again for their 1988 UEFA European Championship campaign. In the finals, the Dutch beat England and the Republic of Ireland to reach the last four, then knocked out hosts West Germany before beating the Soviet Union 2-0 in the final. Michels tookcharge for a third spell as manager when the Netherlands reached the semi-finals of Euro 92. He retired straight after the tournament.

CRUYFF THE MAGICIAN

Johan Cruyff's footballing achievements have made him the most famous living Dutchman. Cruyff (born in Amsterdam on 25 April 1947) was the catalyst for the rise of both Ajax and the national team. As one Dutch paper wrote before the 1974 FIFA World Cup final: "Cruyff woke up the Netherlands and took us to a world-class level." His great opponent, Franz Beckenbauer, said: "He is the best player to have come from Europe." Cruyff joined Ajax as a ten-year-old and made his league debut at 17. He led them to eight championships and the European Cup three years in a row. He and coach Rinus Michels also developed the style of playing known as "Total Football", which became a trademark for club and country. Cruyff made his national debut, against Hungary, on 7 September 1966. He scored 33 goals in 48 appearances and captained his country 33 times. He was named Player of the Tournament in the 1974 FIFA World Cup finals and was voted European Player of the Year three times.

THIS ONE GOES UP TO ELEVEN

The Netherlands' biggest-ever win was an 11-0 thrashing of San Marino in September 2011 during a UEFA European Championship qualifier in Eindhoven. Robin van Persie scored four, while there were braces for **Wesley Sneijder** and Klaas-Jan Huntelaar, and goals apiece for Dirk Kuyt, John Heitinga and Georginio Wijnaldum, who made his international debut as an 86th-minute substitute and scored within four minutes.

LOUIS LOUIS

Louis van Gaal returned for a second spell as Netherlands coach after the 2012 UEFA European Championship. He has enjoyed great success at clubs around Europe, winning the UEFA Champions League with Ajax, two La Liga titles with Barcelona and the Bundesliga with Bayern Munich. After the 2014 FIFA World Cup he took over as manager of Manchester United. The Dutch are no strangers to reappointing former coaches: Karel Kaufman, Friedrich Donenfeld, Leo Beenhakker, Dick Advocaat and Rinus Michels all had more than one spell – and Michels had four. Van Gaal was succeeded by Guus Hiddink, his second spell, too, having been national coach 1995–98.

GOALS GALORE

Only four players have scored five goals in a game for the Netherlands: Jan Vos, as Finland were crushed 9-0 in July 1912; Leen Vente, in a 9-3 defeat of Belgium in March 1934; John Bosman, in an 8-0 home trouncing of Cyprus in October 1987; and Marco van Basten, in an 8-0 win in Malta in December 1990. Bosman scored three separate hat-tricks for the Dutch, as did Mannes Francken, Beb Bakhuys and Faas Wilkes. Two of Wilkes' trebles were scored in 1946 – the third came a full 13 years later.

VAN BASTEN'S TOURNAMENT

Marco van Basten was the hero of the Netherlands' 1988 UEFA European Championship success. He netted a hat-trick to see off England in the group games, scored a semi-final winner against West Germany, and then cracked a spectacular flying volley to clinch a 2-0 victory over the Soviet Union in the final. The Dutch forward also starred in Italy's Serie A with AC Milan, and was twice the league's top scorer before persistent ankle trouble ended his career prematurely.

ALL CHANGE FOR THE ORANJE

Ten of the 11 men who started the 2010 FIFA World Cup final were in the Dutch squad for a disastrous UEFA European Championship in 2012. They lost all three first-round games and missed the knock-out stages of a major tournament for the first time since failing to qualify for Euro 2004. Things improved dramatically at the 2014 FIFA World Cup as the Netherlands finished third after losing the semi-final to Argentina in a penalty shoot-out. Only nine members of the 23-man Euro 2012 squad made it to Brazil 2014. The most memorable Dutch display in Brazil came in their opening match: avenging their 2010 FIFA World Cup final defeat by demolishing champions Spain 5-1 in Salvador. **Robin van Persie**'s fantastic diving header from the edge of the area that looped over goalkeeper Iker Casillas was the highlight. Van Persie thus became the first Dutchman to score at three separate FIFA World Cups. The 2014 FIFA World Cup was the first one which the Netherlands ended with a win: their 3-0 third-place play-off defeat of hosts Brazil. This set another record as the Netherlands became the first country to beat Brazil in FIFA World Cup finals three times.

HERO HAPPEL

Ernst Happel is second only to Rinus Michels for his coaching achievements with Dutch teams. The former Austria defender made history by steering Feyenoord to the European Cup in 1970 – the first Dutch side to win the trophy. He was drafted in to coach the Netherlands at the 1978 FIFA World Cup finals after guiding Belgian side Brugge to the European Cup final. In Johan Cruyff's absence, Happel drew the best from Ruud Krol, Johan Neeskens and Arie Haan as the Netherlands reached the final before losing in extra-time to Argentina in Buenos Aires.

HANGING AROUND

Sander Boschker waited a long time for his full introduction to international football, but set two Dutch records when finally coming on as a second-half substitute against Ghana in a June 2010 friendly. At the age of 39 years and 256 days, he was not only the oldest Dutchman to win his first cap – but also the oldest Dutch international ever. That remains his only cap... so far.

FLYING FEAR DENIED BERGKAMP MORE CAPS

Dennis Bergkamp would have won many more than 79 caps, but for his fear of flying. Bergkamp refused to board aircraft after the Netherlands squad were involved in a bomb hoax incident during the 1994 FIFA World Cup in the United States. He missed every away game for the Netherlands and his clubs unless he could reach the venue by road, rail or boat.

DIFFERENT SIDES OF SNEIJDER

Wesley Sneijder was hoping to achieve an unprecedented quintuple when his Netherlands team took on Spain in the 2010 FIFA World Cup final. No footballer had ever before won the FIFA World Cup in the same season as a domestic league and cup double and the UEFA Champions League or European Cup – let alone adding the FIFA World Cup Golden Boot. Sneijder won the 2009–10 treble with his club side Internazionale before only just missing out on the FIFA World Cup and the Golden Boot. Despite his FIFA World Cup final heartbreak, Sneijder did enjoy some romantic solace six days after defeat to Spain, when he married Dutch actress and TV presenter Yolanthe Cabau van Kasbergen.

VORM WELCOME

The Netherlands became the first country to use all 23 squad players at a FIFA World Cup, when sub keeper Michel Vorm came on for Jasper Cillessen during stoppage-time of their third-place play-off against Brazil. Cillessen set another record as the first goalkeeper to be substituted twice in one tournament. Earlier in the competition, Robin van Persie's suspension from their final first-round match against Chile meant the Dutch played without a single player named 'van' for the first time since 1996, a run lasting 221 matches.

NEESKENS'S EARLY GOAL

The Netherlands took a first-minute lead in the 1974 World Cup final without a West German player having touched the ball. The Dutch built a move of 14 passes from the kick-off and Johan Cruyff was tripped in the box by Uli Hoeness. Johan Neeskens converted the first penalty in a World Cup final history ... but they still went on to lose.

KRUL TO BE KIND

Louis van Gaal pulled a masterstoke when he replaced goalkeeper Jasper Cillessen with **Tim Krul** in the 119th minute of the Netherlands' quarter-final against Costa Rica in the 2014 FIFA World Cup. He reasoned that the Dutch stood a better chance of winning the resulting shoot-out with Krul between the sticks as he is two inches taller than Cillessen. Sure enough, Krul saved two penalties and the Dutch went through. Enforced substitutions during the semi-final against Argentina meant van Gaal could not repeat the trick and Cillessen was unable to emulate Krul's earlier heroics.

NETHERLANDS' DOUBLE LOSERS

Nine Netherlands players were on the losing side in both the 1974 (2-1 to West Germany) and 1978 (3-1 to Argentina) FIFA World Cup finals. Jan Jongbloed, Ruud Krol, Wim Jansen, Arie Haan, Johan Neeskens, Johnny Rep and Rob Rensenbrink started both games. Wim Suurbier started in 1974 and was a substitute in 1978. Rene van de Kerkhof was a sub in 1974 and started in 1978.

THE WINNING CAPTAIN

With his distinctive dreadlocks, Ruud Gullit cut a swathe through world football through the 1980s and '90s. Twice a European Cup winner with AC Milan and a former European Footballer of the Year, he will always be remembered fondly by the Dutch fans as being the first man in a Netherlands shirt to lift a major trophy – the 1988 UEFA European Championship.

NETHERLANDS' EURO STARS

Three Dutch players have won the European Footballer of the Year award: Johan Cruyff, **Ruud Gullit** and Marco van Basten. Cruyff picked up the award in 1971, 1973 and 1974; Gullit was honoured in 1987, and Van Basten was chosen in 1988, 1989 and 1992.

TOP SCORERS

1	Robin van Persie	47
2	Patrick Kluivert	40
3	Dennis Bergkamp	37
4	Klaas-Jan Huntelaar	35
=	Ruud van Nistelrooy	35
=	Faas Wilkes	35
7	Johan Cruyff	33
=	Abe Lenstra	33
9	Beb Bakhuys	28
10	Wesley Sneijder	27

DE BOER BOYS SET RECORD

Twins Frank and Ronald de Boer hold the record for the most games played by brothers together for the Netherlands. Frank won 112 caps, while Ronald won 67.

TOP CAPS

1	Edwin van der Sar	130
2	Frank de Boer	112
3	Rafael van der Vaart	109
4	Gio van Bronckhorst	106
5	Wesley Sneijder	105
6	Dirk Kuyt	103
7	Phillip Cocu	101
8	Robin van Persie	91
9	John Heitinga	87
=	Clarence Seedorf	87

WORK OF VAART

Rafael van der Vaart became the fifth player to make 100 appearances for the Netherlands, following Edwin van der Sar, Frank de Boer, Giovanni van Bronckhorst and Philip Cocu. Yet for a while it looked as if van der Vaart might just miss out on the milestone: he ended the 2012 UEFA European Championship on 99 caps and coach Bert van Marwijk said he may be left out of future squads. But Van Marwijk's departure after Euro 2012 was a boost for van der Vaart, who made his 100th appearance in a 4-2 friendly loss to Belgium in August 2012. Van der Vaart had marked his 99th cap with a stunning long-range goal against Portugal in the Netherlands' final first-round game at Euro 2012, and hit a post, in the 2-1 defeat that ended Dutch interest earlier than expected. Sadly, a calf injury ruled him out of the 2014 FIFA World Cup three days before Louis van Gaal announced his 23-man squad.

ALL-TIME LEADING SCORER

Patrick Kluivert made his Netherlands debut in 1994 and, in the following ten years, won 79 caps and scored a then national record 40 goals. That mark was beaten by Robin van Persie, who was Netherlands captain at the 2014 FIFA World Cup, while Kluivert watched on as Louis van Gaal's assistant coach.

EARLY DAYS

The Netherlands played their first international against Belgium in Brussels on 30 April 1905. Eddy de Neve scored all the goals in the Netherlands' 4-1 win. The Dutch and their Belgian neighbours have been arch-rivals ever since.

BLIND LEADING THE BLIND

Dutch defender **Danny Blind** won 42 caps between 1986 and 1996, and appeared at the FIFA World Cups of 1990 and 1994. He was also involved at the 2014 final, this time as an assistant to coach Louis van Gaal. He thus got to see his son **Daley** – like Danny, a defender playing club football for Ajax Amsterdam – not only feature as a regular starter but score his first international goal, in the third-place play-off victory over Brazil. Danny Blind was appointed as Guus Hiddink's assistant for the 2016 UEFA European Championship qualifying campaign, with the promise of the top job at the end of that tournament.

SIXTH SENSE

Maarten Stekelenburg, Edwin van der Sar's successor as the Netherlands' first-choice goalkeeper, impressed many with his performances at the 2010 FIFA World Cup, conceding just six goals in seven games – two of them penalties. His rise is all the more startling because he is deaf in one ear. He also has the unenviable distinction of being the first Dutch international goalkeeper to be shown a red card. On 6 September 2008, in a 2-1 friendly defeat against Australia in Eindhoven, he was sent off for fouling Josh Kennedy.

KOEMAN PEOPLE

The only man to both play for and manage all of Dutch domestic football's "big three" of Ajax Amsterdam, PSV Eindhoven and Feyenoord is Ronald Koeman. He won the UEFA European Cup twice, with PSV Eindhoven in 1988, and with Barcelona four years later – a game in which he scored the winning goal, a ferocious long-range free-kick. Despite largely playing in defence, he scored 14 goals in 78 games for the Netherlands. Elder brother Erwin played 31 times for the Netherlands and their father Martin won one cap for his country in 1964. Both Ronald and Erwin were part of the Netherlands' 1988 UEFA European Championship-winning side.

MEMPHIS SWELL

Substitute Memphis Depay became the youngest FIFA World Cup goalscorer in Dutch history – aged 20 years and 125 days – by netting in the 3-2 Group B victory over Australia at Porto Alegre in 2014. He also scored against Chile five days later, again as a substitute. Depay was one of three nominees for the Best Young Player award, but lost out to France's Paul Pogba.

JETRO POWERED

Left-back **Jetro Willems** became the youngest player
in UEFA European Championship tournament history
when he started for the Netherlands against
Denmark in their opening Group B game in the
Ukrainian city of Kharkiv on 9 June 2012. He was
18 years and 71 days old, 44 days younger than
Belgium's Enzo Scifo had been at the 1984 finals.
Willems is the fourth-youngest player to be capped
by the Netherlands, with the record held by Jan
van Breda Kolff, who was 17 years and 74 days
old when making his debut against Belgium on
2 April 1911. Van Breda Kolff's goal in a 3-1 win,
the only one of his 11-cap career, means he
remains his country's youngest scorer.

NETHERLANDS SO CLOSE

The Netherlands came within a post's width of winning the 1978
FIFA World Cup final. A Rob Rensenbrink shot bounced off an
upright in the last minute of normal time. It was 1-1 after 90 minutes
and Argentina went on to win 3-1 in extra-time, shattering Dutch final
dreams for the second FIFA World Cup in a row.

PENALTY PLAGUE

Missed penalties have become a Dutch nightmare, causing their
downfall in several tournaments. The jinx started in the 1992
UEFA European Championship semi-final, when Denmark's Peter
Schmeichel won the shoot-out by saving from Marco van Basten.
The Netherlands lost a Euro 96 quarter-final shoot-out to France
and, two years later, went down on penalties to Brazil in a FIFA
World Cup semi-final. And as co-hosts of Euro 2000, the Dutch
missed two penalties in normal time in the semi-final against Italy
and two more in the shoot-out. There was shoot-out joy at the
2014 FIFA World Cup when Costa Rica were beaten, but it turned to
misery in the semi-final when they lost to Argentina on penalties.

KEY PLAYER

Maintaining harmony has often been a tricky task for Dutch coaches
at major international tournaments – but Bert van Marwijk managed
to do so at the 2010 FIFA World Cup, despite rumoured tension
between several of his star players. When not conducting his team
from the touchline, van Marwijk could occasionally be found playing
the piano in the lobby of the squad's Johannesburg hotel.

VAN DER SAR TOPS THE LOT

Goalkeeper **Edwin van der Sar** (born in Voorhout on 29 October 1970) is
the Netherlands' most-capped player, having made 130 appearances for
the national side. He joined Ajax in 1990 and helped them win the European
Cup five years later. He made his Netherlands debut on 7 June 1995, against
Belarus, and was their first-choice keeper for 13 years. He quit international
football after the Netherlands' elimination at Euro 2008, but new coach Bert
van Marwijk persuaded him to return briefly after injuries to his successors,
Maarten Stekelenburg and Henk Timmer. Van der Sar has also won the
UEFA Champions League with Manchester United, as well as spending
spells with Juventus and Fulham.

GOING DUTCH FULL-TIME

Professionalism was not introduced into
Dutch football until 1954. The Netherlands'
emergence as a major power came even
later, after Ajax and Feyenoord decided to
go full-time professional in the early 1960s.
Until then, even stars such as Ajax left-
winger Piet Keizer – who worked in
a tailor's – had part-time jobs outside
the game.

DUTCH CLOGS

The Netherlands became the first team to
be shown as many as nine cards during a
single FIFA World Cup match when they
received eight yellows, including a lenient
one for Nigel de Jong's chest-high challenge
on Xabi Alonso, and a red during the 2010
final against Spain. The Netherlands were
also involved in the FIFA World Cup game
with the most cards: their second-round
defeat to Portugal four years earlier, when
20 cards were shown in total – 16 yellows
and four reds.

WHOLE LOTTA SCHAKEN

Feyenoord winger Ruben Schaken
netted the Netherlands' 1,500th
international goal to complete a 3-0
victory over Estonia in a FIFA World
Cup qualifier in March 2013. It was his
second goal in three appearances for
his country.

SPAIN

Spain is home to some of Europe's strongest club sides (boasting 14 European Cup/UEFA Champions League wins between them) and has produced some of football's biggest names. For years, however, the national team was considered the world game's biggest underachievers (*La Roja's* only success being the 1964 UEFA European Championship). Things changed in 2008, when Spain won the UEFA European Championship, its first international success for 44 years and a first-ever top position in the Coca-Cola/FIFA World Rankings. Even better came with victory in the 2010 FIFA World Cup, and an unprecedented third straight major trophy when the European crown was retained in 2012. But a disappointing first-round exit at the 2014 FIFA World Cup saw the great run end.

"FALSE NINE"

Spain not only began and ended their Euro 2012 campaign against Italy, but also became the first team to win a UEFA European Championship fielding the same starting XI in their opening game as in the final. Perhaps even more surprising was that Vicente del Bosque's men won the tournament so convincingly despite kicking off without an orthodox striker, preferring a 4-6-0 formation with midfielder **Cesc Fabregas** deployed as a "false nine".

DOUBLING UP

Spain's 2010 FIFA World Cup triumph made them the first country since West Germany in 1974 to lift the trophy as the reigning European champions. When France combined the two titles, they did it the other way around, by winning the 1998 FIFA World Cup and then the UEFA European Championship two years later. Yet no country had won three major tournaments in a row until Spain won Euro 2012, trouncing Italy 4-0 in the final. This also made Spain the first team to make a successful defence of their UEFA European Championship title. That scoreline was also the largest victory in a FIFA World Cup or UEFA European Championship final. The clean sheet in the final also stretched their run without conceding a goal in knockout games at major tournaments to 990 minutes.

THREE AND EASY

David Villa and Fernando Torres share Spain's record for most hat-tricks, with three. They even managed one apiece in the same match, the 10-0 crushing of Tahiti at the 2013 FIFA Confederations Cup. It was Spain's third-largest victory, behind only a 13-0 win over Bulgaria in 1933 and a 12-1 rout of Malta in 1983. Torres set another record at the 2009 FIFA Confederations Cup: the fastest ever hat-trick for Spain, all coming in the first 17 minutes of a 5-0 victory over New Zealand.

GROUNDS FOR APPEAL

No single country has provided more venues when hosting a FIFA World Cup finals than the 17 stadiums – in 14 cities – used by Spain in 1982. The 2002 tournament was played at 20 different venues but ten were in Japan and ten in South Korea. The 1982 competition was the first FIFA World Cup to be expanded from 16 to 24 teams. The final was played in Madrid's Estadio Santiago Bernabeu.

NOT TOO SHABY XABI

Passmaster Xabi Alonso scored both goals as Spain beat France 2-0 in their 2012 UEFA European Championship quarter-final – an ideal way for him to celebrate a day in which he became the fifth Spaniard, after Iker Casillas, Raul, Xavi and Andoni Zubizarreta, to make 100 international appearances. The central midfielder's father Periko Alonso won 21 Spanish caps as well as three La Liga titles – two with Real Sociedad and one with Barcelona, though Xabi would later play for Barca's arch-rivals Real Madrid. Xabi's brother Mikel and half-brother Marcos are both professional footballers, while another brother Jon is a referee.

MAJOR TOURNAMENTS

FIFA WORLD CUP:
14 appearances – winners 2010

UEFA EUROPEAN CHAMPIONSHIP:
9 appearances – winners 1964, 2008, 2012

FIRST INTERNATIONAL:
Spain 1 Denmark 0 (Brussels, Belgium, 28 August 1920)

BIGGEST WIN:
Spain 13 Bulgaria 0 (Madrid, 21 May 1933)

BIGGEST DEFEAT:
Italy 7 Spain 1 (Amsterdam, Netherlands, 4 June 1928); England 7 Spain 1 (London, England, 9 December 1931)

RIGHT SAID FRED

When Spain came back from 2-0 and then 3-2 down to win 4-3 in Madrid in May 1929, they became the first non-British team to beat England. Spain's victory, in the Estadio Metropolitano, came with the help of their English coach Fred Pentland, who had moved to Spain in 1920. He had most success with Athletic Bilbao, leading them to league and cup doubles in 1930 and 1931 – and inflicting Barcelona's worst-ever defeat, a 12-1 rout in 1931.

NO DEFENCE

Spain went into the 2014 FIFA World Cup in Brazil aiming not only to successfully retain their crown but also to clinch a historic fourth successive international title, having won the UEFA European Championship in 2008 and 2012. Yet their defence was a disaster – despite taking the lead against the Netherlands in their opening game through a **Xabi Alonso** penalty, they lost the match 5-1: the heaviest FIFA World Cup finals defeat any reigning champion have suffered. A 2-0 defeat to Chile made them the first defending champions to be eliminated with a game remaining, though they gained a token consolation with a 3-0 defeat of Australia. The competition brought to an end the otherwise-glorious international careers of players such as Xavi Hernandez and David Villa.

RED ALERT

Spain refused to play in the first UEFA European Championship in 1960, in protest at having to travel to the Soviet Union, a Communist country. But they changed their minds four years later, not only hosting the tournament but also winning it – by beating the visiting Soviets 2-1 in the final. Spain were captained by Fernando Olivella and managed by Jose Villalonga, who had been the first coach to win the European Cup, with Real Madrid in 1956.

WISE HEAD, OLD SHOULDERS

In 2008, a month short of his 70th birthday, Spain's **Luis Aragones** – full name Luis Aragones Suarez – became the oldest coach to win the UEFA European Championship. A former centre-forward and known only as "Luis" during his playing days, he won 11 caps for Spain. As coach, the "Wise Man of Hortaleza" won 38 matches between 2004 and 2008 – a national record since beaten by his successor Vicente Del Bosque. Aragones died from leukaemia on 1 February 2014, aged 75. Tributes were paid across football, but especially at his former club Atletico Madrid who, that same weekend, went top of La Liga for the first time since 1995–96 – when Aragones was coach. Atletico later won their first title since 1996. The players also wore his name embroidered in gold inside the collars of their shirts during the 2014 UEFA Champions League final.

TORRES! TORRES!

As a child, **Fernando Torres** wanted to be a goalkeeper, but made the wise decision to become a striker instead. He has a penchant for scoring the only goal in the final of a tournament, doing so in the 2008 UEFA European Championship, for Spain against Germany in Vienna, having done the same in the Under-16 UEFA European Championship in 2001 and for the Under-19s the following year. Torres became the most expensive Spanish footballer ever when Chelsea paid €58.5million to sign him from fellow English club Liverpool in January 2011. In 2012, Torres became the first player to score in the final of two different UEFA European Championships, when he came on as a substitute and found the net against Italy. Torres's goal in Spain's 3-0 victory over Australia in June 2014 was his first at a FIFA World Cup finals since Germany 2006. He thus became the ninth Spanish player to have scored four FIFA World Cup goals.

TOP CAPS

1	Iker Casillas	156
2	Xavi Hernandez	133
3	Andoni Zubizarreta	126
4	Sergio Ramos	119
5	Xabi Alonso	114
6	Fernando Torres	110
7	Raul Gonzalez	102
8	Carles Puyol	100
=	Andres Iniesta	100
10	David Villa	97

TOP SCORERS

1	David Villa	59
2	Raul Gonzalez	44
3	Fernando Torres	38
4	Fernando Hierro	29
5	Fernando Morientes	27
6	Emilio Butragueno	26
7	Alfredo Di Stefano	23
8	Julio Salinas	22
9	Michel	21
10	David Silva	20
=	Telmo Zarra	20

HAPPY HERNANDEZ

Relentlessly precise passer **Xavi Hernandez** has proved himself a more than worthy heir to Pep Guardiola at the heart of the Barcelona and Spain midfields. As well as winning the UEFA Champions League with his club in 2006, 2009 and 2011, he was voted Player of the Tournament when Spain won the 2008 UEFA European Championship, and starred as *La Roja* claimed the FIFA World Cup crown two years later and retained their European crown in 2012. Xavi was third, behind club mate Lionel Messi, in the 2010 and 2011 FIFA Ballon d'Or voting. Yet he nearly left Barcelona for Italy's AC Milan when aged just 17 – though Xavi was not keen on the proposed move and later expressed his relief at staying in Spain.

BEST CAS SCENARIO

Spain suffered a rare defeat when goalkeeper and captain Iker Casillas equalled the national record for most international appearances, in a 1-0 friendly defeat to England in November 2011. *La Roja* then drew 2-2 with Costa Rica three days later when he broke the record. Seven months later Casillas was lifting a third trophy in a row, at Euro 2012 – and extending not just his international appearances record but several more. The 4-0 Euro 2012 final victory over Italy made him the first footballer to reach a century of international wins. It was also his 78th clean sheet for his country, more than any other goalkeeper has achieved – the closest challenger was the Netherlands' Edwin van der Sar, on 72. The pair now share the record – nine – for the most UEFA European Championship clean sheets. Casillas went 821 minutes without conceding a goal for Spain until Olivier Giroud scored for France in a FIFA World Cup qualifier in October 2012.

SAVING FOR A REINA DAY

Jose 'Pepe' Reina finally saw action in the FIFA World Cup – at his third finals – when picked for Spain's 3-0 victory over Australia in June 2014. He had been an unused member at Germany 2006 and South Africa 2010. It was Reina's 34th appearance for Spain since making his debut in 2005. His father, Manuel Reina, also a goalkeeper, played in five internationals between 1969 and 1973.

DIES IN HIS BOOTS

David Villa became Spain's all-time top scorer in FIFA World Cups with his ground goal against Chile in 2010, his sixth overall across the 2006 and 2010 tournaments. Villa also became the first Spaniard to miss a penalty in a FIFA World Cup match, when he wasted the chance of a hat-trick against Honduras, also in 2010, by putting his spot-kick wide. Spain had scored their previous 14 FIFA World Cup penalties, not counting shoot-outs. Villa became Spain's all-time leading scorer with a brace against the Czech Republic in March 2011. But a broken leg ruled him out of the 2012 UEFA European Championship, thus missing out on adding to his Euro 2008 and 2010 FIFA World Cup winners' medals. Villa retired from international football as Spain departed the 2014 FIFA World Cup, signing off with a neat backheel goal against Australia – his 59th international in 97 appearances and the first backheeled goal at a FIFA World Cup since Bruno Pezzey against Northern Ireland in 1982.

SERGING SERGIO

Sergio Ramos became the youngest-ever European player to reach 100 international caps, in March 2013, at the age of 26 years and 358 days – and marked the occasion by scoring the opening goal in a 1-1 draw with Finland. He claimed the record from Germany's Lukas Podolski, who was 21 days older when he reached his century of caps. South Korea's Cha Bum-Kun, who was 24 years and 139 days old when he achieved the landmark, holds the global record. Ramos, who can play both at right-back or in central defence, was a member of the Spain team that won the 2008 and 2012 UEFA European Championships, as well as the 2010 FIFA World Cup. He held those trophies in safer hands than he had done when he raised the Spanish Copa del Rey, won by his club Real Madrid, during an open-top bus tour in April 2011: on that occasion, he dropped the cup from the upper deck and saw it crushed beneath the bus's wheels.

FIT FOR PURPOSE

Luis Suarez played through injury for Spain in the 1964 UEFA European Championship final – luckily for his team-mates, since he set up both goals in a 2-1 triumph. He was named European Footballer of the Year in 1960 – the only Spanish-born player to have taken the prize.

TRI-NATIONS

Ladislav Kubala played for not one, not two, but three different countries – though he never appeared in the finals of a major international tournament. Despite being born in Budapest on 10 June 1927, he made his international debut for Czechoslovakia in 1946 – winning five more caps for the country of his parents' birth. He then appeared three times for birthplace Hungary after moving back to the country in 1948, before playing 19 games for Spain after leaving Hungary as a refugee and securing a transfer to Barcelona in 1951.

VICTORY MARCH

Centre-back Carlos Marchena became the first footballer to go 50 internationals in a row unbeaten, when he played in Spain's 3-2 victory over Saudi Arabia in May 2009 – one more than Brazil's 1950s and 1960s winger Garrincha. Marchena was a member of Spain's successful 2010 FIFA World Cup squad, ending the tournament on 54 consecutive internationals without defeat. Marchena's 57-game unbeaten run came to an end when Argentina beat Spain 4-1 in September 2010.

TREASURE CHEST

The Spanish first division goalkeeper who concedes the fewest goals per game each season is awarded the Zamora Trophy. This is named after legendary keeper **Ricardo Zamora**, who played 46 times for Spain between 1920 and 1936 – including the legendary 4-3 win over England in Madrid in 1929. Zamora was the first Spanish star to play for both Barcelona and Real Madrid. Later he was league title-winning coach of ... Atletico Madrid.

LUCKY JUAN

Only one player has failed to score in a FIFA World Cup penalty shoot-out with a spot-kick that would have won the game had it gone in: Spain's Juan Carlos Valeron, whose effort went wide against the Republic of Ireland in 2002. The shoot-out score was 2-1 in Spain's favour, with just an Irish attempt to follow, when he missed – but his team went on to win anyway.

FAMILIAR FACES, UNFAMILIAR OUTCOME

Sixteen players from Spain's triumphant 2010 FIFA World Cup squad were picked for the 2014 tournament and seven who played in the final started against the Netherlands in their opening game four years later – the Dutch had four. It was the first time that the two countries to meet in a FIFA World Cup final played each other in the first-round of the next tournament. Spain's 5-1 defeat at the hands of the Dutch in Salvador was their heaviest FIFA World Cup defeat since losing 6-1 to Brazil in 1950.

SPANISH LEAGUE CHAMPIONSHIPS

Real Madrid	32
Barcelona	22
Atletico Madrid	10
Athletic Bilbao	8
Valencia	6
Real Sociedad	2
Deportivo de la Coruna	1
Sevilla	1
Betis	1

THE RAUL THING

Raul Gonzalez Blanco – known as Raul – is not only Spain's second-most prolific scorer, with 44 goals from 102 games, but also holds the records for the most UEFA European Cup/Champions League goals (71, including five for Schalke 04) and for the most goals for Real Madrid (323), having passed Alfredo di Stefano's tally of 309 in 2008–09. But despite his glittering career, he missed out on international glory for Spain: he was controversially left out of the 2008 UEFA European Championship-winning squad and was also overlooked for the FIFA World Cup two years later.

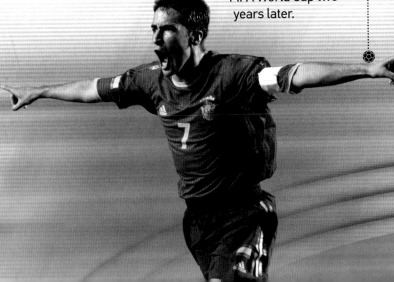

SUPER PED

Spanish winger **Pedro** is the only player to have scored in six separate official club tournaments in one calendar year, managing to hit the net for Barcelona in Spain's Primera Liga, Copa del Rey and Super Cup in 2009, as well as the UEFA Champions League, UEFA European Super Cup and FIFA Club World Cup. He was also in the starting line-up for the 2010 FIFA World Cup final – less than two years after being a member of the Barcelona reserve team in Spain's third division and needing new club manager Pep Guardiola's intervention to prevent him being sent home to Tenerife.

SEMI PRECIOUS

Centre-back **Carles Puyol**'s thumping header not only gave Spain victory in their 2010 FIFA World Cup semi-final – it was also the country's first win over Germany in four FIFA World Cup matches. West Germany had won 2-1 in both 1966 and 1982, before a 1-1 draw at the 1994 tournament. But Spain's 1-0 win in 2010 was a repeat of their triumph over Germany in the UEFA European Championship final two years earlier. Puyol played his 100th and final international against Uruguay in February 2013, and retired from all forms of the game aged 36 in May 2014.

PERFECT PICHICHI

The annual award for top scorer in La Liga is called the "Pichichi" – the nickname of Rafael Moreno, a striker for Athletic Bilbao between 1911 and 1921. He scored 200 goals in 170 games for the club, and once in five matches for Spain. Pichichi, who often took the field wearing a large white cap, died suddenly in 1922 aged just 29.

CLUB SANDWICH

Spanish clubs have won the UEFA European Cup/Champions League 14 times, more than any other country. Italy and England are joint second, on 12 apiece. The 14 include victories in six of the 15 finals since the start of the 21st century, culminating in the first all-Spanish final in 2014 which Real Madrid won 4-1 against local rivals Atletico Madrid. This was Real's 10th European Cup – dubbed "La Decima" – and the first since 2002, having seen Barcelona win three times in the interim.

SPAIN'S PLAYERS IN EURO 2008/FIFA WORLD CUP 2010/EURO 2012 SQUADS

Iker Casillas*
Sergio Ramos*
Andres Iniesta*
Xabi Alonso*
Xavi Hernandez*
Cesc Fabregas*
Fernando Torres*
David Silva
Alvaro Arbeloa
Raul Albiol
Pepe Reina
* = appeared in all three finals.

TOP BOSS DEL BOSQUE

Vicente Del Bosque was an unused substitute during Ladislao Kubala's 68th and final match in charge of Spain in 1980. He was on Spain bench again when *La Roja* played Denmark in March 2013, but this time as manager, and for the 69th time, enabling him to surpass Kubala's record. Del Bosque won the 2010 FIFA World Cup and the 2012 UEFA European Championship as Spain manager, adding to the two UEFA Champions League titles he claimed as Real Madrid boss. He and Italy's Marcelo Lippi are the only men to have won both the UEFA Champions League or European Cup and the FIFA World Cup – but Del Bosque's Euro 2012 triumph gave him an unprecedented hat-trick. Another unmatched feat was his 13 victories in his first 13 matches as Spain manager after he succeeded Luis Aragones in 2008.

FIFA FIRST

Real Madrid were the only Spanish club formally represented at FIFA's first meeting in Paris in 1904 – though the club was then known simply as Madrid FC. Spanish clubs, such as Real Madrid and Real Betis, dropped the word "Real" – meaning "Royal" – from their names during the Second Spanish Republic, between 1931 and 1939.

BELGIUM

Belgium – nicknamed "The Red Devils" – embarked on a golden period in the Eighties after eight decades spent on the fringes of international competition: first a runners-up finish at the 1980 UEFA European Championship, followed by a run to the semi-finals of the 1986 FIFA World Cup. A new crop of elite European stars did, however, help Belgium to reach the 2014 FIFA World Cup quarter-finals – in their first finals appearance since 2002. There is clearly hope for many more impressive performances over the next few years.

BELGIAN LEAGUE CHAMPIONSHIP WINS

33	Anderlecht
13	Club Brugge
11	Union Saint-Gilloise
10	Standard Liege
7	Beerschot
6	Racing de Bruxelles
5	RFC de Liege
5	Daring de Bruxelles
4	Antwerp
4	Mechelen
4	Lierse
3	Genk
3	Cercle Brugge
2	Beveren
1	Molenbeek

ERWIN-WIN SITUATION

Belgium caused a sensation in the opening match of the 1982 FIFA World Cup by defeating the reigning champions Argentina, 1-0, thanks to a 62nd-minute goal by striker **Erwin Vandenburgh** in Barcelona's Camp Nou stadium. The same opponents had their revenge four years later, when two unanswered goals by Diego Maradona were enough to put Argentina into the 1986 FIFA World Cup final. Vandenburgh had also scored in Belgium's opening game of that tournament, a 2-1 Group B defeat to hosts Mexico.

SIXTH SENSE

By qualifying for the 2002 FIFA World Cup, Belgium became the first country to reach six successive tournaments without benefiting once from being either hosts or defending holders.

HE'S OUR GUY

Unquestionably Belgium's greatest manager – as well as their longest-serving – was **Guy Thys**. He led them to the final of the 1980 UEFA European Championship and – with a team featuring the likes of Enzo Scifo and Nico Claesen – the semi-finals of the FIFA World Cup six years later. He spent 13 years in the job from 1976 to 1989, then returned for a second spell just eight months after quitting. He stepped down again after managing Belgium at the 1990 FIFA World Cup. During his playing days in the 1940s and 1950s, he was a striker and won two caps for Belgium. He died at the age of 80 in August 2003.

DIVOCK'S DIVIDEND

Divock Origi was a late choice for Belgium's 2014 FIFA World Cup squad, picked by manager Marc Wilmots to replace the injured Christian Benteke. He justified that faith with the only goal of Belgium's second game, in the 88th minute, against Russia, half an hour after coming on as a substitute. Aged 19 years and 65 days, he became Belgium's youngest FIFA World Cup goalscorer. Divock's father, Mike Origi, was an international for his native Kenya, but spent most of his career in Belgium, where Divock was born and raised. Belgium's oldest FIFA World Cup scorer remains centre-back Leo Clijsters, aged 33 years and 250 days. He headed the opener in a 3-1 win over Uruguay at Italia 90.

CUP CONSOLATIONS

Belgium lost in the second round of the 2002 FIFA World Cup, beaten 2-0 by eventual champions Brazil. But there was some solace as Belgium won the tournament's fair play prize, and they were complemented by coach Luiz Felipe Scolari, who said Belgium were Brazil's toughest opponents en route to lifting the trophy.

TRIUMPHS AND TRAGEDY

The largest football venue in Belgium is the 50,000-capacity **King Baudouin Stadium** in Brussels, which opened under its previous name of the Jubilee Stadium on 23 August 1930 then took the name of Heysel in 1946. It was the scene of tragedy in 1985 when a wall collapsed and 39 fans died in disturbances while attending the European Cup final between Liverpool and Juventus. The stadium was rebuilt and given its current name in 1995. When Belgium and the Netherlands co-hosted the 2000 UEFA European Championship, the stadium staged the opening ceremony and first match, Belgium's 2-1 victory over Sweden. It is now used for Belgium's home internationals.

BARON RUN

The first man given honorary membership of world football's governing body FIFA was Baron Edouard de Laveleye. The Belgian was rewarded for persuading The Football Association in England to join FIFA in 1905 rather than remain independent. De Laveleye was the first chairman of the Belgian FA, founded in 1895, and stayed in post for 29 years. He was also the founder and first chairman of the Belgian Olympic Committee and successfully campaigned for Antwerp to stage the Games in 1920.

CLUB MATES

Belgium ended a 1964 match against neighbours and rivals the Netherlands with a team entirely comprised of Anderlecht players, after Liege goalkeeper Guy Delhasse was substituted by the Brussels club's Jean Trappeniers.

LONGEST-SERVING COACHES*

1 Guy Thys (1976–89, 1990–91)
2 William Maxwell (1910–13, 1920–28)
3 Constant Vanden Stock (1958–68)
4 Raymond Goethals (1968–76)
5 Bill Gormlie (1947–53)
6 Jack Butler (1935–40)
7 Paul Van Himst (1991–96)
8 Hector Goetinck (1930–34)
9 Aime Anthuenis (2002–05)
10 Rene Vandereycken (2006–09)

* Marc Wilmots, who took over in 2012, is contracted until 2018 which would take him to fifth on the list.

THE FOUR-MOST

A collection of players widely described as Belgium's "Golden Generation" helped the country achieve their finest run of victories at a FIFA World Cup when they won four consecutive matches at the 2014 finals – each by a single goal. They defeated Algeria 2-1, Russia and South Korea 1-0 in Group H, then downed the USA 2-1 after extra-time in the second round. The run ended when they fell 1-0 to Argentina in the quarter-finals. None of Belgium's six goals in Brazil came before the 70th minute of a game and four were courtesy of substitutes. Marouane Fellaini and Dries Mertens (both against Algeria), Divock Origi (the 88th minute winner against Russia) and Romelu Lukaku (the second against the USA) all found the net after coming off the bench, whereas **Jan Vertonghen** (to beat South Korea) and Kevin De Bruyne (the opener in the second round) got on the scoresheet having started.

SWINE FEVER

Nicknamed "The Fighting Pig" and "The Bull from Dongelberg", **Marc Wilmots** has hogged more goals for Belgium than all but two compatriots, Paul van Himst and Bernard Voorhoof. His 28 goals in 70 internationals between 1990 and 2002 included a Belgian record five at FIFA World Cups. After retiring, he spent a short spell as an elected Belgian senator before becoming assistant coach for the national team 2009. And, when Georges Leekens suddenly resigned as Belgium coach in 2012, Wilmots was promoted to the top job. He not only successfully qualified Belgium for the 2014 FIFA World Cup in Brazil, but also oversaw record runs of seven wins in a row and 14 consecutive games unbeaten.

SPECS APPEAL

Most footballers with poor vision make do with contact lenses before going out to play, but Belgium captain Jef Jurion stood out in the late 1950s and early 1960s by wearing a pair of specially-made glasses during matches.

VOORHOOF'S A JOLLY GOOD FELLOW

Belgium's scoring record is shared by Bernard Voorhoof and Paul van Himst, both on 30 goals – though Voorhoof's came in 61 games between 1928 and 1940, compared to van Himst's 81 matches from 1960 to 1974. Voorhoof is one of only five players to feature at all three of the pre-Second World War FIFA World Cups, in 1930, 1934 and 1938. The others were Edmond Delfour and Etienne Mattler of France, Nicolae Kovacs of Romania and Brazil's Patesko. Voorhoof's only FIFA World Cup goals were the two he scored in 1934. Van Himst went into management after retiring as a player in 1977, managing Anderlecht when they won the UEFA Cup in 1983 and taking Belgium to the 1994 FIFA World Cup.

SAINT MICHEL

Belgium goalkeeper Michel Preud'homme was the first man to win the Lev Yashin Award for the best goalkeeper at a FIFA World Cup, when it was introduced in 1994. Preud'homme's four displays – conceding four goals – impressed the panel of judges even though Belgium were knocked out in the second round in the USA. He was dubbed "Saint Michel" by supporters when playing for Portuguese club Benfica.

PRINCE FERNAND

Fernand Nisot was part of the Belgium team that won the football gold medal when Antwerp hosted the Olympic Games in 1920. He still holds the record for Belgium's youngest international, being just 16 years and 19 days old on his debut.

THE EDEN PROJECT

Dazzling playmaker **Eden Hazard** made himself one of the hottest properties in world football with his performances for French club Lille. In 2011 he became the youngest footballer to be named the country's player of the year and retained the award 12 months later, just before joining the then-reigning European champions Chelsea. The London club also signed Hazard's brother Thorgan, two years younger than him and a Belgium under-21 international. Eden Hazard – who has been compared to Belgian great **Enzo Scifo** – made his full international debut at the age of 17 years and 316 days, becoming the eighth-youngest player to represent Belgium at full international level. The brothers are the sons of not just one former footballer but two. Their father, Thierry, played as a semi-professional and his mother Carine only retired from the women's game when she was pregnant with Eden.

COURT RISE

Belgium's 1-0 loss against Argentina in their 2014 FIFA World Cup quarter-final in Brasilia was goalkeeper **Thibaut Courtois**'s 22nd appearance for his country – but it was the first time the Red Devils had suffered defeat with him between the sticks. The 22-year-old had made a last-minute save from Lionel Messi, however, which extended to nine games the Argentine's barren run against him. Courtois went into the tournament having just helped Atletico Madrid win the Spanish league title and reach the UEFA Champions League final before being recalled from a three-year loan by his parent club Chelsea. His international debut had come against France in November 2011, when he not only kept a clean sheet in a goalless draw but also became Belgium's youngest ever goalkeeper – aged 19 years and 188 days.

TOP CAPS

1	Jan Ceulemans	96
2	Timmy Simons	93
3	Eric Gerets	86
=	Franky van der Elst	86
5	Enzo Scifo	84
=	Daniel van Buyten	84
7	Paul van Himst	81
8	Bart Goor	78
9	Georges Grun	77
10	Lorenzo Staelens	70
=	Marc Wilmots	70

MOTHER'S BOY

Belgium's most-capped player, **Jan Ceulemans**, is unusual in having turned down a move to Italian giants AC Milan – and he did so on the advice of his mother. He opted to stay loyal to Club Brugge, where he spent most of his playing career, and became a national hero with his linchpin displays at three consecutive FIFA World Cups in 1982, 1986 and 1990. He scored three goals and was captain at Mexico 1986 as Belgium finished fourth. The Lier-born midfielder retired from international football after Belgium's second-round exit at the 1990 FIFA World Cup.

KOMPANY MAN

Belgium's current captain **Vincent Kompany** has emerged as one of the most commanding centre-backs in world football, and one of the most respected and articulate off the football field. He combines his professional career with part-time business administration studies at Manchester Business School. He captained Manchester City to their first English league title for 44 years in 2011-12, and when they won it again in 2013-14. Kompany was recalled by his club, SV Hamburg of Germany, and was forced to miss the semi-final of the men's Beijing 2008 Olympic Games Football tournament. Without him, Belgium lost 4-1 to Nigeria and, after losing 3-0 to Brazil in the third-place match, Belgium were denied a medal to add to the Olympic gold they won as hosts at Antwerp in 1920. Kompany was named Belgium's permanent captain in November 2011, replacing fellow centre-back Thomas Vermaelen.

TOP SCORERS

1	Bernard Voorhoof	30
=	Paul van Himst	30
3	Marc Wilmots	29
4	Joseph Mermans	28
5	Robert De Veen	26
6	Wesley Sonck	24
7	Raymond Braine	23
=	Marc Degryse	23
9	Jan Ceulemans	22
10	Henri Coppens	21

BULGARIA

The glory days of the "golden generation" apart – when Bulgaria finished fourth at the 1994 FIFA World Cup in the United States, sensationally beating defending champions Germany 2–1 in the quarter-finals – a consistent pattern emerges with Bulgarian football. Regular qualifiers for the game's major competitions, and the birthplace of some of the sport's biggest names (such as Hristo Stoichkov and Dimitar Berbatov), the country has too often failed to deliver on the big occasions and make its mark on world football.

TOP SCORERS

1	Dimitar Berbatov	48
=	Hristo Bonev	48
3	Hristo Stoichkov	37
4	Emil Kostadinov	26
5	Ivan Kolev	25
=	Petar Zhekov	25
7	Atanas Mihaylov	23
=	Nasko Sirakov	23
9	Dimitar Milanov	20
=	Martin Petrov	20

MAYOR WITH NO HAIR

Balding Yordan Letchkov headed the winning goal against holders and defending champions Germany in the 1994 FIFA World Cup quarter-final in the United States. At the time, he played for German club Hamburg. He later became mayor of Sliven, the Bulgarian town where he was born in July 1967.

TEETHING TROUBLES

Martin Petrov suffered a terrible start to his international career when he was sent off for two yellow cards just eight minutes into his debut as a substitute in a Euro 2000 qualifier against England. He broke down in tears when leaving the field, but recovered from the experience to become one of his country's most-capped players and enjoyed spells with top clubs such as Atletico Madrid in Spain and Manchester City in England. His 90 caps and 20 goals included Bulgaria's only strike at the 2004 UEFA European Championship, against Italy.

A NATION MOURNS

Bulgaria lost two of its most popular footballing talents when a June 1971 car crash claimed the lives of strikers Georgi Asparukhov (28) and Nikola Kotkov (32). Asparukhov scored 19 goals in 50 internationals, including Bulgaria's only goal of the 1966 FIFA World Cup finals in a 3–1 defeat to Hungary.

MOB RULES

Much-travelled Bulgaria centre-forward **Dimitar Berbatov** claims to have learned English by watching the *Godfather* movies. Berbatov joined Manchester United from Tottenham in 2008 for a club and Bulgarian record fee of £30.75m. Before joining Spurs, he had been a member of the Bayer Leverkusen side who narrowly missed out on a treble in 2002. They lost in the final of both the UEFA Champions League and the German cup and finished runners-up in the German Bundesliga. Berbatov surprised and disappointed fans back home when he announced his international retirement aged just 29, in May 2010, having scored a national-record 48 goals in his 78 appearances for Bulgaria. He briefly considered a return to the national team in 2012, but ultimately opted against the idea, saying that he wanted to "give chances to younger players". After joining Fulham in the summer of that year, he raised eyebrows during one match by revealing a T-shirt with the slogan: "Keep calm and pass me the ball."

STAN THE BURGER VAN MAN

Stiliyan Petrov – nicknamed "Stan" by fans of his English club Aston Villa – was applauded onto the field when he became Bulgaria's first outfield player to reach 100 caps, against Switzerland in March 2011. The midfielder and Bulgaria captain has been playing in Britain since 1999, when he joined Scottish giants Celtic as a 20-year-old – but had to fight hard against a bout of homesickness. He later revealed that his English only improved when he started work behind the counter of a Scottish friend's burger van. Petrov said: "Some of the customers used to stare, thinking: 'That looks like Stiliyan Petrov, but it can't be.' But soon I started to understand things better." Tributes from across football and around the world poured in for Petrov when, in March 2012, he revealed he had been diagnosed with acute leukaemia. After 19 minutes of every home game for the rest of the season Villa fans stood and applauded for 60 seconds – 19 being his squad number.

TOP OF THE POPS

Ivelin Popov has eight international goals to his name. Sofia-born Popov trained with Feyenoord as a 17-year-old, when Netherlands legend Ruud Gullit was the Dutch club's manager, before making his name with Bulgarian team Litex Lovech. He was club captain by the age of 21 and was given the Bulgaria armband in 2012, aged 24. He was soon the skipper of both the national side and Russian club Kuban Krasnodar, who he joined in 2012.

PLAYING LUBO

Bulgaria's current coach is Lubo Penev, nephew of Dimitar Penev who had coached the country to their best-ever FIFA World Cup finish of fourth in 1994. Lubo, a centre-forward, missed out on that tournament after being diagnosed with testicular cancer, but he recovered to play for his country at both the 1996 UEFA European Championship and 1998 FIFA World Cup.

ALL-ROUNDER ALEKSANDAR

Defender Aleksandar Shalamanov played for Bulgaria at the 1966 FIFA World Cup, six years after representing his country as an alpine skier at the Winter Olympics at Lake Placid. He also went to the 1964 Tokyo Summer Olympics as an unused member of the volleyball squad. Shalamanov was voted Bulgaria's best sportsman in both 1967 and 1973.

HRISTO'S HISTORY

Hristo Stoichkov, born in Plovdiv, Bulgaria, on 8 February 1968, shared the 1994 FIFA World Cup Golden Boot, awarded to the tournament's top scorer, with Russia's Oleg Salenko. Both scored six times, though Stoichkov became the sole winner of that year's European Footballer of the Year award. Earlier the same year, he had combined up-front with Brazilian Romario to help Barcelona reach the final of the UEFA Champions League. He was banned for a year after a brawl earlier in his career, during the 1985 Bulgarian cup final between CSKA Sofia and Levski Sofia. Stoichkov won trophies with clubs in Bulgaria, Spain, Saudi Arabia and the United States before retiring as a player in 2003.

TOP CAPS

1	Stiliyan Petrov	106
2	Borislav Mikhailov	102
3	Hristo Bonev	96
4	Krasimir Balakov	92
5	Dimitar Penev	90
=	Martin Petrov	90
7	Radostin Kishishev	88
8	Hristo Stoichkov	83
9	Zlatko Yankov	80
10	Ayan Sadkov	79
=	Nasko Sirakov	79

HEAD BOY

Bulgaria's second most-capped player is **Borislav Mikhailov**, born in Sofia on 12 February 1963, who sometimes wore a wig while playing and later had a hair transplant. After retiring in 2005, he was appointed president of the Bulgarian Football Union. His father Bisser was also a goalkeeper and Borislav's son, Nikolay, made his international debut in goal against Scotland in May 2006. All three have played for Levski Sofia.

CROATIA

Croatia's distinctive red-and-white chequered jersey has become one of the most recognized in world football – just ask England. Croatia broke English hearts not once but twice in the UEFA Euro 2008 qualifying tournament. First Croatia beat England 2–0 in Zagreb and then they shocked them 3–2 at Wembley to secure qualification. Croatia's march to the quarter-finals at the 2008 UEFA European Championship was followed by failure to qualify for the 2010 FIFA World Cup, but they impressed again at Euro 2012, though were edged out in the first round by Spain and Italy.

TOP SCORERS

1	Davor Suker	45
2	Eduardo da Silva	29
3	Darijo Srna	21
4	Ivica Olic	19
5	Niko Kranjcar	16
6	Mario Mandzukic	15
=	Goran Vlaovic	15
8	Niko Kovac	14
9	Mladen Petric	13
10	Zvonimir Boban	12
=	Ivan Klasnic	12

ROCK AND A HARD PLACE

Slaven Bilic and Igor Stimac were formidable central defensive partners as Croatia finished third at the 1998 FIFA World Cup. Bilic was more successful as national coach, taking Croatia to the 2008 and 2012 UEFA European Championships during his six-year reign. Stimac took over in 2012, but an underwhelming 2014 FIFA World Cup qualifying campaign saw him replaced by another former international, **Niko Kovac**, for the play-off tie against Iceland in November 2013, which they won 2–0 on aggregate. Croatia went out in the first round in Brazil – despite taking the lead in the opening game, which they ultimately lost 3–1 to the hosts.

LUKA LOOPY

Luka Modric scored the fastest penalty in UEFA European Championship history: his fourth-minute strike was the only goal of Croatia's first-round victory against co-hosts Austria at the 2008 tournament. But he would miss one of the spot-kicks as Croatia lost a shoot-out to Turkey in the quarter-finals. His much-loved status back home remains unaffected, though, as the diminutive playmaker is now widely seen as one of the world's most skilful midfielders. Modric spent four years with English club Tottenham Hotspur from 2008, before moving to Real Madrid in the summer of 2012, with whom he won a UEFA Champions League medal in 2014.

HAPPY OPENINGS

Few national teams have been as successful in their infancy as Croatia. Formerly part of Yugoslavia, Croatia reached the quarter-finals in their very first senior competition (UEFA Euro 96) and then came third at the 1998 FIFA World Cup. Since becoming eligible to participate in 1993, Croatia qualified for every FIFA World Cup (except for 2010), and missed only one UEFA European Championship (in 2000). Croatia have scored four goals at each of the four UEFA European Championships for which they have qualified, in 1996, 2004, 2008 and 2012. Three of the goals at Euro 2012 came from **Mario Mandzukic**, the first after just two minutes and 38 seconds against the Republic of Ireland – the sixth fastest UEFA European Championship finals goal of all-time. Mandzukic was suspended for Croatia's opening match of the 2014 FIFA World Cup finals, but he did score twice in the next game, a 4–0 defeat of Cameroon in Manaus.

SUPER SUKER

Striker Davor Suker won the Golden Boot for being top scorer at the FIFA World Cup in 1998, scoring six goals in seven games as Croatia finished third. His strikes included the opening goal in Croatia's 2-1 semi-final defeat to eventual champions France, and the winner in a 2-1 triumph over Holland in the third-place play-off. Suker, by far his country's leading scorer of all time, had hit three goals at the UEFA European Championship in 1996 – including an audacious long-distance lob over Denmark goalkeeper Peter Schmeichel. Suker was named president of the Croatian Football Federation in July 2012.

DEER DARIJO

Darijo Srna is Croatia's third top scorer of all time, despite playing many games as a right-back or wing-back. He has a tattoo on his calf in the shape of a deer, the Croatian word for which is "srna". He also has a tattoo on his chest – the name of his brother Igor, who has Down's syndrome and to whom he dedicates each goal he scores. Now Croatia's most capped player, Srna was one of three players to reach 100 appearances for their country against South Korea in February 2013. The other two were goalkeeper Stipe Pletikosa and defender Josip Simunic.

THE KIDNEYS ARE ALL RIGHT

Striker Ivan Klasnic returned to international duty with Croatia despite suffering kidney failure in early 2007. A first attempt at a transplant failed when his body rejected a kidney donated by his mother, but follow-up surgery – using a kidney from his father – proved successful. He recovered enough to play for Croatia again in March 2008 and represented his country in that summer's UEFA European Championship, scoring twice – including a winning goal against Poland.

OLE, OLIC

Croatia's second game at the 2014 FIFA World Cup, a 4-0 trouncing of Cameroon, was doubly notable. It was the first time they had scored as many as four goals in a single FIFA World Cup finals match. It also saw striker Ivica Olic become the first player to score for Croatia at two separate FIFA World Cups, having previously found the net in 2002. His lengthy break between finals goals is matched only by Denmark's Michael Laudrup, who scored at the 1986 tournament and then had to wait until the 1998 finals to do so again.

TOP CAPS

1	Darijo Srna	116
2	Stipe Pletikosa	114
3	Josip Simunic	105
4	Dario Simic	100
5	Ivica Olic	95
6	Robert Kovac	84
7	Niko Kovac	83
8	Robert Jarni	81
=	Niko Kranjcar	81
10	Luka Modric	78

DOUBLE IDENTITY

Robert Jarni and Robert Prosinecki both have the rare distinction of playing for two different countries at different FIFA World Cup tournaments. They both represented Yugoslavia in Italy in 1990, then newly independent Croatia eight years later in France. Full-back Jarni actually played for both Yugoslavia and Croatia in 1990, then only Yugoslavia in 1991, before switching back – and permanently – to Croat colours in 1992 after the country officially joined UEFA and FIFA. He retired with 81 caps for Croatia, seven for Yugoslavia.

MLAD ALL OVER

Mladen Petric is the only player to score four goals in one game for Croatia – in their 7-0 trouncing of Andorra in October 2006. That equalled Croatia's record victory, having previously beaten Australia by the same scoreline in August 1998. **Davor Suker** scored a hat-trick that day, making him the only Croatian to complete two trebles – his first came in a 7-1 defeat of Estonia in September 1995.

CZECH REPUBLIC

The most successful of the former Eastern Bloc countries, as Czechoslovakia they finished as runners-up in the 1934 and 1962 FIFA World Cups, and shocked West Germany in a penalty shoot-out to win the 1976 UEFA European Championship. Playing as the Czech Republic since 1994, they lost – on a golden goal – in the UEFA Euro 96 final, and in the semi-final eight years later. Recent times have been tougher, and although one of Europe's stronger nations, the Czechs failed to qualify for the 2010 or 2014 FIFA World Cups, but were UEFA Euro 2012 quarter-finalists.

EURO-VER AND OVER AND OVER AGAIN

Vladimir Smicer, now general manager of the Czech national team, is one of only seven players to score at three different UEFA European Championships – along with Germany's Jurgen Klinsmann, France's Thierry Henry, Portugal's Nuno Gomes, Helder Postiga and Cristiano Ronaldo, and Sweden's Zlatan Ibrahimovic. Smicer struck at the finals in 1996, 2000 and 2004. Perhaps his other greatest achievement came in his final game for English club Liverpool, during which he scored as a second-half substitute as his team came back from 3-0 down to beat AC Milan in the 2005 UEFA Champions League final. Smicer's wife Pavlina is the daughter of former Czechoslovakia striker Ladislav Vizek, who won footballing gold with his country at the 1980 summer Olympics but who was then sent off against France at the FIFA World Cup two years later.

CHIP WITH EVERYTHING

One of the most famous penalties ever taken was Antonin Panenka's decisive spot-kick for Czechoslovakia against West Germany in the final of the 1976 UEFA European Championship, giving the Czechs victory in the shoot-out. Despite the tension, and the responsibility resting on him, Panenka cheekily chipped the ball into the middle of the goal – as goalkeeper Sepp Maier dived to the side. That style of spot-kick is now widely known as a "Panenka", and has been replicated by the likes of France's Zinedine Zidane, in the 2006 FIFA World Cup final.

CECH CAP

Goalkeeper **Petr Cech** has worn a protective cap while playing ever since suffering a fractured skull during an English Premier League match in October 2006. He later added a chin protector after requiring a facial operation following a training accident. Cech was born as a triplet, along with sister Sarka and brother Michal, who sadly died of an infection at the age of two. Cech served notice of his talents when he was beaten by only one penalty in a shoot-out against France to decide the 2002 UEFA U-21 European Championship final, helping the Czechs to win the trophy. He has also earned winners' medals as Chelsea collected the 2012 UEFA Champions League (he was named man of the match in the penalty shoot-out win over Bayern in their Munich home) and 2013 UEFA Europa League. He celebrated his 100th appearance for the Czech Republic with a clean sheet in a 3-0 March 2013 victory over Armenia.

POPULAR KAREL

UEFA Euro 96 gave **Karel Poborsky** the perfect platform to take his career to new heights as he helped the Czech Republic reach the final and then sealed a dream move to Manchester United. His lob against Portugal in the quarter-finals was rated as one of the finest opportunist goals in the tournament's history. His 118 appearances is a record for his country.

PASSING THE PUC

The final of the 1934 FIFA World Cup was the first to go into extra-time, with Czechoslovakia ultimately losing 2-1 to hosts Italy despite taking a 76th-minute lead through Antonin Puc. Puc was Czechoslovakia/the Czech Republic's top international scorer when he retired in 1938 until he was passed, first by Jan Koller, 67 years later, and, latterly, by Milan Baros.

WALK-OUT

Belgium's 1920 victory in the Olympic Games was overshadowed when Czechoslovakia walked off the pitch after half an hour in protest following what they saw as biased refereeing. Czechoslovakia are the only team in the history of Olympic football to have been disqualified.

SPEED DEMON

Milan Baros, second to Jan Koller in the Czech Republic's all-time goalscoring list, is the only Czech to win the Golden Boot at a FIFA World Cup or a UEFA European Championship. He won the prize after scoring five goals at Euro 2004 in Portugal – when the Czechs lost to eventual winners Greece in the semi-final. Baros helped his country win the 2002 UEFA European U-21 Championship in Switzerland. Three team-mates in the final went on to play in full internationals: Petr Cech, Martin Jiranek and Zdenek Grygera. Baros set a less impressive landmark in November 2007, when his Ferrari was caught travelling at 271 km/h between Lyon and Geneva – the fastest speed ever recorded in France's Ain region. Baros was, inevitably, given a driving ban. He retired from international football in 2012, aged 30, after playing in his third Euro finals.

THE CANNON COLLECTS

Pavel Nedved's election as European Footballer of the Year in 2003 ended an impatient wait for fans in the Czech Republic who had seen a string of outstanding players overlooked since Josef Masopust had been honoured back in 1962. Masopust, a midfield general, had scored the opening goal in the FIFA World Cup final that year before Brazil hit back to win 3-1 in the Chilean capital of Santiago. Years later, Masopust was remembered by Pele and nominated as one of his 125 greatest living footballers. At club level, Masopust won eight Czechoslovak league titles with Dukla Prague, the army club. He was also the winner, in 1962, of the first Czech Golden Ball as domestic footballer of the year. It was another day and in another age. Masopust was presented with his award before the kick-off of a European Cup quarter-final with Benfica – with a minimum of fuss. Years later, Masopust said: "Eusebio just shook hands with me, I put the trophy in my sports bag and went home on the tram."

TOP SCORERS

1	Jan Koller	55
2	Milan Baros	41
3	Vladimir Smicer	27
4	Pavel Kuka	22
=	Tomas Rosicky	22
6	Patrik Berger	18
=	Pavel Nedved	18
8	Vratislav Lokvenc	14
9	Marek Jankulovski	11
10	Michal Kadlec	8
=	Karel Poborsky	8

TOP CAPS

1	Karel Poborsky	118
2	Petr Cech	107
3	Tomas Rosicky	94
4	Milan Baros	93
5	Jan Koller	91
=	Pavel Nedved	91
7	Jaroslav Plasil	89
8	Vladimir Smicer	81
9	Marek Jankulovski	78
=	Tomas Ujfalusi	78

TEN OUT OF TEN

Giant striker **Jan Koller** is Czech football's all-time leading marksman with 55 goals in 91 appearances. Koller scored on his senior debut against Belgium and struck ten goals in ten successive internationals. He scored six goals in each of the 2000, 2004 and 2008 UEFA European Championship qualifying campaigns. He began his career with Sparta Prague, who converted him from goalkeeper to goalscorer. Then, in Belgium, he was top scorer with Lokeren, before scoring 42 goals in two league title-winning campaigns with Anderlecht. Later, with Borussia Dortmund in Germany, he once went in goal after Jens Lehmann had been sent off and kept a clean sheet – having scored in the first half.

DENMARK

Denmark have been playing international football since 1908, but it was not until the mid-1980s that they became competitive at the game's major tournaments. The country's crowning moment came in 1992 when, after being called up as a replacement just ten days before the start of the tournament, they walked away with the UEFA European Championship crown, shocking defending world champions West Germany 2-0 in the final. They may not have been able to repeat that success, but remain a significant player in the world game.

TOP CAPS

#	Player	Caps
1	Peter Schmeichel	129
2	Dennis Rommedahl	126
3	Jon Dahl Tomasson	112
4	Thomas Helveg	108
5	Michael Laudrup	104
6	Martin Jorgensen	102
=	Morten Olsen	102
8	Thomas Sorensen	101
9	Christian Poulsen	92
10	John Sivebaek	87

GOLDEN GLOVES

Peter Schmeichel was rated as the world's best goalkeeper in the early 1990s, winning many club honours with Manchester United and, famously, the UEFA European Championship with his native Denmark. His son Kasper Schmeichel was a member of Denmark's squad at the 2012 UEFA European Championship. Kasper was called up after first-choice Thomas Sorensen suffered a back injury, though began and ended the tournament still waiting for his first cap.

LEADERSHIP STYLE

Morten Olsen captained Denmark at the 1986 FIFA World Cup and later became the first Dane to reach a century of caps, eventually stepping down from the national team with four goals in 102 international appearances between 1970 and 1989. After he retired from playing all football that year, he switched to coaching, first at club level with Brondby, FC Koln and Ajax Amsterdam, before taking on the job as Danish national coach in 2000 and leading them to the 2002 and 2010 FIFA World Cups. Denmark's 2-1 defeat to England in a February 2011 friendly was his 116th international in charge – taking him past the previous record set between 1979 and 1990 by his former national team boss Sepp Piontek. Olsen planned to step down after the 2012 UEFA European Championship, but changed his mind and agreed a new deal extending his stay to the 2014 FIFA World Cup. Posters bearing Olsen's image can often be seen across Denmark – though these are advertising hearing aids, approved by the manager who suffers from deafness.

PENALTY REDEMPTION

Former Dundee, Celtic and Brondby midfielder Morten Wieghorst is the only player to be sent off twice while playing for Denmark – yet has also received a special award for fair play. His first international red card came just three minutes after entering the field as a substitute, against South Africa in the 1998 FIFA World Cup. He was again dismissed after coming on as a sub against Italy in the 2000 UEFA European Championship, though this time he managed a whole 28 minutes of action – and scored a goal in Denmark's 3-2 victory. But the other side of his character was shown during a Carlsberg Cup match against Iran in February 2003, when he deliberately missed a penalty. The spot-kick had been awarded after Iranian defender Jalal Kameli Mofrad had picked the ball up, thinking wrongly that a whistle from the crowd was actually the referee blowing for half-time. The International Olympic Committee later presented Wieghorst with a special fair play prize for deliberately striking his penalty wide – a gesture which looked all the more sporting since Denmark went on to lose the game 1-0.

DANISH DYNAMITE

Denmark's 6-1 defeat of Uruguay in the 1986 FIFA World Cup finals first-round group stage in Neza, Mexico, ranks among the country's finest performances. Sadly, Denmark's adventure was ended by Spain in the last 16, losing 5-1 after a horrendous back pass by Manchester United's Jesper Olsen allowed the Spanish to open the scoring. The Danes had already been hampered by the loss of playmaker Frank Arsesen through suspension, after he was sent off during their final group game, a victory over eventual runners-up West Germany. The side – popularly known as "Danish Dynamite" – was captained by future national coach Morten Olsen and managed by Sepp Piontek, a German who became the Danish national team's first professional coach when appointed in 1979. Michael Laudrup, a star member of the classic mid-1980s side, described them as "Europe's answer to Brazil".

CHRISTIAN AID

Nimble playmaker and free-kick specialist **Christian Eriksen** is the latest in a proud tradition of creative young Danish footballers – and another who has enjoyed a popular and successful association with Dutch giants Ajax Amsterdam. He followed the same career path as Danish stars, such as Soren Lerby and Frank Arnesen in the 1970s and 1980s and the Laudrup brothers, Michael and Brian, in the late 1990s. Eriksen helped inspire the Amsterdam club to a hat-trick of title triumphs before crossing the North Sea to join Tottenham Hotspur in the summer of 2013 – and ended his debut season being voted both player of the year and young player of the year by the London club's supporters. His Danish debut came in March 2010, having only turned 18 the previous month. This made him Denmark's fourth youngest debutant – and he was the youngest player at the 2010 FIFA World Cup. Eriksen's first international goal was scored in a win against Iceland in April 2011. Among his fans is Netherlands and Ajax legend Johan Cruyff, who said: "He's a player I really like with all my heart. You can compare him with Brian and Michael Laudrup."

TOP SCORERS

1	Poul Nielsen	52
=	Jon Dahl Tomasson	52
3	Pauli Jorgensen	44
4	Ole Madsen	42
5	Preben Elkjaer Larsen	38
6	Michael Laudrup	37
7	Henning Enoksen	29
8	Nicklas Bendtner	24
9	Michael Rohde	22
=	Ebbe Sand	22

QUICK DRAW

Ebbe Sand scored the fastest FIFA World Cup goal ever scored by a substitute, when he netted a mere 16 seconds after coming onto the pitch in Denmark's clash against Nigeria at the 1998 FIFA World Cup.

TAKING THE MICHAEL

One Danish player with unhappy memories of a spell with Ajax Amsterdam is Michael Krohn-Dehli, who made just four appearances for the club between 2006 and 2008. But if he felt any resentment for the Netherlands – and the injuries that hampered his progress there and also contributed to his omission from the 2010 FIFA World Cup – then the 2012 UEFA European Championship brought some redemption. Krohn-Dehli scored the only goal in Denmark's surprise opening victory over the Netherlands. He said afterwards: "It's a little bit special for me as I played for eight years in Holland and I have a Dutch girlfriend, so I think the whole family was cheering in Holland." Manager Morten Olsen admitted afterwards that he should have taken Krohn-Dehli to the FIFA World Cup two years earlier. The only other Dane to score – and twice – at Euro 2012 was Nicklas Bendtner, though he was later fined $100,000 and banned for a game after celebrating his second by displaying underpants bearing the name of a betting firm.

THE UNEXPECTED IN 1992

Few Danish football fans will forget June 1992, their national team's finest hour, when they won the UEFA European Championship, despite not qualifying for the finals in Sweden. Ten days before the tournament opened UEFA asked the Danes – who had finished second to Yugoslavia in their qualifying group – to take Yugoslavia's place, following their exclusion in the wake of international sanctions over the Balkan War. Expectations were minimal, but then the inconceivable happened. Relying heavily on goalkeeper Peter Schmeichel, his defence, and the creative spark of Brian Laudrup, Denmark crafted one of the biggest shocks in modern football history by winning the tournament, culminating in a 2-0 victory over world champions Germany. This victory was all the more remarkable in that Brian's brother Michael, their finest player, quit during the qualifying competition after falling out with coach **Richard Moller Nielsen**. Michael revived his international career in 1993, but Denmark failed to qualify for the 1994 FIFA World Cup in the United States. Among those paying their respects at Moller Nielsen's funeral after his death aged 76 in February 2014 were Schmeichel, Brian Laudrup and Euro 92 team-mates Preben Elkjaer Larsen and John Jensen.

BROTHERS IN ARMS

Brian (left) and Michael Laudrup are among the most successful footballing brothers of modern times. As well as making a combined 186 international appearances, they played across Europe at club level. Michael (104 caps, 37 goals) played in Italy with Lazio and Juventus and in Spain with Barcelona and Real Madrid. Brian (82 caps, 21 goals) starred in Germany with Bayer Uerdingen and Bayern Munich, Italy with Fiorentina and Milan, Scotland for Rangers and England for Chelsea.

GREECE

There is no argument about Greece's proudest footballing moment – their shock triumph at the 2004 UEFA European Championship, one of the game's greatest international upsets. Guided by German coach Otto Rehhagel, it was only the Greeks' second appearance at a UEFA Euro finals. Greece also made the last eight at Euro 2012 in Poland and Ukraine. In the FIFA World Cup, South Africa 2010 marked just their second qualification and they reached the second round of a FIFA World Cup for the first time in 2014.

TOP SCORERS

1	Nikos Anastopoulos	29
2	Angelos Charisteas	25
3	Theofanis Gekas	24
4	Dimitris Saravakos	22
5	Mimis Papaioannou	21
6	Nikos Machlas	18
7	Demis Nikolaidis	17
8	Panagiotis Tsalouchidis	16
9	Giorgos Sideris	14
10	Nikos Liberopoulos	13
=	Dimitris Salpingidis	13

SIMPLY THEO BEST

Theodoros "Theo" Zagorakis – born near Kavala on 27 October 1971 – was captain of Greece when they won the UEFA European Championship in 2004 and the defensive midfielder was also given the prize for the tournament's best player. He is the second most-capped Greek footballer of all time, with 120 caps. But it was not until his 101st international appearance – 10 years and five months after his Greek debut – that he scored his first goal for his country, in a FIFA World Cup qualifier against Denmark in February 2005. He retired from international football after making a 15-minute cameo appearance against Spain in August 2007.

PARTY CRASHERS

Shock UEFA Euro 2004 winners Greece became the first team to beat both the holders and the hosts on the way to winning either a UEFA European Championship or FIFA World Cup. In fact, they beat hosts Portugal twice – in both the tournament's opening game and the final, with a quarter-final victory over defending champions France in between.

GORGEOUS GEORGE

Georgios Samaras won and converted the last-minute penalty that sent Greece through to the knock-out stages of a FIFA World Cup for the first time, clinching a dramatic 2-1 victory over Group C opponents Ivory Coast at the 2014 tournament in Brazil. The goal, following a foul by Giovanni Sio, was former Celtic striker Samaras's ninth goal for his country – his first coming on his debut against Belarus in February 2006. Samaras could actually have played international football for Australia, because his father, Ioannis, was born in Melbourne and moved to Greece aged 13. Ioannis actually won 16 caps for Greece between 1986 and 1990, but he is a long way behind his son, who has made 78 appearances.

ALL WHITE NOW

The surprise triumph at UEFA Euro 2004 brought a major change to Greek international football – they switched the national team's kit from blue to white. The former colours had been used since the Hellenic Football Federation was formed in 1926, but the success of Otto Rehhagel's men in their second kit prompted the permanent change of colours.

TOP CAPS

1	Giorgos Karagounis	139
2	Theodoros Zagorakis	120
3	Kostas Katsouranis	114
4	Angelos Basinas	100
5	Stratos Apostolakis	96
6	Antonis Nikopolidis	90
7	Angelos Charisteas	88
8	Dimitris Salpingidis	80
9	Georgios Samaras	78
=	Dimitris Saravakos	78

HONESTY PAYS

Greece's 500th goal in international football was scored by Demis Nikolaidis at Manchester's Old Trafford in October 2001, giving them an unexpected 2–1 lead away to England in a final 2002 FIFA World Cup qualifier – although David Beckham would go on to equalize with a famous last-minute free-kick. In March the following year, striker Nikolaidis was formally acclaimed by the International Committee for Fair Play for admitting to the referee that he handled the ball when scoring for AEK Athens in the final of the Greek Cup. His team still won the match, and the trophy.

DIMI MORE

Striker **Dimitrios Salpingidis** not only struck the only goal of Greece's 2010 FIFA World Cup qualifying play-off victory against Ukraine, sealing their place in South Africa, he also then became the first Greek ever to score at a FIFA World Cup, with a 44th-minute deflected strike in the 2-1 Group B triumph over Nigeria. Yet another notable achievement was added with his equalizer against Poland in the opening game of UEFA Euro 2012: this made him the first Greek ever to score at a FIFA World Cup and a UEFA European Championship.

GEKAS SETBACK

With only two goals, Greece were the lowest scoring team to reach the second round at the 2014 FIFA World Cup. They then faced their first tournament penalty shoot-out, in the round-of-16, and lost to Costa Rica, 5-3 after a 1-1 draw. The only miss was by Theofanis Gekas, who at 34 years and 37 days, was the second-oldest man to miss in a FIFA World Cup shoot-out. Italy captain Franco Baresi was 33 days older when he missed in the 1994 FIFA World Cup final against Brazil.

TOP KAT

Greek football has enjoyed many Portuguese links. National coach Fernando Santos is Portuguese and took over in 2000 after being the Greek league's most successful manager in the 1990s. He was also boss of Portuguese giants Benfica, and their signings this century have included big Greek stars **Kostas Katsouranis** and Giorgios Karagounis. Both players were part of the Greek side that lifted the 2004 UEFA European Championship trophy at Benfica's Estadio da Luz in Lisbon. Katsouranis also played at UEFA Euro 2012, but squandered his best chance of a first goal in a finals tournament when he missed a penalty in the opening game against Poland.

GRIEF AND GLORY FOR GIORGOS

It was a bittersweet day for captain **Giorgos Karagounis** when he equalled the Greek record for international appearances, with his 120th cap against Russia in their final Group A game at the UEFA Euro 2012. The midfielder scored the only goal of the game, giving Greece a place in the quarter-finals at Russia's expense – but a second yellow card of the tournament ruled him out of the next match, in which the Greeks lost to Germany. Karagounis was one of three survivors from Greece's Euro 2004 success, along with fellow midfielder Kostas Katsouranis and goalkeeper Kostas Chalkias – though it was only in Poland that Chalkias made the first of his UEFA European Championship appearances, having been understudy in 2004 and 2008. Manager Fernando Santos also surprised many by leaving the winning goalscoring hero of Euro 2004, Angelos Charisteas, out of the squad. Chalkias, at 38 Euro 2012's oldest player, announced his international retirement once the tournament ended.

KING OTTO

German coach Otto Rehhagel became the first foreigner to be voted "Greek of the Year" in 2004, after leading the country to glory at that year's UEFA European Championship. He was also offered honorary Greek citizenship. His nine years in charge, after being appointed in 2001, made him Greece's longest-serving international manager. The UEFA Euro 2004 triumph was the first time a country coached by a foreigner had triumphed at either the UEFA European Championship or FIFA World Cup. Rehhagel was aged 65 at UEFA Euro 2004, making him the oldest coach to win the UEFA European Championship – though that record was taken off him four years later, when 69-year-old Luis Aragones lifted the trophy with Spain.

HUNGARY

For a period in the early 1950s, Hungary possessed the most talented football team on the planet. They claimed Olympic gold at Helsinki in 1952, inflicted a crushing first-ever Wembley defeat on England the following year, and entered the 1954 FIFA World Cup, unbeaten in almost four years, as firm favourites to win the crown. They lost to West Germany in the final and Hungary's footballing fortunes on the world stage have never been the same again.

TOP SCORERS

1	Ferenc Puskas	84
2	Sandor Kocsis	75
3	Imre Schlosser	59
4	Lajos Tichy	51
5	Gyorgy Sarosi	42
6	Nandor Hidegkuti	39
7	Ferenc Bene	36
8	Tibor Nyilasi	32
=	Gyula Zsengeller	32
10	Florian Albert	31

RETURN TO SANDOR

Sandor Egervari was assistant coach the last time Hungary played at a FIFA World Cup finals, in 1986, and was in charge for one of the success-starved country's most encouraging footballing moments in recent years: third place at the 2009 FIFA U-20 World Cup. Then-Liverpool striker Krisztian Nemeth scored the decisive spot-kick in a play-off defeat of Costa Rica, with only champions Ghana and runners-up Brazil performing better. His reward was promotion to manage the full national team in summer 2010, but he resigned following a national record 8-1 loss to the Netherlands in October 2013 and was succeeded by former international Attila Pinter. Hungary's only comparable defeats were 7-0 trouncings by England in 1908, England Amateurs in 1912 and Germany in 1941.

GERA'S SHARE OF THE SPOILS

While none could compare with Ferenc Puskas, the elegant left-footed playmaker **Zoltan Gera** has been one of Hungary's most noted footballers of recent decades – not only with his performances in the English Premier League (with Fulham and West Bromwich Albion), but also on the international stage. His tally of 76 caps could have been higher but for a brief international retirement in 2009 after a dispute with then-manager Erwin Koeman after Gera arrived late for a team meeting. He returned to the fold when Sandor Egervari took over the following year and was made captain. The first three of his 23 international goals all came in the same game, a 3-0 victory over San Marino in October 2002, eight months after his international debut.

GOLDEN HEAD

Sandor Kocsis, top scorer in the 1954 FIFA World Cup finals with 11 goals, was so good in the air he was known as "The Man with the Golden Head". In 68 internationals he scored an incredible 75 goals, including a record seven hat-tricks. His tally included two decisive extra-time goals in the 1954 FIFA World Cup semi-final against Uruguay, when Hungary had appeared to be on the brink of defeat.

GALLOPING MAJOR

Ferenc Puskas was one of the greatest footballers of all time, scoring a remarkable 84 goals in 85 international matches for Hungary and 514 goals in 529 matches in the Hungarian and Spanish leagues. Possessing the most lethal left-foot shot in the history of football, he was known as the "Galloping Major" – by virtue of his playing for the army team Honved before joining Real Madrid and going on to play for Spain. During the 1950s he was top scorer and captain of the legendary "Mighty Magyars" (the nickname given to the Hungarian national team), as well as of the army club Honved.

HUNGARY FOR IT

Hungary's 6-3 win over England at Wembley in 1953 remains ······················ one of the most significant international results of all time. Hungary became the first team from outside the British Isles to beat England at home, a record that had stood since 1901. The Hungarians had been undefeated for three years and had won the Olympic tournament the year before, while England were the so-called "inventors" of football. The British press dubbed it "The Match of the Century". In the event, the match revolutionized the game in England, Hungary's unequivocal victory exposing the naivete of English football tactics. England captain Billy Wright later summed up the humiliation by saying: "We completely underestimated the advances that Hungary had made, and not only tactically. When we walked out at Wembley ... I looked down and noticed that the Hungarians had on these strange, lightweight boots, cut away like slippers under the ankle bone. I turned to big Stan Mortensen and said: 'We should be all right here, Stan, they haven't got the proper kit.'"

EUROPEAN PIONEERS

While Argentina's match against Uruguay in July 1902 was the first international outside the British Isles, Hungary's 5-0 defeat to Austria in Vienna three months later was the first in Europe between two non-UK sides. Ten of Hungary's first 16 internationals were against Austria, with the Hungarians winning four, drawing one and losing five of them. In total, Hungary have won 66, drawn 30 and lost 40 against their Austrian neighbours.

GLORIOUS FAILURE

Hungary were runaway favourites to win the 1954 FIFA World Cup in Switzerland. They arrived for the finals having been unbeaten for four years. In the first round they thrashed West Germany 8-3, despite finishing with ten men after skipper Ferenc Puskas injured an ankle.

GOODISON LESSON

In the 1966 FIFA World Cup, Hungary gave Brazil a footballing lesson at Goodison Park, running out 3-1 winners before their progress was stopped by the Soviet Union in the quarter-finals. It was Brazil's first defeat in the FIFA World Cup since the 1954 quarter-finals, when they had lost 4-2 to ... Hungary.

YEARS OF PLENTY

Hungary's dazzling line-up of the early 1950s was known as the "*Aranycsapat*" – or "Golden Team". They set a record for international matches unbeaten, going 31 consecutive games without defeat between May 1950 and their July 1954 FIFA World Cup final loss to West Germany – a run that included clinching Olympic gold at Helsinki in Finland in 1952. That 31-match tally has been overtaken since only by Brazil and Spain. Hungary in the 1950s also set a record for most consecutive games scoring at least one goal – 73 matches – while their average of 5.4 goals per game at the 1954 FIFA World Cup remains an all-time high for the tournament.

NERVES AND STEEL

Gabor Kiraly may now have won more caps, and earned more attention for his customary tracksuit bottoms – often compared to pyjama trousers – but **Gyula Grosics** is still recognised ···· as Hungary's greatest goalkeeper. Unusual for a goalkeeper of his era, he was comfortable with the ball at his feet and was willing to rush out of his area. The on-field confidence was not always displayed off it, however – and he was thought to be a nervous character, a hypochondriac and a loner. He allegedly asked to be substituted before the end at Wembley in 1953. He suffered after Hungary's surprise loss to West Germany in the 1954 FIFA World Cup final, being blamed for the equalizer.

TOP CAPS

1	Jozsef Bozsik	101
2	Laszlo Fazekas	92
3	Gabor Kiraly	90
4	Gyula Grosics	86
5	Ferenc Puskas	85
6	Imre Garaba	82
7	Sandor Matrai	81
8	Roland Juhasz	80
9	Vilmos Vanczak	78
10	Zoltan Gera	77
=	Ferenc Sipos	77

NORTHERN IRELAND

Northern Ireland have played as a separate country since 1921 (before that there had been an all-Ireland side). They have qualified for the FIFA World Cup finals on three occasions: in 1958 (when they became the smallest country to reach the quarter-final stage), 1982 (when they reached the second round) and 1986.

GIANT JENNINGS

Pat Jennings's record 119 appearances for Northern Ireland also stood as an international record at one stage. The former Tottenham Hotspur and Arsenal goalkeeper made his international debut, aged just 18, against Wales on 15 April 1964, and played his final game in the 1986 FIFA World Cup, against Brazil, on his 41st birthday.

GEORGE BEST

One of the greatest players never to grace a FIFA World Cup, **George Best** (capped 37 times by Northern Ireland) nevertheless won domestic and European honours with Manchester United – including both a European Champions Cup medal and the European Footballer of the Year award in 1968. He also played in the United States, Hong Kong and Australia before his "final" retirement in 1984.

"PETER THE GREAT"

Former Manchester City and Derby County striker Peter Doherty, one of the most expensive players of his era, won the English league and FA Cup as a player, and earned 19 caps for Northern Ireland in a career interrupted by World War Two. His late goal to earn a 2-2 draw in 1947 ensured Northern Ireland avoided defeat against England for the first time. As manager, he led Northern Ireland to the quarter-finals of the 1958 FIFA World Cup – Northern Ireland remain the smallest country ever to reach that stage of the competition. They were defeated 4-0 by France, who went on to finish third.

OH DANNY BOY

Northern Ireland's captain at the 1958 FIFA World Cup was Tottenham Hotspur's cerebral **Danny Blanchflower** – the first twentieth-century captain of an English club to win both the league and FA Cup in the same season, in 1960–61. When asked the secret of his national team's success in 1958, he offered the explanation: "Our tactic is to equalize before the others have scored." More famously, he offered the philosophy: "The great fallacy is that the game is first and foremost about winning. It's nothing of the kind. The game is about glory. It's about doing things in style, with a flourish, about going out and beating the other lot, not waiting for them to die of boredom."

TOP SCORERS

1	David Healy	36
2	Colin Clarke	13
=	Billy Gillespie	13
4	Gerry Armstrong	12
=	Joe Bambrick	12
=	Iain Dowie	12
=	Jimmy Quinn	12
8	Olphie Stanfield	11
9	Billy Bingham	10
=	Johnny Crossan	10
=	Jimmy McIlroy	10
=	Peter McParland	10

THE BOY DAVIS

Midfielder **Steven Davis** became Northern Ireland's youngest post-war captain when he led out the side against Uruguay in May 2006, aged just 21 years, five months and 20 days. He has remained captain under current coach Michael O'Neill, who replaced Nigel Worthington in 2012 to become Northern Ireland's first Catholic manager for half a century.

TOP CAPS

1	Pat Jennings	119
2	David Healy	95
3	Mal Donaghy	91
4	Aaron Hughes	90
5	Sammy McIlroy	88
=	Maik Taylor	88
7	Keith Gillespie	86
8	Jimmy Nicholl	73
9	Michael Hughes	71
10	Steven Davis	68

"PETER THE LATE"

Peter Watson is thought to have had the shortest Northern Ireland international career, spending two minutes on the pitch in a 5-0 UEFA European Championship qualifying win over Cyprus in April 1971. Coventry-born Watson was playing that season for Northern Irish club Distillery, in a side featuring law student and future international **Martin O'Neill** – who would go on to win 64 caps, including captaining his country at the 1982 FIFA World Cup.

HOSTILE HOSTS

Northern Ireland topped their first-round group at the 1982 FIFA World Cup, thanks to a 1-0 win over hosts Spain at a passionate Mestalla Stadium in Valencia. Watford striker Gerry Armstrong scored the goal and the Irish held on despite defender Mal Donaghy being sent off. A 4-1 second-round loss to France denied Northern Ireland a semi-finals place. Armstrong moved to Spain, joining Mallorca the following year and, predictably, was regularly booed by rival fans.

KEEPING CONNECTED

Maik Taylor is Northern Ireland's fourth most-capped player, though he has no family connection to the country. Born in Germany, to an English father and German mother, his British passport meant he could represent any of the Home Nations – and he chose Northern Ireland. The goalkeeper was skipper for his 88th and final appearance, against Italy, in October 2011.

YOUNG GUN

Norman Whiteside became the then-youngest player at a FIFA World Cup finals (beating Pele's record) when he represented Northern Ireland in Spain in 1982 aged 17 years and 41 days. He won 38 caps, scoring nine goals, before injury forced his retirement aged just 26.

STRIFE OF BRIAN

Brian McLean's Northern Ireland career began and ended with a second-half appearance against Estonia in March 2006. The Scottish-born player had been thought eligible to play for Northern Ireland through family links, but he had played for Scotland Under-17s in a UEFA competition four years earlier and not officially changed his allegiance until after the official deadline of his 21st birthday.

HERO HEALY

Northern Ireland's record goalscorer **David Healy** has scored almost three times as many international goals as the next highest player on the list. He scored twice on his debut against Luxembourg on 23 February 2000, and all three as Northern Ireland stunned Spain 3-2 in a qualifier for UEFA Euro 2008 on 6 September 2006. He also hit the winner against Sven-Goran Eriksson's England in September 2005, Northern Ireland's first victory over them since 1972. Healy would later endure a four-year, 24-game scoring drought between October 2008 and November 2012. His final goal for his country came in a 2-1 home defeat to Israel in March 2013. He retired from all football later that year, aged 34.

NORWAY

Although they played their first international, against Sweden, in 1908 and qualified for the 1938 FIFA World Cup, it would take a further 56 years, and the introduction of a direct brand of football, before Norway reappeared at a major international tournament. Success in such competitions has been rare – they have never progressed beyond the second round – but Norway retains the distinction of being the only nation in history never to have lost to Brazil.

JUVE DONE IT ALL

Jorgen Juve netted his national record 33 international goals in 45 appearances between 1928 and 1937. He did not score as Norway claimed bronze at the Berlin 1936 Olympics, but was playing when Norway beat Germany 2-0 in the quarter-finals, prompting spectators Adolf Hitler and other Nazi leaders to storm out in fury. After retiring in 1938, he worked as a legal scholar, sports journalist and author of books about the Olympics and football.

GOALS FOR EITHER IVERSEN

Steffen Iversen scored the only goal of Norway's only win at a UEFA European Championship – against Spain at the 2000 tournament. Iversen's father Odd had previously been one of the country's leading strikers, hitting memorable strikes in unexpected victories over Yugoslavia in a 1966 FIFA World Cup qualifier and away to France ahead of the 1970 tournament. Odd scored a total of 19 times in 45 games for Norway between 1967 and 1979. Steffen equalled his father's international scoring tally with a hat-trick against Malta in November 2007 – then scored his next two goals against Iceland the following September. He was still playing for Norway in 2011, aged 34, having reached 79 caps and scoring 21 goals.

YOUR BOYS TOOK A HELL OF A BEATING

Bjorge Lillelien's famous commentary after Norway beat England 2-1 in a qualifier for the 1982 FIFA World Cup remains one of the iconic moments of European football. A commentator from 1957 until just before his death from cancer in 1987, he concentrated on winter sports and football. Roughly translated, it sounded as follows: "Lord Nelson, Lord Beaverbrook, Sir Winston Churchill, Sir Anthony Eden, Clement Attlee, Henry Cooper, Lady Diana, Maggie Thatcher, can you hear me? Your boys took a hell of a beating." Although the commentary was for Norwegian radio, it soon made its way to an English audience and has achieved cliché status. In 2002, Lillelien's words were designated the greatest piece of sports commentary ever by the *Observer* newspaper's sports supplement. Such is its place in British sporting culture, parodies of the commentary have been written to celebrate a vast array of domestic sporting victories.

TOP SCORERS

1	Jorgen Juve	33
2	Einar Gundersen	26
3	Harald Hennum	25
4	John Carew	24
5	Tore Andre Flo	23
=	Ole Gunnar Solskjaer	23
7	Gunnar Thoresen	22
8	Steffen Iversen	21
9	Jan Age Fjortoft	20
10	Odd Iversen	19
=	Oyvind Leonhardsen	19
=	Olav Nilsen	19

LONG-DISTANCE RIISE

Fierce-shooting, ex-Liverpool, AS Monaco and AS Roma left-back Jon Arne Riise marked the game in which he matched Thorbjorn Svenssen's Norwegian appearances record, against Greece in August 2012, by getting onto the scoresheet, albeit in a 3-2 losing cause. He was also on the losing side when claiming the record for himself, a 2-0 loss in Iceland the following month, before scoring his 16th international goal in his 106th match four days later as Norway beat Slovenia 2-1. Midfielder Bjorn Helge Riise, Jon Arne's younger brother, joined him at English club Fulham, and has made more than 30 full international appearances.

BOOT CAMPER

Egil Olsen, one of Europe's most eccentric coaches, was signed up for a surprise second spell as national manager when Norway put their faith in the direct-football specialist trying to qualify for the 2010 FIFA World Cup – 15 years after he had led the unfancied Scandinavians to the 1994 finals. That had been Norway's first finals appearance since 1938 and they followed it up by beating Brazil in the first round in France in 1998, making a hero out of the man in Wellington boots who guided his country to No. 2 in FIFA's official rankings. Before answering his country's call for a second stint as manager, Olsen's last job had been as manager of Iraq, but he left after only three months in charge. Remarkably, in his first match back at the helm for Norway, he masterminded a 1-0 win away to Germany with his route-one tactics.

ERIK THE VIKING

Goalkeeper Erik Thorstvedt played at the 1984 Olympic Games in Los Angeles when Norway replaced the boycotting Poland and East Germany. He was also a key member of the team that qualified for the 1994 FIFA World Cup and played a Norwegian goalkeeping record of 97 internationals between 1982 and 1996.

GOAL HANGE

Norway's captain and seventh most-capped player, is commanding centre-back **Brede Hangeland**. He was actually born 5,000 miles from Norway in Houston, Texas, where his father worked for two years for an oil firm, but spent most of his childhood in Stavanger, Norway, making his name with local side Viking and then Danish club Copenhagen. His former Viking manager Roy Hodgson signed him in 2008 for English Premier League team Fulham, where Hangeland became a fans' favourite. He made his international debut in November 2002, but did not score his first goal until his 62nd appearance, against Iceland in September 2010. Another wait followed before his second, third and fourth came in quick succession between August 2012 and October 2012.

TOP CAPS

1	John Arne Riise	110
2	Thorbjorn Svenssen	104
3	Henning Berg	100
4	Erik Thorstvedt	97
5	John Carew	91
=	Brede Hangeland	91
7	Oyvind Leonhardsen	86
8	Kjetil Rekdal	83
9	Morten Gamst Pedersen	80
10	Steffen Iversen	79

LONG STAY TRAVELLERS

Norway's best finish at an international tournament was the bronze medal they clinched at the 1936 Summer Olympics in Berlin, having lost to Italy in the semi-finals but beaten Poland 3-2 in a medal play-off thanks to an Arne Brustad hat-trick. That year's side has gone down in Norwegian football history as the "*Bronselaget*", or "Bronze Team". However, they had entered the tournament with low expectations and were forced to alter their travel plans ahead of the semi-final against Italy on 10 August – Norwegian football authorities had originally booked their trip home for the previous day, not expecting their team to get so far. Italy beat Norway 2-1 in extra-time not only in that summer's Olympic semi-final, but also in the first round of the FIFA World Cup two years later – going on to win both tournaments.

GOLD TIMERS

Any Norway international who reaches 25 appearances for the country is traditionally awarded a gold watch by Norway's football association. This custom began with Gunnar Andersen after he reached his quarter-century on 29 June 1919. Andersen, Norway's football captain at the 1920 Summer Olympics in Antwerp, was also an accomplished ski-jumper.

THE WHOLE HOGMO

Per-Mathias Hogmo, appointed manager of Norway's men's national team in September 2013, also spent three years in charge of Norway's women's team. He coached the women's side 1997–2000, taking them to a fourth-place finish at the 1999 FIFA Women's World Cup and to gold medal glory at the 2000 Sydney Olympics. Hogmo then became coach of Norway's men's U-21 side before returning to club football with Tromso – where the one-cap midfielder had ended his playing days in 1989. He succeeded Egil Olsen as Norway coach after the failure to qualify for the 2014 FIFA World Cup. Hogmo, who combined coaching with doing a PhD in football at Tromso University, vowed: "I see myself as an innovator and will look to put my stamp on how Norway play."

POLAND

The history of Polish football is littered with tremendous highs and depressing lows. Olympic gold-medal success in 1972, and third-place finishes in the 1974 and 1982 FIFA World Cup competitions were followed by failure to qualify for any tournament until 1992. Poland made it to the UEFA European Championship for the first time in 2008 and co-hosted the tournament with Ukraine in 2012, though went out in the first round both times.

TOP SCORERS

1	Wlodzimierz Lubanski	48
2	Grzegorz Lato	45
3	Kazimierz Deyna	41
4	Ernest Pol	39
5	Andrzej Szarmach	32
6	Gerard Cieslik	27
7	Zbigniew Boniek	24
8	Ernest Wilimowski	21
9	Dariusz Dziekanowski	20
=	Euzebiusz Smolarek	20

STAYING ON LATER THAN LATO

Record-breaking Polish stalwart **Michal Zewlakow** bowed out of international football on familiar turf, even though his country were playing an away game. The versatile defender's 102nd and final appearance for his country was a goalless friendly in Greece in March 2011, at the Karaiskakis stadium in Piraeus where he used to play club football for Olympiacos. Zewlakow had overtaken Grzegorz Lato's appearances record for Poland in his previous match, an October 2010 friendly against Ecuador. He had already helped make footballing history for his homeland when he and brother Marcin, a striker, became the first twins to line up together for Poland, against France in February 2000. Marcin would end his international career with 25 appearances and five goals.

TYTON THE TITAN

Two 1-1 draws in a row at the 2012 UEFA European Championship extended Poland's unbeaten run to eight games and filled the tournament co-hosts with high hopes of reaching the knock-out stages for the first time – only for a 1-0 defeat to the Czech Republic to seal their fate. But among those players to emerge from the tournament with credit was goalkeeper **Przemyslaw Tyton**. The stopper, with only five caps to his name, saved a penalty from Greece's Giorgos Karagounis just moments after coming on in the competition's opening match following a red card for first-choice goalkeeper Wojciech Szczesny, and kept his place in the team for the next two games. Szczesny had already conceded an equalizer to Greece's Dimitrios Salpingidis – ending a Polish record run of 512 minutes without allowing opponents to score, stretching back to a 2-1 victory over Hungary in November 2011.

LOVING LEWANDOWSKI

Star striker **Robert Lewandowski** is adept at proving people wrong. He was rejected by Legia Warsaw at the age of 16 and future Poland coach Franciszek Smuda saw nothing in him as a 20-year-old, chiding the man who had recommended him: "You owe me petrol money." Lewandowski's prolific form for Lech Poznan secured a big-money move to Germany's Borussia Dortmund in 2009, but he struggled in his first Bundesliga season. But he soon became one of Europe's top goalscorers, inspiring Dortmund to two Bundesliga titles and the 2013 UEFA Champions League final.

He was even warmly applauded by the Dortmund fans when waving goodbye in spring 2014, having agreed a move to rivals Bayern Munich. He scored on his international debut, as a substitute against San Marino in September 2008, and also struck the opening goal of the 2012 UEFA European Championship. But his sporting exploits should not be a surprise – his father Krzysztof was a footballer and Polish judo champion, both his mother Iwona and his sister Milena have played high-level volleyball and his partner Anna Stachurska is a karate champion.

TOP CAPS

1	Michael Zewlakow	102
2	Grzegorz Lato	100
3	Kazimierz Deyna	97
4	Jacek Bak	96
=	Jacek Krzynowek	96
6	Wladyslaw Zmuda	91
7	Antoni Szymanowski	82
8	Zbigniew Boniek	80
9	Wlodzimierz Lubanski	75
10	Tomasz Waldoch	74

"LITTLE FIGO"

Jacub Blaszczykowski was one of the Polish players to come out of Euro 2012 with the most credit – he scored a spectacular equalising goal against Russia – despite having gone into the tournament in testing circumstances. Before joining the rest of the squad in their training camp, he attended the funeral of his father. His presence at the event was all the more noteworthy because, as a ten-year-old child, Blaszyzkowski had witnessed his mother Anna being stabbed to death by his father, who served a 15-year prison sentence as a result. Polish great Zbigniew Boniek has dubbed Blaszczykowski "Little Figo" – after the Portuguese winger Luis Figo – though he is more commonly known as "Kuba", the name he often wears on the back of his shirt. He had been encouraged to pursue football as a teenager by his uncle Jerzy Brzeczek, who also played for Dortmund and captained Poland, winning 42 caps between 1992 and 1999 and picking up an Olympic silver medal in 1992.

LATO'S MISSION

Grzegorz Lato is not only second in both the tallies of Poland's most-capped and top-scoring players, the only Polish winner of the Golden Boot with his seven goals at the 1974 FIFA World Cup, and a member of the gold medal-winning team at the 1972 Summer Olympics. He was also a leading figure in Poland's co-hosting with Ukraine of the 2012 UEFA European Championship, having become president of the country's football federation in 2008. He vowed: "I am determined to change the image of Polish football, to make it transparent and pure."

FIVE ASIDE

Poland had five different goalscorers when they beat Peru 5-1 at the 1982 FIFA World Cup: Wlodzimierz Smolarek, Grzegorz Lato, Zbigniew Boniek, Andrzej Buncol and Wlodzimierz Ciolek. The feat was not repeated until Phillip Cocu, Marc Overmars, Dennis Bergkamp, Pierre van Hooijdonk and Ronald de Boer gave Holland a 5-0 victory over South Korea at the 1998 FIFA World Cup.

COOL KEEPER

What is it with Polish goalkeepers? The country's outfield players may not always be household names worldwide, but Jerzy Dudek (Liverpool), Artur Boruc and Lukasz Zaluska (both Celtic), Lukasz Fabianski and Wojciech Szczesny (both Arsenal), and Tomasz Kuszczak (Manchester United) have all played roles at four of Britain's most successful clubs.

SUPER ERNEST

Ernest Wilimowski wrote his name into FIFA World Cup history in 1938 when he scored four goals but still finished on the losing side. Poland went down 6-5 after extra-time to Brazil in a first-round tie in Strasbourg, France.

PUNCTUALITY PUNISHMENT

Kazimierz Gorski was the coach – capped once as a player – who led Poland to third place at the 1974 FIFA World Cup, having won gold at the Olympics in Munich, Germany, two years earlier. While winning a reputation for closeness with his players, Gorski could also be ruthless – key player Adam Musial was dropped from the team for a second-round game against Sweden at the 1974 tournament as punishment for turning up 20 minutes late to training. Poland still won the game, 1-0.

BONIEK

Zbigniew Boniek, arguably the best player Poland has ever produced, earned a place among football's legends for his role in the country's progress to third place at the 1982 FIFA World Cup. However, his absence from the tournament's semi-final will go down as one of the great "what ifs" of the competition. Robbed of their star forward through suspension, could Poland have upset both Italy and the odds and reached the final? Instead they lost the match 2-0.

PORTUGAL

Portugal's first experience of international competition almost ended in triumph. Inspired by Eusebio, they marched through to the semi-finals of the 1966 FIFA World Cup, only to lose to eventual champions England. A standout performance in the 1984 UEFA European Championship apart, more than 30 years would pass before Portugal enjoyed such giddy heights again. A "golden" generation of players arrived on the scene and since the turn of the century Portugal have become a consistent force on the world stage.

TOP CAPS

1	Luis Figo	127
2	Cristiano Ronaldo	114
3	Fernando Couto	110
4	Rui Costa	94
5	Pauleta	88
6	Simao	85
7	Joao Pinto	81
8	Vitor Baia	80
9	Nuno Gomes	79
=	Ricardo	79

GOODISON GLORY

At the 1966 FIFA World Cup Portugal beat North Korea 5-3 in an incredible quarter-final at Everton's Goodison Park. The sensational Eusebio spurred an amazing comeback after the Koreans had gone 3-0 ahead in the first 25 minutes. He scored four goals to take Portugal to the semi-finals in their first-ever FIFA World Cup appearance. Despite the tears that flowed after defeat to eventual winners England, Portugal rallied to claim third place with a **2-1 victory over the Soviet Union**.

HAPPY HUNDREDTH BIRTHDAY

Portugal celebrated their 100th birthday as a republic by beating newly crowned world champions Spain in a specially-arranged friendly in November 2010. The match not only marked the anniversary, but also celebrated the two countries' union in an ultimately unsuccessful bid to co-host the 2018 FIFA World Cup. Yet there was little equality in the match, Portugal sweeping to a 4-0 triumph – slight consolation for losing to Spain in the FIFA World Cup second round five months earlier.

TOP SCORERS

1	Cristiano Ronaldo	50
2	Pauleta	47
3	Eusebio	41
4	Luis Figo	32
5	Nuno Gomes	29
6	Helder Postiga	27
7	Rui Costa	26
8	Joao Pinto	23
9	Nene	22
=	Simao	22

THE BLACK PANTHER

Born in Mozambique, **Eusebio** da Silva Ferreira was named Portugal's "Golden Player" to mark UEFA's 50th anniversary in 2004. Signed by Benfica in 1960 at the age of 18, he scored a hat-trick in his second game – against Santos in a friendly tournament in Paris – outshining their young star, Pele. He helped Benfica win a second European Cup in 1962, was named European Footballer of the Year in 1965 and led Portugal to third place in the 1966 FIFA World Cup, finishing as top scorer with nine goals. A phenomenal striker, he scored 320 goals in 313 Portuguese league matches, won the first European Golden Boot in 1968 (and earned a second in 1973). The world of football united in paying tribute to Eusebio after he died aged 71 in January 2014. Portugal declared three days of mourning, his statue at Benfica's Estadio da Luz home was transformed into a shrine, his coffin was carried around the pitch and the Benfica players wore his name on their backs during a 2-0 win over rivals Porto.

PRESIDENTIAL POWER

~~Cristiano Ronaldo dos Santos Aveiro~~ got his second name because his father was a great fan of US President Ronald Reagan. He grew up supporting Benfica, but began his career with arch-rivals Sporting Clube before securing a move to Manchester United in 2003. His best season with United, in 2008, not only brought him the Golden Boot as well as Premier League and Champions League titles, but also helped him become only the second Portuguese player (after Luis Figo) to be named FIFA World Player of the Year (an award he scooped for a second time in 2013). Spanish giants Real Madrid paid €93.9 million to make him the most expensive footballer in history the following year. His club record 60 goals in 2011–12 steered them to the La Liga title, before he hit three for Portugal at the 2012 UEFA European Championship. Ronaldo ended the 2013–14 season with an extra-time goal as Real clinched the UEFA Champions League – in Lisbon – before scoring at his third FIFA World Cup – and sixth international tournament – with the winner against Ghana in Portugal's third and final match. In the previous game he had set up a last-gasp equaliser against the USA for Silvestre Varela – at 94 minutes and 33 seconds, the latest regulation-time goal in FIFA World Cup history, some seven seconds later than Francesco Totti's penalty for Italy against Australia in the round of 16 at the 2006 finals.

THE FAMOUS FIVE

Eusebio, Mario Coluna, Jose Augusto, Antonio Simoes, and Jose Torres were the "Fabulous Five" in Benfica's 1960s Dream Team, who made up the spine of the Portuguese national side at the 1966 FIFA World Cup. Coluna (the "Sacred Monster"), scored the vital third goal in the 1961 European Cup final and captained the national side in 1966. Jose Augusto, who scored two goals in the opening game against Hungary, went on to manage the national side and later the Portuguese women's team. Antonio Simoes (the "Giant Gnome" – just 1.58 metres/5ft 3in tall) made his debut for Portugal and Benfica in 1962, aged just 18. Jose Torres – the only one of the five not to win the European Cup (though he played in the defeats in both 1963 and 1968) – scored the winner against Russia in the 1966 third-place match, and went on to manage the national side to their next appearance at the FIFA World Cup finals in 1986.

THREE AND IN

After suffering a 4-0 trouncing against Germany in their opening game of the 2014 finals – their heaviest FIFA World Cup defeat – Portugal manager Paulo Bento replaced goalkeeper Rui Patricio with Beto for the next match, a 2-2 draw with the USA. Portugal ended their campaign by replacing the injured Beto with Eduardo for the final moments of a 2-1 victory over Ghana. They thus became only the fifth team to use all their goalkeepers in one FIFA World Cup finals and the first since Greece had done so 20 years earlier.

WAY TO GOMES

Portugal have provided three of the seven players to score at three different UEFA European Championships: Nuno Gomes (2000, 2004 and 2008) and Cristiano Ronaldo and **Helder Postiga** (both 2004, 2008 and 2012). Gomes scored four at Euro 2000, the first of which – in a 3-2 victory over England – was actually the first of his 29 goals for Portugal, despite the fact he had made his international debut four years earlier. He was named in the official UEFA team of the tournament for the 2000 event, despite ending it in disgrace: he pushed referee Gunter Benko following Portugal's semi-final defeat to France and was handed a lengthy international ban.

REP. OF IRELAND

It took a combination of astute management and endless searching through ancestral records before the Republic of Ireland finally qualified for the finals of a major tournament, at the 20th time of asking. But ever since Jack Charlton took the team to UEFA Euro 88, Ireland have remained one of Europe's fiercest opponents.

ROBBIE KEEN

The Republic of Ireland's all-time scoring record was taken by much-travelled striker **Robbie Keane** in October 2004 and he has been adding to it ever since – not least with last-minute equalizers against Germany and Spain at the 2006 FIFA World Cup. He marked the final game at the old Lansdowne Road with a hat-trick against San Marino in November 2006 – and, four years later, marked the inaugural game at the revamped replacement ground, the Aviva Stadium, with his 100th cap against Argentina. Ireland's 2-1 win over Macedonia in March 2011 was Keane's 41st match as captain – equalling the record set by Andy Townsend. He followed this up with two more matches as skipper, as Ireland beat Northern Ireland and Scotland in the British-based Carling Nations Cup. Keane also scored three goals in the two games, taking his overall tally to 49, before a double against Macedonia in June 2011 took him to 51. These made him the first player from the British Isles to score a half-century of international goals, and past England's 49-goal top scorer Bobby Charlton. He is now with the Los Angeles Galaxy in the MLS, but still plays for Ireland and has scored 62 times in 133 appearances.

KILBANE KEEPS ON AND ON

Only England's Billy Wright, with 70, has played more consecutive internationals than **Kevin Kilbane**, whose 109th Republic of Ireland cap against Macedonia in March 2011 was also his 65th in a row, covering 11 years and five months. The versatile left-sider – nicknamed "Zinedine Kilbane" by fans – was given a rest for Ireland's next game three days later, though, a friendly against Uruguay.

KEANE CARRY-ON

Few star players have walked out on their country with quite the dramatic impact as Republic of Ireland captain **Roy Keane** in 2002 at their FIFA World Cup training camp in Saipan, Japan. The fiercely intense Manchester United skipper quit before a competitive ball had been kicked, complaining about a perceived lack of professionalism in the Irish preparations – and his loss of faith in manager Mick McCarthy. Ireland reached the second round without him, losing on penalties to Spain, but his behaviour divided a nation. When McCarthy stepped down Keane and the Irish football federation brokered a truce, and he returned to international duty in April 2004 under new boss Brian Kerr. Few expected his second comeback, however, when he was appointed assistant to new manager Martin O'Neill in November 2013. O'Neill, who played 64 times for Northern Ireland between 1971 and 1984 succeeded Italian veteran Giovanni Trapattoni, who resigned after failing to qualify for the 2014 FIFA World Cup finals.

CHAMPION CHARLTON

Jack Charlton became a hero after he took Ireland to their first major finals in 1988, defeating England 1-0 in their first game at the UEFA European Championship. Things got even better at their first FIFA World Cup finals two years later, where the unfancied Irish lost out only to hosts Italy in the quarter-finals.

IT'S A GIVEN

The Republic of Ireland's second-most-capped player, goalkeeper Shay Given, bowed out of international football at the 2012 UEFA European Championship finals – the first major tournament his country had reached since the 1994 FIFA World Cup, when Given was also first-choice in goal. Despite going into UEFA Euro 2012 on a 14-game unbeaten run, the Irish lost all three games, to Croatia, Spain and Italy. The team's final match saw the captain's armband given to winger **Damien Duff**, as he became the fifth man to win a century of caps for Ireland. UEFA president Michel Platini praised the country's boisterous travelling fans and promised them a special award for their enthusiasm. Given, who gave all his international match fees to charity, announced his international retirement in the summer of 2012, following 55 clean sheets in 125 appearances, though he did suggest in January 2013 that he could be available for a comeback. One of his rivals has been Millwall goalkeeper David Forde, who was 33 when he faced Sweden in a FIFA World Cup qualifier in March 2013 – older than any other Ireland debutant in a competitive international.

MORE FOR MOORE

Paddy Moore was the first player ever to score four goals in a FIFA World Cup qualifier when Ireland came from behind to draw 4-4 with Belgium on 25 February 1934. Don Givens became the only Irishman to equal Moore's feat when he scored all four as Ireland beat Turkey 4-0 in October 1975.

CAPTAIN ALL-ROUND

Johnny Carey not only captained Matt Busby's Manchester United to the English league title in 1952, he also captained both Northern Ireland (nine caps) and later the Republic of Ireland (27 caps). He went on to manage the Republic of Ireland between 1955 and 1967.

HOORAY FOR RAY

Ray Houghton may have been born in Glasgow and spoke with a Scottish accent, but he scored two of Ireland's most famous goals. A header gave the Republic a shock 1-0 win over England at UEFA Euro 88 in West Germany and, six years later, his long-range strike was the only goal of the game against eventual finalists Italy, in the first round of the 1994 FIFA World Cup in the USA. It was exactly 18 years to the day from that 1994 shock that Ireland – now managed by Italian Giovanni Trapattoni – lost 2-0 to Italy in their third and final Group C match of the 2012 UEFA European Championship. Playing for Ireland that day was defender John O'Shea, who had previously been part of the Irish team that beat Italy 2-1 in the final of the 1998 UEFA European U-16s Championship final in Scotland. The Republic's only other continental title was the UEFA European U-19s Championship trophy they lifted by beating Germany, also in 1998.

TOP CAPS

1	Robbie Keane	133
2	Shay Given	125
3	Kevin Kilbane	110
4	Steve Staunton	102
5	Damien Duff	100
6	John O'Shea	96
7	Niall Quinn	92
8	Tony Cascarino	88
9	Paul McGrath	83
10	Richard Dunne	80
=	Packie Bonner	80

CROSSING THE CODES

Cornelius "Con" Martin was a Gaelic footballer whose passion for soccer resulted in his expulsion from the Gaelic Athletic Association. His versatility meant he was as good at centre-half as he was in goal, both for club (Aston Villa) and country. He played both in goal and outfield for the fledgling Irish national team, scoring a penalty in the 2-0 victory over England at Goodison Park in 1949 – in what was England's first home defeat to a non-British opponent.

TOP SCORERS

1	Robbie Keane	62
2	Niall Quinn	21
3	Frank Stapleton	20
4	John Aldridge	19
=	Tony Cascarino	19
=	Don Givens	19
7	Noel Cantwell	14
8	Gerry Daly	13
=	Kevin Doyle	13
=	Jimmy Dunne	13

ROMANIA

The history of Romanian football is littered with a series of bright moments – they were one of four countries (with Brazil, France and Belgium) to appear in the first three editions of the FIFA World Cup – followed by spells in the doldrums – since 1938 they have qualified for the finals of the tournament only four times in 14 attempts. The country's highlight came in 1994 when, inspired by Gheorghe Hagi, they reached the quarter-finals of the FIFA World Cup.

TOP CAPS

1	Dorinel Munteanu	134
2	Gheorghe Hagi	125
3	Gheorghe Popescu	115
4	Ladislau Boloni	102
5	Razvan Rat	97
6	Dan Petrescu	95
7	Bogdan Stelea	91
8	Michael Klein	89
9	Bogdan Lobont	85
10	Marius Lacatus	83
=	Mircea Rednic	83

FAMOUS FOURSOME

Gheorghe Hagi, Florin Raducioiu, Ilie Dumitrescu and **Gheorghe "Gica" Popescu** lit up the FIFA World Cup in the United States in 1994. Together they scored nine of Romania's ten goals (Raducioiu four, Hagi three, Dumitrescu two). All three successfully converted their penalties in the quarter-final shoot-out against Sweden, but misses from Dan Petrescu and Miodrag Belodedici sent the Romanians crashing out. All three made big-money moves for the following 1994–95 season: Hagi went from Brescia to Barcelona, Dumitrescu from Steaua Bucharest to Tottenham Hotspur and Raducioiu went from warming the bench at Milan to the first team at Espanyol. Defender/midfielder Popescu followed Dumitrescu to Spurs, and later won the UEFA European Cup Winners' Cup with Barcelona and was captain of Galatasaray when they became the first Turkish team to win a European trophy, the 2000 UEFA Cup. Popescu scored 16 goals in 115 appearances for Romania between 1998 and 2003, playing in the FIFA World Cups of 1990, 1994 and 1998, and the UEFA European Championships of 1996 and 2000. As well as being team-mates, Popescu and Hagi are also brothers-in-law – their wives, Luminita Popescu and Marlilena Hagi, are sisters.

BORDER CROSSING

Some 14 footballers played for both Romania, during the 1930s, and Hungary, during the 1940s – the most prolific being striker Iuliu Bodola, who scored 31 goals in 48 games for Romania, including appearances at the 1934 and 1938 FIFA World Cups, and four in 13 matches for his adopted homeland Hungary.

YELLOW PERIL

Despite topping Group G ahead of England, Colombia and Tunisia at the 1998 FIFA World Cup, Romania's players of that tournament might perhaps be best remembered for their collective decision to dye their hair blond ahead of their final first-round game. The **newly bleached Romanians** struggled to a 1-1 draw against Tunisia, before being knocked out by Croatia in the second round, 1-0.

TOP SCORERS

1	Gheorghe Hagi	35
=	Adrian Mutu	35
3	Iuliu Bodola	31
4	Viorel Moldovan	25
5	Ciprian Marica	24
6	Ladislau Boloni	23
7	Rodion Camataru	21
=	Dudu Georgescu	21
=	Anghel Iordanescu	21
=	Florin Raducioiu	21

CENTURY MAN

Gheorghe Hagi, Romania's "Player of the [twentieth] Century", scored three goals and was named in the Team of the Tournament at the 1994 FIFA World Cup in the United States, at which Romania lost out on penalties to Sweden after a 2-2 draw in the quarter-finals. Hagi made his international debut in 1983, aged just 18, scored his first goal aged 19 (in a 3-2 defeat to Northern Ireland) and remains Romania's joint-top goalscorer with 35 goals in 125 games. Despite retiring from international football after the 1998 FIFA World Cup, Hagi couldn't resist answering his country's call to play in UEFA Euro 2000. Sadly, two yellow-card offences in six minutes in the quarter-final against Italy meant Hagi's final bow on the international stage saw him receive a red card – and leave the field to take an early bath. Farul Constanta, in Hagi's hometown, named their stadium after him in 2000 – but fans stopped referring to it as such after he took the manager's job at rivals Timisoara.

CEMETERY SENTRY

It was second time luckier for former international striker Victor Piturca when he coached Romania at the 2008 UEFA European Championship in Austria and Switzerland, even though they were eliminated in the first round. He had previously been manager when the country qualified for the 2000 UEFA European Championship, but was forced out of the job before the tournament started following arguments with big-name players such as Gheorghe Hagi. Piturca's cousin Florin Piturca was also a professional footballer but died aged only 27 in 1978. Florin's father and Victor's uncle Maximilian, a cobbler, not only built a mausoleum for Florin but also slept at night in the cemetery until his own death in 1994.

ENDURING DORINEL

Dorinel Munteanu has played for Romania more times than any other although at one point his former team-mate Gheorghe Hagi's 125-cap record looked safe. Versatile defensive midfielder Munteanu was stuck on 119 appearances throughout an 18-month absence from the international scene before being surprisingly recalled at the age of 37 by manager Victor Piturca in February 2005. He ended his Romania career two years later, having scored 16 times in 134 games. Yet many Romanians believe he was wrongly denied a goal when a shot against Bulgaria at the 1996 UEFA European Championship appeared to bounce over the line, only to not be given. The match ended 1-0 to Bulgaria and Romania were eliminated in the first round following three straight defeats.

BROUGHT TO BUCHAREST

Romania's new national stadium in the capital Bucharest became the first in the country ever to stage a major European final, when it hosted the 2012 UEFA Europa League final in which Atletico Madrid beat fellow Spanish side Athletic Bilbao. The 55,200-capacity Arena Nationala was opened in September 2011, when Romania drew 0-0 with France. It has also been used by Steaua Bucharest and Dinamo Bucharest for league matches, Otelul Galati for UEFA Champions League games, and both Steaua and Rapid Bucharest for UEFA Europa League fixtures. The venue stands on the site of the old Stadionul National, built in 1953 and demolished 54 years later.

ADRIAN'S AID

Romania have only lost once when **Adrian Mutu** has scored – a fact made all the better for them since, with 35 goals, he is (with Gheorghe Hagi) his country's all-time leading goalscorer. Mutu drew level with Hagi with a FIFA World Cup qualifying game equalizer against Hungary in March 2013, though this was his first international goal in 21 months. Unfortunately for Romania, controversy has followed their finest player of the 21st century: he has been banned twice for failed drugs tests. The first came after a test carried out by his club employers Chelsea in September 2004 showed traces of cocaine and brought about his dismissal. After a seven-month ban he rehabilitated his career in Italy, first with Juventus and then Fiorentina, before receiving a nine-month suspension after he tested positive for a banned anti-obesity drug in January 2010. He did score against Italy at the 2008 UEFA European Championship, Romania's only goal at the last major tournament for which they qualified.

RUSSIA

Before the break-up of the Soviet Union (USSR) in 1992, the team was a world football powerhouse, winning the first UEFA European Championship in 1960, gold at the 1956 and 1988 Olympic Games and qualifying for the FIFA World Cup on seven occasions. Playing as Russia since August 1992, the good times have eluded them – apart from being UEFA Euro 2008 semi-finalists. They did, however, reach the 2014 FIFA World Cup under Italian coach Fabio Capello but will be hoping to better their group round exit when Russia gets to host the tournament for the first time in 2018.

TOP SCORERS
(Russia only)

1	Vladimir Beschastnykh	26
=	Aleksandr Kerzhakov	26
3	Roman Pavlyuchenko	21
4	Andrei Arshavin	17
=	Valeri Karpin	17
6	Dmitri Sychev	15
7	Igor Kolyvanov	12
=	Roman Shorokov	12
9	Sergei Kiryakov	10
=	Aleksandr Mostovoi	10

KERZH LIFTS HIS CURSE

Only one man was in Russia's squads for the 2002 FIFA World Cup finals and the next time they qualified, in 2014: **Aleksandr Kerzhakov**. He was a teenager in 2002, having made his international debut three months earlier, and he played just eight minutes of the finals. Kerzhakov, still only 31 in Brazil, scored his 26th international goal to earn a 1-1 draw in Russia's opener against South Korea. He thus matched Russia's all-time scoring record set by 2002 team-mate Vladimir Beschastnykh. Kerzhakov, with five goals, was Russia's leading scorer in qualifying for the 2014 finals, but unlike in 2008 – when he was five-goal top-scorer in UEFA European Championships qualifying – this time he was not omitted from the finals squad.

HOME RANGE

Russia were the only country at the 2014 FIFA World Cup whose entire 23-man squad played their club football domestically. Dynamo Moscow had six players and CSKA Moscow five, including defender **Sergei Ignashevich** who reached a century of caps in the final Group H game against Algeria. They may have had the highest-paid coach at the tournament, with Fabio Capello earning a reported £6.69million per year. But for the second FIFA World Cup running he was undone by a goalkeeping error in the opening game: in 2010 he watched England's Rob Green fumble in a shot from the USA's Clint Dempsey; in Russia's 2014 opener, keeper Igor Akinfeev did suffer similarly with a long-range effort by South Korea's Lee Keun-Ho. And, by coincidence, both lapses were equalizers in 1-1 draws.

YOUNG PROMISE

Igor Akinfeev became post-Soviet Russia's youngest international footballer when he made his debut in a friendly against Norway on 28 April 2004. The CSKA Moscow goalkeeper was just 18 years and 20 days old. The following season would be perhaps just as memorable for him, clinching a domestic league and cup double with his club while also lifting the UEFA Cup as CSKA Moscow became post-Soviet Russia's first side to win a UEFA club trophy. The youngest Soviet-era debutant was Eduard Streltsov, who hit a hat-trick on his debut against Sweden in June 1956, at the age of 17 years and 340 days and then scored another treble in his second game, against India.

PUTTING ON THE STYLE

As a professional footballer who has a diploma in fashion design, perhaps it is no surprise **Andrei Arshavin** could strut across the pitch with a certain élan as the most skilful of Russia's 21st-century players. Even after missing the first two games of the 2008 UEFA European Championship through suspension, the Russia captain dazzled with his performances in his team's next two matches – especially a 3-1 quarter-final triumph over the Netherlands. Just a month earlier, Arshavin had been central as Zenit St Petersburg lifted the UEFA Cup, although his later spell with English club Arsenal proved patchier before his release in summer 2013. Arshavin's image back home was tainted a little when he argued with fans after their Euro 2012 first-round exit – and he then lost the captaincy under new coach Fabio Capello. Yet, on his day, this natty man with an eye for an outfit could prove a cut above.

TOP CAPS
(Russia only)

1	Viktor Onopko	109
2	Sergei Ignashevich	100
3	Aleksandr Kerzhakov	84
4	Vasili Berezutskiy	81
5	Aleksandr Anyukov	77
8	Andrei Arshavin	75
7	Igor Akinfeev	72
=	Valeri Karpin	72
9	Vladimir Beschastnykh	71
10	Sergei Semak	65

PAV A GO HERO

Roman Pavlyuchenko's thumping strike as a substitute to wrap up a 4-1 victory over the Czech Republic in Russia's opening game of the 2012 UEFA European Championship took him to within five goals of Vladimir Beschastnykh's post-Soviet scoring record. Pavlyuchenko also scored Russia's first goal of Euro 2008, this time in a 4-1 defeat at the hands of eventual champions Spain. Despite the loss, Russia still managed to reach the semi-finals that year; in 2012 they failed to make it beyond the group stages. Pavlyuchenko is Russia's top scorer in UEFA European Championships, with four overall – three in 2008 and one in 2012.

SUPER STOPPER

FIFA declared **Lev Yashin** to be the finest goalkeeper of the 20th century – naturally, he made it into their Century XI team, too. In a career spanning 20 years, Yashin played 326 league games for Dynamo Moscow – the only club side he ever played for – and won 78 caps for the Soviet Union, conceding on average less than a goal a game (only 70 in total). With Dynamo, he won five Soviet championships and three Soviet cups, the last of which came in his final full season in 1970. He saved around 150 penalties in his long career, and kept four clean sheets in his 12 FIFA World Cup matches. Such was Yashin's worldwide reputation, Chilean international Eladio Rojas was so excited at scoring past the legendary Yashin in the 1962 FIFA World Cup that he gave the surprised keeper a big hug with the ball still sitting in the back of the net. Yashin was nicknamed the "Black Spider" for his distinctive black jersey and his uncanny ability to get a hand, arm, leg or foot in the way of shots and headers of all kinds. In 1963, Yashin became the first, and so far only, keeper to be named European Footballer of the Year, the same year in which he won his fifth Soviet championship and starred for the Rest of the World XI in the English FA's Centenary Match at Wembley.

CAPPING IT ALL

Viktor Onopko, despite being born in the Ukraine, played all his career for the CIS and Russian national football teams. The first of Onopko's 113 international caps (the first four for the CIS) came in a 2-2 draw against England in Moscow on 29 April 1992. He played in the 1994 and 1998 FIFA World Cups, as well as the UEFA European Championship in 1996. He was due to join the squad for the UEFA European Championship in 2004 but missed out through injury. Onopko's club career, spanning 19 years, took him to Shakhtar Donetsk, Spartak Moscow, Real Oviedo, Rayo Vallecano, Alania Vladikavkaz and FC Saturn. He was Russian footballer of the year in 1993 and 1994.

GOLDEN BOY

Igor Netto captained the USSR national side to their greatest successes: gold at the 1956 Olympics in Melbourne and victory in the first-ever UEFA European Championship in France in 1960. Born in Moscow in 1930, Netto was awarded the Order of Lenin in 1957 and became an ice hockey coach after retiring from football.

SCOTLAND

A country with a vibrant domestic league and a rich football tradition – it played host to the first-ever international football match, against England, in November 1872 – Scotland have never put in the performances on the international stage to match their lofty ambitions. There have been moments of triumph, such as an unexpected victory over Holland at the 1978 FIFA World Cup, but far too many moments of despair. Scotland have not qualified for the finals of a major tournament since 1998.

TOP SCORERS

1	Kenny Dalglish	30
=	Denis Law	30
3	Hughie Gallacher	23
4	Lawrie Reilly	22
5	Ally McCoist	19
6	Kenny Miller	18
7	Robert Hamilton	15
=	James McFadden	15
9	Maurice Johnston	14
10	Bob McColl	13
=	Andrew Wilson	13

KING KENNY

Kenny Dalglish is Scotland's joint-top international goalscorer (with Denis Law) and remains the only player to have won more than a century of caps for the national side, with 102 in total – 11 more than the next highest cap-winner, goalkeeper Jim Leighton. Despite growing up a Rangers fan (he was born in Glasgow on 4 March 1951), Dalglish made his name spear-heading Celtic's domestic dominance in the 1970s, winning four league titles, four Scottish Cups and one League Cup. He then went on to become a legend at Liverpool, winning a hat-trick of European Cups (1978, 1981 and 1984) and leading the side as player-manager to their first-ever league and cup double in 1986. He later joined Herbert Chapman and Brian Clough as one of the few managers to lead two different sides to the league title – guiding Blackburn Rovers to the summit of English football in 1994–95. For Scotland, Dalglish scored at both the 1978 and 1982 FIFA World Cup finals, netting the first goal in the famous 3-2 victory over eventual runners-up Holland in the 1978 group stages. He played his last international in 1986.

DON'T COME HOME TOO SOON

Scotland's 2-0 defeat to Serbia in March 2013 gave them the unenviable record of being the first European country eliminated from the 2014 FIFA World Cup – denying them a chance to get beyond the first round of the finals for the first time. **Gordon Strachan**, who scored five goals in 50 games for Scotland in midfield between 1980 and 1992, had replaced the sacked Craig Levein in January 2013.

THE LAWMAN

Denis Law is joint top scorer for Scotland with Kenny Dalglish, scoring 30 goals in only 55 games compared to the 102 it took Dalglish to do the same. Law twice scored four goals in a match for Scotland. First against Northern Ireland on 7 November 1962, helping win the British Home Championships. He repeated the feat against Norway in a friendly on 7 November 1963. Law clearly enjoyed playing against Norway, having grabbed a hat-trick in Bergen just five months earlier.

ROOM FOR ONE MORE?

Hampden Park, Scotland's national stadium, boasts the record for the highest-ever football attendance in Europe. The crowd was so huge no one can be quite sure how many squeezed in to watch Scotland v England in 1937, though the official figure is usually quoted as 149,415. Scotland won the British Home Championship tie 3-1, though they ended runners-up to Wales in the overall tournament. Since being redeveloped in 1999, Hampden Park has hosted almost all of Scotland's home internationals. The first to be played elsewhere was a 2008 UEFA European Championship qualifier against the Faroe Islands in September 2006, when Celtic Park in Glasgow was used instead – Hampden having been pre-booked for a concert by pop star Robbie Williams.

DIVIDED LOYALTIES

Scottish-born winger Jim Brown played and scored for the USA side which lost to Argentina in the first FIFA World Cup in 1930. He had moved to New Jersey three years earlier and qualified through his US citizen father. Two of his brothers also played professionally: younger brother John, a goalkeeper, was capped by Scotland, but Tom did not play at international level. Jim's son George appeared once for the USA, in 1957, while two of John's sons, Peter and Gordon, both played rugby for Scotland.

The first brothers to play for different countries, were John and Archie Goodall – members of Preston North End's 1888–89 league and FA Cup double-winning squad – and although their parents were both Scottish, London-born John played for England and Belfast-born Archie represented Ireland. Another pair of brothers with Scottish parents were Joe and Gerry Baker – though Joe chose to play for England in the 1960s and Gerry appeared for the USA.

TOP CAPS

1	Kenny Dalglish	102
2	Jim Leighton	91
3	Alex McLeish	77
4	Paul McStay	76
5	Tom Boyd	72
6	Kenny Miller	69
=	David Weir	69
8	Christian Dailly	67
9	Willie Miller	65
10	Darren Fletcher	62
=	Danny McGrain	62

I HAVEN'T FELT THIS GOOD SINCE ARCHIE GEMMILL SCORED AGAINST HOLLAND

Archie Gemmill scored Scotland's greatest goal on the world stage in the surprise 3-2 victory over Holland at the 1978 FIFA World Cup. He jinked past three defenders before chipping the ball neatly over Dutch goalkeeper Jan Jongbloed. Amazingly, in 2008, this magical moment was turned into a dance in the English National Ballet's "The Beautiful Game".

RECENT REMATCH

The world's oldest international fixture was staged for the first time in 14 years when England and Scotland met at Wembley in an August 2013 friendly. Gordon Strachan's Scotland twice came from behind but lost 3-2 thanks to a late winner by England's debutant substitute Rickie Lambert. This was the first England–Scotland game in which both teams scored at least twice since Scotland's famous 3-2 win in 1967.

WEIR ON THE BALL

Rugged Rangers centre-back **David Weir** became Scotland's oldest international footballer when he faced Lithuania in a 2012 UEFA European Championship qualifier on 3 September 2010, aged 40 years and 111 days, for his 66th appearance. He was still representing his country three caps and 39 days later, against reigning world and European champions Spain.

UNOFFICIAL WORLD CHAMPIONS

One of the victories most cherished by Scotland fans is the **3-2 triumph** over arch-rivals and reigning world champions England in April 1967 at Wembley – the first time Sir Alf Ramsey's team had lost since clinching the 1966 FIFA World Cup. Scotland's man of the match that day was ball-juggling left-half/midfielder Jim Baxter, while it was also the first game in charge for Scotland's first full-time manager, Bobby Brown. Less fondly recalled is Scotland's 9-3 trouncing by the same opposition at the same stadium in April 1961, which made unfortunate goalkeeper Frank Haffey the butt of a popular joke that did the rounds across the border in England: "What's the time? Nearly 10 past Haffey." The game was Haffey's second – and last – for Scotland.

⚽ SERBIA

The former Yugoslavia was one of the strongest football nations in eastern Europe. They reached the FIFA World Cup semi-finals in 1930 and 1962, they were also runners-up in the UEFA European Championships of 1960 and 1968. In addition, Yugoslavia's leading club, Red Star Belgrade, were only the second team from eastern Europe (after Romania's Steaua Bucharest in 1986) to win the European Cup, when they beat Marseille on penalties in the 1991 final.

⚙ MAGIC DRAGAN

Yugoslavia's greatest player was Red Star left winger **Dragan Dzajic**, who later went on to become the club's president. He made his international debut at 18, won a national record 85 caps and scored 23 goals. The most important was his last-minute winner against world champions England in the 1968 UEFA European Championship semi-final in Florence, which took Yugoslavia to the final against Italy. Pele said of Dzajic: "He's a real wizard. I'm sorry he's not Brazilian."

⚙ SAVICEVIC STRIKES

Dejan Savicevic is Serbia's greatest player of the modern era. The attacking midfielder was a key member of Red Star Belgrade's 1991 European Cup-winning team. He also inspired them to three consecutive championships. He moved on to Milan and starred as his new club beat Barcelona 4-0 in the 1994 European Cup final. He created the opening goal, then crashed home a 35-yard volley. Savicevic later became a prominent supporter of the drive for Montenegrin independence from Serbia and was credited with playing an influential role in the referendum vote on 21 May 2006 that led to the establishment of a separate Montenegrin state.

⚽ TOP CAPS

#	Player	Caps
1	Dejan Stankovic	103
2	Savo Milosevic	102
3	Dragan Djazic	85
4	Dragan Stojkovic	84
5	Predrag Mijatovic	73
6	Branislav Ivanovic	71
7	Zlatko Vujovic	70
8	Branko Zebec	65
9	Slavisa Jokanovic	64
10	Stjepan Bobek	63
=	Sinisa Mihajlovic	63

⚙ YUGOSLAVIA HIT BY BOYCOTT

The rivalry between Serbia and Croatia was apparent even in the early days of the old federation. Yugoslavia reached the last four of the inaugural FIFA World Cup in 1930, but they did so without any Croat players, who boycotted the squad for the finals in protest at the new federal association headquarters being located in the Serb capital, Belgrade.

TOP SCORERS

1	Stjepan Bobek	38
2	Mian Galic	37
=	Savo Milosevic	37
4	Blagoje Marjanovic	36
5	Rajko Mitic	32
6	Dusan Bajevic	29
7	Todor Veselinovic	28
8	Borivoje Kostic	26
=	Predrag Mijatovic	26
10	Zlatko Vujovic	25

STAN'S THE MAN

Midfielder **Dejan Stankovic** is the only man to have represented three different countries at separate FIFA World Cups, playing for Yugoslavia in 2002, Serbia and Montenegro in 2006, and Serbia in 2010. His pragmatic comment on his achievement was: "I'm happy with the record, but I'd rather win. It's OK to have been in three World Cups, but I would have liked to have better results." Stankovic scored twice on his international debut for Yugoslavia in 1998. He has also twice scored memorable volleyed goals from virtually on the halfway line – once for Internazionale against Genoa in 2009–10, with a first-time shot from the opposing goalkeeper's clearance, and an almost identical finish against German club FC Schalke 04 in the UEFA Champions League the following season. Stankovic tied Savo Milosevic's Serbian appearances record with his final competitive international in October 2011, but went one better in October 2013, when playing the first ten minutes of a 2-0 friendly defeat of Japan at Novi Sad.

SAV A GO HERO

Savo Milosevic was the first Serbian player to reach a century of international appearances – and he can claim to have played for his country in four different guises, representing Yugoslavia before and after it broke up, Serbia & Montenegro and finally Serbia alone. Milosevic's 100th international appearance was memorable for the wrong reasons, coming in a 6-0 defeat to Argentina at the 2006 FIFA World Cup. He returned to the fold for a final, farewell match: a friendly against Bulgaria on 19 November 2008. Milosevic played only the first 34 minutes yet managed not only to score twice but also miss two penalties. He joked: "Maybe those 34 minutes sum up my career, in the best possible way, with good moments and bad times, when you are at the top and at the bottom. Believe me, I have never missed two penalties before – not even in training."

BRAN POWER

Versatile Chelsea defender and Serbia captain **Branislav Ivanovic** has enjoyed scoring significant late goals against Portuguese opposition. His first goal for his country was an 88th-minute equalizer in a UEFA European Championship qualifier away to Portugal in 2007. His stoppage-time header gave Chelsea victory over Benfica in the final of the 2013 UEFA Europa League, a year after suspension ruled him out of the club's UEFA Champions League triumph over Bayern Munich.

MILORAD'S MILESTONE

The first man to captain and then coach his country at the FIFA World Cup was Milorad Arsenijevic, who captained Yugoslavia to the semi-finals at the inaugural tournament in Uruguay in 1930 and then managed their squad in Brazil 20 years later.

GOING IT ALONE

After Serbia and Montenegro competed at the 2006 FIFA World Cup, the 2010 tournament was the first featuring Serbia alone following Montenegro's independence. Topping their qualifying group ahead of France, Radomir Antic's Serbian side failed to make it through to the knockout stages in South Africa, despite a single-goal victory over Group D rivals Germany. A Serbian working for an opposing team was partly to blame – Milovan Rajevac was coach of the Ghana side that beat Serbia 1-0 in their opening first-round match. A mainstay in the Serbian defence was dominating centre-back **Nemanja Vidic**, a 2008 UEFA Champions League-winner and hero at Manchester United – but he announced his retirement from international football in October 2011.

SLOVAKIA

Slovakia have finally begun claiming bragging rights over their neighbours, the Czech Republic. A Slovak team did play games during the Second World War but then had to wait until post-war Czechoslovakia divided into Slovakia and the Czech Republic in 1993 before their next match. They returned to competitive action in qualifiers for the 1996 UEFA European Championship, finishing a promising third in their group. Continuing gradual progress culminated in qualification for their first FIFA World Cup, in 2010, at which they upset defending champions Italy 3-2 and reached the second round.

VLAD ALL OVER

Three relatives named Vladimir Weiss – different generations of the same family – have represented their country in international football, with two of them featuring at the 2010 FIFA World Cup. The first Vladimir won a footballing silver medal with Czechoslovakia at the 1964 Olympics, before his son Vladimir played for the same country at the 1990 FIFA World Cup. This second Vladimir then led Slovakia to the 2010 tournament as coach, picking his Manchester City winger son – yet another Vladimir – for three of the team's four matches. The first Vladimir made three appearances for Czechoslovakia, including the 1964 Olympics final in which he scored an own goal as Hungary triumped 2-1. The second Vladimir won 19 caps for Czechoslavakia and 12 for Slovakia, and the third, then aged only 20, ended the 2010 FIFA World Cup with 12. By the summer of 2014, the youngest Weiss had moved on 33 appearances. The coach described their 3-2 victory over holders Italy at the 2010 FIFA World Cup as the second happiest day of his life – only beaten by the day his son was born. He stepped down as boss after failing to qualify for the 2012 UEFA European Championship.

HOMEMADE MARIAN

Marian Masny holds the international appearances record for Slovak-born footballers who played for the united Czechoslovakia, earning 75 caps between 1974 and 1982. Masny, from Rybany, was also the second-highest-scoring Slovak during the united Czechoslovakia era. His 18 goals were only bettered by the 22 in 36 matches struck by Vrutky-born Adolf Scherer from 1958 to 1964. Scherer's tally included three at the 1962 FIFA World Cup, when Czechoslovakia finished runners-up. Scherer scored the winner against Hungary in the quarter-finals and Czechoslovakia's final goal in their 3-1 semi-final victory over Yugoslavia.

TOP SCORERS

1	Robert Vittek	23
2	Szilard Nemeth	22
3	Miroslav Karhan	14
=	Marek Mintal	14
5	Peter Dubovsky	12
=	Stanislav Sestak	12
7	Marek Hamsik	11
8	Martin Jakubko	9
=	Tibor Jancula	9
=	Lubomir Reiter	9

MAREK OFF THE MARK

Slovakia's biggest win is 7-0, a result they have achieved three times – with wing-back Marek Cech the only man to play in all three games: against Liechtenstein in September 2004 and twice versus San Marino, in October 2007 and June 2009. He scored twice in the most recent match and in fact four of his five international goals since his 2004 debut came against San Marino – he also scored a brace in a 5-0 victory in November 2007.

CZECH EIGHT

Eight Slovakia players played in Czechoslovakia's triumphant 1976 UEFA European Championship final against West Germany, including captain Anton Ondrus and both their scorers in the 2-2 draw: Jan Svehlik and Karol Dobias. Three of the team's successful penalty-takers in their 5-3 shoot-out win were Slovak-born: Marian Masny, Ondrus and substitute Ladislav Jurkemik. The other Slovaks to feature were Jan Pivarnik, Jozef Capkovic and Jozef Moder. Defender Koloman Gogh was born in what is now the Czech Republic, but had Slovak family ties and played most of his club football for Slovan Bratislava in the Slovak capital.

TOP CAPS		
1	Miroslav Karhan	108
2	Robert Vittek	80
3	Marek Hamsik	69
4	Martin Skrtel	66
5	Jan Durica	64
6	Filip Holosko	63
7	Szilard Nemeth	58
8	Radoslav Zabavnik	57
9	Stanislav Varga	54
10	Stanislav Sestak	53

SKRTEL'S A CERT

Slovakia captain and centre-back **Martin Skrtel** has won his country's Footballer of the Year award more times than any other Slovak player, since it was introduced in 1993. He collected the prize in 2007, 2008, 2011 and 2012 – with national team-mate Marek Hamsik the winner in 2009, 2010 and 2013. The only man named Slovak Footballer of the Year three years in a row was defender Dusan Tittel – in 1993, 1994 and 1995.

ROBERT THE HERO

Slovakia's **Robert Vittek** became only the fourth player from a country making their FIFA World Cup debut to score as many as four goals in one tournament, at the 2010 event in South Africa. He hit one against New Zealand, two against defending champions Italy, and a late penalty in a second-round defeat to Holland. The previous three players to have done so were Portugal's Eusebio in 1966, Denmark's Preben Elkjaer Larsen in 1986 and Croatia's Davor Suker in 1998. Vittek's last-minute penalty against Holland made him Slovakia's all-time leading scorer with 23 goals, overtaking former Sparta Prague and Middlesbrough striker Szilard Nemeth. His 2010 FIFA World Cup form was all the more striking since he had failed to score at all in the qualifiers.

CUTTING EDGE HAMSIK

Playmaker Marek Hamsik was just 17 when he left Slovakia in 2004 – after only six games for Slovan Bratislava – and moved to Italy, joining Brescia, then Napoli. After helping Napoli to win the 2012 Coppa Italia, he fulfilled a promise to shave off his Mohawk hairstyle. Hamsik captained Slovakia at the 2010 FIFA World Cup, where he helped to eliminate Italy in the opening round. It was a less happy story for Hamsik and Slovakia when it came to qualifying for the 2014 FIFA World Cup. Slovakia finished a disappointing third behind Greece and group G winners Bosnia & Herzegovina. Hamsik scored twice in eight appearances, but was absent for the final two matches.

BROKEN-DOWN KARHAN

Slovakia's defensive midfielder **Miroslav Karhan** helped his country qualify for the 2010 FIFA World Cup, taking his appearances tally to a national-record 95. But an Achilles tendon injury meant the team captain was ruled out of the tournament itself. After returning to action later in 2010, Karhan became the first Slovakia player to pass 100 caps.

SWEDEN

Eleven appearances at the FIFA World Cup finals (with a best result of second, as tournament hosts, in 1958) and three Olympic medals (including gold in London in 1948), bear testament to Sweden's rich history on the world football stage. Recent success has been harder to find, however, with semi-final appearances at the 1992 UEFA European Championship (again as hosts) and the 1994 FIFA World Cup the country's best performances in recent years.

GRE-NO-LI OLYMPIC AND ITALIAN GLORY

Having conquered the world by leading Sweden to gold in the 1948 Olympics in London, Gunnar Gren, Gunnar Nordahl and **Nils Liedholm** were snapped up by AC Milan. Their three-pronged "Gre-No-Li" forward line led the Italian giants to their 1951 scudetto win. Nordahl, who topped the Serie A scoring charts five times between 1950 and 1955, remains Milan's all-time top scorer with 221 goals in 268 games. Gren and Liedholm went on to appear for the Swedish national team in the 1958 FIFA World Cup – where they finished runners-up.

ONE MORE ENCORE, AGAIN!

One of the most famous and decorated Swedish footballers of modern times, **Henrik Larsson** (a star on the club scene with both Celtic and Barcelona) quit international football after the 2002 FIFA World Cup ... and again after the 2006 FIFA World Cup in Germany. He then made a further comeback in the 2010 FIFA World Cup qualifiers. With 37 goals in his 106 appearances, including five in his three FIFA World Cups, fans and officials clamoured for his return each time he tried to walk away. Sweden's failure to qualify for the tournament in 1998 meant a record-equalling 12 years elapsed between Larsson's first FIFA World Cup finals goal against Bulgaria in 1994 and his last, a dramatic late equalizer in a 2-2 group-stage draw with England in 2006. After finally retiring for good in 2009, he became manager of Swedish second-tier club Landskrona BoIS.

TOP CAPS

1	Anders Svensson	148
2	Thomas Ravelli	143
3	Olof Mellberg	117
4	Roland Nilsson	116
5	Bjorn Nordqvist	115
6	Andreas Isaksson	113
7	Kim Kallstrom	110
8	Niclas Alexandersson	109
9	Henrik Larsson	106
10	Zlatan Ibrahimovic	98

TOP-STOPPER RAVELLI

Thomas Ravelli kept goal for Sweden a record 143 times – conceding 143 goals. He saved two penalties in a shoot-out against Romania in the 1994 FIFA World Cup quarter-final to send Sweden into the last four, where they lost 1-0 to Brazil. Sweden went on to finish third, and were also the tournament's highest scorers with 15 goals in all – four more than eventual champions Brazil. Sweden's tally included five for Kennet Andersson, four for Martin Dahlin and three for Tomas Brolin.

IBRA-CADABRA

Few footballers these days can claim such consistent success – nor boast such an ego – as Swedish forward **Zlatan Ibrahimovic**. His proclamations have included "There's only one Zlatan", "I am like Muhammad Ali" and – in response to criticism from Norway's John Carew – "What Carew does with a football, I can do with an orange." Yet his clubs, including Ajax in the Netherlands, Juventus, Internazionale and AC Milan in Italy, Barcelona in Spain and Paris Saint-Germain in France, have all benefited from his presence; he has won 11 league titles since 2002. He christened the newly built Friends Arena in Solna with all four goals as Sweden beat England 4-2 in a November 2012 friendly – his final goal topping the lot, a 30-yard overhead kick which won the FIFA Ferenc Puskas goal of the year award. Ibrahimovic thus became the first player in 915 matches to score four goals in one game against England. Other notable strikes include a back-heel volley against Italy at the 2004 UEFA European Championship and a long-range volley versus France at Euro 2012. Despite also qualifying for Bosnia and for Croatia through his family, Malmo-born Ibrahimovic made his Sweden debut in January 2001 and has scored 48 goals in 98 appearances. His success in Paris since signing for €20million in 2012 prompted a local restaurateur to introduce a new €30 burger, "La Zlatan", comprising 600g of beef, three slices of cheese and extravagant toppings of onions and ham.

ANDERS KEEPERS

Midfielder Anders Svensson celebrated equalling Thomas Ravelli's Sweden appearances record by scoring in both his 142nd and 143rd games for his country: a long-range strike as Norway were beaten 4-2 and then the winning goal against the Republic of Ireland in a qualifier for the 2014 FIFA World Cup. He then became his country's most-capped player in a 1-0 victory over Kazakhstan, but he didn't score. Svensson retired from international football in 2013, aged 37, after Sweden lost to Portugal in the qualifying play-off. He made 148 appearances, and scored 21 goals.

MAGICAL MELL

Commanding centre-back **Olof Mellberg** became one of only seven players to appear at four different UEFA European Championship finals when he took part at Euro 2012 – and was the first Swede to achieve the feat. The 34-year-old also became Sweden's oldest UEFA European Championship goalscorer when he headed them into a 2-1 lead against England, ten minutes after his shot led to Glen Johnson scoring an own goal to draw the Swedes level. Unfortunately for Mellberg, and Sweden, however, England hit back to win 3-2. Mellberg's six previous goals for his country had all come in qualifying matches for either the UEFA European Championship or the FIFA World Cup.

TOP SCORERS

1	Sven Rydell	49
2	Zlatan Ibrahimovic	48
3	Gunnar Nordahl	43
4	Henrik Larsson	37
5	Gunnar Gren	32
6	Kennet Andersson	31
7	Marcus Allback	30
8	Martin Dahlin	29
9	Tomas Brolin	27
=	Agne Simonsson	27

FOUR SQUARE

In October 2012, Sweden became the first team to claw back a four-goal deficit against Germany, when they recovered from 4-0 down to finish 4-4 in a 2014 FIFA World Cup qualifier – thanks to second-half goals from Zlatan Ibrahimovic, Mikael Lustig, Johan Elmander and Rasmus Elm.

MANAGER SWAP

The most successful manager Sweden ever had was Englishman **George Raynor**, who led them to Olympic gold in London in 1948 and steered Sweden to third place and the runners-up spot in the 1950 and 1958 FIFA World Cups respectively. Raynor got one over on the country of his birth when Sweden became only the second foreign side to win at Wembley, with a 3-2 victory over England in 1959. Working in the opposite direction, in 2001 Sven-Goran Eriksson left Serie A side Lazio to become England's first foreign coach. He led the side to three consecutive quarter-finals – in the FIFA World Cups of 2002 and 2006 and, in between, the 2004 UEFA European Championship. Eriksson, however, failed to lead England to a win over his home country, recording three draws (1-1 in a 2001 friendly; 1-1 in a 2002 FIFA World Cup group game; 2-2 in a 2006 FIFA World Cup group game) and one defeat (0-1 in a 2004 friendly).

KLAS ACT

Midfielder Klas Ingesson helped Sweden finish third at the 1994 FIFA World Cup but after retiring in 2001 opted for a very different career: working as a lumberjack on his farm and 815-hectare wood. Yet he was tempted back into football, in management, and pursued that path even after being diagnosed with an incurable form of cancer in 1999. He took joint charge of IF Elfsborg in September 2013, despite being told by doctors he would have to use a wheelchair.

SWITZERLAND

Switzerland set a record in 2006 when they became the first side in FIFA World Cup finals history to depart the tournament without conceding a goal. It sums up the country's football history: despite three FIFA World Cup quarter-final appearances (in 1934, 1938 and 1954 – the latter as tournament hosts) and the second round in 2006 and 2014, Switzerland have failed to establish themselves on the international football stage. The country co-hosted the 2008 UEFA European Championship, with Austria, and is better known as being the home of both FIFA and UEFA.

CLEAN SHEET WIPE-OUT

The Swiss national team made history in 2006 by becoming the first – and to date only – team to exit the FIFA World Cup without conceding a single goal in regulation time. However, in the shoot-out defeat to Ukraine in the second round, following a goalless 120 minutes, they failed to score a single penalty and lost 3-0. Despite being beaten three times in the shoot-out, goalkeeper **Pascal Zuberbuhler**'s performances in Germany earned him a Swiss record for consecutive clean sheets at an international tournament.

DERDIYOK AT THE DOZEN

Nineteen-year-old striker **Eren Derdiyok** scored with his very first kick of the ball in international football after coming on as a substitute against England at Wembley in a February 2009 friendly. But England won 2-1. He scored three of Switzerland's goals in a thrilling 5-3 friendly victory over Germany in May 2012 – making him the first player to score a hat-trick against the Germans since England's Michael Owen almost 11 years earlier. He was playing his club football at the time for German side Hoffenheim – and all three of his goals were set up by another Bundesliga-based player, Bayer Leverkusen's Tranquillo Barnetta.

TOP SCORERS

1	Alexander Frei	42
2	Max Abegglen	34
=	Kubilay Turkyilmaz	34
4	Andre Abegglen	29
=	Jacques Fatton	29
6	Adrian Knup	26
7	Josef Hugi	23
8	Charles Antenen	22
9	Lauro Amado	21
=	Stephane Chapuisat	21

LLAMA FARMER FREI-ING HIGH

After being compared to a llama by an angry Swiss sports press for spitting at Steven Gerrard at UEFA Euro 2004, **Alexander Frei**, Switzerland's all-time top scorer, adopted a llama at Basel zoo as part of his apology to the nation. Frei appeared to abandon all hope of adding to his record Swiss goal tally of 42 in 84 games when he announced his retirement from international football in April 2011, blaming abuse from his own fans during recent matches. These included a goalless draw against minnows Malta, when both Frei and team-mate Gokhan Inler missed penalties. Frei was joined in international retirement by strike partner Marco Streller, who had scored 12 goals in 37 games.

CHAMPION CHAPPI

Stephane "Chappi" Chapuisat – the third man to make 100 appearances for Switzerland – was the first Swiss player to win a UEFA Champions League medal when he led the line for Borussia Dortmund in their 3-1 victory over Juventus in 1997. But his most significant contribution in the final was to make way for Lars Ricken, whose goal with his first touch put the game beyond Juventus. Stephane's father, Pierre-Albert Chapuisat, was also a successful Swiss international – earning 34 caps for the national side in the 1970s and 1980s – but he failed to reach the heights of Stephane, who would later add both the Club World Cup and the Swiss super league (while playing for Grasshoppers) to his winners' medal collection.

YAK ATTACK

Brothers Murat and **Hakan Yakin** were both born in the Swiss city of Basel to Turkish parents and both opted to play for the country of their birth. Midfielder Murat, almost three years older than his brother, hit four goals and won 49 caps between 1994 and 2004, while Hakan – who played slightly further forward – made his international debut in 2000 and bowed out 11 years later. Hakan scored the opening goal of Switzerland's 2008 UEFA European Championship first-round 2-1 defeat to Turkey – in rain-sodden conditions and despite the ball sticking in the mud – but declined to celebrate. He ended his international career with 20 goals from 87 appearances.

SEF ESTEEM

Switzerland not only set their 2014 FIFA World Cup campaign off to a dramatic and victorious beginning with a 2-1 triumph over Ecuador in Brasilia. They did so thanks to a strike three minutes into stoppage-time by substitute striker Haris Seferovic. This new mark for the latest winning goal recorded in the group stages of a FIFA World Cup lasted all of seven days – when Portugal equalized in the fifth minute of added time against the USA.

SHAQIRI SHAQIRI

Twenty-two-year-old **Xerdan Shaqiri** scored the 50th hat-trick in FIFA World Cup finals history during Switzerland's 3-0 triumph over Honduras in Manaus, in the first round of the 2014 tournament. The Bayern Munich playmaker was the second Swiss footballer to hit a FIFA World Cup treble, the previous one being Josef Hugi in their 7-5 defeat to Austria in the 1954 quarter-finals. Hugi remains the last Swiss scorer in the knock-out stages of a FIFA World Cup – since then they have lost 3-0 to Spain in 1994, on penalties following a second-round goalless draw with Ukraine in 2006 and 1-0 after extra time against Argentina eight years later.

TOP CAPS

1	Heinz Hermann	117
2	Alain Geiger	112
3	Stephane Chapuisat	103
4	Johann Vogel	94
5	Hakan Yakin	87
6	Alexander Frei	84
7	Patrick Muller	81
8	Severino Minelli	80
9	Andy Egli	79
=	Ciriaco Sforza	79

THE ORIGINAL BOLT

Karl Rappan did so much for Swiss football – including founding its first national football fan club – that it is often forgotten that he was Austrian. After a moderately successful career as a player and coach in Austria, Rappan achieved lasting fame as an innovative manager in Switzerland, leading the national side in the 1938 and 1954 FIFA World Cups, as well as securing league titles and cups as manager of Grasshopper Club, FC Servette and FC Zurich. He developed a flexible tactical system – which allowed players to switch positions depending on the situation and putting greater pressure on their opponents. This revolutionary new idea became known as the "Swiss bolt" and helped the unfancied hosts defeat Italy on the way to the quarter-finals of the 1954 FIFA World Cup, before losing out to Rappan's home country, Austria. An early advocate of a European league, Rappan eventually settled for the simpler knockout tournament, the Intertoto Cup, which he helped devise and launch in 1961. Rappan was, until Kobi Kuhn, Switzerland's longest-serving and statistically most successful manager, with 29 victories in 77 games in charge.

"MERCI KOBI"

Former Swiss international player and manager, **Jakob "Kobi" Kuhn**, was left close to tears as his players unfurled a "thank you" banner at the end of his final game as Swiss national manager – the 2-0 victory over Portugal in the final group game of UEFA Euro 2008. How times have changed for Kuhn: while now a much-loved elder statesmen of the Swiss game, when he was just 22 years old, he was sent home from the 1966 FIFA World Cup for missing a curfew. He was then banned from the national side for a year.

The shoe was on the other foot when Kuhn had to send Alexander Frei home from UEFA Euro 2004 after the centre-forward spat at England's Steven Gerrard. Kuhn spent most of his playing career, where he was described as playing "with honey in his boots", with FC Zurich, winning six league titles and five Swiss Cups. He played 63 times for the national side, scoring five goals. He then worked his way up through the ranks of the Swiss national team, leading first the Under-18s, then the Under-21s and finally the senior national team. He retired, aged 64, with a record of 32 victories, 18 draws and 23 defeats in 73 matches as Swiss coach.

TURKEY

Galatasaray's penalty shoot-out success over Arsenal in the 2000 UEFA Cup final signalled a change in fortune for Turkish football. Prior to that night in Copenhagen, Turkey had qualified for the FIFA World Cup only twice (in 1950, when they withdrew, and 1954), and had consistently underachieved on the world stage. Since 2000, however, Turkish fans have had plenty to cheer about, including a third-place finish at the 2002 FIFA World Cup, and a semi-final appearance at the 2008 UEFA European Championship.

GUESS WHO'S BACK?

Rustu Recber doesn't know the meaning of the word "quit". Less than a year after retiring from international football after UEFA Euro 2008, Turkey's most-capped player came out of retirement to join the national team once more in the qualifying campaign for the 2010 FIFA World Cup in South Africa. This was not his first international comeback – for UEFA Euro 2008, Rustu had been relegated to the bench, but played in the quarter-final against Croatia after first-choice keeper Volkan Demirel was sent off in the final group game. Rustu was the hero of the penalty shoot-out, saving from Mladen Petric to send Turkey through to their first-ever UEFA European Championship semi-final, in which they lost to Germany. Back in 1993, Rustu came back from an even more devastating set-back after he was seriously injured in a car crash that resulted in the death of a friend. The accident also scuppered a potential move to Besiktas, although he went on to star for Fenerbahce, winning five Turkish league titles in 12 years with them. With his distinctive pony-tail and charcoal-black war paint, Rustu has always stood out, but perhaps never more so than as a star performer in Turkey's third-place performance at the 2002 FIFA World Cup finals. He was elected into the Team of the Tournament and was named FIFA's Goalkeeper of the Year.

SPOREL SPORTS

Zeki Riza Sporel scored Turkey's first goal in international football, against Romania on 26 October 1923. He actually hit a brace that day in a 2-2 draw, the first of 16 games for Turkey in which he hit 15 goals. Turkey's captain for their first international was his older brother Hasan Kamil Sporel.

OLD GOLD

The last FIFA World Cup "golden goal" was scored by Turkey substitute **Ilhan Mansiz**, in the 94th minute of their 2002 quarter-final against Senegal – giving his side a 1-0 win on their way to finishing third overall. The "golden goal" rule was abandoned ahead of the 2006 FIFA World Cup, which went back to two guaranteed 15-minute periods of extra-time if a knockout fixture ended level after 90 minutes.

QUICK OFF THE MARK

Hakan Sukur scored the fastest-ever FIFA World Cup finals goal – taking only 11 seconds to score Turkey's first goal in their third-place play-off match against South Korea at the 2002 FIFA World Cup. Turkey went on to win the game 3-2 to claim third place, their finest-ever performance in the competition. His total of 51 goals (in 112 games) is more than double his nearest competitor in the national team ranking. His first goal came in only his second appearance, as Turkey beat Denmark 2-1 on 8 April 1992. He went on to score four goals in a single game twice – in the 6-4 win over Wales on 20 August 1997 and in the 5-0 crushing of Moldova on 11 October 2006.

TWIN TURKS

Hamit Altintop (right) was born 10 minutes before identical twin brother **Halil** (left) – and he has been just about leading the way throughout their parallel professional footballing careers since their birth in the city of Gelsenkirchen, Germany, on 8 December 1982. Both began playing for German amateur side Wattenscheid, before defender-cum-midfielder Hamit signed for FC Schalke 04 in the summer of 2006 and striker Halil followed suit shortly afterwards. Hamit would stay just a season there, though, before being bought by Bayern Munich. Both helped Turkey reach the semi-finals of the 2008 UEFA European Championship – losing to adopted homeland Germany – though only Hamit was voted among UEFA's 23 best players of the tournament.

TAKE FAT

Having coached Galatasaray to their UEFA Cup triumph in 2000, **Fatih Terim** led Turkey in their amazing run to the 2008 UEFA European Championship semi-finals. Defeat to Portugal in the opening game left the Turks with an uphill task, but stunning successive comebacks against Switzerland and the Czech Republic took them through to the quarter-finals. A 119th-minute goal seemed to have clinched the tie for Croatia, but, as the Croatian players celebrated, "Emperor" Fatih urged his players to get up, pick the ball out of the net and fight on to the very end. They did just that, and Semih Senturk's improbable equalizer took the match to penalties. The semi-final against Germany provided yet another rollercoaster ride, but this time there was no answer to the Germans' last-minute winner. When Fatih said "there is something special about this team" few could disagree. Terim followed this up with a third spell managing Galatasaray, before returning to international duty in August 2013 for a third stint in charge of Turkey. He won eight games and lost one before stepping aside to become the national team director. His tally as Turkey coach totalled 101 matches, comprising 51 wins, 26 draws and 24 defeats.

TOP SCORERS

1	Hakan Sukur	51
2	Tuncay Sanli	22
3	Lefter Kucukandonyadis	21
4	Nihat Kahveci	19
=	Metin Oktay	19
=	Cemil Turan	19
7	Zeki Riza Sporel	15
8	Arda Turan	14
9	Burak Yilmaz	13
10	Arif Erdem	11
=	Ertugrul Saglam	11

TOP CAPS

1	Rustu Recber	120
2	Hakan Sukur	112
3	Bulent Korkmaz	102
4	Tugay Kerimoglu	94
5	Emre Belozoglu	91
6	Alpay Ozalan	90
7	Hamit Altintop	80
=	Tuncay Sanli	80
9	Ogun Temizkanoglu	76
10	Arda Turan	72

500 MILESTONE

Turkey played their 500th match in international football on 14 November 2012, a friendly that ended in a 1-1 draw against Denmark. The game, played at Istanbul's Turk Telekom Arena, was preceded by pop star Hadise's performance and appearances by Turkish football legends. Turkey's first international match was also a draw in Istanbul: 2-2 against Romania on 26 October 1923.

WORK HARD, PLAY ARDA

Wing wizard **Arda Turan** has survived cardiac arrhythmia, swine flu and a car crash to emerge as one of Turkish football's leading lights. His international achievements include key goals at t he 2008 UEFA European Championship, the first a stoppage-time winner against Switzerland, then Turkey's late opener when overturning a two-goal deficit against the Czech Republic in a first-round qualification decider. After leaving boyhood club Galatasaray for Spain's Atletico Madrid in 2011, he has helped the club to glory in the UEFA Europa League and UEFA Super Cup in 2013 and La Liga in 2014, as well as the 2013–14 UEFA Champions League final, though he missed that match through injury. He mixes in prestigious circles – guests at his June 2013 wedding to TV presenter Sinem Kobal included Turkish prime minister Recep Tayyip Erdogan.

UKRAINE

Ukraine has been a stronghold of football in eastern Europe for many years. A steady flow of talent from Ukrainian clubs with a rich European pedigree, such as Dynamo Kiev, provided the Soviet national team with many standout players in the years before independence. Since separating from the Soviet Union in 1991, Ukraine has become a football force in its own right, qualifying for the FIFA World Cup for the first time in 2006, reaching the quarter-finals.

DEVASTATING DEVIC

Ukraine enjoyed their biggest win on 6 September 2013 thrashing San Marino 9-0 in a FIFA World Cup qualifier – then rubbed salt into the wounds by winning 8-0 away to the same opposition the following month, on 25 October 2013. There were eight different scorers in the first game, with the opening goal struck by striker Marko Devic – and he then went on to hit a hat-trick in the rematch. Devic was actually born in Belgrade and brought up in Serbia but transferred to Ukrainian club Volyn Lutsk in 2005 and switched nationalities three years later.

ROCKET MAN

Andriy Shevchenko beat team-mate **Anatoliy Tymoshchuk** to become the first Ukrainian footballer to reach a century of international appearances, but the defensive midfielder later overtook the striker to become the country's most-capped player with 132 appearances. He also enjoyed the rare honour of seeing his name in space, when Ukrainian cosmonaut Yuri Malenchenko launched into orbit wearing a Zenit St Petersburg shirt with "Tymoshchuk" on the back in 2007. After leaving Zenit in 2009 for Bayern Munich, he won the 2013 UEFA Champions League with the German club before announcing his return to his previous St Petersburg side.

HARD START

With the newly independent Ukraine unable to register with FIFA in time for the qualifying rounds for the 1994 FIFA World Cup, many of their stars opted to play for Russia and went to the finals in the United States representing that country. Andrei Kanchelskis, Viktor Onopko, Sergei Yuran and Oleg Salenko could all have played for the new Ukraine side, but decided not to. Ukraine then failed to qualify for an international tournament until the **2006 FIFA World Cup** in Germany, where they lost 3-0 in the quarter-finals to eventual winners Italy.

YURI-KA MOMENT

Denys Harmash and Dmytro Korkishko scored the goals against England that gave Ukraine their first major international footballing title, in the final of the 2009 UEFA Under-19 European Championship. The coach was Yuri Kalitvintsev, later assistant to Oleg Blokhin with the senior international side.

SUPER SHEVA

In 2004, **Andriy Shevchenko** became the third Ukrainian to win the Ballon D'Or. The first to do so, in 1975, was his 2006 FIFA World Cup coach Oleg Blokhin (second was Igor Belanov in 1986), but he was the first to win the award since Ukraine's independence from the Soviet Union. Born on 29 September 1976, Shevchenko was a promising boxer as a youngster, before deciding to focus on football full-time. He has won trophies at every club he's played for, including five titles in a row with Dynamo Kiev, the Serie A and the Champions League with AC Milan, and even two cups in his "disappointing" time at Chelsea. Shevchenko is Ukraine's second most-capped player and leading goalscorer, with 48 goals in 111 games. This includes two at the 2006 FIFA World Cup, where he captained his country in their first-ever major finals appearance, and a double to secure a 2-1 comeback win over Sweden in Ukraine's first match co-hosting the 2012 UEFA European Championship.

LEADING FROM THE FRONT

Oleg Blokhin, Ukraine's coach on their first appearance at a major tournament finals, made his name as a star striker with his hometown club Dynamo Kiev. Born on 5 November 1952, when Ukraine was part of the Soviet Union, Blokhin scored a record 211 goals in another record 432 appearances in the USSR national league. He also holds the goals and caps records for the USSR, with 42 in 112 games. He led Kiev to two victory in the European Cup-Winners' Cup in 1975 and 1986, scoring in both finals, and was named the 1975 European Footballer of the Year. Always an over-achiever, Blokhin managed Ukraine to the finals of the 2006 FIFA World Cup in Germany, where they lost out to eventual winners Italy 3-0 in the quarter-finals after knocking out Switzerland in the second round – also on penalties. Blokhin was renowned for his speed – when Olympic gold medallist Valeriy Borzov trained the Kiev squad in the 1970s, Blokhin recorded a 100 metres time of 11 seconds, just 0.46 seconds slower than Borzov's own 1972 medal-winning run. Blokhin quit as Ukraine manager in December 2007, but returned to the job in April 2011. Ukraine's manager since December 2012 has been former USSR international defender Mykhaylo Fomenko, whose 24 caps for the ex-Soviet Union included reaching the final of the 1972 UEFA European Championship and winning bronze at the Montreal 1976 Olympic Games.

REBROV REBORN

Serhiy Rebrov, who retired in 2009, was Andriy Shevchenko's dynamic strike partner for both club and country. The forward pair starred for Dynamo Kiev in the late 1990s before making big-money moves across Europe. Like Shevchenko at Chelsea, Rebrov struggled in London, first at Tottenham Hotspur and then at West Ham United. But after returning to Ukraine in 2005, he earned a late-career recall to the international team – and scored a memorable long-range strike against Saudi Arabia at the 2006 FIFA World Cup. Having dropped back into midfield, he then crossed the border and helped outsiders Rubin Kazan win their first Russian league title in 2008. But Rebrov, a keen amateur radio "ham", remains the Ukrainian Premier League's all-time leading scorer, with 125 goals in 268 games.

TOP SCORERS

1	Andriy Shevchenko	48
2	Serhiy Rebrov	15
=	Andriy Yarmolenko	15
4	Oleh Husyev	13
5	Serhiy Nazarenko	12
6	Andriy Husin	9
=	Yevhen Seleznyov	9
=	Andriy Vorobey	9
9	Tymerlan Huseynov	8
=	Yevhen Konoplyanka	8
=	Artem Milevskiy	8
=	Andriy Voronin	8

PY IN THE SKY

Goalkeeper **Andriy Pyatov** set a national record by going 752 minutes without conceding a goal for his country, between March 2013 and November 2013. The previous best had been Oleksandr Shovkovskiy's 728 minutes. Pyatov's resistance was finally ended by Mamadou Sakho's opener in a 3-0 play-off defeat that took France instead of Ukraine to the 2014 FIFA World Cup.

TOP CAPS

1	Anatoliy Tymoshchuk	132
2	Andriy Shevchenko	111
3	Oleksandr Shovkovskiy	92
4	Oleh Husyev	91
5	Serhiy Rebrov	75
6	Ruslan Rotan	74
=	Andriy Voronin	74
7	Andriy Husin	71
=	Andriy Vorobey	68
10	Andriy Nesmachniy	67

⚽ WALES

In a land where rugby union remains the national obsession, Wales have struggled to impose themselves on the world of international football. Despite having produced a number of hugely talented players, Wales have only ever played once in the finals of a major tournament – at the 1958 FIFA World Cup finals in Sweden.

GOOD ON RAMSEY

Arsenal midfielder **Aaron Ramsey** became Wales's youngest captain when appointed to the role in March 2011 by new manager Gary Speed. Ramsey was 20 years 90 days old when he led the side out for the first time at Cardiff's Millennium Stadium in a 2012 UEFA European Championship qualifier that ended in a 2-0 win for England. The record had previously been held by centre-back Mike England, who was 22 years 135 days old when skipper against Northern Ireland in April 1964. Ramsey had not long returned to full fitness after a potentially career-threatening broken leg suffered while playing for Arsenal against Stoke City in February 2010.

WHERE'S OUR GOLDEN BOY?

One of the most skilful and successful players never to appear at the FIFA World Cup, **Ryan Giggs** somehow missed 18 consecutive friendlies for Wales. He made his Manchester United debut in 1990 and appeared in his 1,000th competitive match in a 2-1 UEFA Champions League defeat to Real Madrid. His tally by then included 932 club matches, 64 for Wales and four for Great Britain at the London 2012 Summer Olympics. Giggs finally hung up his boots aged 40 at the end of the 2013–14 season, the last four games of which he had spent as Manchester United's caretaker-manager following the dismissal of David Moyes. He made the announcement as the club revealed he would now be assistant-manager to new boss Louis Van Gaal.

BRICKS TO BRILLIANCE

Goalkeeper **Neville Southall** made the first of his record 92 appearances for Wales in a 3-2 win over Northern Ireland on 27 May 1982. The former hod-carrier and bin man kept 34 clean sheets in 15 years playing for Wales and won the English Football Writers' Player of the Year in 1985 thanks to his performances alongside Welsh captain Kevin Ratcliffe at Everton. In his final match for Wales, on 20 August 1997, he was substituted halfway through a 6-4 defeat against Turkey in Istanbul.

RUSH FOR GOAL

Ian Rush is Wales's leading goalscorer, with 28 goals in 73 games. His first came in a 3-0 win over Northern Ireland on 27 May 1982; he scored the 28th and final goal in a 2-1 win over Estonia in Tallinn in 1994.

CAUGHT ON CAMERA

Pioneer movie-makers Sagar Mitchell and James Kenyon captured Wales playing Ireland in March 1906, making it the first filmed international football match.

TOP CAPS

1	Neville Southall	92
2	Gary Speed	85
3	Craig Bellamy	78
4	Dean Saunders	75
5	Peter Nicholas	73
=	Ian Rush	73
7	Mark Hughes	72
=	Joey Jones	72
9	Ivor Allchurch	68
10	Brian Flynn	66

TOP SCORERS

1	Ian Rush	28
2	Ivor Allchurch	23
=	Trevor Ford	23
4	Dean Saunders	22
5	Craig Bellamy	19
6	Robert Earnshaw	16
=	Mark Hughes	16
=	Cliff Jones	16
9	John Charles	15
10	John Hartson	14

KEEPING UP WITH THE JONESES

Cliff Jones, left-winger for Wales at the 1958 FIFA World Cup and for Tottenham Hotspur's league and cup "Double" winners in 1961, was part of a Welsh footballing dynasty. His father Ivor Jones had previously played for Wales, as did Ivor's brother Bryn. Cliff's cousin Ken, a goalkeeper, was another member of the 1958 FIFA World Cup squad, but never actually played for his country.

ALL HAIL BALE

Wales' long wait to return to a major international tournament stretches on yet they can now boast one of the world's authentic football superstars – and the most expensive player of all-time. Blessed with dramatic bursts of acceleration and piledriving long-range shooting, wing wizard **Gareth Bale** cost Real Madrid £86million to buy from England's Tottenham Hotspur in August 2013. Yet even that extravagant sum looked like money well-spent when he scored the crucial extra-time goal that put Real Madrid ahead in the 2014 UEFA Champions League final against rivals Atletico Madrid. Real went on to win the match in Lisbon 4-1. Bale had previously scored a stunning solo winner in that season's Spanish Cup final against Barcelona. He had begun his career at Southampton as a left-back, then blossomed as a dynamic left-winger at Spurs before flourishing as an all-round forward. He was named English football's player of the year in 2011 and 2013 – voted so by both the Premier League's footballers and the nation's journalists – thanks to dazzling performances and strikes for both Spurs and Wales. Despite being eligible to play for England through one grandmother, the Cardiff-born patriot became Wales' youngest international when making his debut against Trinidad and Tobago in May 2006, aged 16 years and 315 days.

HAT-TRICK HERO

Welsh striker Robert Earnshaw holds the remarkable record of having scored hat-tricks in all four divisions of English football, the FA Cup, the League Cup, as well as scoring three for the national team against Scotland on 18 February 2004.

SHOCK LOSS OF A MODEL PROFESSIONAL

Welsh and world football were united in shock and grief at the sudden death of Wales manager **Gary Speed** in November 2011. Former Leeds United, Everton, Newcastle United and Bolton Wanderers midfielder Speed, the country's most-capped outfield player, was found at his home in Cheshire, England. The 42-year-old had been manager for 11 months, overseeing a series of encouraging performances that saw a rise in the world rankings from 116th to 48th and a prize for FIFA's "Best Movers" of 2011. An official memorial game was played in Cardiff in February 2012 between Wales and Costa Rica – the country against whom he had made his international debut in May 1990. Among the tributes paid to Speed was one from FIFA president Sepp Blatter, who called him "a model professional and a fantastic ambassador for the game". Former Wales centre-back Chris Coleman was appointed as Speed's successor.

OTHER TEAMS EUROPE

For the major European football powers, a qualifying campaign for one of the game's major international tournaments would not be the same without an awkward trip to one of the former Eastern Bloc countries or the chance of a goal-fest against the likes of San Marino or Luxembourg. For these countries' players, the thrill of representing their nation is more important than harbouring dreams of world domination.

SELVA SERVICE

San Marino, with a population of under 30,000, is the smallest country to be a member of UEFA. Striker **Andy Selva** is not only San Marino's top scorer with eight goals and for a long time was the country's only player to score twice – until midfielder Manuel Marani followed up his February 2007 goal against the Republic of Ireland with another, against Malta, in August 2012.

MOSQUITO STINGS

Malta ended a 20-year wait for an away win in a competitive international when they shocked Armenia 1-0 in a 2014 FIFA World Cup qualifier in June 2013. Appropriately enough, the decisive strike came from veteran forward **Michael Mifsud** – his country's captain and all-time leading scorer, who made his international debut in February 2000 and made his name in Germany with Kaiserslautern and in England with Coventry City. Nicknamed "Mosquito", the 1.65m-tall player's international exploits include five goals in the 7-1 trouncing of Liechtenstein in March 2008 – including a hat-trick within the first 21 minutes. Before Armenia, the last time Malta won a FIFA World Cup or UEFA European Championship away qualifier had been a 1-0 success in Estonia in May 1993.

UNDERDOGS HAVE THEIR DAY

Slovenia were the only unseeded team to win a UEFA qualifying play-off for the 2010 FIFA World Cup, beating Russia on away goals. Slovenia lost 2-1 in Moscow, thanks to substitute Nejc Pecnik's crucial away goal late in the first leg and Ztlatko Dedic scored the only goal in Maribor to give Slovenia victory. With a population of two million and just 429 registered professional players, Slovenia was the smallest nation in the finals.

LIT'S A KNOCK-OUT

Perhaps it's not be too surprising that **Jari Litmanen** should have become a football star – both his parents played for the Lahti-based club Reipas while Litmanen's father Olavi also won five caps for the national team. But Jari's skills and achievements far outstripped them both – and, arguably, any other player the country has produced. It was fitting that Litmanen became the first Finnish player to get his hands on the UEFA European Cup – or Champions League trophy – when his Ajax Amsterdam side beat AC Milan in 1995. Litmanen had left Finland at the age of 21 to make his name and mark with the legendary Dutch club Ajax, inheriting the great Dennis Bergkamp's support-striker role – and number 10 shirt. Litmanen scored in the 1996 UEFA Champions League final, though Ajax lost on penalties to Juventus. He remains the Dutch club's record scorer in European competition, with 24 goals in 44 games. Litmanen joined Barcelona in 1999 and then Liverpool two years later, though his time in England was hampered by a wrist injury he suffered on international duty and he returned to Ajax in 2002. Despite a series of injuries, he remained dedicated to his country, captaining the side between 1996 and 2008, and was still playing and scoring in 2010, aged 39 – having recorded more international goals and games than any other Finn, scoring 32 times in 137 appearances.

GIVING IT UP

Lithuania and Estonia did not bother playing their final group game against each other in the 1934 FIFA World Cup qualifying competition. Sweden had already guaranteed themselves top spot, and the sole finals place available, by beating Lithuania 2-0 and Estonia 6-2.

BEYOND THE IRON CURTAIN

The break-up of the Soviet Union in 1990 led to 15 new footballing nations, though initially Russia played on at the 1992 UEFA European Championship as CIS, or the Commonwealth of Independent States – without the involvement of Estonia, Latvia and Lithuania. In the coming years, UEFA and FIFA approved the creation of separate teams for Russia, Armenia, Azerbaijan, Belarus, Estonia, Georgia, Kazakhstan, Kyrgyzstan, Latvia, Lithuania, Moldova, Tajikstan, Turkmenistan, Ukraine and Uzbekistan. Upheavals in the early 1990s would also fragment the former Yugoslavia into Croatia, Serbia, Bosnia-Herzegovina, Macedonia, Slovenia and Montenegro, while Czechoslovakia split into Slovakia and the Czech Republic.

YEAR AFFILIATED TO FIFA

Albania	1932
Andorra	1996
Austria	1905
Belarus	1992
Bosnia-Herzegovina	1996
Cyprus	1948
Estonia	1923
Faroe Islands	1988
Finland	1908
Georgia	1992
Greece	1927
Iceland	1947
Israel	1929
Kazakhstan	1994
Latvia	1922
Liechtenstein	1974
Luxembourg	1910
Macedonia	1994
Malta	1959
Moldova	1994
Montenegro	2007
San Marino	1988
Slovenia	1992

REBORN BOURG

A long and painful wait finally ended for traditional whipping-boys Luxembourg when they beat Northern Ireland 3-2 in September 2013. It was the "Red Lions" first home win in a FIFA World Cup qualifier for 41 years, since overcoming Turkey 2-0 in October 1972. It was also five years to the day since their last FIFA World Cup qualifying victory, a 2-1 triumph in Switzerland in 2008. Luxembourg's goals came from Aurelien Joachim, Stefano Bensi and **Mathias Janisch**. The winning goal, with three minutes remaining, was the first of Janisch's international career.

THE FULL MONTY AND THE FULL MONTY

Estonia may have lost their June 2012 friendly against France 4-0, despite the presence of all-time top scorer **Andres Oper**, but they did make history that night, becoming the first country to play all 52 fellow UEFA nations. The 52nd addition to the UEFA family was Montenegro, who became a FIFA member in 2007, a year after competing as part of Serbia and Montenegro in the 2006 FIFA World Cup. Both Estonia and Montenegro came close to a major tournament in their own right by reaching the play-offs for the 2012 UEFA European Championship, but lote over two legs to the Republic of Ireland and the Czech Republic respectively. In 2013 Gibraltar became the 54th member of UEFA.

TRAVELLING MEN

Israel looked like qualifying for the 1958 FIFA World Cup without kicking a ball, because scheduled opponents Turkey, Indonesia and Sudan refused to play them. But FIFA ordered them into a two-legged play-off against a European side – which Israel lost 4-0 on aggregate to Wales. Israel were unfortunate again in the 2006 FIFA World Cup qualifiers, ending the campaign unbeaten – yet failing even to make the play-offs, finishing third in their group behind France and Switzerland. Coach Avram Grant later went on to manage Chelsea, losing the 2008 UEFA Champions League final on penalties to Manchester United. Israel hosted, and won, the 1964 Asian Nations Cup, and qualified for the 1970 FIFA World Cup through a combined Asia/Oceania qualifying competition, but are now members of the European Federation.

HIT AND SWISS

When defender Elsad Zverotic made his 44th appearance, he passed Simon Vukcevic to become Montenegro's most-capped international. He was born in Behane, in what is now Serbia, but played for Switzerland U-18s, where he also played his club football from 2004. Zverotic moved to English Premier League Fulham in 2013.

AD ENOUGH

Temuri Ketsbaia scored 16 times for Georgia, more than anyone other than 26-goal Shota Arveladze, and was also the first coach to lead a Cypriot side – Anorthosis Famagusta – into the UEFA Champions League before taking over as Georgia's national coach in 2009. Yet to many fans – those in England especially – he might be best remembered for his bizarre celebration after scoring a last-minute winner for Newcastle United against Bolton Wanderers in January 1998, when instead of looking pleased he flung off his shirt and furiously kicked out at pitchside advertising hoardings. After receiving the ball when the game kicked off again, he instantly booted it high into the crowd.

MORE SIND AGAINST

Austria's star player **Matthias Sindelar** refused to play for a new, merged national team when Germany annexed Austria in 1938. Sindelar, born in modern-day Czech Republic in February 1903, was the inspirational leader of Austria's so-called Wunderteam of the 1930s. He scored 27 goals in 43 games for Austria, who went 14 internationals unbeaten between April 1931 and December 1932, won the 1932 Central European International Cup and silver at the 1936 Olympics. During a special reunification match between the Austrian and German teams in Vienna in April 1938, Sindelar disobeyed orders and scored a spectacular solo goal. Austria went on to win 2-0 in a game which might have been expected to end in a diplomatic draw. Sindelar was mysteriously found dead from carbon monoxide poisoning in his Vienna apartment in January 1939.

YURA STAR

Armenia equalled their biggest ever win with a 4-0 triumph away to Denmark in FIFA World Cup qualifying in June 2013. **Yura Movsisyan** opened the scoring after only 24 seconds, later added another goal and was applauded off even by the home fans when substituted with seven minutes remaining. The Spartak Moscow forward used to play club football in Denmark, for Randers. He had begun his football career in the USA, having moved there as a child with his Armenian family after being born in the capital of Azerbaijan, Baku. Armenia's unexpected and emphatic victory over the Danes came just four days after an embarrassing 1-0 defeat to Malta, only their opponents' fifth ever victory in a competitive match.

THE GUD SON

Iceland striker **Eidur Gudjohnsen** made history on his international debut away to Estonia in April 1996, by coming on as a substitute for his own father, Arnor Gudjohnsen. Eidur was 17 at the time, his father 34 – though both were disappointed they did not get to play on the pitch at the same time. The Icelandic Football Association thought they would get a chance to do so in Iceland's next home game, but Eidur was ruled out by an ankle injury and the opportunity never arose again.

REIM AND REASONING

Before being overtaken by Latvia's Vitalijs Astafjevs, the European record for most international appearances was held by another Baltic veteran – Estonian holding midfielder Martin Reim scored 14 goals in 157 games for his country between June 1992 and June 2009. Yet he could even have closed in on an unprecedented double-century of international appearances, had he not missed 40 games following a dispute with Latvia's Dutch manager Jelle Goes between 2004 and 2007. He retired from international football after matching the 150-cap record of Germany's Lothar Matthaus in February 2007, but was persuaded to return by new national boss Viggo Jensen. His 157th and final match, a testimonial played in his honour, came against Equatorial Guinea on 6 June 2009, a day that was also said to mark the centenary of football in Estonia.

VITAL VITALIJS

Midfielder Vitalijs Astafjevs put Latvia on the map when he became the most-capped European footballer of all time, with 167 appearances for his country – including three at the 2004 UEFA European Championship. He also scored 16 goals for Latvia. Astafjevs made his international debut in 1992, the year the Latvian football team was revived after independence following the break-up of the Soviet Union. He was still playing for his country at the age of 38 in November 2009, when his appearance in a friendly against Honduras saw him to overtake Estonian Martin Reim's record for most European caps.

MOST INTERNATIONAL APPEARANCES

Albania	Altin Lala	79
Andorra	Oscar Sonejee	97
Austria	Andreas Herzog	103
Belarus	Alyaksandr Kulchy	102
Bosnia-Herz.	Zvejzdan Misimovic	83
Cyprus	Ioannis Okkas	106
Estonia	Martin Reim	157
Faroe Islands	Oli Johannesen	83
Finland	Jari Litmanen	137
Georgia	Levan Kobiashvili	100
Iceland	Runar Kristinsson	104
Israel	Yossi Benayoun	96
Kazakhstan	Ruslan Baltiev	73
Latvia	Vitalijs Astafjevs	167
Liechtenstein	Mario Frick	113
	Martin Stocklasa	113
Lithuania	Andrius Skerla	84
Luxembourg	Jeff Strasser	98
Macedonia	Goce Sedloski	100
Malta	David Carabott	121
Moldova	Radu Rabeja	74
Montenegro	Elsad Zverotic	47
San Marino	Damiano Vannucci	68
Slovenia	Zlatko Zahovic	80

ED BOY

Edin Dzeko became Bosnia-Herzegovina's all-time leading scorer with a second-half hat-trick in an 8-1 2014 FIFA World Cup qualifier victory over Liechtenstein in September 2012. The goals not only took him past previous record-holder Elvir Bolic, but also ahead of Dzeko's international team-mate Zvejdan Misimovic whose brace earlier in the game had briefly put him in the lead. Midfielder Misimovic drew level again with Dzeko in the following game, scoring twice in a 4-1 win, before Dzeko's last-minute strike put him ahead again. Not bad for a forward sold by Bosnian club Zeljeznicar to the Czech Republic's FK Teplice for a cut-price €25,000 in 2005 – six years before English club Manchester City handed over €32million to sign him from Germany's VfL Wolfsburg. Dzeko's off-field activities include a role as a UNICEF ambassador – and he donated almost €25,000 in 2012 towards the care of a 17-year-old Bosnian boy fighting bone marrow disease.

SUPER PAN

Macedonia celebrated 100 years of football in the country with a friendly against world champions Spain in August 2009 – and star striker **Goran Pandev** marked the occasion by becoming his country's all-time leading scorer. His first-half brace gave the hosts a 2-0 lead and although Spain came back to win 3-2, he replaced 16-goal Gorgi Hristov at the top of Macedonia's scoring charts. Pandev has played the majority of his club career in Italy, after signing for Internazionale from local team FK Belasica as an 18-year-old in 2001. Pandev helped Inter win a treble of the UEFA Champions League, Serie A and the Coppa Italia in 2009–10, before scoring in their 2010 FIFA Club World Cup victory. Now with Napoli, he also played for Ancona and Lazio.

LAT'S ENTERTAINMENT

The 1938 FIFA World Cup went ahead with 15 instead of 16 teams after qualifiers Austria found themselves annexed by Germany – to the frustration of Latvia, who had finished runners-up in the Austrians' qualification group. Latvia was subsumed by the Soviet Union between 1940 and 1991, but qualified for their first major finals by beating Turkey in a play-off to reach the 2004 UEFA European Championship. Their team at that tournament featured all-time leading scorer Maris Verpakovskis, still playing for Latvia in 2013, and their most-capped player Vitalijs Astafjevs.

BASKET CASE

Captain **Rashad Sadygov** not only secured Azerbaijan's biggest win in their history when he scored the only goal against Turkey in a UEFA Euro 2012 qualifier in October 2010 – he was also delivering a blow against the country in which he was making his living. Having previously played for Turkish top-flight side Kayserispor, he had since moved on to rivals Eskisehirspor. Not every transfer has worked out well for Sadygov: he missed the transfer deadline when signing for Azeri side PFC Neftchi in 2006, so he decided to play basketball for a season to keep himself fit until allowed to resume football.

MOST INTERNATIONAL GOALS

Albania	Erjon Bogdani	18
Andorra	Ildefons Lima	7
Austria	Toni Polster	44
Belarus	Maksim Romashenko	20
Bosnia-Herz.	Edin Dzeko	36
Cyprus	Michalis Konstantinou	32
Estonia	Andres Oper	38
Faroe Islands	Rogvi Jacobsen	10
Finland	Jari Litmanen	32
Georgia	Shota Arveladze	26
Iceland	Eidur Gudjohnsen	24
Israel	Mordechai Spiegler	33
Kazakhstan	Ruslan Baltiev	13
Latvia	Maris Verpakovskis	29
Liechtenstein	Mario Frick	16
Lithuania	Tomas Danilevicius	19
Luxembourg	Leon Mart	16
Macedonia	Goran Pandev	26
Malta	Michael Mifsud	39
Moldova	Serghei Clescenco	11
Montenegro	Mirko Vucinic	15
San Marino	Andy Selva	8
Slovenia	Zlatko Zahovic	35

TU-WHIT TWO-NIL

Finland's adopted lucky mascot is an eagle owl called "Bubi" that occasionally swoops down on the Helsinki Olympic Stadium during international matches – making his debut during a 2-0 UEFA European Championship qualifier win over Belgium in June 2007 and holding up the game for several minutes as he flew about the pitch and perched on goalposts. The eagle owl was later voted the Finnish capital's "Resident of the Year".

HIGH LIFE

At 64°09'N, Reykjavik, in Iceland, is the northernmost city to host a FIFA World Cup match – though so far only in qualifiers. The northernmost FIFA World Cup finals venue is Sandviken in Sweden, at 60°37'N – while Christchurch in New Zealand (43°32'S) holds the record for southernmost FIFA World Cup venue, with the finals record held by Mar del Plata in Argentina (38°01'S). Iceland's 9,800-seater national stadium, the Laugardalsvollur, was opened in 1958 and then renovated 39 years later.

BOHEMIAN RHAPSODY

Striker **Josef "Pepi" Bican** is, for many Austrian fans, the most prolific goalscorer of all time. Some authorities put his total tally in officially recognized matches at 805 goals, higher in the rankings than Romario, Pele and Gerd Muller. Bican played for Austrian clubs Rapid Vienna and Admira in the 1930s, but the bulk of his strikes came for Czech-based Slavia Prague between 1937 and 1948. He also scored 19 goals in 19 games for Austria from 1933 to 1936, before switching citizenship and hitting 21 in 14 matches for Czechoslovakia between 1938 and 1949. Although he reached the semi-finals of the 1934 FIFA World Cup with Austria, an administrative error meant he was not registered with his new country in time for the 1938 tournament. He also played one international match for a representative Bohemia and Moravia side in 1939, scoring a hat-trick.

LIVING HAND TO FOOT

The part-time international footballers of the Faroe Islands have a motley collection of day jobs – and other sporting achievements. Bobble hat-wearing goalkeeper **Jens Martin Knudsen,** man of the match in their shock 1-0 win over Austria in 1989, made his living as a forklift truck driver – while also winning a national gymnastics title and playing handball. Team-mates who have also played both football and handball include journalist/musician Uni Arge, the Faroes' fourth-top-scorer, and third-placed John Petersen.

POWER GAME

Albert Gudmundsson was Iceland's first professional footballer. He enjoyed a distinguished career in the 1940s and 1950s, including spells with Rangers in Scotland, Arsenal in England and AC Milan in Italy. After retiring from football, he entered politics and ran – unsuccessfully – for president in 1980 before being appointed minister for finance in 1983 and minister for industry two years later. His son Ingi Bjorn Albertsson played as a striker for Iceland in the 1970s then joined his father as a member of parliament in 1987.

A SEQUEL TO HAMLET

Striker Hamlet Mkhitaryan played twice for post-Soviet state Armenia in 1994, though died two years later from a brain tumour at the age of just 33. His son Henrikh, seven when his father died, has gone on to become the country's all-time leading scorer – and one who often dedicates his achievements to his late parent. The younger Mkhitaryan became Armenia's joint top scorer, alongside Artur Petrosyan, with a goal against Denmark in June 2013. While Petrosyan's goals came in 69 games, Mkhitaryan's 11 were scored in 39 – and he pulled away on his own, with a 12th international strike, in a 2-2 draw with Italy in October 2012. **Henrikh Mkhitaryan** made his Armenia debut in 2007, and his international career overlapped with an unrelated player also named Hamlet Mkhitaryan – a midfielder who won 56 caps between 1994 and 2008.

RECORD WINS

Albania	5-0	v	Vietnam (A, December 2003);
	6-1	v	Cyprus (H, August 2009)
Andorra	2-0	v	Belarus (H, April 2000);
	2-0	v	Albania (H, April 2002)
Austria	9-0	v	Malta (H, April 1977)
Belarus	5-0	v	Lithuania (H, June 1998)
Bosnia-Herzegovina	7-0	v	Estonia (H, September 2008)
Cyprus	5-0	v	Andorra (H, November 2000)
Estonia	6-0	v	Lithuana (H, July 1928)
Faroe Islands	3-0	v	San Marino (H, May 1995)
	4-1	v	Gibraltar (A, March 2014)
Finland	10-2	v	Estonia (H, August 1922)
Georgia	7-0	v	Armenia (H, March 1997)
Iceland	9-0	v	Faroe Islands (H, July 1985)
Israel	9-0	v	Chinese Taipei (A, March 1988)
Kazakhstan	7-0	v	Pakistan (H, June 1997)
Latvia	8-1	v	Estonia (A, August 1942)
Liechtenstein	4-0	v	Luxembourg (A, October 2004)
Luxembourg	6-0	v	Afghanistan (A, July 1948)
Macedonia	11-1	v	Liechtenstein (A, November 1996)
Malta	7-1	v	Liechtenstein (H, March 2008)
Moldova	5-0	v	Pakistan (A, August 1992)
Montenegro	6-0	v	San Marino (A, September 2012)
San Marino	1-0	v	Liechtenstein (H, April 2004)
Slovenia	7-0	v	Oman (A, February 1999)

RECORD DEFEATS

Albania	0-12	v	Hungary (A, September 1950)
Andorra	1-8	v	Czech Republic (A, June 2005);
	0-7	v	Croatia (A, October 2006)
Austria	1-11	v	England (H, June 1908)
Belarus	0-5	v	Austria (A, June 2003)
Bosnia-Herzegovina	0-5	v	Argentina (A, May 1998)
Cyprus	0-12	v	West Germany (A, May 1969)
Estonia	2-10	v	Finland (A, August 1922)
Faroe Islands	0-7	v	Yugoslavia (A, May 1991);
	0-7	v	Romania (A, May 1992);
	0-7	v	Norway (H, August 1993);
	1-8	v	Yugoslavia (H, October 1996)
Finland	0-13	v	Germany (A, September 1940)
Georgia	0-5	v	Romania (A, April 1996);
	1-6	v	Denmark (A, September 2005)
Iceland	2-14	v	Denmark (A, August 1967)
Israel*	1-7	v	Egypt (A, March 1934)
Kazakhstan	0-6	v	Turkey (H, June 2006);
	0-6	v	Russia (A, May 2008)
Latvia	0-12	v	Sweden (A, May 1927)
Liechtenstein	1-11	v	Macedonia (H, November 1996)
Luxembourg	0-9	v	England (H, October 1960);
	0-9	v	England (A, December 1982)
Macedonia	0-5	v	Belgium (H, June 1995)
Malta	1-12	v	Spain (A, December 1983)
Moldova	0-6	v	Sweden (A, June 2001)
Montenegro	0-4	v	Romania (A, May 2008)
	0-4	v	Ukraine (H, June 2013)
San Marino	0-13	v	Germany (H, September 2006)
Slovenia	0-5	v	France (A, October 2002)

* Played under the British Mandate of Palestine.

KULCHY COUP

Midfielder **Alyaksandr Kulchy** became the first player to win 100 caps for Belarus, skippering the side against Lithuania in a June 2012 friendly. He also ended ex-Arsenal and Barcelona playmaker Alexander Hleb's run of four successive Belarus footballer of the year awards by claiming the prize in 2009. Hleb, whose younger brother Vyacheslav has also played for Belarus, had previously won the accolade in 2002 and 2003 as well, only for Belarus's all-time top scorer Maksim Romashenko to take it in 2004.

NO-SCORE ANDORRA

Since playing their first international on New Year's Day 1996 – a 6-1 home defeat to Estonia – Andorra have won only three matches, two of them friendlies. Their only competitive triumph was a 1-0 success over Macedonia in an October 2004 FIFA World Cup qualifying match, when left-back Marc Bernaus struck the only goal of the game. Perhaps their lack of strength should come as no surprise – the principality is the sixth-smallest country in Europe, with a population of just 71,822 and they have played their most high-profile games, against England, across the Spanish border in Barcelona.

CAUGHT SHORT

If Montenegro are scoring, then fans can "put their shirt" on captain and all-time leading scorer **Mirko Vucinic** being among the goals. He celebrated scoring the winner against Switzerland in a UEFA Euro 2012 qualifier by removing not his top, but his shorts – and wearing them on his head, antics that earned him a yellow card. Vucinic had previously celebrated a goal for his Italian club side by taking off both his shorts and his shirt, revealing another AS Roma shirt underneath.

MASSIMO BETTER BLUES

Massimo Bonini was unable to inspire a win or even a draw as San Marino manager between 1996 and 1998. But his own playing career was far more effective, including seven years, 192 matches and three Serie A league titles at Italian giants Juventus during the 1980s. Bonini played all 90 minutes of Juventus's 1-0 victory over Liverpool in the 1985 UEFA European Cup final – making him the only San Marino footballer to lift the trophy, or even feature at such a high-flown footballing occasion.

SARG'S 20-YEAR SERVICE

Armenia's first international was a goalless draw at home to Moldova on 14 October 1992. In their starting line-up that day was centre-back Sargis Hovsepyan, who went on to win a record 132 caps for the country before his international retirement in November 2012. He was then appointed the Armenian national team's football director.

SOUTH AMERICA

Brazil hosted a spectacularly vivid and exciting FIFA World Cup in 2014, returning there for the first time since 1950. Appropriately one of the continent's giants reached the final, albeit arch-enemy neighbours Argentina. Brazil have lifted the trophy five times and Argentina twice, as have Uruguay, inaugural FIFA World Cup hosts and winners. Argentina and Uruguay may bid to co-host the centenary tournament in 2030. A special centenary Copa America is due in 2016, with central and north American teams joining in, and the US will host it.

Brazil's high hopes for a sixth FIFA World Cup were not fulfilled in 2014 but it was not for any lack of passion, fervour and support among home fans.

ARGENTINA

Copa America champions on 14 occasions, FIFA Confederations Cup winners in 1992, Olympic gold medallists in 2004 and 2008 and, most treasured of all, FIFA World Cup winners in 1978 and 1986: few countries have won as many international titles as Argentina. The country has a long and rich football history (the first Argentine league was contested in 1891) and has produced some of the greatest footballers ever to have played the game.

LONGEST-SERVING MANAGERS

Guillermo Stabile	1939–60
Cesar Luis Menotti	1974–83
Carlos Bilardo	1983–90
Alfio Basile	1990–94
	2006–08
Marcelo Bielsa	1998–2004
Jose Maria Minella	1964–68
Daniel Passarella	1994–98
Manuel Seoane	1934–37
Juan Jose Pizzuti	1969–72
Alejandro Sabella	2011–14

HAPPY AND SAB

Argentina's 2014 FIFA World Cup squad received a rapturous welcome home from thousands of fans and national president Cristina Fernandez de Kirchner after their final loss to Germany. There had already been mass celebrations and relief across Argentina at qualifying for their first FIFA World Cup final since 1990. The 2014 coach was **Alejandro "Alex" Sabella**, who succeeded Sergio Batista in 2011. Sabella, who stepped down after the tournament, led the first Argentina side to win all of their first five games at a FIFA World Cup, before relying on the penalty saves of goalkeeper Sergio Romero in the semi-final. Sabella's two predecessors, Batista and Diego Maradona, were both FIFA World Cup winners as Argentina players in 1986 – two years after midfielder Sabella won the last of his eight caps.

FRINGE PLAYERS

Daniel Passarella was a demanding captain when he led his country to glory at the 1978 FIFA World Cup. He was the same as coach. After taking over the national side in 1994, he refused to pick anyone unless they had their hair cut short – and ordered striker Claudio Caniggia to get rid of his "girl's hair".

GONZALO'S HIGHS AND LOWS

Striker Gonzalo Higuain ended the longest scoring drought of his international career – 528 minutes and six matches – when he netted the only goal with an opportunist's strike against Belgium in the 2014 FIFA World Cup quarter-final. Higuain was born in Brest, France, where his ex-footballer father Jorge Higuain was playing, but left the country aged ten months. Higuain holds dual French-Argentina nationality, but took up Argentine citizenship in 2007. His goal against Belgium was his only one of the 2014 FIFA World Cup though he did think he had given Argentina the lead in the final against Germany, only for it to be ruled out for offside.

WORTH WAITING FOR

Argentina's national stadium, "El Monumental" in Buenos Aires, hosted its first game in 1938. But the original design was not completed until 20 years later – largely thanks to the £97,000 River Plate received for a transfer fee from Juventus for **Omar Sivori**. The stadium is a must-see stop on the itinerary of many global football tourists for the "Superclasico" derby between hosts River Plate and cross-city rivals Boca Juniors.

NUMBERS GAME

Argentina's FIFA World Cup squads of 1978 and 1982 were given numbers based on alphabetical order rather than positions, which meant the No. 1 shirt was worn by midfielders Norberto Alonso in 1978 and Osvaldo Ardiles in 1982. The only member of the 1982 squad whose shirt number broke the alphabetical order was No. 10, Diego Maradona.

DO YOU COME HERE OFTEN?

Argentina and Uruguay have played each other more often than any other two nations, beginning with Argentina's 3-2 victory in Uruguay's capital Montevideo in 1901 – the first international staged outside the United Kingdom. The two teams have clashed another 179 times in official international matches since then, with Argentina winning 82 times in all, Uruguay 54, and 44 ending as draws.

A ROUND DOZEN

Argentina were responsible for the biggest win in Copa America history, when five goals by Jose Manuel Moreno helped them thrash Ecuador 12-0 in 1942. The much-travelled Moreno won domestic league titles in Argentina, Mexico, Chile and Colombia.

CHINA IN YOUR HAND

In an unusual move, the two 2008 Olympics football finalists Argentina and Nigeria were allowed to take two drinks breaks during the match, which was watched by 89,102 spectators. The game was played in stifling heat in Chinese host city Beijing. Angel Di Maria scored the only goal for Argentina, allowing them to retain the title they won in Athens – for the first time – four years earlier.

THE KIDS ARE ALL RIGHT

Sergio Aguero struck in the final, and ended the tournament as six-goal top scorer, when Argentina won the FIFA World U-20 Championship for a record sixth time in 2007, in Canada, beating the Czech Republic 2-1. Two years later, Aguero married Giannina Maradona – the youngest daughter of Argentina legend Diego – and in February 2009 she gave birth to Diego's first grandchild, Benjamin. Sergio Aguero is widely known by his nickname of "Kun", after a cartoon character he was said to resemble as a child.

BEGINNER'S LUCK

Aged just 27 years and 267 days old, Juan Jose Tramutola became the FIFA World Cup's youngest-ever coach when Argentina opened their 1930 campaign by beating France 1-0. Argentina went on to reach the final, only to lose 4-2 to Uruguay. Top-scorer at the 1930 FIFA World Cup was Argentina's Guillermo Stabile, with eight goals in four games – the only internationals he played. He later won six Copa America titles as his country's longest-serving coach between 1939 and 1960.

TARNISHED GOLD

Despite winning Olympics football gold in 2004 and 2008 – with **Javier Mascherano** becoming the first male footballer since 1928 to collect two Olympic golds – Argentina surprisingly failed to qualify for the 2012 tournament in London. South America's two places went instead to Brazil and Uruguay, based on performances at the 2011 South American Youth Championship staged in Peru. Argentina had finished third in the final group of six.

MAJOR TOURNAMENTS

FIFA WORLD CUP Winners (2)	16 appearances – 1978, 1986
COPA AMERICA Winners (14)	39 appearances – 1921, 1925, 1927, 1929, 1937, 1941, 1945, 1946, 1947, 1955, 1957, 1959, 1991, 1993
CONFEDERATIONS CUP Winners (1)	Three appearances – 1992
FIRST INTERNATIONAL	Uruguay 2 Argentina 3 (Montevideo, Uruguay, 16 May 1901)
BIGGEST WIN	Argentina 12 Ecuador 0 (Montevideo, Uruguay, 22 January 1942)
BIGGEST DEFEATS	Czechoslovakia 6 Argentina 1 (Helsingborg, Sweden, 15 June 1958); Argentina 0, Colombia 5 (Buenos Aires, 5 September 1993) Bolivia 6 Argentina 1 (La Paz, Bolivia, 1 April 2009)

YELLOW GOODBYE

Some 20 years before France were forced to wear local Argentine club Atletico Kimberly's kit at the 1978 FIFA World Cup, Argentina themselves faced similar embarrassment for their first-round match against West Germany. The Argentines had neglected to bring along a second kit and a colour-clash with their opponents meant borrowing the yellow shirts of Swedish side IFK Malmo. Despite taking a third-minute lead, Argentina lost 3-1 and departed the tournament bottom of Group A.

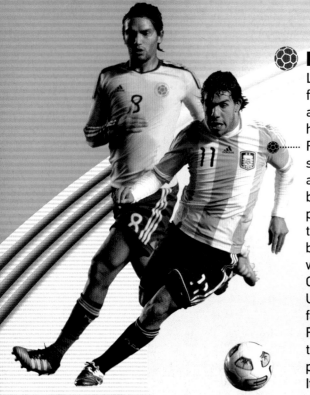

PEOPLE'S FAVOURITE

Lionel Messi may be acclaimed as the finest footballer in the world – and one of the best of all-time – yet back home in Argentina the real hero for many fans is three-time South American Footballer of the Year **Carlos Tevez**. When Argentina staged the 2011 Copa America, team line-up announcements in stadia described Messi as "the best in the world" but Tevez as "the player of the people". Tevez grew up in poverty in Buenos Aires' tough "Fuerte Apache" neighbourhood and still bears scars on his neck from when boiling water was spilled on him as a child. Yet he ended the 2011 Copa America as a villain – his missed penalty gave Uruguay shoot-out victory in the quarter-final. Tevez failed even to make Argentina's squad for the 2014 FIFA World Cup, despite having scored 21 club goals the preceding season and been named Juventus's player of the year as they won their third consecutive Italian league title.

SPOT-KICK FLOP

If at first you don't succeed, try and try again – unfortunately Martin Palermo missed all three penalties he took during Argentina's 1999 Copa America clash with Colombia. The first hit the crossbar, the second flew over the bar and the third was saved. Colombia won the match 3-0.

WINNING TOUCH

Midfielder Marcelo Trobbiani played just two minutes of FIFA World Cup football – the last two minutes of the 1986 final, after replacing winning goalscorer Jorge Burruchaga. Trobbiani touched the ball once, a backheel. The former Boca star ended his international career with 15 caps and one goal to his name.

TOP SCORERS

1	Gabriel Batistuta	56
2	Lionel Messi	42
3	Hernan Crespo	35
4	Diego Maradona	34
5	Luis Artime	24
6	Gonzalo Higuain	22
=	Leopoldo Luque	22
=	Daniel Passarella	22
9	Sergio Aguero	21
=	Herminio Masantonio	21
=	Jose Sanfilippo	21

SECOND TIME LUCKY

Luisito Monti is the only man to play in the the FIFA World Cup final for two different countries. The centre-half, born in Buenos Aires on 15 May 1901 but with Italian family origins, was highly influential in Argentina's run to the 1930 final. They lost the game 4-2 to Uruguay – after Monti allegedly received mysterious pre-match death threats. Following a transfer to Juventus the following year, he was allowed to play for Italy and was on the winning side when the *Azzurri* beat Czechoslovakia in the 1934 final. Another member of the 1934 team was Raimundo Orsi, who had also played for Argentina before switching countries in 1929.

DIVINE DIEGO

To many people **Diego Armando Maradona** is the greatest footballer the world has ever seen, better even than Pele. The Argentine legend, born in Lanus on 30 October 1960, first became famous as a ball-juggling child during half-time intervals at Argentinos Juniors matches. He was distraught to be left out of Argentina's 1978 FIFA World Cup squad and was then sent off for retaliation at the 1982 tournament. Maradona, as triumphant Argentina captain in Mexico in 1986, scored the notorious "Hand of God" goal and then a spectacular individual strike within five minutes of each other in a quarter-final win over England. He again captained Argentina to the final in 1990, in Italy – the country where he inspired Napoli to Serie A and UEFA Cup success. He was thrown out of the 1994 FIFA World Cup finals in disgrace after failing a drugs test. Maradona captained Argentina 16 times in FIFA World Cup matches, a record, and was surprisingly appointed national coach in 2008, despite scant previous experience as a manager.

FITTER, JAVIER

Javier Zanetti is Argentina's most-capped player, with 145 international appearances – despite being surprisingly left out of squads for both the 2006 and 2010 FIFA World Cups. Zanetti, who can play at full-back or in midfield, has also played more Serie A matches than any other non-Italian – and all for Internazionale of Milan, with whom he won the treble of Italian league, Italian Cup and UEFA Champions League in 2009–10. Despite those achievements, he and Inter team-mate Esteban Cambiasso failed to make Diego Maradona's squad for the 2010 FIFA World Cup – but Zanetti returned to the fold under Maradona's successor Sergio Batista and captained his country at the 2011 Copa America. Zanetti made his 600th appearance in Italy's Serie A in 2013.

THE ANGEL GABRIEL

Gabriel Batistuta, nicknamed "Batigol" and Argentina's all-time leading scorer, is the only man to have scored hat-tricks in two separate FIFA World Cups. He scored the first against Greece in 1994 and the second against Jamaica four years later. Hungary's Sandor Kocsis, France's Just Fontaine and Germany's Gerd Muller each scored two hat-tricks in the same FIFA World Cup. Batistuta, born in Reconquista on 1 February 1969, also set an Italian league record during his time with Fiorentina, by scoring in 11 consecutive Serie A matches at the start of the 1994–95 season.

SUPER MARIO

Mario Kempes, who scored twice in the 1978 FIFA World Cup final and won the Golden Boot, was the only member of Cesar Menotti's squad who played for a non-Argentine club. Playing for Valencia, he had been the Spanish league's top scorer for the previous two seasons.

LEO BRAVO

Lionel Messi passed the international appearances tally of Diego Maradona during the 2014 FIFA World Cup, having edged ahead of him in goalscoring a year earlier. But his wait to lift the FIFA World Cup – as his predecessor did – goes on, after Argentina lost the final in Rio de Janeiro 1-0 to Germany. The FIFA World Cup remains a rare accolade to have escaped Messi's grasp and he left the Maracana with the Golden Ball prize after being named tournament's best player. As coach, Maradona made Messi Argentina's youngest-ever captain, giving him the armband, two days before his 23rd birthday, during the 2010 FIFA World Cup. He was captain under both of Maradona's successors, Sergio Batista and Alex Sabella, as he continued to be a world superstar. He scored four times at the 2014 FIFA World Cup, including a last-minute winner in the first-round against Iran. His four Man Of The Match awards were the most in finals. But the four-time FIFA Ballon d'Or winner may have just one more shot to win the FIFA World Cup, in Russia in 2018 when he will be 31.

TOP CAPS

1	Javier Zanetti	145
2	Roberto Ayala	115
3	Diego Simeone	106
4	Javier Mascherano	105
5	Oscar Ruggeri	97
6	Lionel Messi	93
7	Diego Maradona	91
8	Ariel Ortega	87
9	Gabriel Batistuta	78
10	Juan Pablo Sorin	76

SAINTED PALERMO

Veteran striker Martin Palermo waited 10 years between international appearances before being called up again by his former Boca Juniors team-mate Diego Maradona in 2009. He justified the surprise recall with a stoppage-time winner in the penultimate qualifier against Peru, prompting Maradona to take a celebratory dive in rain-sodden mud on the touchline and then hail it as "the miracle of St Palermo". Palermo also became his country's oldest-ever FIFA World Cup scorer, at the 2010 tournament in South Africa. He was 36 years and 227 days old when he came on as a substitute in the first round against Greece and completed the scoring in a 2-0 victory – a year and 358 days older than Maradona had been when scoring against the same country 16 years earlier.

BRAZIL

No country has captured the soul of the game to the same extent as Brazil. The country's distinctive yellow-shirted players have thrilled generations of football fans and produced some of the game's greatest moments. No FIFA World Cup tournament would be the same without Brazil – the nation that gave birth to Pele, Garrincha, Zico, Ronaldo and Kaka. The only nation to appear in every FIFA World Cup finals and competition winners a record five times, Brazil's widely-admired hosting of the 2014 tournament did not end with the sixth triumph they craved.

FIERCEST RIVALS

Brazil's oldest club classic is Fluminense versus Botafogo in Rio de Janeiro. The clubs faced each other for the first time on 22 October 1905, when Fluminense won 6-0. One particular match stirred a controversy that lasted 89 years. The two teams disagreed on the result of the 1907 championship, whose title was disputed up to 1996... when they finally decided to share it.

TAKING AIM WITH NEYMAR

Brazil's triumph in the 2013 FIFA Confederations Cup, a record third in a row, was consolation for their failure in 2012 to break their Olympic hoodoo, Mexico beating them in the London Games final. This remains the only FIFA-approved prize to elude Brazil but they will be the hosts at Rio de Janeiro in 2016. **Neymar** was nine-goal top scorer at London 2012, voted South American Footballer of the Year for the second successive year and then, in 2013, was named player of the FIFA Confederations Cup. Those were his last matches as a Santos player before he joined Spanish giants Barcelona. He was Brazil's undoubted star man at the 2014 FIFA World Cup, with four goals in four games before suffering a tournament-ending broken bone in his back during the quarter-final win against Colombia.

CLOSE ENCOUNTERS

Brazil have been involved in many memorable games. Their 3-2 defeat to Italy in 1982 is regarded as one of the classic games in FIFA World Cup finals history. Paolo Rossi scored all three of Italy's goals with Brazil coach Tele Santana much criticized for going all out in attack when only a 2-2 draw was needed. Brazil's 1982 squad, with players such as **Socrates**, Zico and **Falcao**, is considered one of the greatest teams never to win the tournament. In 1994, a 3-2 win over the Netherlands in the quarter-finals – their first competitive meeting in 20 years – was just as thrilling, with all the goals coming in the second half. Socrates – a qualified medical doctor, as well as elder brother to 1994 FIFA World Cup-winner Rai – was mourned across the globe when he died at the age of 57 in December 2011.

BRAZIL'S RECORD

FIFA WORLD CUP	20 appearances (every finals)
Matches (104)	W70, D17, L17, GF221, GA102
Winners (5)	1958, 1962, 1970, 1994, 2002
Runners-up (2)	1950, 1998
Third place (2)	1938, 1978
Fourth place (1)	1974, 2014
COPA AMERICA	33 appearances
Winners (8)	1919, 1922, 1949, 1989, 1997, 1999, 2004, 2007
CONFEDERATIONS CUP	Seven appearances
Winners (4)	1997, 2005, 2009, 2013
FIRST INTERNATIONAL	Argentina 3 Brazil 0 (Buenos Aires, 20 September 1914)
BIGGEST WIN	Brazil 10 Bolivia 1 (Sao Paulo, 10 April 1949)
HEAVIEST DEFEAT	Uruguay 6 Brazil 0 (Vina del Mar Chile, 18 September 1920) Brazil 1, Germany 7 (Belo Horizonte, 8 July 2014)

LAND OF FOOTBALL

No country is more deeply identified with football success than Brazil, who have won the FIFA World Cup a record five times – in 1958, 1962, 1970, 1994 and 2002. They are also the only team never to have missed a FIFA World Cup finals and are favourites virtually every time the competition is staged. After winning the trophy for a third time in Mexico in 1970, Brazil kept the **Jules Rimet Trophy** permanently. Sadly, it was stolen from the federation's headquarters in 1983 and was never recovered. Brazilians often refer to their country as "o país do futebol" ("the country of football"). It is the favourite pastime of youngsters, while general elections are often held in the same year as the FIFA World Cup, with critics arguing that political parties try to take advantage of the nationalistic surge created by football and bring it into politics. Charles Miller, the son of a Scottish engineer, is credited with bringing football to Brazil in 1894. Yet the sport would only truly become Brazilian when blacks were able to play at the top level in 1933. At first, because of the game's European origin, it was the sport of Brazil's urban white elite. However, it quickly spread among the urban poor as Brazilians realized the only thing they needed to play was a ball, which could be substituted inexpensively with a bundle of socks, an orange, or even a cloth filled with paper.

CAPTAIN TO COACH

Brazil's 1994 FIFA World Cup-winning captain **Dunga** was appointed national coach in 2006 despite having no previous management experience. He led the team to 2007 Copa America and 2009 FIFA Confederations Cup success. But he lost his job after Brazil were knocked out of the 2010 FIFA World Cup in a 2-1 quarter-final defeat to the Netherlands. Dunga – real name Carlos Caetano Bledorn Verri, but widely known by the Portuguese for "Dopey" – had already faced criticism back home for his team's defensive style and decisions not to take Ronaldinho, Adriano or Alexandre Pato to South Africa.

TOP OF THE FLOPS

Brazil's dreams of winning a sixth FIFA World Cup, but first on home soil, became a nightmare in 2014 – 64 years on from the trauma caused by Uruguay's surprise triumph at Rio de Janeiro's Maracana stadium. Luiz Felipe Scolari's 2014 vintage set a series of unenviable records as they crashed out, 7-1 to Germany, in the semi-final in Belo Horizonte. This was not only Brazil's heaviest FIFA World Cup defeat, but also the biggest any semi-finalist had ever suffered. It equalled the 6-0 trouncing by Uruguay at the 1920 Copa America as Brazil's worst defeat of all-time. Finally, it was Brazil's first home loss in a competitive international since Peru beat them 3-1 – also in Belo Horizonte – in a 1975 Copa America semi-final. A 3-0 setback against the Netherlands in the third-place play-off meant Brazil lost consecutive internationals at home for the first time since 1940, when Argentina, 3-0, and Uruguay 4-3, were victorious. The 14 goals Brazil conceded was their worst ever in a FIFA World Cup, three worse than in 1938, and they became the first FIFA World Cup hosts to concede the most goals in a tournament.

EYE FOR GOAL

Centre-forward **Tostao** – full name Eduardo Goncalves de Andrade – was one of the stars of Brazil's legendary 1970 FIFA World Cup-winning team but almost did not make the tournament. He had suffered a detached retina when hit in the face by a football the previous year, prompting some doctors' warnings that he should be left out. Tostao eventually retired at the age of 26 in 1973, after another eye injury, and went to work as a doctor instead. His 1970 team-mate Pele also experienced failing eyesight.

JOY OF THE PEOPLE

Garrincha, one of Brazil's greatest legends, was really Manuel Francisco dos Santos at birth but his nickname meant 'Little Bird' – inspired by his slender, bent legs. Despite the legacy of childhood illness, he was a star right-winger at Botafogo from 1953 to 1965. He and Pele were explosively decisive newcomers for Brazil at the 1958 FIFA World Cup finals. In 1962 Garrincha was voted player of the tournament four years later. He died in January 1983 at just 49. His epitaph was the title often bestowed on him in life: "The Joy of the People."

TOP CAPS

1	Cafu	142
2	Roberto Carlos	125
3	Lucio	105
4	Claudio Taffarel	101
5	Djalma Santos	98
=	Ronaldo	98
=	Ronaldinho	98
7	Gilmar	94
9	Gilberto Silva	93
10	Pele	92
=	Rivelino	92

TOP SCORERS

1	Pele	77
2	Ronaldo	62
3	Romario	55
4	Zico	48
5	Bebeto	39
6	Neymar	35
7	Rivaldo	34
8	Jairzinho	33
=	Ronaldinho	33
10	Ademir	32
=	Tostao	32

THE KING

Pele is considered by many as the greatest player of all time, a sporting icon *par excellence* and not only for his exploits on the pitch. When, for instance, he scored his 1,000th goal, Pele dedicated it to the poor children of Brazil. He began playing for Santos at the age of 15 and won his first FIFA World Cup two years later, scoring twice in the final. Despite numerous offers from European clubs, the economic conditions and Brazilian football regulations at the time allowed Santos to keep hold of their prized asset for almost two decades, until 1974. All-time leading scorer of the Brazilian national team, he is the only footballer to be a member of three FIFA World Cup-winning teams. Despite being in the Brazilian squad at the start of the 1962 tournament, an injury suffered in the second match meant he was not able to play on and, initially, he missed out on a winner's medal. However, FIFA announced in November 2007 that he would be awarded a medal retrospectively. After the disastrous 1966 tournament, when Brazil fell in the first round, Pele said he did not wish to play in the FIFA World Cup again. He was finally talked round and ended up, in 1970, playing a key role in what is widely considered as one of the greatest sides ever. Since his retirement in 1977, Pele has been a worldwide ambassador for football, as well undertaking various acting roles and commercial ventures.

PARTY ANIMAL

Brazil's captain when they played Argentina (twice), Costa Rica and Mexico in autumn 2011 was a man many had not even expected to be in the international side again – former two-time FIFA World Footballer of the Year, Ronaldinho. Having amazed the world with his fancy footwork and prolific goalscoring for Paris Saint-Germain in France, Barcelona in Spain and AC Milan in Italy, he returned to his homeland with Flamengo in 2011 – but was widely accused of being more interested in partying than playing. But a return to form won him a recall under Mano Menezes. That appearance against Mexico took him to 33 goals, level with 1970 FIFA World Cup winner Jairzinho, then his next match – his 94th for Brazil – equalled the caps tally of 1958 and 1962 FIFA World Cup champion goalkeeper Gilmar. Ronaldinho himself became a FIFA World Cup winner in 2002, aged 22, when his long-range goal against England gave Brazil victory in the quarter-finals – though he was sent off seven minutes later and had to sit out the semi-final, before returning for the final.

WHITHER RONALDO?

Only one person knows exactly what happened to **Ronaldo** in the hours before the 1998 FIFA World Cup final – the man himself. He sparked one of the biggest mysteries in FIFA World Cup history when his name was left off the teamsheet before the game, only for it to reappear just in time for kick-off. It was initially reported that Ronaldo had an ankle injury, and then a upset stomach. Finally team doctor Lidio Toledo revealed the striker had been rushed to hospital after suffering a convulsion in his sleep, but that he had been cleared to play after neurological and cardiac tests. The most dramatic account came from Ronaldo's roommate Roberto Carlos. "Ronaldo was scared about what lay ahead. The pressure had got to him and he couldn't stop crying," said the legendary full-back. "At about four o'clock, he became ill. That's when I called the team doctor and told him to get over to our room as fast as he could."

HOME COMFORTS

The hosts of the FIFA World Cup have never lost their first match of that tournament, and Brazil continued that run by beating Croatia 3-1 in what was also the opening match of the 2014 FIFA World Cup. It was Brazil's ninth consecutive victory in their finals opener. Neymar scored twice against Croatia, making him the first Brazil player to hit a brace in his FIFA World Cup debut.

THAT'S MY BOY

When Bebeto scored for Brazil against the Netherlands in their 1994 FIFA World Cup quarter-final, he and strike partner Romario celebrated with a "cradling the baby" dance that would be much-imitated for years to come. Bebeto's wife had just given birth to their son Matheus – who would grow up to become a footballer himself, joining Flamengo's youth set-up in 2011. By this time, both **Bebeto** (middle) and **Romario** (right, Mazinho is left) were in tandem again – as elected politicians in Brazil.

INAUSPICIOUS START

Left-back/left-winger **Marcelo** achieved the dubious "honour" of being the first player to score the opening goal of a FIFA World Cup finals in his own net. He inadvertently gave Croatia the lead in the 2014 tournament's curtain-raiser in Sao Paulo, but Brazil did come back to win 3-1, thanks to a pair of goals from Neymar and one from Oscar. Marcelo, who a couple of weeks earlier had scored for his club, Real Madrid, as they won the UEFA Champions League final, also became the first Brazil player ever to score past his own goalkeeper in the FIFA World Cup finals.

BRAZIL'S YOUNGEST PLAYERS

1 Pele, 16 years and 257 days
   (v Argentina, 7 July 1958)
2 Ronaldo, 17 years and 182 days
   (v Argentina, 24 March 1994)
3 Adriano, 17 years and 272 days
   (v Australia, 17 November 1999)
4 Toninho, 17 years and 343 days
   (v Uruguay, 28 April 1976)
5 Carvalho Leite, 18 years and 26 days
   (v Bolivia, 22 July 1930)
6 Diego, 18 years and 60 days
   (v Mexico, 30 April 2003)
7 Marcelo, 18 years and 115 days
   (v Wales, 5 September 2006)
8 Philippe Coutinho, 18 years and 116 days
   (v Iran, 7 October 2010)
9 Doria, 18 years and 149 days
   (v Bolivia, 6 April 2013)
10 Neymar, 18 years and 186 days
    (v USA, 10 August 2010)

ROLLING RIVA

Brazilian legend **Rivaldo** was still playing into his 40s – a decade after the highlight of his career, helping Brazil win the 2002 FIFA World Cup. He scored 34 goals in 74 matches for his country between 1993 and 2003, including three goals at the 1998 FIFA World Cup and five more in Japan and South Korea four years later. His 2002 FIFA World Cup was marred only by blatant play–acting that helped get Turkey's Hakan Unsal sent off and earned Rivaldo a fine. Rivaldo – full name Rivaldo Vitor Borba Ferreira – became one of the world's finest footballers despite suffering malnourishment in a poverty-stricken childhood. His individual achievements including FIFA World Footballer of the Year and European Footballer of the Year prizes in 1999 while playing for Spanish giants Barcelona. His later clubs included AC Milan in Italy, Olympiacos and AEK Athens in Greece, Bunyodkor in Uzbekistan, Kabuscorp in Angola and – in 2013, at the age of 40, Brazilian second division side Sao Caetano.

WORLD-BEATING SAINTS

Right-back **Djalma Santos** is one of only two players to be voted into the official all-star team of a FIFA World Cup on three different occasions. He was honoured for his performances at the 1954, 1958 and 1958 finals – even though his only appearance in 1958 was in the final. West Germany's Franz Beckenbauer was the other, chosen in 1966, 1970 and 1974. On the opposite flank to Djalma Santos was the left-back Nilton Santos – no relation – who also played in 1954, 1958 and 1962 and had also been a member of Brazil's runners-up squad on home turf in 1950.

ON THE SLIDE?

As 2014 FIFA World Cup hosts, Brazil qualified automatically and so saw little competitive action after the 2012 Copa America. This explained their plunge out of the FIFA World Rankings top ten, to 11th, in July 2012. Brazil reached an all-time low of 22nd in June 2013, though entered the 2014 FIFA World Cup third behind Spain and Germany, but fell to seventh in the first post-tournament update.

YELLOW FEVER

The world-renowned yellow and blue kit now worn by Brazil was not adopted until 1954, as a replacement for their former all-white strip. The *Correio da Manha* newspaper organised a design competition which was won by 19-year-old Aldyr Garcia Schlee and the new colours were worn for the first time in March 1954 against Chile. Schlee was from Pelotas, close to Brazil's border with Uruguay and actually supported Uruguayan sides against Brazil.

THE OLD RIVALS: BRAZIL V ARGENTINA

Matches played: 95
Brazil wins: 35
Argentina wins: 36
Draws: 24
Brazil goals: 145
Argentina goals: 151
First match: Argentina 3 Brazil 0 (20 September 1914)
Latest match: Argentina 2 Brazil 1 (21 November 2012)
Biggest Brazil win: Brazil 6 Argentina 2 (20 December 1945)
Biggest Argentina win: Argentina 6 Brazil 1 (5 March 1940)

GRAND ACHIEVEMENT

Brazil played their 1,000th match on 14 November 2012, with Neymar's second-half equaliser securing a 1-1 draw against Colombia in New Jersey, United States. Brazil's first match is considered generally to have been a 2-0 victory over visiting English club Exeter City on 21 July 1914, at the Estadio das Laranjeiras in Rio – still used by Fluminense. Brazil won that day despite star striker **Arthur Friedenreich** losing two teeth in a collision. Brazil's first international against another country was a 3-0 defeat to Argentina on 20 September 1914.

LUIZ STREAK

Crazy-haired Brazil centre-back **David Luiz** went 39 international appearances without a goal. His first goal came against Chile in the 2014 FIFA World Cup second-round – and his second came in the next match, a long-range free-kick, in the quarter-final win over Colombia. Just before the tournament began he had left English club Chelsea for France's Paris Saint-Germain, where he would play next to his regular Brazil central defensive partner Thiago Silva. Luiz stood in as captain for the suspended Silva in the 7-1 semi-final defeat to Germany.

BRAZIL'S 2014 WORLD CUP STADIA

1 Maracana, Rio de Janeiro (76,804)
2 Brasilia, Estadio Nacional Mane Garrincha (70,064)
3 Mineirao, Belo Horizonte (62,547, Atletico Mineiro and Cruzeiro)
4 Arena Corinthians, Sao Paulo (65,807)
5 Estadio Castelao, Fortaleza (64,846)
6 Estadio Beira-Rio, Porto Alegre (48,849)
7 Arena Fonte Neva, Salvador (48,747)
8 Arena Pernambuco, Recife (46,000)
9 Arena Pantanal, Cuiaba (42,968)
10 Arena da Amazonia, Manaus (42,374)
11 Arena das Dunas, Natal (42,086)
12 Arena da Baixaba, Curitiba (41,456)

BRAZIL HAVE HAD THEIR PHIL

The return of "Big Phil" **Luiz Felipe Scolari** as Brazil coach in November 2012 was meant to culminate, in 2014, with a repeat of his success spearheading the country to triumph at the 2002 FIFA World Cup. Yet although his second reign did bring glory at the 2013 FIFA Confederations Cup, the following year's FIFA World Cup on home turf will be remembered for the many unwanted records his team set and the embarrassment with which their efforts ended – most notably, the 7-1 defeat by Germany in their Belo Horizonte semi-final. Scolari was relieved of his role just days after a 3-0 defeat to the Netherlands in the third-place play-off. However, the tournament gave him a second fourth-place finish, achieving that mark as Portugal boss in 2006, and he became the first coach to be in charge in three different FIFA World Cup semi-finals.

LETTING LUCIO

Elegant centre-back **Lucio** set a FIFA World Cup record during the 2006 tournament by playing for 386 minutes without conceding a foul – only ending in Brazil's 1-0 quarter-final defeat to France. While mostly noted for leadership and control at the back, he also had an eye for goal – heading the late winner that gave Brazil a 3-2 triumph over the USA in the 2009 FIFA Confederations Cup final. The following year he was part of Italian club Internazionale's treble success, clinching the Italian league and cup as well as the UEFA Champions League.

SUPER-POWERS' POWER CUT

There was a new addition to the annual international calendar in 2011: the Superclasico de los Americas, a two-legged event between Brazil and Argentina. Brazil were the first winners, thanks to a goalless draw followed by a 2-0 win. They dramatically retained the crown in 2012. Brazil won the first leg at home, 2-1, but the return game in Chaco was postponed after a power cut – possibly because Brazil's team bus hit an electricity trailer. The rearranged game ended 2-1 to Argentina, but Brazil won 4-3 on penalties, their goal being scored by Fred, while strike partner Neymar netted the winning spot-kick. For Brazil's coach Mano Menezes, however, his "reward" was the sack. There was no Superclasico in 2013 and the next edition was due to be a one-off match, in the Chinese capital Beijing in October 2014.

CHILE

Chile were one of four founding members of CONMEBOL, South America's football confederation, in 1916. They played in the first match at a South American football championship – losing the opener of the unofficial 1910 tournament 3-0 to Uruguay – and they played in the first official Copa America, in 1916. Never winners, they have been runners-up on four occasions, in 1955, 1956, 1979 and 1987. Their greatest glory was hosting – and taking third place at – the 1962 FIFA World Cup.

TOP SCORERS

1	Marcelo Salas	37
2	Ivan Zamorano	34
3	Carlos Caszely	29
4	Alexis Sanchez	24
5	Leonel Sanchez	23
6	Jorge Aravena	22
7	Humberto Suazo	21
8	Juan Carlos Letelier	18
9	Enrique Hormazabal	17
10	Matias Fernandez	14

BRAVO, BEAUSEJOUR

Chile went precisely 48 years between victories at a FIFA World Cup, from a 1-0 third-place play-off success against Yugoslavia on 16 June 1962 to a first-round victory by the same scoreline over Honduras on 16 June 2010. That long-awaited winner in South Africa came from **Jean Beausejour**, who then hit Chile's third in their opening-game 3-1 triumph over Australia in Brazil four years later. It meant he became the first Chilean player ever to score at more than one FIFA World Cup. Goalkeeper and captain at both tournaments was Claudio Bravo, Chile's second-most-capped player.

CENTRE-BACK'S HAT-TRICK

The first player to be named South American Footballer of the Year three times was not Pele, Garrincha or Diego Maradona but Chilean centre-back **Elias Figueroa**, who took the prize in three consecutive years from 1974 to 1976 while playing for Brazilian club Internacional. The only players to emulate such a hat-trick were Brazil's Zico, in 1977, 1981 and 1982, and Argentina forward Carlos Tevez, in 2003, 2004 and 2005. Two more Chileans have won the award: Marcelo Salas in 1997 and Matias Fernandez in 2006. Outside of Brazil and Argentina, the most winners of the prize have come from Chile and Paraguay, with five apiece. Although Figueroa started and ended his playing career in Chile, he also played for clubs in Brazil, Uruguay and the US, while also representing his country for 16 years from 1966 to 1982 – including FIFA World Cup appearances in 1966, 1974 and 1982.

ALEXIS IS YOUNGEST

Chile's youngest-ever international is also now their most exciting star, Arsenal winger **Alexis Sanchez**. He was just 17 years and four months old when he made his debut against New Zealand in April 2006, the month before he left South America to sign for Italy's Udinese. He spent loan spells back in Chile and Argentina before making his breakthrough in Serie A with eye-catching displays that earned a move to Barcelona in 2011. Sanchez is now fourth, with 24 goals, among the all-time scorers for Chile, his tally including three in qualifying for the 2010 FIFA World Cup and two in the finals four years later, when they again reached the second round. Chile won many admirers with their attacking style of play, though their tougher edge could be found in the nicknames of other stars, such as Gary "The Pitbull" Medel and Arturo "The Warrior" Vidal. Sanchez showed more tender emotions after scoring Chile's final goal, in a 4-0 friendly victory over Estonia in June 2011. He revealed a T-shirt bearing a photo of his adoptive father Jose Delaigue, who had died days earlier.

⚽ SALAS DAYS

Chile's all-time leading scorer **Marcelo Salas** formed a much-feared striking partnership with Ivan Zamorano during the late 1990s and early 21st century. Salas scored four goals as Chile reached the second round of the 1998 FIFA World Cup in France despite not winning a game. The striker spent two years in international retirement, from 2005 to 2007, but returned for the first four games of qualification for the 2010 FIFA World Cup. His scored twice in Chile's 2-2 draw with Uruguay on 18 November 2007, but his international career ended for good three days later, following a 3-0 defeat to Paraguay.

⚽ HAPPY SAMP

Chile had never reached the knock-out stages of consecutive FIFA World Cups until their 2014 vintage in Brazil matched the 2010 squad's achievement. And both times they had coaches from Argentina: Marcelo Bielsa was in charge in 2010 and Jorge Sampaoli four years later – and another compatriot, Claudio Borghi, served a spell in between. Sampaoli retired from playing aged 19, because of tibia and fibula injuries, and devoted himself to a coaching career that took in Peru and Ecuador before he took the Chilean hotseat in 2012.

⚽ SURFACE APPEAL

Football helped keep up the spirits of 33 Chilean miners trapped underground for 69 days after an explosion at a mine in the Atacama desert on 5 August 2010. The men were initially given up for dead, but after news of their survival emerged, supplies sent underground included footage of Chile's 2-1 defeat to Ukraine in a friendly on 7 September. Some of the rescued miners played "keepy-uppies" with footballs on finally emerging into daylight at the surface and, two weeks later, played an exhibition match against their rescuers.

⚽ LUCKY LEO

Leonel Sanchez holds the Chilean record for international appearances, scoring 23 goals in 84 games. But he was lucky to remain on the pitch for one of them. Sanchez escaped an early bath despite punching Italy's Humberto Maschio in the face during their so-called "Battle of Santiago" clash at the 1962 FIFA World Cup, when English referee Ken Aston could have sent off more than just the two players he did dismiss. Sanchez, a left-winger born in Santiago on 25 April 1936, finished the tournament as one of its six four-goal leading scorers – along with Brazilians Garrincha and Vava, Russian Valentin Ivanov, Yugoslav Drazan Jerkovic and Hungarian Florian Albert.

URUGUAY

Uruguay was the first country to win a FIFA World Cup, in 1930, and with a population of under four million, they remain the smallest to do so. They claimed the game's greatest prize for a second time in 1950, having already won Olympic gold in 1924 and 1928. Recent years were less productive, until a fourth-place finish at the 2010 FIFA World Cup and a record-breaking 15th Copa America triumph the following year.

TOP SCORERS

1	Luis Suarez	40
2	Diego Forlan	36
3	Hector Scarone	31
4	Angel Romano	28
5	Oscar Miguez	27
6	Sebastian Abreu	26
7	Pedro Petrone	24
8	Carlos Aguilera	22
=	Edinson Cavani	22
=	Fernando Morena	22

FORLAN HERO

Diego Forlan was Uruguay's star man at the 2010 FIFA World Cup, scoring five goals – including three from outside the penalty area, the first player to achieve that feat at a FIFA World Cup since Germany's Lothar Matthaus in 1990. He also hit the crossbar with a free-kick, the final touch of his country's 3-2 defeat to Germany in the 2010 third-place play-off. Uruguay's fourth-place finish in South Africa meant Diego fared better than his father Pablo, who had played in the Uruguay team that was knocked out in the first round of the 1974 FIFA World Cup.

GET IN, GODIN

Centre-back **Diego Godin's** crucial late headed goal gave Uruguay a 1-0 Group D win over Italy at the 2014 FIFA World Cup and a place in the second round at Italy's expense. Godin developed an knack for crucial strikes in 2014: his goal secured a first Spanish league title in 18 years for Atletico Madrid in May 2014 and he gave them the lead in the UEFA Champions League final, only to lose ultimately 4-1 to Real Madrid.

DIFFERENT BALL GAME

Uruguay were the inaugural hosts – and the first winners – of the FIFA World Cup in 1930, having won football gold at the Olympics of 1924 in Paris and 1928 in Amsterdam. Among the players who won all three of those titles was forward Hector Scarone, who remains Uruguay's second-highest scorer with 31 goals in 52 internationals. Uruguay beat arch-rivals Argentina 4-2 in the 1930 final, in a game which used two different footballs – Argentina's choice in the first half, in which they led 2-1, before Uruguay's was used for their second-half comeback.

HAPPY ANNIVERSARY

A so-called "Mundialito", or "Little World Cup", was staged in December 1980 and January 1981 to mark the 50th anniversary of the FIFA World Cup – and, as in 1930, Uruguay emerged triumphant. The tournament was meant to involve all six countries who had previously won the tournament, though 1966 champions England turned down the invitation and were replaced by 1978 runners-up Holland. Uruguay beat Brazil 2-1 in the final, a repeat of the scoreline from the two teams' final match of the 1950 FIFA World Cup. The Mundialito-winning Uruguay side was captained by goalkeeper Rodolfo Rodriguez and coached by Roque Maspoli, who had played in goal in that 1950 final.

TOP CAPS

1	Diego Forlan	112
2	Diego Lugano	95
3	Maxi Pereira	93
4	Diego Perez	89
5	Diego Godin	81
6	Luis Suarez	79
7	Rodolfo Rodriguez	78
8	Cristian Rodriguez	77
9	Fabian Carini	74
10	Enzo Francescoli	73

CAV FAITH

It took just three minutes for **Edinson Cavani** to score his first international goal, after coming on as a substitute for his Uruguay debut against Colombia in February 2008. He not only helped Uruguay finish fourth at the 2010 FIFA World Cup and win a record 15th Copa America in 2011, but his scoring exploits in club football for Italy's Napoli and Paris Saint-Germain in France have established him as one of the world's finest modern strikers. Cavani, a devout Christian, received high praise from the Archbishop of Naples, Crescenzio Sepe, who said: "God serves himself by having Cavani score goals." The forward was given his Uruguay debut by Oscar Tabarez, a former schoolteacher known as "The Maestro", whose second spell as international boss began in 2006. Cavani was aged just three when Tabarez led Uruguay at their most recent FIFA World Cup before 2010, reaching the second round in 1990.

BITE RETURN

Notoriety has cast many shadows over the career of **Luis Suarez** and the controversy he caused at the 2010 FIFA World Cup was mild compared to what followed in Brazil four years later. Uruguay's all-time leading scorer is one of the world's most talented strikers but is also a danger not only to others but to himself and team-mates. He earned infamy with a deliberate goal-line handball to concede a penalty when Uruguay and Ghana were level in their 2010 FIFA World Cup quarter-final – then celebrated wildly when Asamoah Gyan missed – and Uruguay won the resulting shoot-out. Worse followed, however, at the 2014 FIFA World Cup, when he bit into the shoulder of Italian defender Giorgio Chiellini, earning himself a nine-match international ban and a four-month suspension from all football. Astonishingly, this was the third time Suarez had bitten someone on the football field – having previously done so while playing for both Ajax Amsterdam and Liverpool. His scoring instincts, are much more admirable – his 40 international goals include four during Uruguay's triumphant 2011 Copa America campaign. Suarez does inspire loyalty among supporters and team-mates, who even pegged his shirt up in the dressing-room before their 2014 second-round clash with Colombia despite his enforced departure from Brazil the previous day.

BOYS IN BLUE

Uruguay's 3-2 home loss to Argentina, in Montevideo on 16 May 1901, was the first international match staged outside the UK. The second, on 20 July 1902, ended 6-0 to Argentina – still the *Celeste*'s heaviest loss. They have played each other another 176 times in official internationals – a world record – with Uruguay winning 53, Argentina 80, and 43 draws. Before an agreed kit-swap in 1910, Uruguay often wore vertical light-blue and white stripes and arch-rivals Argentina would don pale-blue shirts.

OLE, FRANCESCOLI

Until Diego Forlan passed him in 2011, no outfield player had represented Uruguay more often than **Enzo Francescoli** (73 caps) – and few can have taken the field quite so gracefully as the playmaker whose club career included stints with River Plate in Argentina, Racing and Marseille in France and Cagliari and Torino in Italy. His international swansong for Uruguay brought Copa America glory in 1995, when he starred as both midfielder and emergency striker and also scored one of Uruguay's spot-kicks in their penalty shoot-out final victory over Brazil. Among Francescoli's high-profile fans was Zinedine Zidane, who later named his first-born son Enzo, in honour of the Uruguayan maestro.

TRAVEL SICKNESS

Despite winning the 1930 FIFA World Cup, Uruguay turned down the chance to defend their crown four years later, when the tournament was held in Italy. Uruguayan football authorities were unhappy that only four European countries had made the effort to travel to Uruguay and take part in 1930.

OTHER TEAMS SOUTH AMERICA

GOING CARACAS FOR FOOTBALL

Baseball and boxing may have held more sway with Venezuelans in recent decades but football fever has been on the rise in the twenty-first century – given a big boost by the country staging its first Copa America in 2007. This not only saw extravagant investment in new stadia but also Venezuela's first Copa America victory since 1967 – and unprecedented progress into the knock-out stages. **Juan Arango,** a popular success in Spain with La Liga club RCD Mallorca, scored Venezuela's goal in a 4-1 quarter-final loss to Uruguay. They followed this relative breakthrough by finishing eighth out of 10 in South America's qualification campaign for the 2010 FIFA World Cup, then sixth of nine for 2014 – above Peru, Bolivia and Paraguay.

NATIONAL STADIUMS

Bolivia:
Estadio Hernando Siles,
La Paz (45,000 capacity)

Chile:
Estadio Nacional,
Santiago (63,379)

Colombia:
Estadio El Campin,
Bogota (48,600)

Ecuador:
Estadio Olimpico Atahualpa,
Quito (40,948)

Paraguay:
Estadio Defensores del Chaco,
Asuncion (36,000)

Peru:
Estadio Nacional,
Lima (45,574)

Venezuela:
Estadio Polideportivo
de Pueblo Nuevo,
San Cristobal (38,755)

BOLIVIA LEAVE IT LATE

Bolivia have only ever won the Copa America once, but did so in dramatic and memorable style when playing host in 1963. They were the only team to finish the competition unbeaten in all six matches, topping the league table. But they almost threw away glory on the competition's final day, twice squandering two-goal leads against Brazil. Bolivia led 2-0 before being pegged back to 2-2, then saw a 4-2 advantage turn to 4-4, before Maximo Alcocer scored what proved to be Bolivia's winning goal with four minutes remaining.

ENNER THE OTHER VALENCIA

Ecuador striker **Enner Valencia**'s hot scoring streak in 2014 saw him find the net six times across five consecutive matches – including three strikes at that summer's FIFA World Cup. His brace in the 2-1 Group E win over Honduras made him the first Ecuadorian to score more than once in a FIFA World Cup game. His fortunes were in stark contrast to those of his namesake, Ecuador captain Antonia Valencia. The Manchester United winger was sent off in their final first-round game against France – and it was his second red card in four internationals, having been dismissed in a pre-tournament friendly against England.

YEP MAN

Two of Colombia's most-capped players are **Carlos Valderrama** (first, with 111 appearances) and Leonel Alvarez (third, with 101). Valderrama led the criticism when Alvarez was fired after just three games as national coach in 2011. But his successor, ex-Argentina boss Jose Pekerman, led Colombia to the 2014 FIFA World Cup quarter-finals – their best ever performance. Colombia defender Mario Yepes, at 38 one of the finals' oldest players, won four more caps to take him to 102. He had been worried about playing on, but right-back Camilo Zuniga said: "You have to be there – we'll do the running for you."

RE-ENTER THE MONDRAGON

Colombia goalkeeper **Faryd Mondragon** set a number of records at the 2014 FIFA World Cup. He became the oldest player to appear in the finals when he came on as a substitute with five minutes remaining of their first-round match against Japan, on 24 June, aged 43 years and three days, breaking the record formerly held by Cameroon's 42-year-old Roger Milla in 1994. Mondragon also set a new mark for the longest gap between FIFA World Cup appearances, two days short of 16 years. His last game had been in Colombia's final match at the 1998 tournament – a 2-0 defeat to England. This was actually Mondragon's third FIFA World Cup finals, spanning a record 20 years, but he did not appear in the 1994 tournament.

BIGGEST WINS

Bolivia 7 Venezuela 0
(22 August 1993)

Argentina 0 Colombia 5
(5 September 1993)

Colombia 5 Uruguay 0
(6 June 2004)

Colombia 5 Peru 0
(4 June 2006)

Ecuador 6 Peru 0
(22 June 1975)

Paraguay 7 Bolivia 0
(30 April 1949)

Hong Kong 0 Paraguay 7
(17 November 2010)

Peru 9 Ecuador 1
(11 August 1938)

Venezuela 6 Puerto Rico 0
(26 December 1946)

ABOVE-PAR PARAGUAY

In their eighth appearance at a FIFA World Cup, Paraguay topped their first-round group for the first time in 2010. Not only that, they went on to reach a later stage of the tournament than ever before, the quarter-finals, before narrowly losing 1-0 to Spain. Their penalty shoot-out victory over Japan in the second round (Oscar Cardozo converting the decisive kick) meant four South American countries made the quarter-finals – outnumbering the three European nations – for the first time. That said, there were no quarter-finals in 1930, 1950, 1974, 1978 or 1982. Paraguay followed up their impressive FIFA World Cup display by reaching the final of the following year's Copa America, only losing in the end to Uruguay (3-0).

TIM'S TIME

Peru were coached at the 1982 FIFA World Cup by Tim, who had been waiting an unprecedented 44 years to return to the FIFA World Cup finals – after playing once as striker for his native Brazil in the 1938 tournament.

HIGH LIFE

Bolivia and Ecuador play their home internationals at higher altitudes than any other teams on earth. Bolivia's showpiece Estadio Hernando Siles stadium, in the capital La Paz, is 3,637 metres (11,932ft) above sea level, while Ecuador's main Estadio Olimpico Atahualpa, in Quito, sits 2,800 metres (9,185ft) above sea level. Opposing teams have complained that the rarefied nature of the air makes it difficult to breathe, let alone play, but a FIFA ban on playing competitive internationals at least 2,500 metres (8,200ft) above sea level, first introduced in May 2007, was amended a month later – adjusting the limit to 3,000 metres (9,840ft) and allowing Estadio Hernando Siles to be used as a special case. The altitude ban was suspended entirely in May 2008. FIFA had changed its mind after protests by Bolivia, Ecuador and other affected nations Colombia and Peru. Other campaigners to overturn the law included Argentina legend Diego Maradona. He may have regretted his decision. In March 2009 Bolivia scored a 6-1 home win against Argentina in a FIFA World Cup qualifier. The Argentina coach was... Diego Maradona.

STUDYING THE FORM

Peru captain **Claudio Pizarro** is the highest-scoring foreign-born footballer in Germany's Bundesliga, his successful spells – two apiece – with Werder Bremen and Bayern Munich bringing him 176 goals in 370 league games, as well as a 2012–13 UEFA Champions League winners' medal with Bayern. His international career has been patchier, hampered by a fractured skull suffered against Venezuela at the 2004 Copa America and a three-month ban for joining a hotel party while on international duty in 2007. But he did score Peru's fastest international goal, after 18 seconds of their 3-1 friendly victory over Mexico in August 2003. He has also enjoyed success off the football field and on the racing track, as co-owner – with English footballer Joey Barton – of a racehorse named Crying Lightning, after a song by the rock band the Arctic Monkeys.

BIGGEST DEFEATS

Brazil 10 Bolivia 1
(10 April 1949)

Brazil 9 Colombia 0
(24 March 1997)

Argentina 12 Ecuador 0
(22 January 1942)

Argentina 8 Paraguay 0
(20 October 1926)

Brazil 7 Peru 0
(26 June 1997)

Argentina 11 Venezuela 0
(10 August 1975)

BOTERO'S ERA

Bolivia failed to reach the 2010 FIFA World Cup but did pull off one of the most eye-catching results of the qualifying campaign – a 6–1 thrashing of Argentina, who had previously been unbeaten under new coach Diego Maradona. The 1 April 2009 game in La Paz made an April fool of Maradona but a national icon of striker **Joaquin Botero,** who hit a hat-trick. A month later, however, the 31-year-old decided to quit international football, bowing out after 48 caps and a Bolivian-record 20 goals.

ELITE CUB

Peru forward Teofilo Cubillas became the first player to twice end a FIFA World Cup finals with at least five goals – he scored five apiece in 1970 and 1978, but did not win the Golden Boot on either occasion. Germany's Miroslav Klose emulated the achievement, scoring five times in both 2002 and 2006, as did compatriot, Thomas Muller, who scored five in 2010 and 2014. Klose and Muller, however, did win the Golden Boot, Klose in 2006 and Muller four years later.

COOL DUDAMEL

Venezuela suffered some bad defeats when missing out on the 1998 FIFA World Cup. They ended with no wins and 13 defeats in 16 games, scoring 13 and conceding 41 goals. The losses included 4–1 to Peru, 6–1 to Bolivia and 6–0 to Chile, for whom Ivan Zamorano scored five. But their goalkeeper Rafael Dudamel had a moment to savour against Argentina in October 1996, when he scored with a direct free-kick late in the game. Venezuela still lost 5–2.

HOT ROD

Colombia's most expensive ever player was cruelly denied a role at the 2014 FIFA World Cup. Star striker Radamel Falcao failed to recover in time from a knee injury suffered at the start of that year. This gave the chance for his AS Monaco team-mate **James Rodriguez** to emerge not only as Colombia's main man, but also one of the most dazzling players at the whole tournament. The 22-year-old playmaker scored in all five of Colombia's matches, six goals in all – including a long-range volley against Uruguay, which opposing manager Oscar Tabarez described as one of the finest the FIFA World Cup had ever seen. Rodriguez joined Monaco for €45 million from FC Porto in May 2013. There he was joined, a few weeks later, by compatriot Falcao, who cost Monaco €60 million when they signed him from Atletico Madrid. The striker – named after the 1980s Brazil midfielder Falcao – has scored 20 goals in 57 games for Colombia, behind only Arnoldo Iguaran who managed 25 in 68.

CHRISTIAN TRIBUTE

Ecuador's footballers dedicated their 2014 FIFA World Cup campaign to former team-mate Christian "Chucho" Benitez, who died suddenly from a cardiac arrest in July 2013 at the age of only 27. Team-mate, and Ecuador's captain at the 2014 FIFA World Cup finals, Antonio Valencia had Benitez's number 11 tattooed on his arm in tribute and the number was officially "retired" by the Ecuador FA. FIFA World Cup rules, however, meant the number had to be worn, and it was given to striker Felipe Caicedo at the 2014 finals.

MOST INTERNATIONAL CAPS

Bolivia	Luis Cristaldo	93
	Marco Sandy	93
Colombia	Carlos Valderrama	111
Ecuador	Ivan Hurtado	167
Paraguay	Paulo Da Silva	112
Peru	Roberto Palacios	128
Venezuela	Juan Arango	120

FIVE-STAR PARAGUAY

The South American Footballer of the Year award dates back to 1971 and has been dominated by players from Brazil and Argentina. However, five Paraguayan players have won the award, all since 1985 – and the honours have come roughly every five years. The first was attacking midfielder Romerito (Julio Cesar Romero) – the only Paraguayan named in Pele's top 125 living players in 2004 – who claimed the prize in 1985. Five years later, it went to Raul Vicente Amarilla who, although Paraguayan, did not win a cap for his country (he had won two Spanish Under-21 caps when playing club football over there). Prolific goalscoring goalkeeper Jose Luis Chilavert won the award in 1996 and he was followed by two strikers, Jose Cardozo, in 2002, and Salvador Cabanas, in 2007.

IVAN THE ADMIRABLE

Ecuador defender Ivan Hurtado is South America's most-capped footballer, playing 167 games after making his debut in 1992 – including five goals. He was one of Ecuador's most influential players at their first FIFA World Cup finals, in 2002, and captained them as they reached the second round of the competition four years later.

MEDELLIN MURDER

Tragic Colombian defender Andres Escobar, 27, was shot dead outside a Medellin bar ten days after scoring an own goal in a 1994 FIFA World Cup first-round match against the United States. Colombia lost the game 2-1 and were eliminated from a tournament some observers – including Pele – had tipped them to win.

MARKSMAN SPENCER

Ecuador's greatest player of all time is arguably prolific striker **Alberto Spencer,** even though he played much of his club football in Uruguay. Spencer holds the record for most goals in South America's Copa Libertadores club championship, scoring 54 times between 1960 and 1972 and lifting the trophy three times with Uruguay's Penarol. He also scored four goals in 11 games for Ecuador and once in four appearances for Uruguay. Spencer was nicknamed "Magic Head" and was even praised as a better header of the ball than Pele – the tribute coming from Pele himself.

MOST INTERNATIONAL GOALS

Bolivia	Joaquin Botero	20
Colombia	Arnoldo Iguaran	25
Ecuador	Agustin Delgado	31
Paraguay	Roque Santa Cruz	29
Peru	Teofilo Cubillas	26
Venezuela	Juan Arango	22
	Giancarlo Maldonado	22

SAFE HANDS OSCAR

Keeping clean sheets for Colombia all the way through the 2001 Copa America was **Oscar Cordoba**, who went on to become his country's most-capped goalkeeper – with 73 appearances between 1993 and 2006.

HIGHS AND LOWS FOR LOLO

Teodoro "Lolo" Fernandez scored six goals in two games for Peru at the 1936 Summer Olympics, including five in a 7–3 defeat of Finland and another in a 4–2 victory over Austria. But Peru were outraged when the Austrians claimed that fans had been invading the pitch and were even more upset when officials ordered the match to be replayed. Peru withdrew from the tournament in protest, while Austria went on to claim silver. But Fernandez and his team-mates had a happier ending at the Copa America three years later, with Peru crowned champions and Fernandez finishing as top scorer with seven goals. Only Teofilo Cubillas, with 26 goals in 81 games, has scored more for Peru than Fernandez's 24 from 32 appearances.

CANIZA CAN DO

Centre-back and captain Denis Caniza, 36, became the first Paraguayan to play at four different FIFA World Cups, with his one appearance against New Zealand during the 2010 tournament. The same event brought a milestone for team-mate Roque Santa Cruz – his goal in the first-round game against Brazil equalled Jose Saturnino Cardozo's all-time Paraguayan scoring record of 25. Fellow striker Salvador Cabanas missed out on the tournament after being shot in the head with a gun in a nightclub five months earlier – though he did recover well enough to return to professional football in 2012.

AFRICA

The African confederation organized its inaugural Cup of Nations in 1957, only a year after it was founded. Egypt, with a record seven victories, were the first winners while most recent include first-timers Zambia then Nigeria in 2013. In the FIFA World Cup, South Africa, in 2010, were Africa's first finals hosts but it is still waiting for a semi-finalist (Cameroon, Senegal and Ghana have all lost quarter-finals). And in 2014, only two teams made it to the second round, where Algeria and Nigeria both lost.

Ghana reached the quarter-finals of the FIFA World Cup in 2010 but, despite colourful vocal support, the Black Stars failed narrowly to progress beyond the group stage at Brazil 2014.

NORTH AFRICA FIFA WORLD CUP RECORDS

FAWZI'S FIRST

Abdelrahman Fawzi became the first African footballer to score at a FIFA World Cup, when he pulled a goal back for Egypt against Hungary in the first round of the 1934 tournament – then scored an equalizer eight minutes later, to make it 2-2 at half-time. Egypt went on to lose the match 4-2, and would not return to the finals for another 56 years.

PLAY-OFF PIQUE

Morocco's qualification for the 1970 FIFA World Cup ended a 36-year African exile from the finals. No African countries played at the 1966 FIFA World Cup in Africa, with 16 possible candidate countries all boycotting the event because FIFA wanted the top African team to face a side from Asia or Oceania in a qualification play-off.

AGELESS ALI

Tunisian goalkeeper **Ali Boumnijel** played in all three of his country's games at the 2006 FIFA World Cup – making him the oldest player to feature in Germany that summer, as well as only the fifth man over the age of 40 to play at a FIFA World Cup. Boumnijel conceded six goals in those three matches, against Saudi Arabia (two, in a 2-2 draw), Spain (three, in a 3-1 defeat) and Ukraine (one, in a 1-0 loss).

REDS IN A ROW

When Antar Yahia was sent off for a second bookable offence, three minutes into stoppage-time of Algeria's 1-0 defeat to the USA at the 2010 FIFA World Cup, it was not only the latest red card shown in any World Cup game not featuring extra-time. It also meant at least one player had been sent off on eight consecutive days of the 2010 tournament – a record run for any FIFA World Cup.

DJAB FAB

Barring penalty shoot-outs, no African has scored a later FIFA World Cup goal than Algerian midfielder **Abdelmoumene Djabou**. His consolation strike in a 2-1 second-round loss to Germany on 30 June 2014 was timed at 120 minutes and 50 seconds. This was the third meeting between the two teams. Algeria had followed a 2-0 friendly win in 1964 with a shock 2-1 success at the 1982 FIFA World Cup.

HAIL HALLICHE

Algeria became the first African nation to score four goals in one game at a FIFA World Cup finals when they defeated South Korea 4-2 at Porto Alegre in their Group H contest in the Brazil 2014 tournament. The Algerians went on to finish second in the group, behind winners Belgium, and thus qualified for the knock-out stages for the first time. In the second round they faced one of the tournament favourites, Germany, and Algeria only departed after losing a thrilling match 2-1 after extra time. One of Algeria's scorers in the victory over South Korea on 22 June – they had raced into a 3-0 half-time lead – was centre-back **Rafik Halliche** (he headed the second goal), who by the end of the 2014 tournament had made eight FIFA World Cup appearances – a new Algerian record.

MOROCCAN ROLL

Morocco were the first North African country to reach the second round of a FIFA World Cup, though they were knocked out, 1-0, by eventual finalists West Germany. It was in Mexico in 1986 that Morocco were the first African team to top a FIFA World Cup group, finishing above England, Poland and Portugal. Crucial was their 3-1 victory over Portugal in their final group game, following goalless draws against the other two teams – including an England side who lost captain Bryan Robson to a dislocated shoulder and vice-captain Ray Wilkins to a red card. **Abderrazak Khairi** scored two of the goals against Portugal, while Lothar Matthaus's winning strike for Germany came with just three minutes remaining.

NORTH AFRICAN COUNTRIES' BEST FIFA WORLD CUP PERFORMANCES

ALGERIA: Second round 2014
EGYPT: First round 1934, 1990
MOROCCO: Second round 2006
TUNISIA: First round 1978, 1998, 2002, 2006

NORTH AFRICAN COUNTRIES' FIFA WORLD CUP QUALIFICATIONS

ALGERIA: 4 (1982, 1986, 2010, 2014)
MOROCCO: 4 (1970, 1986, 1994, 1998)
TUNISIA: 4 (1978, 1998, 2002, 2006)
EGYPT: 2 (1934, 1990)

NORTH AFRICA: TOP FIFA WORLD CUP GOALSCORERS

Salah Assad	(Algeria)	2
Salaheddine Bassir	(Morocco)	2
Abdelmoumene Djabou	(Algeria)	2
Abdelrahman Fawzi	(Egypt)	2
Abdeljalil Hadda	(Morocco)	2
Abderrazak Khairi	(Morocco)	2
Islam Slimani	(Algeria)	2

NO WAITING GAME

Morocco's 2-1 defeat to Saudi Arabia in 1994 was one of the last two games to be played simultaneously at a FIFA World Cup, without falling on a final match-day of a group. Belgium were beating Holland 1-0 at the same time, with every team in Group F having still one game to play. At later tournaments, every match has been played separately until the climactic two fixtures of any group.

HOMEGROWN HERO

Of the six African countries at the 2010 FIFA World Cup, Algeria's was the only squad with an African coach – **Rabah Saadane**, in his fifth separate stint in charge since 1981. He previously led his country to the 1986 FIFA World Cup in Mexico, where they were also eliminated in the first round. Along with Honduras, the Algeria team of 2010 were one of only two countries failing to score a single goal. However, they did concede just twice in their three games: 1-0 defeats to Slovakia and the USA, and a surprise goalless draw with England – Algeria's first-ever FIFA World Cup clean sheet.

MOKHTAR RUNS AMOK

Egypt had to play only two matches to qualify for the 1934 FIFA World Cup, becoming the first African representatives at the tournament. Both games were against a Palestine side under the British mandate – and the Egyptians won both games handsomely, 7-1 in Cairo and 4-1 in Palestine. Captain and striker Mahmoud Mokhtar scored a hat-trick in the first leg, a brace in the second. Turkey were also meant to contest qualifiers against the two sides, but withdrew, leaving the path to the finals free for Egypt.

TUNISIA IN TUNE

Tunisia became the first African team to win a match at a FIFA World Cup finals, when they beat Mexico 3-1 in Rosario, Argentina, in 1978 – thanks to goals from Ali Kaabi, Nejib Ghommidh and Mokhtar Dhouib. While they share with Morocco and Algeria the North African record of reaching four different FIFA World Cups, they are the only nation from that part of the continent to qualify for three finals in a row – in 1998, 2002 and 2006. Among the players to feature in all three tournaments were 2006 captain Riadh Bouazizi, Hatem Trabelsi and **Radhi Jaidi**.

NORTH AFRICA NATIONAL RECORDS

FRENCH CONNECTIONS

Algeria were the only North African country to qualify for the 2014 FIFA World Cup, as Ethiopia, Egypt and Tunisia all fell short in the final play-offs. The Algerians' victory over Burkina Faso gave their Bosnian coach Vahid Halilhodzic the chance to finally manage at a finals, having led the Ivory Coast through qualifying four years earlier only to be fired before the finals. All three Algeria goalscorers against Burkina Faso were born in France but with family connections to Algeria: Sofiane Feghouli, former France U21s captain Carl Medjani and skipper **Madjid Bougherra**.

ABOUD AWAKENING

After the political upheaval in Libya in 2011, little was expected of the country's footballers at the 2012 Africa Cup of Nations. Yet they brought some joy to supporters with a surprise 2-1 victory over Senegal in their final first-round match – the first time Libya had ever won an Africa Cup of Nations match outside their own country. Their kit bore the new flag of the country's National Transitional Council. Among the star performers were Ihaab al Boussefi – scorer of both goals against Senegal – and goalkeeper and captain **Samir Aboud**, at 39 the oldest player at the tournament. Libya played their first competitive home game in the capital Tripoli since 2010 when they hosted the Democratic Republic of Congo in a 2014 FIFA World Cup qualifier in June 2013, the game ending in a 0-0 draw.

OFFICIAL INFLUENCE

The first African to referee a FIFA World Cup final was Morocco's **Said Belqola**, who controlled the 1998 climax in which hosts France beat Brazil 3-0. Perhaps his most notable moment was sending off France's **Marcel Desailly** in the 68th minute – brandishing only the third red card to be shown in a FIFA World Cup final. Belqola was 41 at the time. He died from cancer just under four years later.

FOUNDING FATHERS

The Confederation of African Football was officially established at a meeting in the Sudanese capital Khartoum, in the city's Grand Hotel on 7 February 1957 – three days before the first Africa Cup of Nations kicked off in the same city. Representatives of Sudan, South Africa, Ethiopia and Egypt were present at the first assembly, and Egypt's Abdel Aziz Salem became CAF's first president.

SUDAN IMPACT

After two second-place and one third-place finishes, Sudan became the third and last of the Africa Cup of Nations founders to lift the trophy, when they beat Ghana in the 1970 final. Hosts Sudan left it late to reach the final, with two goals from El-Issed – the second 12 minutes into extra-time – seeing off Egypt. The same player scored the only goal of the final, after 12 minutes.

NORTH AFRICA: SELECTED TOP GOALSCORERS

ALGERIA: Abdelhafid Tasfaout		35
EGYPT: Hossam Hassan		68
LIBYA: Tarik El Taib		23
MOROCCO: Ahmed Faras		42
SUDAN: Haytham Tambal		26
TUNISIA: Issam Jemaa		36

THE BLACK EAGLES HAVE LANDED

The Confederation of African Football welcomed a new and 54th member state on 10 February 2012, when the newly-independent nation of South Sudan created a new team and football association. The "Black Eagles" were not admitted in time to take part in qualifiers for the 2013 Africa Cup of Nations but hope to take part in future events – and win FIFA membership as well. Football association president Oliver Benjamin said: "We are a country that has just come out of war. We lack even the balls and the T-shirts – we don't have these in our country. Some of our players use their socks, put clothes in them, wrap them up and play with them. That is our love of football."

HURRAH FOR SALAH

Egypt have a rising star in **Mohamed Salah**. His performances at the London 2012 Olympic Games helped win him that year's Most Promising Talent award from the African Football Confederation. A week before his 21st birthday in June 2013 he scored a hat-trick against Zimbabwe in a 4-2 FIFA World Cup qualifier win and ended the campaign with six goals – only equalled by compatriot Mohamed Aboutrika and Ghana's Asamoah Gyan in Africa's 2014 qualifying rounds. His performances for both country and Swiss club Basel earned him an £11million move to English Premier League giants Chelsea in January 2014.

HEAD-TO-HEAD

The international career of Algeria's leading scorer **Abdelhafid Tasfaout** came to an end at the 2002 Africa Cup of Nations – though it could have been a lot worse. Tasfaout was knocked out by a collision with Mali defender Boubacar Diarra which caused him to swallow his tongue, prompting fears he might not even survive – though, thankfully, he did recover. Tasfaout, who played French league football for six years, scored 34 goals in 62 games for Algeria between 1990 and 2002.

SORE LOSERS

Libya could claim the record for highest-scoring victory by an African side, having racked up a 21-0 lead over Oman during the Arab Nations Cup in April 1966. But the Oman players walked off with 10 minutes remaining, in protest at Libya being awarded a penalty, and played no further part in the competition.

NORTH AFRICA: SELECTED TOP APPEARANCES

ALGERIA: Lakhdar Belloumi		101
EGYPT: Ahmed Hassan		184
LIBYA: Tarik El Taib		77
MOROCCO: Abdelmajid Dolmy		140
SUDAN: Haitham Mustafa		103
TUNISIA: Radhi Jaidi		105

STRIKING RIVALS

A homegrown hero is back at the top of Tunisia's scoring ranks after Gabes-born **Issam Jemaa** overtook Francileudo Santos and now has 34 goals from 73 appearances since his debut in 2005. Jemma began his career with Esperance but since 2005 has played his club football in France, for Lens and Auxerre. Brazil-born Santos, by contrast, did not visit Tunisia until his late teens and only accepted citizenship at the age of 24 in 2004. Within weeks he was helping his new nation not only to host but win the 2004 Africa Cup of Nations, scoring four goals including the opener in the final against Morocco. Both Jemaa and Santos were hampered by injury ahead of the 2006 FIFA World Cup – Santos played only 11 minutes at the tournament, while Jemaa missed out all together. He has recovered to continue scoring ever since, including the winner against Niger at the 2012 Africa Cup of Nations.

FIFA WORLD CUP SUB-SAHARAN AFRICA

MAD FOR 'MADIBA'

Apart from the Dutch and Spanish sides competing in the 2010 FIFA World Cup final, one of the star attractions in Johannesburg's Soccer City stadium on 11 July 2010 was South Africa's legendary former president **Nelson Mandela**. The frail 91-year-old – known affectionately by his tribal name of "Madiba" – was driven on to the pitch before the game in a golf cart and given a rapturous reception by the crowd. It marked his one and only public appearance at the tournament. Mandela had hoped to attend the opening ceremony and game on 11 June, but was mourning the death of his 13-year-old great-granddaughter in a car crash the previous evening. He had been a high-profile presence at the FIFA vote in 2004 which awarded South Africa hosting rights for 2010.

GOING FOR A SONG

Two players have been sent off at two separate FIFA World Cups: Cameroon's Rigobert Song, against Brazil in 1994 and Chile four years later, and France's Zinedine Zidane – red-carded against Saudi Arabia in 1998 and against Italy in the 2006 final. Song's red card against Brazil made him the youngest player to be dismissed at a FIFA World Cup – he was just 17 years and 358 days old. Song, born in Nkanglikock on 1 July 1976, is Cameroon's most-capped player, with 137 appearances – including winning displays in the 2000 and 2002 finals of the Africa Cup of Nations. He has been joined in the national team by his nephew, Arsenal utility player Alexandre Song Billong.

SUB-SAHARAN AFRICAN COUNTRIES' BEST FIFA WORLD CUP PERFORMANCES

ANGOLA:	First round 2006
CAMEROON:	Quarter-finals 1990
GHANA:	Quarter-finals 2010
IVORY COAST:	First round 2006, 2010, 2014
NIGERIA:	Second round 1994, 1998, 2014
SENEGAL:	Quarter-finals 2002
SOUTH AFRICA:	First round 1998, 2002, 2010
TOGO:	First round 2006
ZAIRE/CONGO DR:	First round 1974

MORE FOR ASAMOAH

Ghana's Asamoah Gyan has scored more FIFA World Cup goals than any other player representing an African nation. He took his overall tally to six with two strikes at the Brazil 2014 FIFA World Cup – putting him one ahead of Cameroon's Roger Milla. He also became the first African to score at three separate FIFA World Cups and his 11 matches took him level with Cameroon's Francois Omam-Biyik.

JOLLY ROGER

Cameroon striker **Roger Milla**, famous for dancing around corner flags after each goal, became the FIFA World Cup's oldest scorer against Russia in 1994 – aged 42 years and 39 days. He came on as substitute during that tournament with his surname handwritten, rather than printed, on the back of his shirt. Milla, born in Yaounde on 20 May 1952, had retired from professional football for a year before Cameroon's president, Paul Biya, persuaded him to join the 1990 FIFA World Cup squad. His goals in that tournament helped him win the African Footballer of the Year award for an unprecedented second time – 14 years after he had first received the trophy. He finally ended his international career after the 1994 FIFA World Cup in the United States, finishing with 102 caps and 28 goals to his name.

SUB-SAHARAN AFRICAN COUNTRIES' FIFA WORLD CUP QUALIFICATIONS

CAMEROON:	7	(1982, 1990, 1994, 1998, 2002, 2010, 2014)
NIGERIA:	5	(1994, 1998, 2002, 2010, 2014)
SOUTH AFRICA:	3	(1998, 2002, 2010)
GHANA:	3	(2006, 2010, 2014)
IVORY COAST:	3	(2006, 2010, 2014)
ANGOLA:	1	(2006)
SENEGAL:	1	(2002)
TOGO:	1	(2006)
ZAIRE/CONGO DR:	1	(1974)

OH NO, YOBO

Nigeria captain Joseph Yobo set two national records when he played a second-round tie against France at the 2014 FIFA World Cup – yet his late own goal in a 2-0 defeat may make it a match he would rather forget. His appearance that day not only made him the first Nigerian international to reach a century of caps, but also meant he had played 10 FIFA World Cup games – one more than previous national record-holder Jay-Jay Okocha.

RATOMIR GETS IT RIGHT

Ghana went through four different managers during qualifiers for the 2006 FIFA World Cup, with Serbian coach Ratomir Dujkovic finally clinching the country a place at the finals for the very first time. He led them through the whole of 2005 unbeaten, winning a FIFA prize for being the most-improved team of the year. Ghana were the only African country to make it through the first round of both the 2006 and 2010 FIFA World Cups, despite having the youngest average age of any squad each time. They were again coached by a Serb in 2010, this time Milovan Rajevac.

BROTHERS AT ARMS

The Boateng brothers made FIFA World Cup history in playing against each other at the 2010 finals in South Africa. Both were also selected for the 'replay' in 2014. In 2010 Jerome played left-back for Germany while elder half-brother **Kevin-Prince**, who had switched nationalities a month earlier, was in the Ghana midfield. In the group match in 2010 Jerome Boateng switched to right-back. Germany won 1-0 in South Africa while the return in Brazil ended up 2-2. Kevin-Prince was the only brother to play a full 90 minutes, in South Africa. He was substituted during the game in Brazil while Jerome was replaced during both games. In the total 180 minutes they were on the pitch together for 'only' 117 minutes.

SUB-SAHARAN AFRICAN COUNTRIES: TOP FIFA WORLD CUP GOALSCORERS

Asamoah Gyan (Ghana) 6
Roger Milla (Cameroon) 5
Papa Bouba Diop (Senegal) 3
Samuel Eto'o (Cameroon) 3
Daniel Amokachi (Nigeria) 2
Emmanuel Amunike (Nigeria) 2
Andre Ayew (Ghana) 2
Shaun Bartlett (South Africa) 2
Wilfried Bony (Ivory Coast) 2
Henri Camara (Senegal) 2
Aruna Dindane (Ivory Coast) 2
Didier Drogba (Ivory Coast) 2
Gervinho (Ivory Coast) 2
Patrick Mboma (Cameroon) 2
Benni McCarthy (South Africa) 2
Sulley Muntari (Ghana) 2
Ahmed Musa (Nigeria) 2
Francois Omam-Biyik (Cameroon) 2

KESHI JOB

Nigeria's Stephen Keshi became the first African manager to reach the knock-out stages of a FIFA World Cup when he steered his country through Group F at the 2014 tournament in Brazil. The feat also meant Nigeria were the first African country to reach the second round of three separate FIFA World Cups, having previously done so in 1994 – when Keshi was in the team – and 1998. He announced his resignation after their second-round 2-0 defeat to France, which came despite one of several brave displays by goalkeeper **Vincent Enyeama**.

THE FOURMOST

The only two African footballers to play at four FIFA World Cups – and the only three to be named in the squads for four – are all from Cameroon. Striker Samuel Eto'o became the latest in 2014, after playing in 1998, 2002 and 2010. He emulated defender Rigobert Song, who was in the Cameroon team in 1994, 1998, 2002 and 2010. Goalkeeper Jacques Songo'o was named in the country's squads for the four FIFA World Cups between 1990 and 2002, but he only actually played in the 1994 and 1998 versions.

SUB-SAHARAN AFRICA NATIONAL RECORDS

HOT DROG

Didier Drogba may have been raised in France but he was born in Ivory Coast and remains one of the African country's favourite sons for his actions both on and off the pitch. The Ivory Coast captain has a record 65 goals in 104 appearances for the Elephants. He has been credited with influence off the pitch, too, when he called for a ceasefire in the civil war-torn nation. He also pushed for an Africa Cup of Nations qualifier against Madagascar in June 2007 to be moved from the capital Abidjan to rebel army stronghold Bouake, in an effort to encourage reconciliation. Drogba, a two-time CAF African Footballer of the Year, captained the Ivory Coast team at the three FIFA World Cups they have reached, in 2006, 2010 and 2014, but he started only the third game in 2014.

SUB-SAHARAN AFRICA: SELECTED TOP GOALSCORERS

ANGOLA: Akwa	36
BOTSWANA: Jerome Ramatlhakwane	19
CAMEROON: Samuel Eto'o	56
GHANA: Asamoah Gyan	42
IVORY COAST: Didier Drogba	65
NIGERIA: Rashidi Yekini	37
SENEGAL: Henri Camara	29
SOUTH AFRICA: Benni McCarthy	32
TOGO: Emmanuel Adabayor	27
ZAMBIA: Godfrey Chitalu	79
ZIMBABWE: Peter Ndlovu	38

KNOCKED OUT ON PENALTIES

Botswana goalkeeper and captain Modiri Marumo was sent off in the middle of a penalty shoot-out against Malawi in May 2003, after punching the opposing goalkeeper Philip Nyasulu in the face. Botswana defender Michael Mogaladi had to go in goal for the rest of the shoot-out, which Malawi won 4-1.

FIFTEEN LOVE

Fifteen-year-old Samuel Kuffour became the youngest footballer to win an Olympic medal when Ghana took bronze at the 1992 Olympics in Barcelona – 27 days before his 16th birthday.

EAGLETS SOAR

The first African country to win an official FIFA tournament was Nigeria, when their "Golden Eaglets" beat Germany 2-0 in the final of the 1985 World Under-17 Championships.

SO LONG, PITSO

South Africa went through four different foreign coaches – in five separate spells – between 2004 and 2010 before the top job went to South African Pitso Mosimane. He had previously won four caps as a player, then assisted Brazilian Carlos Alberto Parreira at the 2010 FIFA World Cup. Mosimane's first nine games in charge brought six wins, two draws and just one defeat, but he lost the post in 2012 after a winless nine-game streak cost South Africa the chance of competing at the 2014 FIFA World Cup and was replaced by Gordon Igesund.

GENEROUS GEORGE

In 1995 Liberia's George Weah became the first African to be named FIFA World Player of the Year, an award that recognized his prolific goalscoring exploits for Paris Saint-Germain and AC Milan. That same year he added the European Footballer of the Year and African Footballer of the Year prizes to his collection. Weah not only captained his country, but often funded the team's travels – though he remains the only FIFA World Player of the Year whose country has never qualified for a FIFA World Cup. After retiring in 2003 after 60 caps and 22 international goals, he moved into politics and ran unsuccessfully for the Liberian presidency in 2005.

SUPER FRED

In 2007, **Frederic Kanoute** became the first non-African-born player to be named African Footballer of the Year. The striker was born in Lyon, France, and played for France U-21s. But the son of a French mother and Malian father opted to play for Mali in 2004, scoring 23 goals in 37 appearances before retiring from international football after the 2010 Africa Cup of Nations. As well as going down in history as one of Mali's greatest-ever players, he is also a hero to fans of Spanish side CF Sevilla, for whom he scored 143 goals, winning two UEFA Cups along the way. Only three men have scored more goals for the club.

SUB-SAHARAN AFRICA: SELECTED TOP APPEARANCES

ANGOLA: Akwa		80
BOTSWANA: Mompati Thuma		66
CAMEROON: Rigobert Song		137
GHANA: Richard Kingson		90
IVORY COAST: Didier Zokora		121
NIGERIA: Joseph Yobo		100
SENEGAL: Henri Camara		99
SOUTH AFRICA: Aaron Mokoena		107
TOGO: Dare Nibombe		71
ZAMBIA: David Chabala		108
ZIMBABWE: Peter Ndlovu		100

DRAMATIC TURNAROUNDS

Ghana managed to concede three goals in a minute to world champions Germany in an April 1993 friendly. Ghana had been 1-0 up with 20 minutes left, before losing the game 6-1. In the 1989 FIFA World Youth Championships, Nigeria were 4-0 down with 25 minutes left in their quarter-final against the Soviet Union, but hit back to draw 4-4 before winning 5-3 on penalties.

MAESTRO'S MEMORIALS

Didier Zokora, the Ivory Coast's most-capped player, bears several tattoos cherishing members of his family – chiefly his tragic younger brother Armand, whose name is inked on Didier's right forearm. The duo had both just signed professional contracts with local side ASEC Mimosas when Armand drowned off a beach in 1997 at the age of 14. On his left forearm Zokora – himself nicknamed "Maestro" – has the names of his children Sarah and Nadya while a tattoo of his wife Mariam is just above his heart. Zokora has scored just once in 121 international appearances, in a 4-0 FIFA World Cup qualifier victory over Botswana in June 2008.

MAD FOR "MADIBA"

The world of football united in paying tribute to one of the game's greatest fans, when former South African president and anti-apartheid leader Nelson Mandela died aged 94 on 5 December 2013. His final public appearance had been at the 2010 FIFA World Cup final, when he and wife Graca Machel were driven around the pitch and given a rapturous reception by the crowd. Mandela – known affectionately by his tribal name of 'Madiba' – had played a crucial role in convincing FIFA to award the 2010 hosting rights to South Africa. He had often spoken of how, when imprisoned on Robben Island, he and fellow inmates kept their spirits up by playing football. He recalled: "The only access to the World Cup was on radio. Football was the only joy to prisoners." Former South Africa captain Lucas Radebe described Mandela as "my hero", David Beckham said meeting him was "the highlight of my career" and Pele called him "one of the most influential people in my life". The week of Mandela's death, every UEFA Champions League game began with the unfurling of 12m by 2m banners proclaiming: "Madiba, the world will never forget you."

ASIA & OCEANIA

Asia wrote a major chapter in football history in 2002 when Japan and South Korea became the FIFA World Cup's first co-hosts and the Koreans produced Asia's best-ever finish, fourth. Asia's World Cup strength improved when Australia moved from Oceania in 2006. However, the 2014 FIFA World Cup was depressing for the Asian region as all four nations went out at the group stage, and Oceania was not even represented. Asia's two most populous nations, China and India, have yet to catch up with their neighbours in football terms.

Korea's dynamic fans proved as much of a sensation as their team did co-hosting the 2002 FIFA World Cup with Japan, but there was no such luck at Brazil 2014, as Korea went home after the group stage.

AUSTRALIA

Victims, perhaps, of an overcomplicated qualifying system that has limited the country's FIFA World Cup finals appearances, and hampered by its geographical isolation that, in the early years, saw other sports prosper in the country at football's expense, it has taken many years for Australia to establish itself on the world football map. However, driven by a new generation of players, many based with top European clubs, the Socceroos delivered for the first time at the 2006 FIFA World Cup and briefly were ranked No. 1 in Asia.

AUSTRALIA RECORDS

Honours: Oceania champions 1980, 1996, 2000, 2004
First international: v New Zealand (lost 3-1), Auckland, 17 June 1922
Biggest win: 31-0 v American Samoa, Coffs Harbour, 11 April 2001
Biggest defeat: 7-0 v Croatia, Zagreb, 6 June 1998

NATIVE HERO

Harry Williams holds a proud place in Australian football history as the first Aboriginal player to represent the country in internationals. He made his debut in 1970 and was part of the first Australian squad to compete at a FIFA World Cup finals, in West Germany in 1974.

MOMENTOUS MORI

Damian Mori's then-Australian record tally of 29 goals, in just 45 internationals, included no fewer than five hat-tricks: trebles against Fiji and Tahiti, four-goal hauls against the Cook Islands and Tonga, and five in Australia's 13-0 trouncing of the Solomon Islands in a 1998 FIFA World Cup qualifier. His international career spanned from 1992 to 2002, but he never played in a FIFA World Cup finals as Australia didn't qualify. He did, though, claim a world record for scoring the fastest goal – after just 3.69 seconds for his club side Adelaide City against Sydney United in 1996.

NEILL APPEAL

Tough-tackling Australia veteran **Lucas Neill** had to wait until his 91st international appearance before scoring his first goal for his country: the final strike in a 4-0 victory over Jordan in June 2013 that boosted their chances of reaching the 2014 FIFA World Cup. Qualification was clinched in the next game, thanks to a lone goal by Josh Kennedy to defeat Iraq – making Australia the third team, after hosts Brazil and Japan, to secure a place at the finals. Former Blackburn Rovers, West Ham United and Galatasary defender Neill made his Australia debut in October 1996, becoming the country's third-youngest international. His scoring record, though, pales alongside that of fellow centre-back Robbie Cornthwaite, his goal against Romania in February 2013 was his third in his first six games for Australia.

TOP CAPS

#	Player	Caps
1	Mark Schwarzer	109
2	Lucas Neill	96
3	Brett Emerton	95
4	Alex Tobin	87
5	Paul Wade	84
6	Luke Wilkshire	80
7	Mark Bresciano	76
=	Tony Vidmar	76
9	Tim Cahill	71
10	Scott Chipperfield	68

CAHILL MAKES HISTORY

Tim Cahill's FIFA World Cup goals total is only one fewer than all other Australians combined. He scored the Socceroos' first ever finals goals, netting in the 84th (and 89th) minutes of a comeback 3-1 win over Japan in 2006. His most spectacular goal was his last, a first-time volley in a 3-2 defeat to the Netherlands at Porto Alegre in 2014. Sadly for Cahill he later received his second yellow card of the finals and so missed Australia's final match. He scored twice in 2006, once in 2010 – and received a red card in Australia's opening game – and twice in 2014. Australia's other FIFA World Cup finals scorers are Brett Holman (two), John Aloisi, Craig Moore, Harry Kewell and Mile Jedinak (all one).

AUSTRALIA'S SHOOT-OUT RECORD

Australia are the only team to reach the FIFA World Cup finals via a penalty shoot-out – in the final qualifying play-off in November 2005. They had lost the first leg 1-0 to Uruguay in Montevideo. Mark Bresciano's goal levelled the aggregate score, which remained 1-1 after extra-time. Goalkeeper **Mark Schwarzer** made two crucial saves as Australia won the shoot-out 4-2, with John Aloisi scoring the winning spot-kick. Schwarzer passed Alex Tobin to become Australia's most-capped footballer with his 88th appearance, in January 2011, in the AFC Asian Cup final defeat to Japan. Tobin had been in defence when Schwarzer made his Australia debut against Canada in 1993.

COME TO A LAND DOWN UNDER

After reaching the quarter-finals of their first AFC Asian Cup in 2007 and finishing runners-up to Japan four years later, Australia will want to make it third time lucky at the 2015 tournament – especially as this time the country will be playing host. Australia was the only country to bid for staging rights.

THREE-CARD TRICK

Graham Poll, in 2006, was not the first referee at a FIFA World Cup to show the same player three yellow cards. It happened in another game involving Australia, when their English-born midfielder Ray Richards was belatedly sent off against Chile at the 1974 FIFA World Cup. Reserve official Clive Thomas, from Wales, informed Iranian referee Jafar Namdar he had booked Richards three times without dismissing him. Richards played four unwarranted minutes before eventually receiving his marching orders.

PRECEDENT KENNEDY

Australian newspapers acclaimed a player nicknamed "Jesus" as their "saviour" when Josh Kennedy's 83rd-minute goal against Iraq in June 2013 clinched a place at the 2014 FIFA World Cup for his country – ensuring a third consecutive appearance at the finals. Lofty striker Kennedy, given the nickname for his former styling of long hair and a beard, had entered the field just six minutes earlier as a replacement for Tim Cahill. It was his 16th – and most significant – goal in 30 appearances for Australia.

BET ON BRETT

Brett Holman's goal against Ghana, in a 1-1 draw at the 2010 tournament, made him Australia's youngest marksman at a FIFA World Cup. He was 26 years 84 days old at the time, 105 days younger than Tim Cahill had been when striking against Japan in 2006. Holman added to his tally five days later, when Australia beat Serbia 2-1. Cahill himself was also on the scoresheet, though goal difference meant Australia failed to reach the second round.

TOP SCORERS

1	Tim Cahill	34
2	Damian Mori	29
3	Archie Thompson	28
4	John Aloisi	27
5	Attila Abonyi	25
=	John Kosima	25
7	Brett Emerton	20
=	David Zdrilic	20
9	Graham Arnold	19
10	Ray Baartz	18

KEWELL THE TOPS

Harry Kewell (born on 22 September 1978) is widely regarded as Australia's best-ever player. The left winger has scored 13 goals in 39 international appearances, including the equalizer against Croatia that took Australia to the last 16 of the 2006 FIFA World Cup finals. Kewell has enjoyed a successful club career with Leeds United, Liverpool and Galatasaray. He is also the only Australian-born player to gain a Champions League winner's medal, with Liverpool in 2005. He endured an unhappier time at the 2010 FIFA World Cup, when he lasted just 22 minutes before being red-carded for handball against Ghana – the 150th sending-off in the history of the finals.

JAPAN

The past two decades have seen great breakthroughs for Japanese football. Until the first professional league was introduced in 1993, clubs had been amateur and football was overshadowed in Japan's affections by other sports such as baseball, martial arts, table tennis and golf. Even more significantly, Japan co-hosted the 2002 FIFA World Cup – where the team reached the second round for the first time. And AFC Asian Cup wins in 1992, 2000, 2004 and 2011 were celebrated keenly as proof of surging standards.

TOP SCORERS

1	Kunishige Kamamoto	80
2	Kazuyoshi Miura	55
3	Shinji Okazaki	39
4	Hiromi Hara	37
5	Takuya Takagi	27
6	Kazushi Kimura	26
7	Shunsuke Nakamura	24
8	Keisuke Honda	23
=	Naohiro Takahara	23
10	Masashi Nakayama	21

NAKATA BLAZES THE TRAIL

Hidetoshi Nakata ranks among Japan's best-ever players. The midfielder set up all three goals in a 3-2 FIFA World Cup qualifying play-off win over Iran in November 1997. Nakata moved to Perugia in Italy after the 1998 finals, becoming the first Japanese player to star in Europe, and won a Serie A championship medal with Roma in 2001. He was followed abroad by international team-mates such as Shinji Ono, who joined Feyenoord in the Netherlands, and midfielder Shunsuke Nakamura, whose European employers included Reggina in Italy, Celtic in Scotland and Espanyol in Spain. Nakata started in three FIFA World Cup finals tournaments, making ten appearances and scoring one goal – the second in a 2-0 win over Tunisia that took Japan to the last 16 in 2002. Nakata won 77 caps and scored 11 goals, before surprisingly retiring from all forms of football after the 2006 FIFA World Cup, aged just 29.

POLITICAL FOOTBALL

Japan were surprise bronze medallists in the football tournament at the 1968 summer Olympics in Mexico City, and star striker **Kunishige Kamamoto** finished top scorer overall with seven goals. He remains Japan's all-time leading scorer, with 76 goals in 75 matches. Since retirement, he has combined coaching with being elected to Japan's parliament and serving as vice-president of the country's football association.

HONDA INSPIRES

After hosts Brazil, Japan were the first country to qualify for the 2014 FIFA World Cup, after Keisuke Honda's late penalty secured a 1-1 draw with Australia in June 2013. Honda had previously won two man-of-the-match awards at the 2010 FIFA World Cup and was named player of the tournament when Japan, under Italian-born coach Alberto Zaccheroni, won the 2011 AFC Asian Cup. He scored Japan's first goal at the 2014 finals, against Ivory Coast, but they lost 2-1 and exited the tournament after two defeats and a draw, prompting Zaccheroni's resignation. Honda was the first Japanese player to score at two FIFA World Cups and the first to reach three goals.

⚽ TOP CAPS

1	Yasuhito Endo	146
2	Masami Ihara	122
3	Yoshikatsu Kawaguchi	116
4	Yuji Nakazawa	110
5	Shunsuke Nakamura	98
6	Kazuyoshi Miura	89
7	Kunishige Kamamoto	84
8	Yasuyuki Konno	83
9	Junichi Inamoto	82
=	Alessandro Santos	82

CLEAN SWEEP

Japan's footballers may not have made much of an impact on the pitch at the 2014 FIFA World Cup – all four Asian teams went out in the first round, the first time this had happened. But their supporters certainly made a good impression in the stands. The fans were widely acclaimed for sticking around after each of their three group games to tidy the terraces around them. One "Blue Samurai" supporter, Kei Kawai, said: "We try to do a little bit of clean-up to show respect to the host country and just, you know, show off how clean things are in Japan. And we like to make it so here, too."

THREE AND IN

Japan's 3-1 Group E victory over Denmark in Bloemfontein at the 2010 FIFA World Cup made them the first Asian side to score three times in one FIFA World Cup match since North Korea's 5-3 defeat to Portugal in their 1966 quarter-final. Japan's goals came from Keisuke Honda, Yasuhito Endo and Shinji Okazaki. Honda and Endo both scored directly from free-kicks, the first time a team has managed such a double in one FIFA World Cup game since Yugoslavia hit three when beating Zaire 9-0 in 1974. Endo has gone on to become Japan's most-capped player, surpassing Masami Ihara's tally by appearing in an October 2012 friendly against Brazil.

SHINJI BENEFITS

Playmaker **Shinji Kagawa** became the first Japanese footballer to be part of an English league championship-winning side, when securing the Premier League title with Manchester United in 2012-13 – 12 months after helping his former club Borussia Dortmund win the Bundesliga in Germany. Kagawa was named 2012 AFC International Player of the Year. Yet he suffered for his art during Japan's triumphant 2011 AFC Asian Cup campaign, scoring twice in their victorious quarter-final but breaking his foot in the next game and thus missing the final.

TA-DA, TADANARI

The goalscoring hero whose extra-time strike clinched a record fourth AFC Asian Cup for Japan in 2011 was a man who had not even played for his country before the tournament began. Striker Tadanari Lee made his international debut in the first-round match against Jordan – and conjured perfect timing for his first Japan goal, with 11 minutes of extra-time left in the final against Australia. His midfield team-mate **Kaisuke Honda** took the prize for the event's most valuable player, while forward Shinji Okazaki's first-round hat-trick against Saudi Arabia helped earn him a place in the team of the tournament.

JAPANESE GOAL GLUT

No team have scored more goals in one AFC Asian Cup tournament than Japan's 21 in six games on their way to winning the title for the second time, in Lebanon in 2000 – though the final against Saudi Arabia was settled with just a single goal, by Shigeyoshi Mochizuki. Nine different players scored for Japan during the tournament – including Akinori Nishizawa and Naohiro Takahara, who each managed five – while their team-mate Ryuzo Morioka scored once in his own net. Japan's most emphatic victory of the tournament came in the first round, 8-1 against Uzbekistan, with both Nishizawa and Takahara hitting hat-tricks.

SOUTH KOREA

"Be the Reds!" was the rallying cry of South Korea as they co-hosted the 2002 FIFA World Cup ... energetic team become the first Asian side to ... finals, ultimately finishing fourth. South Korea ... AFC Asian Cup the first two times it was held ... and 1960). South Korea could reflect on ... continent's leading football side, ... Cup triumphs have been thin on the ... then. The country's professional ... making progress and South Korea ... have won the Asian club championship ... 10 times.

HWANG'S THE MAN

A rare veteran among South Korea's young guns at the 2002 FIFA World Cup was 33-year-old **Hwang Sun-Hong**, after Cha Bum-Kun the only other player to score a half-century of goals for the country. His 50th goal came in the 2-0 win over Poland that clinched South Korea's place in the second round. Hwang had also played in the 1990 and 1994 FIFA World Cups, but missed the 1998 event through injury. Eight of Hwang's goals came in one game, an 11-0 crushing of Nepal in October 1994. South Korea's record victory was also against poor Nepal, in September 2003 – this time ending 16-0, with five for Park Jin-Sub and three apiece for Woo Sung-Yong and Kim Do-Hoon.

HERE COMES THE SON

South Korea have played more FIFA World Cup finals matches than any other Asian team, taking their tally to 31 with three games in 2014 – though they finished bottom of Group H. Only twice has South Korea made it past the first round and their overall record is five wins, nine draws and 17 defeats. Their 30th game, which fell on 22 June 2014, a 4-2 defeat to Algeria, was an unhappier outcome than their two previous matches on the same date: a penalty shoot-out victory over Spain in a 2002 quarter-final and a 2-2 group-stage draw with Nigeria eight years later. South Korea's second goal against Algeria was scored by Bayer Leverkusen striker **Son Heung-Min**. His father, Son Woong-Chun, a former international footballer, had unsuccessfully urged coaches during qualifying to leave his son out of the team and allow him more time to develop as a player.

SPIDER CATCHER

Goalkeeper **Lee Woon-Jae** – nicknamed "Spider Hands" – made himself a national hero by making the crucial penalty save that took co-hosts South Korea into the semi-finals of the 2002 FIFA World Cup. He blocked Spain's fourth spot-kick, taken by winger Joaquin, in a quarter-final shoot-out. Lee, who also played in the 1994, 2006 and 2010 FIFA World Cups, provided more penalty saves at the 2007 AFC Asian Cup – stopping three spot-kicks in shoot-outs on South Korea's way to third place. Lee's form restricted his frequent back-up, Kim Byung-Ji, to just 62 international appearances. But Kim did at least set a new South Korean top-flight landmark of 200 clean sheets in June 2012, at the age of 42.

PARK LIFE

The tirelessly-energetic midfielder **Park Ji-Sung** can claim to be the most successful Asian footballer of all time. He became the first Asian player to lift the UEFA Champions League trophy when his club Manchester United beat Chelsea in 2008, despite missing the final. He also became the first Asian footballer to score at three successive FIFA World Cups – beginning on home turf in 2002, when his goal broke the deadlock in a first-round game against Portugal, putting South Korea through to the knock-out stages for the first time ever. International team-mate Ahn Jung-Hwan and Saudi Arabia's Sami Al-Jaber are the only other Asian footballers to have scored three FIFA World Cup goals. Park became the eighth South Korean to reach a century of caps when he captained the side in their 2011 AFC Asian Cup semi-final defeat to Japan, before announcing his international retirement to allow a younger generation to emerge.

⚽ TOP CAPS

1	Hong Myung-Bo	136
2	Lee Woon-Jae	132
3	Lee Young-Pyo	127
4	Yoo Sang-Chul	122
5	Cha Bum-Kun	121
6	Kim Tae-Young	106
7	Hwang Sun-Hong	103
8	Park Ji-Sung	100
9	Lee Dong-Gook	99
10	Kim Nam-Il	98

⚽ TOP SCORERS

1	Cha Bum-Kun	55
2	Hwang Sun-Hong	50
3	Park Lee-Chun	36
4	Kim Jae-Han	33
5	Kim Do-Hoon	30
=	Lee Dong-Gook	30
=	Choi Soon-Ho	30
8	Huh Jung-Moo	29
9	Choi Yong-Soo	27
10	Park Chu-Young	24

HONG SETS FIFA WORLD CUP RECORD

South Korea defender **Hong Myung-Bo** was the first Asian footballer to appear in four consecutive FIFA World Cup finals tournaments. He played all three games as South Korea lost to Belgium, Spain and Uruguay in 1990. He scored twice in three appearances in 1994 – his goal against Spain sparking a Korean fightback from 2-0 down to draw 2-2. In 1998 he started all three group games as South Korea were eliminated at the group stage. Four years later, on home soil, he captained South Korea to fourth place in the finals and was voted third-best player of the tournament. Hong coached South Korea's U-23 side to Olympic bronze at the 2012 Summer Games – beating Japan 2-0 in the medal play-off. Those goals were scored by Arsenal's Park Chu-Young and WfL Wolfsburg Koo Ja-Cheol. Hong became South Korea manager in June 2013, and was in charge of the team at the 2014 FIFA World Cup, where one group game pitted him against Belgium and their coach Marc Wilmots – the pair having played against each other at the 1998 finals.

CHA BOOM AND BUST

Even before South Korea made their FIFA World Cup breakthrough under Guus Hiddink, the country had a homegrown hero of world renown – thunderous striker **Cha Bum-Kun**, known for his fierce shots and suitable nickname "Cha Boom". He helped pave the way for more Asian players to make their name in Europe by signing for German club Eintracht Frankfurt in 1979 and later played for Bundesliga rivals Bayer Leverkusen. His achievements in Germany included two UEFA Cup triumphs – with Frankfurt in 1980 and with Leverkusen eight years later – while his performances helped make him a childhood idol for future German internationals such as Jurgen Klinsmann and Michael Ballack. His record 55 goals for the national team, in 121 appearances, included a seven-minute hat-trick against Malaysia in the 1977 Park's Cup tournament – levelling the score after South Korea had been trailing 4-1. "Cha Boom" later served as national coach, winning 22, losing 11 and drawing eight during his time in charge between January 1997 and June 1998 – but there was an unhappy ending when he was sacked two games into the 1998 FIFA World Cup, after South Korea's 5-0 defeat to the Netherlands.

OTHER ASIAN COUNTRIES

The lesser-known Asian footballing nations represent the backwaters of world football. These may well be the areas in which true football obsession has yet to take hold, but competition between, and achievements by, these teams are no less vibrant. The regions are the home to many of the game's record-breakers – from the most goals in a single game to the most career appearances – and some of these records may never be broken.

SAUDIS MAKE FLYING START

Saudi Arabia reached the last 16 in their first FIFA World Cup finals appearance in 1994. **Saeed Owairan**'s winner against Belgium enabled them to finish level on points with the Netherlands in Group F. After the Saudis lost their opening game 2-1 to the Dutch, Sami Al-Jaber and Fuad Amin then scored in a 2-1 win over Morocco before they lost 3-1 to Sweden in the last 16. Substitute Fahad Al-Ghesheyan scored in the 85th minute after the Swedes led 2-0. Kennet Andersson grabbed Sweden's decisive third goal three minutes later. The Saudis have failed to advance beyond the group stages in their three subsequent appearances.

IRAN TOP SCORERS

1	Ali Daei	109
2	Karim Bagheri	50
3	Ali Karimi	38
4	Javad Nekounam	37
5	Gholam Hossein Mazloomi	19
=	Farshad Pious	19
7	Nasser Mohammadkhani	18
=	Ali Asghar Modir Roosta	18
9	Vahid Hashemian	15
10	Hamid Alidoosti	14

NEK'S THE NEXT IN LINE

Iran midfielder Javad Nekounam is second behind striker Ali Daei not only in caps won, but also in matches as captain. He led Iran 49 times in 143 games, compared to 149-cap Daei's 80 as skipper. Only Ali Parvin, in 1978, can match Nekounam for the most FIFA World Cup matches as Iran captain, three. But only two Iran players have made six FIFA World Cup appearances: Mehdi Mahdavikia (in 1998 and 2006) and Andranik Teymourian (in 2006 and 2014).

IRAN'S WINNING RUN

Iran won all 13 matches across their hat-trick of AFC Asian Cup triumphs in 1968, 1972 and 1976 – and their 8-0 win over South Yemen in 1976 remains a tournament record. Among the players who enjoyed repeat success was Homayoun Behzadi, who scored in all four games in 1968 and was again on the winning side four years later. Iran's manager in 1976 was Heshmat Mohajerani, who also led the team to the quarter-finals of that year's Summer Olympics in Montreal before steering Iran to their first-ever FIFA World Cup appearance in 1978. Iran's captain at the tournament in Argentina was midfielder Ali Parvin – who had scored the only goal of the 1976 AFC Asian Cup final against Kuwait.

RANK OUTSIDERS

North Korea only narrowly lost their first game of the 2010 FIFA World Cup, 2-1 to Brazil – **Ji Yun-Nam** scoring late on for the Koreans. The match was between the tournament's highest- and lowest-ranked qualifying teams. Brazil were in first place in the FIFA rankings, while North Korea were 105th.

IRAN TOP CAPS

1	Ali Daei	149
2	Javad Nekounam	143
3	Ali Karimi	127
4	Mehdi Mahdavikia	111
5	Hossein Kaebi	89
6	Jalal Hosseini	88
7	Karim Bagheri	87
8	Mohammad Nosrati	83
9	Hamid Reza Estili	82
=	Andranik Taymourian	82

APPEARANCES IN THE FIFA WORLD CUP FINALS

Saudi Arabia	4 (1994, 1998, 2002, 2006)
New Zealand	2 (1982*, 2010*)
North Korea	2 (1966, 2010)
China	1 (2002)
Indonesia**	1 (1938)
Iraq	1 (1986)
Israel	1 (1970)
Kuwait	1 (1982)
United Arab Emirates	1 (1990)

* Qualified for FIFA World Cup as Oceania Confederation member
** Played in the 1938 FIFA World Cup as Dutch East Indies

SHAKEN SHEIKH

Kuwait have qualified for the FIFA World Cup just once, in 1982 – though they made a memorable appearance when they almost walked off the field in protest at a decision. Kuwait's chief Olympic official, Sheikh Fahad Al-Ahmed, even stomped on to the pitch in Valladolid, Spain, when France's Alain Giresse scored a goal that would have given les Bleus a 4-1 lead. The Kuwaitis claimed they had heard a whistle and stopped playing and ultimately convinced referee Myroslav Stupar to disallow the strike. The game still finished 4-1 to France, though, and Kuwait were eliminated in the first round.

CHINA YET TO REALIZE POTENTIAL

China, the world's most populous nation, have qualified just once for the FIFA World Cup finals, in 2002. They topped their final qualifying group by eight points from the United Arab Emirates, but coach Bora Milutinovic's team slumped in the finals, failing to score a goal in defeats by Costa Rica (2-0), Brazil (4-0) and Turkey (3-0). Their 2002 side included record caps-holder **Li Weifeng** (112 appearances) and all-time leading scorer Hao Haidong (37 goals).

IRAN STOP AT 19

Iran hold the record for the highest score in an Asian zone FIFA World Cup qualifier. They thrashed Guam 19-0 in Tabriz on 24 November 2000. Karim Bagheri scored six goals and Ali Karimi four. Future national coach Ali Daei and Farhad Majidi both netted three. This was two goals better than Iran's previous highest qualifying win – 17-0 against the Maldives on 2 June 1997, during which Bagheri scored seven times. Two days after their 19-goal thrashing, Guam crashed 16-0 to Tajikistan.

PALESTINE THE PIONEERS

Palestine, then under British rule, were the first Asian team to enter the FIFA World Cup qualifiers. They lost 7-1 away to Egypt on 16 March 1934. They lost the return match at home on 6 April, 4-1. Four years later, they were eliminated by Greece, who won 3-1 in Tel Aviv and 1-0 at home.

WORLD'S WORST

On the same day that Brazil and Germany contested the FIFA World Cup final on 30 June 2002, the two lowest-ranked FIFA countries were also taking each other on. Asian side Bhutan ran out 4-0 winners over CONCACAF's Montserrat, in a match staged in the Bhutan capital Thimphu. The winning side's captain, striker Wangay Dorji, scored a hat-trick.

IRAQ AND ROLL

One of the greatest – and most heart-warming – surprises of recent international football was Iraq's unexpected triumph at the 2007 AFC Asian Cup, barely a year after the end of the war that ravaged the country and forced them to play "home" games elsewhere. Despite disrupted preparations, they eliminated Vietnam and South Korea on the way to the 2007 final in which captain **Younis Mahmoud**'s goal proved decisive against Saudi Arabia. They were unable to retain their title four years later, losing to Australia in the quarter-finals. Mahmoud retired from international football in March 2014, ending his Iraq career with 50 goals in 124 matches – second in both categories – behind only Hussein Saeed, who scored 61 goals in 126 appearances between 1977 and 1990.

AL-DEAYEA CAPS THEM ALL

Saudi goalkeeper Mohamed Al-Deayea had to choose between football and handball as a youngster. He was persuaded by his elder brother Abdullah to pick football and he went on to make 181 appearances for his country: the first coming against Bangladesh in 1990 and the last against Belgium in May 2006. He also appeared in the FIFA World Cup finals tournaments of 1994, 1998 and 2002. He played his last finals game in a 3-0 defeat by the Republic of Ireland on 11 June 2002 and was recalled to the squad for the 2006 finals, although he did not play.

HAPPY DAEI

Iran striker **Ali Daei** became the first footballer to score a century of international goals, when his four in a 7-0 defeat of Laos on 17 November 2004 took him to 102. He ended his career having scored 109 times for Iran in 149 internationals between 1993 and 2006 – though none of his goals came during FIFA World Cup appearances in 1998 and 2006. He is also the all-time leading scorer in the AFC Asian Cup, with 14 goals, despite failing ever to win the tournament. His time as national coach was less auspicious – he lasted only a year from March 2008 to March 2009 before being fired, as Iran struggled in qualifiers for the 2010 FIFA World Cup.

ONE OF BARCA'S BEST

The first Asian footballer ever to play for a European club was also, for almost a century, the all-time leading scorer for Spanish giants Barcelona, before being finally overtaken by Lionel Messi in March 2014. Paulino Alcantara, from the Philippines, scored 369 goals in 357 matches for the Catalan club between 1912 and 1927. He made his debut aged just 15, and remains Barcelona's youngest-ever first-team player. Alcantara was born in the Philippines, but had a Spanish father, and appeared in internationals for Catalonia, Spain and the Philippines, for whom he featured in a record 15-2 trouncing of Japan in 1917. Alcantara became a doctor after retiring from football at the age of 31, though he did briefly manage Spain in 1951.

SURPRISE SEVEN

The top scorer in the Asian qualification campaign for the 2014 FIFA World Cup was Japan's eight-goal Shinji Okazaki, but he was followed by players from outside the Asian Confederation's traditional superpowers. Tied on seven goals apiece were Iraq's Younis Mahmoud, Jordan's Ahmad Hayel and Hassan Abdel-Fattah and Vietnam's **Le Cong Vinh**, whose strikes helped him to an all-time national record of 31. Jordan had never reached the fourth and final round of AFC qualifiers before and did so this time coached by Adnan Hamad, who had previously served five different stints as manager of his native Iraq.

KUWAIT IN GOLD

Kuwait's one and only AFC Asian Cup triumph came in 1980, when they also hosted the tournament. They beat South Korea 3-0 in the final – having lost by the same scoreline, to the same opponents, in a first-round group game. Faisal Al-Dakhil was Kuwait's hero in the final, scoring two of their goals, his fourth and fifth of the tournament. He had also struck what proved to be the winner in a 2-1 semi-final victory over Iran.

THE JONG TURNING

North Korea's star striker at the 2010 FIFA World Cup, Jong Tae-Se, sobbed when their anthem was played before the first game against Brazil, but he had never actually visited the country he was playing for. Jong was born in Japan, where he continues to play his club football for Kawasaki Frontale, and has parents who are South Korean citizens. But he chose to pursue his family right to a North Korean passport.

AFC ASIAN CUP ALL-TIME TOP SCORERS

1	Ali Daei (Iran)	14
2	Lee Dong-Gook (South Korea)	10
3	Naohiro Takahara (Japan)	9
4	Jassem Al-Houwaidi (Kuwait)	8
5	Behtash Fariba (Iran)	7
=	Hossein Kalani (Iran)	7
=	Choi Soon-Ho (South Korea)	7
=	Faisal Al-Dakhil (Kuwait)	7
9	Yasser Al-Qahtani (Saudi Arabia)	6
=	Alexander Geynrikh (Uzbekistan)	6

PAK STRIKE MAKES HISTORY

North Korea's **Pak Doo Ik** earned legendary status by scoring the goal that eliminated Italy from the 1966 FIFA World Cup finals. The shockwaves caused by the victory were comparable to those caused by the United States' 1-0 win over England in 1950. Pak netted the only goal of the game in the 42nd minute at Middlesbrough on 19 July. North Korea thus became the first Asian team to reach the quarter-finals. Pak, an army corporal, was promoted to sergeant after the victory and later became a gymnastics coach.

ASIAN FOOTBALLER OF THE YEAR

Year	Player	Country
1988	Ahmed Radhi	Iraq
1989	Kim Joo-Sung	South Korea
1990	Kim Joo-Sung	South Korea
1991	Kim Joo-Sung	South Korea
1992	not awarded	
1993	Kazuyoshi Miura	Japan
1994	Saeed Owarain	Saudi Arabia
1995	Masami Ihara	Japan
1996	Khodadad Azizi	Iran
1997	Hidetoshi Nakata	Japan
1998	Hidetoshi Nakata	Japan
1999	Ali Daei	Iran
2000	Nawaf Al Temyat	Saudi Arabia
2001	Fan Zhiyi	China
2002	Shinji Ono	Japan
2003	Mehdi Mahdavikia	Iran
2004	Ali Karimi	Iran
2005	Hamad Al-Montashari	Saudi Arabia
2006	Khalfan Ibrahim	Qatar
2007	Yasser Al-Qahtani	Saudi Arabia
2008	Server Djeparov	Uzbekistan
2009	Yasuhito Endo	Japan
2010	Sasa Ognenovski	Australia
2011	Server Djeparov	Uzbekistan
2012	Lee Keun-Ho	South Korea
2013	Zheng Zhi	China

SO NEAR AND SO FAR

The Asian Confederation's two-legged qualifying final for a place at the Brazil 2014 FIFA World Cup pitted two teams still waiting for their first finals appearance: Uzbekistan and Jordan. The Uzbeks ended their final group level on points with automatic qualifiers South Korea but with an inferior goal difference of one, despite a 5-1 win over Qatar, when Basodir Nasimov equalized just 18 seconds after he came on as substitute. Jordan, with **Amer Shafi** heroic in goal, won 9-8 on penalties, after two 1-1 draws, but lost to Uruguay 5-0 on aggregate and missed out on the finals.

AFC ASIAN CUP-WINNING COACHES

1956	Lee Yoo-Hyung	(South Korea)
1960	Wi Hye-Deok	(South Korea)
1964	Gyula Mandl	(Israel)
1968	Mahmoud Bayati	(Iran)
1972	Mohammad Ranjbar	(Iran)
1976	Heshmat Mohajerani	(Iran)
1980	Carlos Alberto Parreira	(Kuwait)
1984	Khalil Al-Zayani	(Saudi Arabia)
1988	Carlos Alberto Parreira	(Saudi Arabia)
1992	Hans Ooft	(Japan)
1996	Nelo Vingada	(Saudi Arabia)
2000	Philippe Troussier	(Japan)
2004	Zico	(Japan)
2007	Jorvan Vieira	(Iraq)
2011	Alberto Zaccheroni	(Japan)

AL-JABER TO THE FORE

Sami Al-Jaber (born on 11 December 1972 in Riyadh) became only the second Asian player to appear in four FIFA World Cup finals tournaments when he started against Tunisia in Munich on 14 June 2006. He scored in a 2-2 draw, his third goal in nine appearances at the finals. Al-Jaber played only one game in 1998 before he was rushed to hospital with a burst appendix, which ruled him out of the competition. He became Saudi Arabia's record scorer, with 44 goals in 163 matches.

A LONG JOURNEY FOR A BEATING

The first Asian country to play in a FIFA World Cup finals was Indonesia, who played in France in 1938 as the Dutch East Indies. The tournament was a straight knockout and, on 5 June in Reims, Hungary beat them 6-0, with goals from Gyorgy Sarosi, Gyula Zsengeller (two each), Vilmos Kohut and Geza Toldi.

⚽ A RESULT FOR REZA

No AFC nation reached the 2014 FIFA World Cup knock-out stages for the first time since 1998. Japan, South Korea, Australia and Iran all went out in the first-round, but Iran forward **Reza Ghoochannejhad**'s consolation goal in their final game, a 3-1 loss to Bosnia-Herzegovina, meant that all the finalists had scored. This had not happened at a FIFA World Cup since 1998, when the tournament first expanded to 32 teams. Ghoochannejhad also scored Iran's goal in the 1-0 win against South Korea in June 2013 that ensured they finished at the top of their final Asian qualification group.

⚽ FOREIGN DOUBLE AGENT

Brazilian Carlos Alberto Parreira is the only coach to win the AFC Asian Cup twice – and he did so with two different countries. His Kuwait side won in 1980 and he got his hands on the trophy again eight years later, this time in charge of Saudi Arabia.

⚽ LOCAL COACHES MAKE THEIR MARK

No one has won the AFC Coach of the Year award more than once since it was introduced in 1994 – though Asians have claimed the prize every year except when it went to Japan's French boss Philipppe Troussier in 2000 and South Korea's Dutch manager Guus Hiddink two years later. The women's game was recognized with triumphs for China coach Ma Yuanan in 1996, North Korea's U-20 manager Choe Kwang-Sok ten years later and Japan's FIFA Women's World Cup-winning coach Norio Sasaki in 2011. The award 12 months later went to Kim Ho-Gon, in charge of South Korean club Ulsan Hyundai.

⚽ HIGHEST ... AND LOWEST

The highest attendance for an Asian team in a home FIFA World Cup qualifier was the 130,000 who watched Iran draw 1-1 with Australia in the Azadi Stadium, Tehran, on 22 November 1997. The game was the first leg of a final playoff for the last place in the 1998 finals. Iran advanced on away goals after drawing the second leg 2-2 in Melbourne. The lowest attendance was the "crowd" of 20 that turned out for Turkmenistan's 1-0 win over Taiwan, played in Amman, Jordan, on 7 May 2001.

⚽ HUGE FOLLOWING FOR FOOTBALL IN CHINA

China's national team boasts a massive fan base – as was demonstrated when they reached the FIFA World Cup finals for the only time in 2002. Between their qualification on 19 October 2001 and their opening game of the finals against Costa Rica on 4 June 2002, an estimated 170 million new TV sets were sold throughout China. TV audiences for the team's three matches regularly topped 300 million, even though China lost all three matches and failed to score a goal.

⚽ ABOUT UZ

Uzbekistan's four most-capped internationals are still active: midfielders Timur Kapadze (109 appearances) and two-time Asian Footballer of the Year Server Djeparov (100), striker Alexander Geynrikh (84) and goalkeeper Ignatiy Nesterov (83). Striker **Maksim Shatskikh** leads the nation's scoring list, with 34 goals in 61 games. He has also enjoyed success in Ukraine with several sides including Dynamo Kiev – with whom he became the second Uzbek, after Mirjalol Qosimov, to score in UEFA club competitions. Qosimov, who struck 31 goals for his country, is now the national team coach.

⚽ CHINA'S 4X4

Four teams carry the name of China. The China national team receives the most attention, but Hong Kong (a former British colony) and Macau (a former Portuguese colony) both retain their autonomous status for football – as Hong Kong China and Macau China respectively. Meanwhile, the independent island state of Taiwan competes in the FIFA World Cup and other competitions as Chinese Taipei.

UAE KO ZAGALLO

Brazilian great Mario Zagallo, who won the FIFA World Cup as both player and manager, coached the United Arab Emirates when they qualified for their one and only FIFA World Cup finals in 1990. But despite his success in the Asian qualifiers, he was sacked on the eve of the FIFA World Cup itself. Zagallo was replaced by Polish coach Bernard Blaut, whose UAE team lost all three matches at Italia 90. Other big names to have managed the UAE over the years include Brazil's Carlos Alberto Parreira (another FIFA World Cup winner with Brazil), England's Don Revie and Roy Hodgson, Ukraine's Valery Lobanovsky and Portugal's Carlos Queiroz.

SOVIET REPUBLICS FIND NEW HOME

The break-up of the former Soviet Union swelled the ranks of the Asian Confederation in the early 1990s. Former Soviet republics Kazakhstan, Kyrgyzstan, Tajikistan, Turkmenistan and Uzbekistan all joined in 1994, though the Kazaks switched to UEFA in 2002. **Uzbekistan** have been the most successful, reaching the quarter-finals in 2004 and 2007 and finishing fourth in 2011. Australia became the AFC's 46th – and newest – member, entering the Confederation on 1 January 2006, a few months after East Timor had become the 45th.

DOUBLE AGENT

Although North Korea's Kim Myong-Won usually plays as a striker, he was named as one of three goalkeepers in the country's 23-man squad for the 2010 FIFA World Cup. FIFA told North Korea he would only be able to play in goal, rather than outfield, though he failed to make it on to the pitch in any form during his country's three Group G matches.

THE ISRAEL ISSUE

Israel is, geographically, an Asian nation. It hosted – and won – the Asian Cup in 1964. But, over the years, many Asian confederation countries refused to play Israel on political grounds. When Israel reached the 1970 FIFA World Cup finals they came through a qualifying tournament involving two Asian nations – Japan and South Korea – and two from Oceania – Australia and New Zealand. In 1989, Israel topped the Oceania group, but lost a final play-off to Colombia for a place in the 1990 finals. They switched to the European zone qualifiers in 1992 and have been a full member of the European federation, UEFA, since 1994.

ASIAN CUP WINNERS

The Asian Cup is Asia's continental championship

Year	Winners
1956	South Korea
1960	South Korea
1964	Israel
1968	Iran
1972	Iran
1976	Iran
1980	Kuwait
1984	Saudi Arabia
1988	Saudi Arabia
1992	Japan
1996	Saudi Arabia
2000	Japan
2004	Japan
2007	Iraq
2011	Japan

FROZEN OUT

Mongolia went 38 years without playing a single international between 1960 and 1998 and the country still barely stages any action, international or domestic, due to below-freezing conditions between October and June.

OCEANIA

Football in Oceania can claim some of the most eye-catching football statistics – though not necessarily in a way many there would welcome, especially the long-suffering goalkeepers from minnow islands on the end of cricket-style scorelines. The departure to the Asian Football Confederation of Australia, seeking more testing competition, was a morale blow – but benefited New Zealand out on the pitch. The finals tournament of the 2010 FIFA World Cup was the first to feature both Australia and New Zealand.

KAREMBEU THE FIFA WORLD CUP WINNER

Christian Karembeu, born in New Caledonia, is the only FIFA World Cup winner to come from the Oceania region. He started for France in their 3-0 final victory over Brazil on 12 July 1998. The defensive midfielder had earlier begun against Denmark (group), Italy (quarter-finals) and Croatia (semi-finals). He played 53 times for France, scoring one goal, and was also a double European Champions League Cup winner with Real Madrid in 1998 in 2000.

RYAN'S SISTER

New Zealand's captain **Ryan Nelsen** flew back from Blackburn in England to his native city of Christchurch in March 2011 after the city was devastated by an earthquake. Nelsen was worried for the safety of his family, especially his pregnant sister Stephanie Martin – but after being "knocked down" by the 6.3-magnitude quake, she safely gave birth to a healthy baby boy.

PAIA FIRE IN VAIN

No team from Oceania other than Australia or New Zealand has ever qualified for the men's football tournament at the Summer Olympics – but Fiji came close to reaching the 2012 event, only losing 1-0 to New Zealand in the final of the qualifying competition. The top scorers were the Solomon Islands, but they didn't make it out of their opening group. They recorded a best first-round goal difference of +12 – thanks to a 16-1 destruction of American Samoa, including seven goals by Ian Paia. However, defeats by Fiji and Vanuatu left them third in the four-team section.

TOP CAPS: NEW ZEALAND

#	Name	Caps
1	Ivan Vicelich	88
2	Simon Elliott	69
3	Vaughan Coveney	64
4	Ricki Herbert	61
5	Chris Jackson	60
6	Brian Turner	59
7	Duncan Cole	58
=	Steve Sumner	58
9	Chris Zoricich	57
10	Leo Bertos	56
=	Ceri Evans	56

TOP SCORERS: NEW ZEALAND

#	Name	Goals
1	Vaughan Coveney	28
2	Shane Smeltz	23
3	Steve Sumner	22
4	Brian Turner	21
5	Jock Newall	17
6	Chris Killen	16
=	Keith Nelson	16
8	Grant Turner	15
9	Darren McClennan	12
=	Michael McGarry	12
=	Wynton Rufer	12
=	Chris Wood	12

RETURNING RICKI

Ricki Herbert is the only footballer from New Zealand to reach a FIFA World Cup twice – he played left-back at the 1982 tournament in Spain, then coached the country to their second World Cup appearance, in 2010. Qualification second time around came courtesy of a play-off win over Asian Football Confederation representatives Bahrain – though the New Zealand football authorities have been pondering whether to follow Australia in defecting from Oceania and joining the AFC. Herbert, born in Auckland in 1961, combined qualifying for the 2010 FIFA World Cup with coaching New Zealand-based club Wellington Phoenix, who play in Australia's A-League.

TEHAU ABOUT THAT?

The Pacific Island underdogs of Tahiti finally broke the stranglehold Australia and New Zealand had over the OFC Nations Cup by winning the tournament when it was held for the ninth time in 2012, following four previous triumphs for Australia and four for New Zealand. Tahiti scored 20 goals in their five games at the event in the Solomon Islands – 15 of which came from the Tehau family: brothers Lorenzo (five), Alvin and **Jonathan Tehau** (four each) and their cousin Teaonui (two). Steevy Chong Hue scored the only goal of the final, against New Caledonia, to give the team managed by Eddy Etaeta not only the trophy but a place at the 2013 FIFA Confederations Cup in Brazil.

PIERRE'S PERFECT START

The very first goal of the 2010 FIFA World Cup was scored, in qualifying, by New Caledonia's Pierre Wajoka – the only strike of an August 2007 match against Tahiti, the country of his birth.

BAD LUCK OF THE DRAW

Despite featuring at only their second-ever FIFA World Cup – and their first since 1982 – New Zealand did not lose a game in South Africa in 2010. They drew all three first-round matches, against Slovakia, Italy and Paraguay. The three points were not enough to secure a top-two finish in Group F, but third-placed New Zealand did finish above defending world champions Italy. The only other three teams to have gone out despite going unbeaten in their three first-round group games were Scotland (1974), Cameroon(1982) and Belgium (1998).

LAUGHING ALL THE WAY TO THE BANK

New Zealand went to the 2010 FIFA World Cup with four amateur players in their 23-man squad. Midfielder **Andy Barron**, who worked as an investment adviser at a bank in Wellington, even made it on to the pitch as a stoppage-time substitute against reigning world champions Italy.

"WORLD'S WORST TEAM" TO SILVER SCREEN

Nicky Salapu was in goal when American Samoa set an unwanted international record, losing 31-0 to Australia in April 2001 – two days after Australia had crushed Tonga 22-0. Passport problems had denied American Samoa some of their best players for the Australia game and they had to field three 15-year-olds in a side with an average age of 18. Salapu was also playing when American Samoa finally won their first competitive international, 2-1 against Tonga in November 2011 thanks to goals by Ramin Ott and Shamin Luani. This was followed by a 1-1 draw with the Cook Islands, during a 2014 FIFA World Cup qualification campaign during which American Samoa were managed by Dutch coach Thomas Rongen and followed by film crews making a documentary movie, *Next Goal Wins*. It was released in 2014 to widespread critical acclaim – including for Jaiyah Saelua, the world's first transgender international footballer. He was born biologically male but is from the Fa'afafine people, a traditional American Samoan group with both masculine and feminine traits and often described as "third-gender".

THE WHITE STUFF

New Zealand's national football team is known as the "All-Whites" – not just a recognition of their kit colours, but also a counterpoint to the "All-Blacks" nickname of the country's more famous and successful rugby union side.

⚽ CONCACAF

The power and passion of football in the Caribbean, Central and North America was illustrated dramatically at the 2014 FIFA World Cup finals. Costa Rica, Mexico and the United States all progressed beyond the group stage in Brazil, with the popular adventurers of Costa Rica going the furthest. Los Ticos reached the quarter-finals for the first time in their history, only to lose to Netherlands on the lottery of a penalty shoot-out. Keeping CONCACAF in focus, Canada hosts the FIFA Women's World Cup in 2015.

Record TV ratings back home followed the United States' run to the round-of-16 at the 2014 FIFA World Cup in Brazil, where US fans also topped the foreign tickets "ranking".

MEXICO

Mexico may well be the powerhouse of the CONCACAF region and are regular qualifiers for the FIFA World Cup – they did not play in the finals of the tournament on just three occasions (1934, 1974 and 1982) – but they have always struggled to impose themselves on the international stage. Two FIFA World Cup quarter-final appearances (both times as tournament hosts, in 1970 and 1986) represent their best performances to date. A football-mad nation expects more.

TOP SCORERS

1	Jared Borghetti	46
2	Cuauhtemoc Blanco	39
3	Javier Hernandez	35
=	Carlos Hermosillo	35
=	Luis Hernandez	35
6	Enrique Borja	31
7	Luis Roberto Alves	30
8	Luis Flores	29
=	Benjamin Galindo	29
=	Luis Garcia	29
=	Hugo Sanchez	29

VICTOR HUGO

Jared Borgetti may hold the record as Mexico's all-time leading scorer, but perhaps the country's most inspirational striker remains **Hugo Sanchez,** famed for his acrobatic bicycle-kick finishes and somersaulting celebrations. Sanchez played for Mexico at the 1978, 1986 and 1994 FIFA World Cups and would surely have done so had they qualified in 1982 and 1990. During spells in Spain with Atletico Madrid and Real Madrid he finished as La Liga's top scorer five years out of six between 1985 and 1990. He was less successful as Mexico coach from 2006 to 2008, the best result being third in the 2007 Copa America.

MAKING HIS MARQUEZ

Commanding centre-back **Rafael Marquez** made history in 2014 as the first player to captain his country at four consecutive FIFA World Cups. His four games in 2014 took him to 16 FIFA World Cup appearances, beyond Antonio Carbajal – whose 11 were spread across five not four tournaments. Marquez, who scored against Cameroon in 2014, having also registered in 2006 and 2010, is also the second Mexican to score at three different FIFA World Cups, after Cuauhtemoc Blanco.

PRECOCIOUS PEREZ

Mexico's youngest international remains midfielder **Luis Ernesto Perez,** who won the first of his 69 caps at the age of 17 years and 308 days, against El Salvador on 17 November 1998. Less impressive was his red card in Mexico's third first-round match against Portugal at the 2006 FIFA World Cup. Hugo Sanchez was the nation's oldest player, 39 years and 251 days old for his final international, against Paraguay on 19 March 1998 – though this was a farewell game for Sanchez, four years after his previous Mexico appearance, and he was replaced in the first minute by Luis Garcia.

TOP CAPS

1	Claudio Suarez	178
2	Pavel Pardo	148
3	Gerardo Torrado	146
4	Jorge Campos	130
5	Rafael Marquez	124
=	Carlos Salcido	124
7	Ramon Ramirez	121
8	Cuauhtemoc Blanco	120
9	Alberto Garcia-Aspe	109
10	Andres Guardado	108

LITTLE PEA FROM A POD

When Javier Hernandez appeared for Mexico against South Africa on 11 June 2010, he became the third generation of his family to play at a FIFA World Cup. Hernandez – nicknamed "Chicharito", or "Little Pea" – is the son of Javier Hernandez who reached the quarter-finals with Mexico in 1986 and the grandson of Tomas Balcazar, a member of the country's 1954 squad. Another Mexican pair were the first grandfather-grandson pairing to each play at the finals. Luis Perez represented Mexico in 1930 in Uruguay. His grandson Mario Perez played for Mexico, on home turf, 40 years later. Hernandez scored all three of Mexico's goals at the 2013 FIFA Confederations Cup – in a 2-1 defeat to Italy and a 2-1 win over Japan – taking him to joint-third in his country's scoring ranks, alongside Carlos Hermosillo and Luis Hernandez. Chicharito reached the tally in 53 games, compared to Hermosillo's 90 and Luis Hernandez's 85.

FAMILY SPLIT

Winger **Giovani dos Santos** was distraught when Mexico's 30-man preliminary squad was reduced to 23 for the 2010 FIFA World Cup – though not for the obvious reason. He actually made the cut, and played in all four of Mexico's matches, but his brother Jonathan dos Santos was left out by coach Javier Aguirre. Gio was again the only brother to make the cut in 2014, when he was among Mexico's most impressive performers and looked like putting them through to the quarter-finals with a stunning volley against the Netherlands – only for his side to concede twice in the closing moments.

MEXICO BEATS EARTHQUAKE

Mexico stepped in to host the 1986 FIFA World Cup finals after the original choice, Colombia, pulled out in November 1982. FIFA chose Mexico as the replacement venue because of its stadiums and infrastructure, still in place from the 1970 finals. The governing body turned down rival bids from Canada and the United States. Mexico had to work overtime to be ready for the finals, after the earthquake of 19 September 1985, which killed an estimated 10,000 people in central Mexico and destroyed many buildings in Mexico City.

SUAREZ IS NUMBER TWO ALL-TIME

Only Egyptian midfielder Ahmed Hassan played more internationals than Mexico defender **Claudio Suarez**, who made 178 appearances. Suarez – nicknamed "The Emperor" – played in all of Mexico's four games at the 1994 and the 1998 FIFA World Cups, but had to miss the 2002 finals after suffering a broken leg. He was a member of the squad for the 2006 tournament in Germany, but did not play.

ROSAS NETS HISTORIC PENALTY

Mexico's Manuel Rosas scored the first penalty ever awarded in the FIFA World Cup finals when he converted a 42nd-minute spot-kick in his country's match against Argentina in 1930. Rosas scored again in the 65th minute, but it was too little too late for the Mexicans: they crashed to a 6-3 defeat.

SO NEAR, SO FAR

Mexico have proved to be experts at getting out of the first round at the FIFA World Cup – but, in recent years thus far and no further. They have now gone out at the round of 16 stage six tournaments in a row, the latest their last-gasp 2-1 defeat to the Netherlands in Fortaleza in 2014. Their manager in 2014 was the excitable **Miguel Herrera**, whose extravagant touchline antics caught the eye almost as compellingly as the on-pitch action. Herrera, who played 14 times for Mexico in 1993 and 1994, took charge in October 2013 – the country's fourth different coach within the space of a month, at a time when qualification for Brazil 2014 had seemed unlikely. But he guided the team into the finals, after beating New Zealand 9-3 in a playoff.

UNITED STATES

Some of football's biggest names – from Pele to David Beckham – have graced the United States' domestic leagues over the years, and the country is one of only 15 countries to have had the honour of hosting a FIFA World Cup, but it is still a minority sport in the world's most powerful country. However, following a series of impressive performances on the world stage, especially at the Brazil 2014 World Cup, and a huge upsurge in support, the expectation is that the situation will soon change.

TOP CAPS

1	Cobi Jones	164
2	Landon Donovan	156
3	Jeff Agoos	134
4	Marcelo Balboa	128
5	DaMarcus Beasley	120
6	Claudio Reyna	112
7	Carlos Bocanegra	110
=	Paul Caligiuri	110
9	Clint Dempsey	109
10	Eric Wynalda	106

ALTIDORE OPENS THE FLOODGATES

Jozy Altidore became the United States' youngest scorer of an international hat-trick in a 3-0 victory over Trinidad and Tobago on 1 April 2009, aged 19 years and 146 days. But he endured a 15-month barren spell between November 2011 and June 2013, when he scored the opener in a 4-3 defeat of Germany in a Washington DC friendly marking America's Centennial. He then scored against Jamaica, Panama and Honduras to equal a national record of scoring four games in a row, joining William Lubb, Eric Wynalda, Eddie Johnson, **Brian McBride** and Landon Donovan. Altidore's scoring spree came in a 2012–13 season in which he also set a US record for goals in a European club league, with 31 for Dutch club AZ Alkmaar. Sadly his 2014 FIFA World Cup was ended by a hamstring injury 23 minutes into the opening game against Ghana.

CALIGIURI'S SHOT MAKES HISTORY

The US's FIFA World Cup qualifying win in Trinidad, on 19 November 1989, is regarded as a turning point in the country's football history. The team included just one full-time professional, Paul Caligiuri, of (West) German second division club Meppen. He scored the only goal of the game with a looping shot after 31 minutes to take the US to their first finals for 40 years. Trinidad's goalkeeper, Michael Maurice, claimed to have been blinded by the sun, but the win raised the profile of the US team hugely, despite a first-round elimination in the 1990 FIFA World Cup.

LANDON HOPE AND GLORY

The US's all-time leading scorer **Landon Donovan** was the undoubted star of their 2010 FIFA World Cup campaign. He scored three goals in four matches, including a stoppage-time winner against Algeria that meant his side finished top of Group C. His four displays at the tournament meant he has now featured in 13 FIFA World Cup matches for the USA, two ahead of compatriots Earnie Stewart and Cobi Jones. His successful penalty in a second-round defeat to Ghana also made him the USA's all-time top scorer in the competition, with five goals – one more than 1930 hat-trick hero Bert Patenaude. He remains the only man to score more than one hat-trick for the US, having hit four goals against Cuba in July 2003 then trebles versus Ecuador in March 2007 and Scotland in May 2012. Nine others have scored individual hat-tricks.

HIGH-POWERED BACKING

US president Barack Obama was among the millions of Americans who enthused over the 2014 FIFA World Cup like never before. Many millions tuned in to watch the games in their homes – it was estimated 25 million for the team's 2-2 draw with Portugal in the group stage – and millions more watched in bars and clubs. Team USA also faced Joachim Low's Germany in the first round – pitting coach Jurgen Klinsmann against his native land, the country he had led at the 2006 FIFA World Cup with Low as his assistant. Low's men won 1-0 to top Group G, with the USA second. Then some 28,000 fans crowded into Chicago's Soldier Field for big-screen coverage of the USA's second-round match against Belgium. They lost, bravely, 2-1 after extra-time – despite goalkeeper Tim Howard making a FIFA World Cup record 16 saves.

PAYING HIS DEUCE

Clint Dempsey got the USA's 2014 FIFA World Cup off to the ideal start by scoring against Ghana after just 30 seconds. This was not only the fifth fastest goal in the tournament's history but also made him the first man to score for the USA at three different FIFA World Cups. The striker nicknamed "Deuce" is second only to Landon Donovan in the nation's international scoring records. Donovan, having played at the 2002, 2006 and 2010 finals, was contentiously left out of the 2014 squad by manager Jurgen Klinsmann – allowing DaMarcus Beasley to become the first USA player to appear in four FIFA World Cup finals.

ENGLAND STUNNED BY GAETJENS

The US's 1-0 win over England on 29 June 1950 ranks among the biggest surprises in FIFA World Cup history. England, along with hosts Brazil, were joint favourites to win the trophy. The US had lost their last seven matches, scoring just two goals. Joe Gaetjens scored the only goal, in the 37th minute, diving to head Walter Bahr's cross past goalkeeper Bert Williams. England dominated the game, but US keeper Frank Borghi made save after save. Defeats by Chile and Spain eliminated the US at the group stage, but their victory over England remains the greatest result in the country's football history.

MILITARY SUB

Berlin-born defender **John Brooks**, who represented both the USA and Germany at U20s level, opted to play full international football for the American homeland of his armed forces-serving parents. His first goal for his country proved decisive in their first 2014 FIFA World Cup game against Ghana, securing a 2-1 victory in the 86th minute at Natal's Estadio das Dunas. Brooks also became the first USA substitute to score in the FIFA World Cup, after replacing Matt Besler for the second half.

TOP SCORERS

1	Landon Donovan	57
2	Clint Dempsey	39
3	Eric Wynalda	34
4	Brian McBride	30
5	Joe-Max Moore	24
6	Jozy Altidore	23
7	Bruce Murray	21
8	Eddie Johnson	19
9	DaMarcus Beasley	17
=	Earnie Stewart	17

"OLD MAN" HAHNEMANN

Goalkeeper Marcus Hahnemann became the US's oldest international when he faced Paraguay on 29 March 2011 at the age of 38 years and 286 days. That was the last of his nine caps, testament to the US's strength in depth when it comes to goalkeepers in recent years – Kasey Keller (101 caps), Tim Howard (90) and Brad Friedel (82) were among the competition. Hahnemann's debut was in 1994, followed by two more appearances that year, but he then had to wait until 2004 for his next international action.

KEEPING UP WITH JONES

His dreadlocked hair helped catch the attention, but **Cobi Jones**'s raiding runs down the wing also made him one of the host country's most high-profile performers at the 1994 FIFA World Cup. Jones went on to become the US's most-capped player, with 164 international appearances between 1992 and 2004. When he finally retired from all forms of the game in 2007, his number 13 shirt was officially "retired" by the Los Angeles Galaxy – the first time a Major League Soccer club had honoured a player in such a way. Jones had been with the Galaxy since the MLS was launched in 1996 and later served the club as assistant coach and caretaker manager.

CONCACAF OTHER TEAMS

Mexico and the United States (with 25 FIFA World Cup finals appearances between them) are clearly the powerhouses of the CONCACAF region, which takes in North and Central America and the Caribbean. But Mexico only reached the 2014 finals via a play-off, after finishing behind automatic qualifiers USA, Honduras and Costa Rica. The surprising Costa Ricans were one of the stand-out performers in the finals, outdoing their Confederation rivals by reaching the quarter-finals.

PAVON ... AND ON ... AND ON

Striker **Carlos Pavon**, with 101, is one of four Honduras players to win 100 caps. The others are defender Maynor Figueroa (108), goalkeeper Noel Valladares (125) and midfielder Amado Guevara (138). Guevara, in 2010, and Valladares, in 2014, also captained Honduras in the FIFA World Cup finals. Pavon scored seven goals in the 2010 qualifying tournament, as Honduras reached their first FIFA World Cup finals since 1982. But then aged 36, he played just 60 minutes in the finals. Nicknamed "The Shadow", Pavon played club football in seven countries before he retired in 2013: Honduras, Mexico, Spain, Italy, Colombia, Guatemala and the USA, where he was an LA Galaxy team-mate of David Beckham.

WAITING GAMES

Patience is the watchword for many of Central America's smaller nations when it comes to footballing achievement – or even participation. International matches are rare in Montserrat due to the risk of volcanic activity on the 5,000-population Caribbean island. The team has played just 15 international matches in the 21st century, none between November 2004 and March 2008. More positively, Puerto Rico finally ended a 14-year wait for a win when they beat Bermuda 2-0 in January 2008, before reaching the second round of CONCACAF's qualifiers for the 2010 FIFA World Cup. The British Virgin Islands were eliminated from those qualifiers despite not losing a game – their two-legged first-round tie against the Bahamas ended 5-5 on aggregate, with the British Virgin Islands knocked out on away goals.

COSTA RICA WIN WITHOUT A CROWD

The lowest-ever attendance for a CONCACAF FIFA World Cup qualifier was for the Costa Rica–Panama game on 26 March 2005. FIFA ordered the game, staged at the Saprissa Stadium in San Jose, to be played behind closed doors after missiles were thrown at visiting players and the match officials when Mexico won there 2-1 on 9 February. The game was known as "the ghost match". Costa Rica beat Panama 2-1, thanks to a **Roy Myrie** goal in the first minute of stoppage time.

KEYLOR IS KEY

Costa Rica made their FIFA World Cup finals debut in 1990 and goalkeeper Luis Gabelo Conejo shared the best goalkeeper award with Argentina's Sergio Goycochea as his displays helped his team reach the knock-out stages. "Los Ticos" did even better in 2014 and while goalscorers **Joel Campbell** and Bryan Ruiz impressed, again a goalkeeper was crucial: **Keylor Navas** was named man of the match four times in five games. Costa Rica went to the quarter-finals, where the Netherlands beat them, but only on penalties. They had topped the so-called "Group Of Death" by beating two former FIFA World Cup winners, Uruguay and Italy, and drawing with another, England. Navas conceded only two goals at the finals and his penalty shoot-out save from Theofanis Gekas helped his side past Greece in the second-round. Costa Rica became only the second CONCACAF side, after Mexico in 1986, to go out without losing a game in regulation-time.

CONCACAF TEAMS IN THE FIFA WORLD CUP FINALS

Appearances made by teams from the CONCACAF region at the FIFA World Cup finals

1	Mexico	15
2	US	10
3	Costa Rica	4
4	Honduras	3
5	El Salvador	2
6	Canada	1
=	Cuba	1
=	Haiti	1
=	Jamaica	1
=	Trinidad & Tobago	1

CELSO LIKE HIS FATHER

Costa Rica playmaker Celso Borges was delighted, in 2014, to emulate his father by reaching the knock-out stages of the FIFA World Cup. He actually went one better as he scored the first penalty of Los Ticos' 5-3 shoot-out defeat of Greece in the second round. His Brazilian-born father, Alexandre Borges Guimares, played at the 1990 FIFA World Cup and set up the late winner scored by Hernan Medford against Sweden to take the FIFA World Cup finals debutants beyond the first round. The man affectionately known as "Guima" was Costa Rica's coach at both the 2002 and 2006 FIFA World Cup finals, but they failed to go beyond the group stage on either occasion.

REGGAE BOYZ STEP UP

In 1998, Jamaica became the first team from the English-speaking Caribbean to reach the FIFA World Cup finals. The "Reggae Boyz", as they were nicknamed, included several players based in England. They were eliminated at the group stage, despite beating Japan 2-1 in their final game thanks to two goals by **Theodore Whitmore**. They had earlier lost 3-1 to Croatia and 5-0 against Argentina.

BROTHERS IN ARMS

Honduras became the first team to field not one, not two, but three siblings at a FIFA World Cup, when they picked defender Johnny, midfielder Wilson and striker Jerry Palacios in the 2010 squad. Stoke City defensive midfielder Wilson Palacios was perhaps the most famous and acclaimed player in the first Honduras side to reach a FIFA World Cup in 28 years. Like the 1982 side, though, Reinaldo Rueda's men went three games without a win. An older brother, Milton Palacios, played 14 times as a defender for Honduras between 2003 and 2006. Both Jerry and Wilson made it into the 2014 FIFA World Cup squad, but it was not a happy time, especially for Wilson, who was sent off in the opener against France, and Honduras lost all three matches, but did at least score in the defeat against Ecuador.

CUBA SHOW THE WAY

In 1938, Cuba became the first island state of the CONCACAF region to reach the FIFA World Cup quarter-finals. They drew 3-3 with Romania after extra-time in the first round, then won the replay 2-1 with goals by Hector Socorro and Carlos Oliveira after trailing at half-time. They were thrashed 8-0 by Sweden in the last eight. Haiti were the next Caribbean island to play in the finals, in 1974. They lost all three group games, 3-1 to Italy, 7-0 against Poland and 4-1 to Argentina.

RUIZ ON TARGETS

Guatemala's all-time leading scorer **Carlos Ruiz** had double cause for celebration when scoring in their 3-3 draw with Paraguay in August 2012: the game gave him not only a century of international appearances, but a half-century of goals. The player nicknamed "Pescado", or "Fish", announced his international retirement two months later, finishing with a record of 104 matches and 55 goals.

STERN OPPOSITION

Only eight internationals have claimed more goals than the 70 in 114 matches scored by Trinidad and Tobago's **Stern John** between his debut in 1995 and his final game for his country in 2011. The former Columbus Crew, Nottingham Forest and Sunderland striker was Trinidad and Tobago's top scorer and second-highest appearance-maker, behind midfielder Angus Eve. John was part of the country's squad for the 2006 FIFA World Cup, though Eve missed out – prompting him to retire from international football after 117 appearances.

TRINIDAD'S FIRST TIME

Trinidad & Tobago reached the FIFA World Cup finals for the first time in 2006 after a marathon qualifying competition that ended with their 1-0 play-off victory in Bahrain. The team, nicknamed the "Socca Warriors", held Sweden 0-0 in their opening game, but lost 2-0 to England and 2-0 to Paraguay.

PART 3: UEFA EUROPEAN CHAMPIONSHIP

THE UEFA EUROPEAN Championship finals have gone from being a four-team curiosity, snubbed by major nations, to perhaps the third-biggest sporting event on earth, behind only the FIFA World Cup and the Summer Olympic Games. UEFA, the European football confederation, was founded during the 1954 FIFA World Cup in Switzerland and initially set itself the task of creating a championship for national teams. Many major European nations – such as Italy, West Germany and England – refused to take part in the initial competition, launched in 1958, because their national associations feared fixture congestion. So the first finals, featuring four nations, were staged in France and saw the Soviet Union end up as first winners after defeating Yugoslavia in the final in Paris's original Parc des Princes.

Now the map of Europe has changed so remarkably that, while UEFA's membership has more than doubled, the Soviet Union and Yugoslavia no longer exist. The Soviets also reached the second finals in 1964 but lost their crown in the final against their Spanish hosts in the Estadio Bernabeu in Madrid. Spain's playmaker Luis Suarez, from Italy's Internazionale, thus became the first player to win the European Championship and the European Cup in the same season.

In the tournament's early years, qualifying was based on a simple two-legged knockout system, but this was amended to a group-based format and then, in 1980, the finals were expanded to eight nations. That year saw West Germany win for a second time, having previously triumphed in 1972. The next expansion, to 16 teams in England in 1996, saw a unified Germany win their record third title, defeating the Czech Republic (once half of Czechoslovakia) with an extra-time golden goal.

Belgium and the Netherlands organized the first co-hosted finals in 2000. Eight years later Austria and Switzerland were co-hosts, and Spain then became the first team to retain the trophy when they triumphed again at Euro 2012, a tournament co-hosted behind the old Iron Curtain in Poland and Ukraine. France are due to stage the 2016 event with, for the first time, 24 teams.

Goals from David Silva, Jordi Alba, Fernando Torres and Juan Mata meant Spain's goalkeeper-captain Iker Casillas lifted the Henri Delaunay Trophy, his third international cup in a row, at the climax of Euro 2012.

FANCY SEEING YOU AGAIN

When Spain and Italy met in the 2012 final it was the fourth time UEFA European Championship opponents had faced each other twice in the same tournament. Each time, it followed a first-round encounter. The Netherlands lost to the Soviet Union, then beat them in the final in 1988; Germany beat the Czech Republic twice at Euro 96, including the final; and Greece did the same to Portugal in 2004. Spain and Italy drew in Euro 2012's Group C, with Cesc Fabregas replying to Antonio Di Natale's opener for Italy. Their second showdown was rather less even.

THREE OFF AS CZECHS ADVANCE

Czechoslovakia's 3-1 semi-final win over the Netherlands in Zagreb, on 16 June 1976, featured a record three red cards. The Czechs' Jaroslav Pollak was dismissed for a second yellow card – a foul on Johan Neeskens – after an hour. Neeskens followed in the 76th minute for kicking Zdenek Nehoda. Wim van Hanegem became the second Dutchman dismissed, for dissent, after Nehoda scored the Czechs' second goal with six minutes of extra-time left.

DENMARK'S UNEXPECTED EURO TRIUMPH

Denmark were unlikely winners of UEFA Euro 1992. They had not even expected to take part after finishing behind Yugoslavia in their qualifying group, but they were invited to complete the final eight when Yugoslavia were barred for security fears following the country's collapse. Goalkeeper **Peter Schmeichel** was their hero – in the semi-final shoot-out win over the Netherlands and again in the final against Germany, when goals by John Jensen and Kim Vilfort earned Denmark a 2-0 win.

GERMANS DOMINATE AS COMPETITION TAKES OFF

In 52 years, the UEFA European Championship has grown to become the most important international football tournament after the FIFA World Cup. Only 17 teams entered the first tournament, won by the Soviet Union in 1960, yet 51 took part in qualifying for the right to join co-hosts Poland and Ukraine at Euro 2012. Germany (formerly West Germany) and Spain have each won the competition three times, though the Germans have played and won more matches (43 and 23, respectively), as well as scoring and conceding more goals (63 and 45) than any other country. Defender Berti Vogts is the only man to win the tournament as a player (1972) and coach (1996), both with the Germans, the latter after unification. Some of Europe's most famous teams have under-achieved: Italy only claimed the title on home soil in 1968 and England have never reached the final, finishing third in 1968 and reaching the semi-finals in 1996.

DOMENGHINI RESCUES ITALY

The most controversial goal in the history of the final came on 8 June 1968. Hosts Italy were trailing 1-0 to Yugoslavia with ten minutes left. The Yugoslavs seemed still to be organizing their wall when Angelo Domenghini curled a free-kick past goalkeeper Ilja Pantelic for the equalizer. Yugoslavia protested but the goal was allowed to stand. Italy won the only replay in finals history 2-0, two days later, with goals from Gigi Riva and Pietro Anastasi.

FRANCE BOAST PERFECT RECORD

France, on home soil in 1984, are the only side to win all their matches since the finals expanded beyond four teams. They won them without any shoot-outs, too, beating Denmark 1-0, Belgium 5-0 and Yugoslavia 3-2 in their group, Portugal 3-2 after extra-time in the semi-finals and Spain 2-0 in the final.

CZECHS WIN LONGEST SHOOT-OUT

The longest penalty shoot-out in finals history came in the 1980 third-place play-off between hosts Italy and Czechoslovakia, in Naples on 21 June. The Czechs won 9-8, following a 1-1 draw. After eight successful spot-kicks each, Czech goalkeeper **Jaroslav Netolicka** saved Fulvio Collovati's kick.

FRANCE STRIKE, WITHOUT STRIKERS

France still hold the record for the most goals scored by one team in a finals tournament, 14 in 1984. Yet only one of those goals was netted by a recognized striker – Bruno Bellone, who hit the second in their 2-0 final win over Spain. France's inspirational captain, Michel Platini, supplied most of the French firepower, scoring an incredible nine goals in five appearances. He hit hat-tricks against Belgium and Denmark and a last-gasp winner in the semi-final against Portugal. Midfielders Alain Giresse and Luis Fernandez chipped in with goals in the 5-0 win over Belgium. Defender Jean-Francois Domergue gave France the lead against Portugal in the semi-finals, and added another in extra-time after Jordao had put Portugal 2-1 ahead.

TOP TEAM SCORERS IN THE FINALS

1960	Yugoslavia	6
1964	Spain, Soviet Union, Hungary	4
1968	Italy	4
1972	West Germany	5
1976	West Germany	6
1980	West Germany	6
1984	France	14
1988	Netherlands	8
1992	Germany	7
1996	Germany	10
2000	France, Netherlands	13
2004	Czech Republic	9
2008	Spain	12
2012	Spain	12

SPAIN REFUSE TO MEET SOVIETS

Political rivalries wrecked the planned clash between Spain and the Soviet Union in the 1960 quarter-finals. The fascist Spanish leader, General Francisco Franco, refused to allow Spain to go to the communist Soviet Union – and banned the Soviets from entering Spain. The Soviet Union were handed a walkover on the grounds that Spain had refused to play. Franco relented four years later, allowing the Soviets to come to Spain for the finals. He was spared the embarrassment of presenting the trophy to them, however, as Spain beat the Soviet Union 2-1 in the final.

UEFA EUROPEAN CHAMPIONSHIP WINNERS

3	West Germany/Germany (1972, 1980, 1996)
	Spain (1964, 2008, 2012)
2	France (1984, 2000)
1	Soviet Union (1960)
	Czechoslovakia (1976)
	Italy (1968)
	Netherlands (1998)
	Denmark (1992)
	Greece (2004)

SAME OLD SPAIN

Spain not only cruised their way to the largest winning margin of any UEFA European Championship final by trouncing Italy 4-0 in the climax to 2012 – they also became the first country to successfully defend the title. David Silva, **Jordi Alba** – with his first international goal – and substitutes Fernando Torres and Juan Mata got the goals in Kiev's Olympic Stadium on 1 July. Spain thus landed their third major trophy in a row, having won Euro 2008 and the 2010 FIFA World Cup.

BIGGEST WINS IN THE FINALS

Netherlands 6, Yugoslavia 1, 2000
France 5, Belgium 0, 1984
Denmark 5, Yugoslavia 0, 1984
Sweden 5, Bulgaria 0, 2004

TOSS FAVOURS HOSTS ITALY

Italy reached the 1968 final on home soil thanks to the toss of a coin. It was the only game in finals history decided in such fashion. Italy drew 0-0 against the Soviet Union after extra-time in Naples on 5 June 1968. The Soviet captain, Albert Shesternev, made the wrong call at the toss – so Italy reached the final where they beat Yugoslavia.

DELLAS TIMES IT RIGHT FOR GREECE

Greece scored the only "silver goal" victory in the history of the competition in the UEFA Euro 2004 semi-finals. (The silver goal rule meant that a team leading after the first period of extra-time won the match.) Traianos Dellas headed Greece's winner seconds before the end of the first period of extra-time against the Czech Republic in Porto on 1 July. Both golden goals and silver goals were abandoned for UEFA Euro 2008, and drawn knockout matches reverted to being decided over the full 30 minutes of extra-time, and penalties if necessary.

UEFA EUROPEAN CHAMPIONSHIP PLAYER RECORDS

SHEARER TALLY BOOSTS ENGLAND

Alan Shearer is the only Englishman to top the finals scoring chart. Shearer led the scorers with five goals as England went out on penalties to Germany in the Euro 96 semi-final at Wembley. He netted against Switzerland, Scotland and the Netherlands (2) in the group and gave England a third-minute lead against the Germans. Shearer added two more goals at Euro 2000, to stand second behind Michel Platini in the all-time scorers' list.

ILYIN GOAL MAKES HISTORY

Anatoly Ilyin of the Soviet Union scored the first goal in UEFA European Championship history when he netted after four minutes against Hungary on 29 September 1958. A crowd of 100,572 watched the Soviets win 3-1 in the Lenin Stadium, Moscow. The Soviet Union went on to win the first final, in 1960.

GOLDEN ONE-TOUCH

Spain striker **Fernando Torres** claimed the Golden Boot, despite scoring the same number of goals – three – as Italy's Mario Balotelli, Russia's Alan Dzagoev, Germany's Mario Gomez, Croatia's Mario Mandzukic and Portugal's Cristiano Ronaldo. The decision came down to number of assists – with Torres and Gomez level on one apiece – then amount of time played. The 92 minutes spent on the pitch by Torres, compared to Gomez, meant his contributions were deemed better value for the prize.

VONLANTHEN BEATS ROONEY RECORD

The youngest scorer in finals history was Switzerland midfielder **Johan Vonlanthen**. He was 18 years 141 days when he netted in their 3-1 defeat by France on 21 June 2004. He beat the record set by England forward Wayne Rooney four days earlier. Rooney was 18 years 229 days when he scored the first goal in England's 3-0 win over the Swiss. Vonlanthen retired from football at the age of 26 in May 2012 due to a knee injury.

KIRICHENKO NETS QUICKEST GOAL

The fastest goal in the history of the finals was scored by Russia forward Dmitri Kirichenko. He netted after just 67 seconds to give his side the lead against Greece on 20 June 2004. Russia won 2-1, but Greece still qualified for the quarter-finals – and went on to become shock winners. The fastest goal in the final was Spain midfielder Jesus Pereda's sixth-minute strike in 1964, when Spain beat the Soviet Union 2-1.

GROOM FOR SUCCESS

Spanish playmaker Andres Iniesta, scorer of the winner in the 2010 FIFA World Cup, followed that tournament in style by being named the best player of Euro 2012 – despite not appearing on the scoresheet in any of his team's six matches. Six days after the final against Italy, Iniesta had more cause for celebration. This time the occasion was back home in Spain, where he got married in a ceremony attended by international team-mates Cesc Fabregas and Sergio Busquets.

TOP SCORERS IN FINALS HISTORY

1	Michel Platini (France)	9
2	Alan Shearer (England)	7
3	Nuno Gomes (Portugal)	6
=	Thierry Henry (France)	
=	Patrick Kluivert (Netherlands)	
=	Zlatan Ibrahimovic (Sweden)	
=	Cristiano Ronaldo (Portugal)	
=	Ruud van Nistelrooy (Netherlands)	
9	Milan Baros (Czech Republic)	5
=	Jurgen Klinsmann (W Germany/Germany)	
=	Savo Milosevic (Yugoslavia)	
=	Wayne Rooney (England)	
=	Fernando Torres (Spain)	
=	Marco van Basten (Netherlands)	
=	Zinedine Zidane (France)	

BIERHOFF NETS FIRST "GOLDEN GOAL"

Germany's **Oliver Bierhoff** scored the first golden goal in the history of the tournament when he hit the winner against the Czech Republic in the Euro 96 final at Wembley on 30 June. The golden goal rule meant the first team to score in extra-time won the match. Bierhoff netted in the fifth minute of extra-time. His shot from 20 yards deflected off defender Michal Hornak and slipped through goalkeeper Petr Kouba's fingers.

PONEDELNIK'S MONDAY MORNING FEELING

Striker Viktor Ponedelnik headed the Soviet Union's extra-time winner to beat Yugoslavia 2-1 in the first final on 10 July 1960 – and sparked some famous headlines in the Soviet media. The game in Paris kicked off at 10pm Moscow time on Sunday. It was running into Monday morning there by the time Ponedelnik – whose name means "Monday" in Russian – scored. He said: "When I scored, all the journalists wrote the headline 'Ponedelnik zabivayet v Ponedelnik' – 'Monday scores on Monday'."

MARCHING ORDERS

Only one man has ever been sent off in a UEFA European Championship final: France defender Yvon Le Roux, who received a second yellow card with five minutes remaining of his team's 2-0 triumph over Spain in 1984. The most red cards were shown at Euro 2000, when then ten dismissals included Romania's Gheorghe Hagi, Portugal's **Nuno Gomes**, Italy's Gianluca Zambrotta and the Czech Republic's Radoslav Latal – an unprecedented second sending-off for Latal, who was also given his marching orders at Euro 96.

VASTIC THE OLDEST

The oldest scorer in finals history is Austria's Ivica Vastic. He was 38 years and 257 days old when he equalized in the 1-1 draw with Poland at UEFA Euro 2008.

TOP SCORERS IN THE FINALS

1960	Francois Heutte (France)	2
	Milan Galic (Yugoslavia)	
	Valentin Ivanov (Soviet Union)	
	Drazan Jerkovic (Yugoslavia)	
	Slava Metreveli (Soviet Union)	
	Viktor Ponedelnik (Soviet Union)	
1964	Ferenc Bene (Hungary)	2
	Dezso Novak (Hungary)	
	Jesus Pereda (Spain)	
1968	Dragan Dzajic (Yugoslavia)	2
1972	Gerd Muller (West Germany)	4
1976	Dieter Muller (West Germany)	4
1980	Klaus Allofs (West Germany)	3
1984	Michel Platini (France)	9
1988	Marco van Basten (Netherlands)	5
1992	Dennis Bergkamp (Netherlands)	3
	Tomas Brolin (Sweden)	
	Henrik Larsen (Denmark)	
	Karlheinz Riedle (Germany)	
1996	Alan Shearer (England)	5
2000	Patrick Kluivert (Netherlands)	5
	Savo Milosevic (Yugoslavia)	
2004	Milan Baros (Czech Republic)	5
2008	David Villa (Spain)	4
2012	Mario Balotelli (Italy)	3
	Alan Dzagoev (Russia)	
	Mario Gomez (Germany)	
	Mario Mandzukic (Croatia)	
	Cristiano Ronaldo (Portugal)	
	Fernando Torres (Spain)	

MATTHAUS MIRRORS TOURNAMENT GROWTH

The career of Lothar Matthaus straddles the growth of the European Championship. He appeared in four tournaments between 1980 and 2000. He missed Euro 92 because of injury and stayed at home for Euro 96 after falling out with coach Berti Vogts and skipper Jurgen Klinsmann. He had made his entry as a 19-year-old substitute for Bernd Dietz in West Germany's 3-2 group win over the Netherlands in Naples on 14 June 1980. That was the first tournament which involved eight teams and two groups rather than the previous four semi-finalists. He ended his association with the championship at the age of 39, playing for a reunited Germany as they were eliminated 3-0 by Portugal at Euro 2000. By now the tournament had expanded to include 16 teams in four groups. Despite featuring in four tournaments, Matthaus made only 11 appearances in total. He did, however, enter the tournament when it was taking its first steps to expansion and left it when the European Championship had become second only to the FIFA World Cup as football's most important international competition.

BROTHERS IN ARMS

Four pairs of brothers went to Euro 2000: Gary and Phil Neville (England), Frank and Ronald de Boer (Netherlands), Daniel and Patrik Andersson (Sweden) and Belgium's Emile and Mbo Mpenza.

BECKENBAUER'S 100th ENDS IN DEFEAT

West Germany legend Franz Beckenbauer won his 100th cap in the 1976 final against Czechoslovakia. After his side's shoot-out defeat, he played only three more games for his country before retiring from international football.

PORTUGAL TRIO BANNED FOR THE LONGEST

The longest suspensions in the history of the finals were handed out to three Portugal players after their Euro 2000 semi-final defeat by France. Zinedine Zidane's "Golden Goal" penalty infuriated the Portuguese, who surrounded referee Gunter Benko and assistant Igor Sramka. The three Portuguese players – **Abel Xavier**, Nuno Gomes and Paulo Bento – were banned for "physically and verbally intimidating" the officials. Xavier was suspended from European football for nine months. Gomes, who was also sent off, was banned for eight months. Bento received a six-month suspension.

CLEAN SHEETS FOR CASILLAS

Spain saw out the 2012 tournament conceding just one goal, emulating the achievement of Italy in 1980 and Norway in 2000 – neither of whom achieved what Spain did and lifted the trophy. That successful 2012 campaign took Spanish captain and goalkeeper Iker Casillas to nine clean sheets in UEFA European Championships, from 14 games – equalling the record held by the Netherlands' Edwin van der Sar, with his nine clean sheets from 16 matches.

MOST FINALS TOURNAMENTS PLAYED

Eight players have appeared in four finals tournaments:

Name	Country	Years
Lothar Matthaus	(West Germany/Germany)	1980, 1984, 1988, 2000
Peter Schmeichel	(Denmark)	1988, 1992, 1996, 2000
Aron Winter	(Netherlands)	1988, 1992, 1996, 2000
Alessandro del Piero	(Italy)	1996, 2000, 2004, 2008
Edwin van der Sar	(Netherlands)	1996, 2000, 2004, 2008
Lilian Thuram	(France)	1996, 2000, 2004, 2008
Olof Mellberg	(Sweden)	2000, 2004, 2008, 2012
Iker Casillas	(Spain)	2000, 2004, 2008, 2012

MULLERY THE FIRST TO GO

Wing-half Alan Mullery became the first England player ever to be sent off when he was dismissed in the 89th minute of their 1-0 semi-final defeat by Yugoslavia in Florence on 5 June 1968. Mullery was sent off for a foul on Dobrivoje Trivic, three minutes after Dragan Dzajic had scored Yugoslavia's winner. His dismissal came in England's 424th official international match.

HAGI'S JOURNEY ENDS IN RED

Romania's greatest player, Gheorghe Hagi won the last of his 125 caps in a 2-0 UEFA Euro 2000 quarter-final defeat by Italy on 24 June. However, his international career would end in sad circumstances: he was sent off in the 59th minute for two yellow-card offences. Hagi had previously been booked against Germany and Portugal – and had missed Romania's 3-2 group win over England through suspension.

MOST MATCHES PLAYED IN THE FINALS

- 16 Edwin van der Sar (Netherlands)
- Lilian Thuram (France)
- 14 Iker Casillas (Spain)
- Luis Figo (Portugal)
- Nuno Gomes (Portugal)
- Philipp Lahm (Germany)
- Karel Poborsky (Czech Republic)
- Cristiano Ronaldo (Portugal)
- Zinedine Zidane (France)

BACK OF THE WRONG NET

 Glen Johnson became only the fifth man to score an own goal at a UEFA European Championship, when the England right-back put through his own net against Sweden in their Euro 2012 first-round clash. The earlier unfortunates were Czechoslovakia's Anton Ondrus in 1976, Bulgaria's Dimitar Penev in 1996, Yugoslavia's Dejan Govedarica in 2000 and Portugal's Jorge Andrade in 2004.

ARAGONES THE VETERAN COACH

Luis Aragones, Spain's coach in 2008, is the oldest boss of a European champion team. Aragones (born in Madrid on 28 July 1938) was 29 days short of his 70th birthday when Spain beat Germany 1-0 in the final on 29 June. That was his last match in charge. He had taken over the national team after Euro 2004.

KADLEC FATHER AND SON

Czech defenders Miroslav and Michal Kadlec are the only father and son to have played in the finals. Miroslav (born on 22 June 1964 in Uherkse Hradiste) captained the Czech Republic side that finished as runners-up to Germany at Euro 96. He also scored the winning penalty in the semi-final shoot-out against France. Michal (born on 13 December 1984 in Vyskov) made his first appearance as an 80th-minute substitute for Jaroslav Plasil in the Group A game against Turkey in Geneva on 15 June 2008.

SUAREZ GAINS FIRST DOUBLE

The first man to earn winners' medals in the European Championship and the European Cup in the same season was Spain's **Luis Suarez**. He helped Spain beat the Soviet Union 2-1 in the final on 21 June 1964. A few weeks earlier, Suarez had been in the Internazionale team that beat Real Madrid 3-1 in the European Cup final. Four players were in both PSV Eindhoven's 1988 European Cup final victory over Benfica and the Netherlands' UEFA Euro 88 final defeat of Russia. Nicolas Anelka won the Champions League with Real Madrid in 2000 and was in the France squad that won Euro 2000, but he did not appear in the final.

KARAGOUNIS A GONER

The yellow card shown to Greece's Giorgos Karagounis in their final first-round match of Euro 2012, against Russia, achieved even more than ruling him out of their quarter-final against Germany. It was also his eighth in UEFA European Championship history, a competition record. He had previously been able to play in the final of Euro 2004 after collecting two bookings beforehand.

MATTHAUS THE OLDEST

The oldest player to appear in a game at the UEFA European Championship finals was Germany's Lothar Matthaus. He was 39 years 91 days when he played in their 3-0 defeat by Portugal on 20 June 2000.

UEFA EUROPEAN CHAMPIONSHIP OTHER RECORDS

LOW CONQUERS ALMOST ALL

Germany coach Joachim Low claimed the record for most UEFA European Championship victories in charge, when his side beat Greece 4-2 in the Euro 2012 quarter-finals. This took him to eight wins from ten games, across Euro 2008 and Euro 2012. The semi-final defeat against Italy also equalled Berti Vogts's record of 11 UEFA European Championship games as a manager.

NAMES ON THEIR SHIRTS

Players wore their names as well as their numbers on the back of their shirts for the first time at Euro 92. They had previously been identified only by numbers.

REPEAT PROENCA

Portuguese official Pedro Proenca achieved the double feat of refereeing the 2012 UEFA Champions League final between Chelsea and Bayern Munich and the 2012 UEFA European Championship final between Spain and Italy. He also became the third man to referee four matches in one UEFA European Championship, after Sweden's Anders Frisk (2004) and Italy's Roberto Rosetti (2008). Frisk's eight matches overall is a UEFA European Championship record.

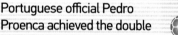

GREEKS HAND ALBANIA WALKOVER

When Greece were drawn against Albania in the first round of the 1964 tournament, the Greeks immediately withdrew, handing Albania a 3-0 walkover win. The countries had technically been at war since 1940. The Greek government did not formally lift the state of war until 1987, although diplomatic relations were re-established in 1971.

ITALY HOSTS TWICE

Italy were the first country to host the finals twice – in 1968 and 1980. They were awarded the finals in 1968 in recognition of the 60th anniversary of the Italian football federation. Belgium have also hosted the finals twice: first, alone, in 1972, and then in partnership with the Netherlands for Euro 2000.

RECORD EURO GOAL DROUGHT

Between **Xabi Alonso**'s added-time penalty in Spain's 2-0 quarter-final defeat of France and Mario Balotelli's 20th-minute semi-final strike for Italy in their 2-1 victory against Germany, Euro 2012's goalless spell lasted 260 minutes – a UEFA European Championship record.

ELLIS BLOWS THE WHISTLE

English referee **Arthur Ellis** took charge of the first UEFA European Championship final between the Soviet Union and Yugoslavia in 1960. Ellis had also refereed the first-ever European Cup final, between Real Madrid and Reims, four years earlier. After he retired from football, he became the "referee" on the British version of the Europe-wide game show *It's a Knock-out.*

FINALS HOSTS

1960	France
1964	Spain
1968	Italy
1972	Belgium
1976	Yugoslavia
1980	Italy
1984	France
1988	West Germany
1992	Sweden
1996	England
2000	Netherlands and Belgium
2004	Portugal
2008	Austria and Switzerland
2012	Poland and Ukraine

HOSTS WITH (ALMOST) THE MOST

In 2000, Belgium and the Netherlands began the trend for dual hosting the UEFA European Championship finals – it was the first time the tournament was staged in more than one country. The opening game was Belgium's 2-1 win over Sweden in Brussels on 10 June, with the final in Rotterdam. Austria and Switzerland co-hosted Euro 2008, starting in Basel and climaxing in Vienna, before Poland and Ukraine teamed up in 2012. Warsaw staged the opening match and Kiev was the host city for the final.

SINGING IN UKRAINE

The eight venues – four apiece – in Poland and Ukraine matched the number used when Belgium and the Netherlands shared hosting rights at Euro 2000 and when Austria and Switzerland did so eight years later. Only Euro 2004 in Portugal had more venues (10). Poland's 56,070-capacity National Stadium in Warsaw staged the opening game between Poland and Greece, while Kiev's 64,640-seater Olympic Stadium was the setting for the final. France will stage Euro 2016, while the final tournament in 2020 will be played – for the first time – in as many as 13 different cities across 13 different countries.

WELL DONE, WELBECK

Perhaps surprisingly, the biggest official attendance at Euro 2012 was not for the final but for a first-round Group D match, when 64,640 saw England beat Sweden 3-2 thanks to a late back-heeled winner by **Danny Welbeck**.

UEFA EUROPEAN CHAMPIONSHIP FINAL REFEREES

Year	Referee
1960	Arthur Ellis (England)
1964	Arthur Holland (England)
1968	Gottfried Dienst (Switzerland)
	Replay: Jose Maria Ortiz de Mendibil (Spain)
1972	Ferdinand Marschall (Austria)
1976	Sergio Gonella (Italy)
1980	Nicolae Rainea (Romania)
1984	Vojtech Christov (Czechoslovakia)
1988	Michel Vautrot (France)
1992	Bruno Galler (Switzerland)
1996	Pierluigi Pairetto (Italy)
2000	Anders Frisk (Sweden)
2004	Markus Merk (Germany)
2008	Roberto Rosetti (Italy)
2012	Pedro Proenca (Portugal)

THE "ITALIAN JOB"

The 1968 finals in Italy were used as the backdrop to a famous English-language film – *The Italian Job*, starring Michael Caine – about a British gang who use the cover of the finals to stage a daring gold robbery in Turin. The film was released in England on 2 June 1969.

GOALS AREN'T EVERYTHING

Despite being widely praised for the quality of attacking football on display, Euro 2012 actually had the lowest average of goals per game for any UEFA European Championship since Euro 96 in England. The 76 goals across 31 matches in Poland and Ukraine was one fewer than was scored at each of the 2004 and 2008 tournaments, and meant an average of 2.45 goals per game. It was not until the fourth of the four quarter-finals that Euro 2012 witnessed its first goalless draw, between England and Italy – but this was followed by another stalemate in the next game, three days later, between Spain and Portugal in the first of the semi-finals.

KEEPING IT CLEAN

Only three red cards were shown during Euro 2012 – Greece's Sokratis Papastathopoulos and Poland's **Wojciech Szczesny** in the opening game, and Keith Andrews for the Republic of Ireland against Italy. This equalled the sendings-off total in the 2008 UEFA European Championship but was half the tally of Euro 2004.

PART 4: COPA AMERICA

THE WORLD'S OLDEST surviving international championship finds its rich history repeating itself even in a modern world much-transformed since the inaugural Copa America – with both the 1916 and 2011 tournaments being won by Uruguay. Their 15th Copa America triumph in 2011 made them the competition's most successful country – flying high on the football field once more.

More literal jet travel was missing, however, when they first hoisted the trophy – one of the factors that helped make a continental championship such a worthwhile idea for its South American founders. Before jet travel became commonplace in the last half-century, major footballing events were difficult to organize – and that played an influence in FIFA's founding membership in 1904 being entirely European. Although South American nations such as Brazil, Argentina and Uruguay were not slow in signing up, the opportunities available to them to play against their European cousins were scarce – open only to those willing to endure laborious journeys by sea.

The South Americans thus decided to organize their own international competitions, which led to the creation in 1916 of the South American Championship, now known as the Copa America. Communications not being what they are today, even then organization was far from simple – and many of the early championships are now considered unofficial. Further problems arose over scheduling which meant that countries could not secure the release of their best players who were under contract to European clubs. Argentina were champions in 1957 and considered favourites for the following year's FIFA World Cup. But they soon lost all their inspirational forward trio – Humberto Maschio, Antonio Valentin Angelillo and Enrique Omar Sivori – to Italian clubs.

Now, however, the club-versus-country issue has been largely resolved by FIFA's enforcement of a unified international calendar, recognizing the priority status of the Copa America.

Uruguay might have been South America's most successful nation at the 2010 FIFA World Cup, but their 2011 Copa America triumph, in Argentina, was still considered a big surprise.

COPA AMERICA TEAM RECORDS

LITTLE NAPOLEON

In 1942, Ecuador and their goalkeeper Napoleon Medina conceded more goals in one tournament than any other team, when they let in 31 goals across six games – and six defeats. Three years later he and his team-mates finally managed to keep a clean sheet, in a goalless draw against Bolivia – but still managed to let in another 27 goals in their five other matches.

LUCK OF THE DRAW

Paraguay reached the 2011 final despite not winning a single game in normal play. Instead, they drew all three matches in the first-round group stage, then needed penalties to win their quarter-final against Brazil and semi-final versus Venezuela after both games ended goalless. Perhaps not surprisingly, their captain **Justo Villar** was voted the tournament's best goalkeeper.

COPA AMERICA WINNERS

1916	Uruguay (league format)
1917	Uruguay (league format)
1919	Brazil 1 Uruguay 0
1920	Uruguay (league format)
1921	Argentina (league format)
1922	Brazil 3 Paraguay 1
1923	Uruguay (league format)
1924	Uruguay (league format)
1925	Argentina (league format)
1926	Uruguay (league format)
1927	Argentina (league format)
1929	Argentina (league format)
1935	Uruguay (league format)
1937	Argentina 2 Brazil 0
1939	Peru (league format)
1941	Argentina (league format)
1942	Uruguay (league format)
1945	Argentina (league format)
1946	Argentina (league format)
1947	Argentina (league format)
1949	Brazil 7 Paraguay 0
1953	Paraguay 3 Brazil 2
1955	Argentina (league format)
1956	Uruguay (league format)
1957	Argentina (league format)
1959	Argentina (league format)
1959	Uruguay (league format)
1963	Bolivia (league format)
1967	Uruguay (league format)
1975	Peru 4 Colombia 1 (on aggregate, after three games)
1979	Paraguay 3 Chile 1 (on aggregate, after three games)
1983	Uruguay 3 Brazil 1 (on aggregate, after two games)
1987	Uruguay 1 Chile 0
1989	Brazil (league format)
1991	Argentina (league format)
1993	Argentina 2 Mexico 1
1995	Uruguay 1 Brazil 1 (Uruguay won 5-3 on penalties)
1997	Brazil 3 Bolivia 1
1999	Brazil 3 Uruguay 0
2001	Colombia 1 Mexico 0
2004	Brazil 2 Argentina 2 (Brazil won 4-2 on penalties)
2007	Brazil 3 Argentina 0
2011	Uruguay 3 Paraguay 0

HOSTING RIGHTS BY COUNTRY

Argentina	9	(1916, 1921, 1925, 1929, 1937, 1946, 1959, 1987, 2011)
Uruguay	7	(1917, 1923, 1924, 1942, 1956, 1967, 1995)
Chile	6	(1920, 1926, 1941, 1945, 1955, 1991)
Peru	6	(1927, 1935, 1939, 1953, 1957, 2004)
Brazil	4	(1919, 1922, 1949, 1989)
Ecuador	3	(1947, 1959, 1993)
Bolivia	2	(1963, 1997)
Paraguay	1	(1999)
Colombia	1	(2001)
Venezuela	1	(2007)

EXTRA TIME

The longest match in the history of the Copa America was the 1919 final between Brazil and Uruguay. It lasted 150 minutes, 90 minutes of regular time plus two extra-time periods of 30 minutes each.

HOW IT STARTED

The first South American "Championship of Nations", as it was then known, was held in Argentina from 2–17 July 1916, during the country's independence centenary commemorations. The tournament was won by Uruguay, who drew with Argentina in the last match of the tournament. It was an inauspicious beginning. The 16 July encounter had to be abandoned at 0-0 when fans invaded the pitch and set the wooden stands on fire. The match was continued at a different stadium the following day and still ended goalless ... but Uruguay ended up topping the mini-league table and were hailed the first champions. Isabelino Gradin was the inaugural tournament's top scorer. The event also saw the foundation of the South American federation CONMEBOL, which took place a week into the competition on 9 July 1916. From that point on the tournament was held every two years, though some tournaments are now considered to have been unofficial. There was, a three-year gap between the 2004 and 2007 tournaments, and the competition is now staged every four years instead.

SUB-STANDARD

During the 1953 Copa America, Peru were awarded a walkover win when Paraguay tried to make one more substitution than they were allowed. Would-be substitute Milner Ayala was so incensed, he kicked English referee Richard Maddison and was banned from football for three years. Yet Paraguay remained in the tournament and went on to beat Brazil in the final – minus, of course, the disgraced Ayala.

ROTATING RIGHTS

The Campeonato Sudamericano de Selecciones was rebaptized the Copa America from 1975. Between then and 1983 there was no host nation, before CONMEBOL adopted the policy of rotating the right to host the Copa America among the ten member confederations. The first rotation was complete after Venezuela hosted the 2007 edition, with Argentina lined up to play host for the ninth time in 2011.

HISTORY MEN

The Copa America is the world's oldest surviving international football tournament, having been launched in 1916 when the participating nations were Argentina, Bolivia, Brazil, Chile, Colombia, Ecuador, Paraguay, Peru, Uruguay and Venezuela. In 1910, an unofficial South American championship had been won by Argentina, who beat Uruguay 4-1 in the decider – though the final match had been delayed a day after rioting fans burnt down a stand at the Gimnasia stadium in Buenos Aires.

FALLEN ANGELS

Argentina's 1957 Copa America-winning forward trio of Humberto Maschio, Omar Sivori and Antonio Valentin Angelillo became known by the nickname "the angels with dirty faces". At least one of them scored in each of the side's six matches – Maschio finished with nine, Angelillo eight and Sivori three. Argentina's most convincing performance was an opening 8-2 win over Colombia, in which Argentina had scored four goals and missed a penalty within the first 25 minutes. The dazzling displays made Argentina, not eventual winners Brazil, favourites for the following year's FIFA World Cup. Before then, however, Maschio, Sivori and Angelillo had all been lured away to Europe by Italian clubs and the Argentine federation subsequently refused to pick them for the trip to Sweden for the FIFA World Cup. Sivori and Maschio ultimately made it to the FIFA World Cup, in 1962. However, to fury back home, they did so wearing not the light blue-and-white stripes of Argentina, but the Azzurri blue of their newly adopted Italy.

CONSISTENT COLOMBIANS

In 2001, Colombia, who went on to win the trophy for the first and only time in their history, became the only country to go through an entire Copa America campaign without conceding a single goal. They scored 11 goals themselves, more than half of them from six-goal tournament top scorer **Victor Aristazabal**. Keeping the clean sheets was goalkeeper Oscar Cordoba, who had previously spent much of his international career as back-up to the eccentric Rene Higuita. Just a month earlier, Cordoba had won the South American club championship, the Copa Libertadores, with Argentine side Boca Juniors.

TRIUMPHS BY COUNTRY

Uruguay 15 (1916, 1917, 1920, 1923, 1924, 1926, 1935, 1942, 1956, 1959, 1967, 1983, 1987, 1995, 2011)
Argentina 14 (1921, 1925, 1927, 1929, 1937, 1941, 1945, 1946, 1947, 1955, 1957, 1959, 1991, 1993)
Brazil 8 (1919, 1922, 1949, 1989, 1997, 1999, 2004, 2007)
Peru 2 (1939, 1975)
Paraguay 2 (1953, 1979)
Bolivia 1 (1963)
Colombia 1 (2001)

MORE FROM MORENO

Argentina were not only responsible for the Copa America's biggest win, but also the tournament's highest-scoring game, when they put 12 past Ecuador in 1942 – to no reply. Jose Manuel Moreno's five strikes in that game included the 500th goal in the competition's history. Moreno, born in Buenos Aires on 3 August 1916, ended that tournament as joint top scorer with team-mate Herminio Masantonio – hitting seven goals. Both men ended their international careers with 19 goals for their country, though Moreno did so in 34 appearances – compared to Masantonio's 21. Masantonio scored four in the Ecuador thrashing.

URUGUAY AGAIN

Inaugural Copa America winners Uruguay claimed their 15th triumph in 2011 – pulling one clear of neighbours and rivals Argentina. What made the glory even sweeter was that it came on Argentine turf and included a quarter-final victory on penalties over their hosts. Argentina and Brazil had gone into the tournament as favourites, with many expecting them to contest the final for the third time running – but instead both were knocked out in the quarter-finals, producing an unlikely last four of Uruguay, Paraguay, Venezuela and Peru. Uruguay proved their fourth place finish at the 2010 FIFA World Cup – South America's best team at that tournament – was no one-off fluke, as they savoured success again under coach Oscar Washington Tabarez.

COPA AMERICA PLAYER RECORDS

FROG PRINCE

Chilean goalkeeper Sergio Livingstone holds the record for most Copa America appearances, with 34 games, across the 1941, 1942, 1945, 1947, 1949 and 1953 tournaments. Livingstone, nicknamed "The Frog", was voted player of the tournament in 1941 – becoming the first goalkeeper to win the award – and might have played even more Copa America matches had he not missed out on the 1946 competition. Livingstone, born in Santiago on 26 March 1920, spent almost his entire career in his home country – save for a season with Argentina's Racing Club in 1943–44. Overall, he made 52 appearances for Chile between 1941 and 1954, before retiring and becoming a popular TV journalist and commentator.

CHILE'S ILL FORTUNE

The first Copa America own goal was scored by Chile's Luis Garcia, giving Argentina a 1-0 win in 1917, in the second edition of the tournament. Even more unfortunately for Chile, Garcia's strike was the only goal by one of their players throughout the tournament – making Chile the first team to fail to score a single goal in a Copa America competition.

MOST GAMES PLAYED

1	Sergio Livingstone (Chile)	34
2	Zizinho (Brazil)	33
3	Leonel Alvarez (Colombia)	27
4	Carlos Valderrama (Colombia)	27
5	Alex Aguinaga (Ecuador)	25
6	Claudio Taffarel (Brazil)	25
7	Teodoro Fernandez (Peru)	24
8	Angel Romano (Uruguay)	23
9	Djalma Santos (Brazil)	22
10	Claudio Suarez (Mexico)	22

OVERALL TOP SCORERS

1	Norberto Mendez (Argentina)	17
=	Zizinho (Brazil)	17
3	Teodoro Fernandez (Peru)	15
=	Severino Varela (Uruguay)	15
5	Ademir (Brazil)	13
=	Jair da Rosa Pinto (Brazil)	13
=	Gabriel Batistuta (Argentina)	13
=	Jose Manuel Moreno (Argentina)	13
=	Hector Scarone (Uruguay)	13

REPEATING THE FEAT

Uruguay's Pedro Petrone (in 1923 and 1924) and **Gabriel Batistuta** of Argentina (in 1991 and 1995) are the only players to finish as top scorers in the Copa America on two occasions. Batistuta made his Argentina debut just a few days before the 1991 Copa America, in which his starring performances – including a decisive goal in the final – helped him win a transfer from Boca Juniors to Italy's Fiorentina.

LIKE GRANDFATHER, LIKE FATHER, LIKE SON

Diego Forlan's two goals in the 2011 Copa America final helped Uruguay to a 3-0 victory over Paraguay and their record 15th South American championship. They also ensured he followed in family footsteps in lifting the trophy – his father **Pablo** was part of the Uruguay side who won in 1967, when his grandfather Juan Carlos Corazzo was the triumphant coach. Corazzo had previously managed Uruguay's winning team in 1959. The brace against Paraguay put the youngest Forlan level with Hector Scarone as Uruguay's all-time leading scorer, with 31 goals. Yet it was Forlan's strike partner Luis Suarez – opening goal-scorer in the final – who was voted best player of the 2011 tournament.

MAGIC ALEX

When Alex Aguinaga lined up for Ecuador against Uruguay in his country's opening game at the 2004 event, he became only the second man to take part in eight different Copa Americas – joining legendary Uruguayan goalscorer Angel Romano. Aguinaga, a midfielder born in Ibarra on 9 July 1969, played a total of 109 times for his country – 25 of them in the Copa America, a competition that yielded four of his 23 international goals. His Copa America career certainly began well: Ecuador went undefeated for his first four appearances, at the 1987 and 1989 events, but his luck had ran out by the time his Ecuador career was coming to an end: he lost his final seven Copa America matches.

START TO FINISH

Colombia playmaker Carlos Valderrama and defensive midfielder **Leonel Alvarez** played in all 27 of their country's Copa America matches between 1987 and 1995, winning ten, drawing ten and losing seven – including third-place finishes in 1987, 1993 and 1995. Valderrama's two Copa America goals came in his first and final appearances in the competition – in a 2-0 victory over Bolivia in 1987 and a 4-1 thrashing of the United States eight years later.

GUERRERO'S RARE ACHIEVEMENT

Peru endured a disastrous qualification campaign for the 2010 FIFA World Cup, finishing bottom of the South American table – which made their third-place finish at the 2011 Copa America all the more remarkable. There was even more joy for striker **Paolo Guerrero,** whose five goals made him only the third Peruvian ever to finish top scorer at a Copa America – following Teodoro Fernandez in 1939 and Eduardo Malasquez in 1983. Guerrero's haul included a hat-trick in a 4-1 defeat of Venezuela in the third-place play-off.

FANTASTIC FIVES

Four players have scored five goals in one Copa America game: Hector Scarone in Uruguay's 6-0 win over Bolivia in 1926; Juan Marvezzi in Argentina's 6-1 win over Ecuador in 1941; Jose Manuel Moreno in Argentina's 12-0 win over Ecuador in 1942; and Evaristo de Macedo in Brazil's 9-0 win over Colombia in 1957.

LOW-KEY JOSE

The first-ever Copa America goal, in 1916, was scored by Jose Piendibene – setting Uruguay on the way to a 4-0 triumph over Chile. But he is not thought to have marked the moment with any great extravagance – Piendibene, renowned for his sense of fair play, made a point of not celebrating goals, to avoid offending his opponents.

PELE'S INSPIRATION

Brazilian forward **Zizinho** jointly holds the all-time goalscoring record for the Copa America, along with Argentina's Norberto Mendez. Both men struck 17 goals, Zizinho across six tournaments and Mendez three – including the 1945 and 1946 tournaments, which featured both men. Mendez was top scorer once and runner-up twice and won championship medals on all three occasions, while Zizinho's goals helped Brazil take the title only once, in 1949. Zizinho, Pele's footballing idol, would emerge from the 1950 FIFA World Cup as Brazil's top scorer and was also voted the tournament's best player – but was forever traumatized by the hosts' surprise defeat to Uruguay that cost Brazil the title.

SUCCESSFUL INVADERS

Only two foreign coaches have led a country to Copa America glory – Brazilian Danilo Alvim, whose Bolivian side won in 1963, and Englishman Jack Greenwell, Peru coach in 1939. Alvim, who won the tournament as a centre-half with Brazil in 1949, not only coached Bolivia to their one and only Copa America triumph – he did it by beating his native land 5-4 in the final match.

HOME COMFORTS

Uruguay have a unique record in remaining unbeaten in 38 Copa America games on home turf, all played in the country's capital Montevideo – comprising 31 wins, seven draws. The last tournament match they hosted was both a draw and a win – 1-1 against Brazil in 1995, with Uruguay emerging as champions, 5-3 on penalties after Fernando Alvez saved Tulio's penalty.

INVITED GUESTS

1993	Mexico (runners-up), United States
1995	Mexico, United States (fourth)
1997	Costa Rica, Mexico (third)
1999	Japan, Mexico (third)
2001	Costa Rica, Honduras (third), Mexico (runners-up)
2004	Costa Rica, Mexico
2007	Mexico (third), United States
2011	Costa Rica, Mexico

WRONG JUAN

It took 21 years, but Uruguay's Juan Emilio Piriz became the first Copa America player sent off, against Chile in 1937 – the first of 170 dismissals so far. Some 127 of those disgraced players have had a red card flourished in their face, since FIFA introduced the card system for referees in 1970.

MULTI-TASKING

Argentina's **Guillermo Stabile** not only holds the record for most Copa America triumphs as coach – he trounces all opposition. He led his country to the title on no fewer than six occasions – in 1941, 1945, 1946, 1947, 1955 and 1957. No other coach has lifted the trophy more than twice. Stabile coached Argentina from 1939 to 1960, having been appointed at the age of just 34. He lasted for 123 games in charge, winning 83 of them – and still managed to coach three clubs on the side at different times throughout his reign. He remained as Red Star Paris manager during his first year in the Argentina role, then led Argentine club Huracan for the next nine years – before leading domestic rivals Racing Club from 1949 to 1960. Stabile's Argentina may have, unusually, missed out on Copa America success in 1949, but that year brought the first of three Argentina league championships in a row for Stabile's Racing Club.

CAPTAIN CONSISTENT

Uruguay's 1930 World Cup-winning captain **Jose Nasazzi** is the only footballer to be voted player of the tournament at two different Copa America tournaments. Even more impressively, he achieved the feat 12 years apart – first taking the prize in 1923, then again in 1935. He was a Cup winner in 1923, 1924, 1926 and 1935. Nasazzi also captained Uruguay to victory in the 1924 and 1928 Olympic Games and in the 1930 World Cup.

EXTENDED INVITE

Japan are the Copa America participants – as guests – who have featured in fewer games than any other nation, playing three matches at the 1999 competition. They were invited to take part in the 2011 tournament, but pulled out following the devastating 9.0 magnitude earthquake and tsunami that struck the country four months beforehand, and were replaced by Costa Rica – whose up-and-coming stars included striker **Joel Campbell**, who signed for English giants Arsenal just after the tournament.

GOALS AT A PREMIUM

In terms of goals per game, the 2011 Copa America was the second tightest of all time – with only 54 strikes hitting the back of the net in 26 matches, an average of 2.08 per game. Only the 1922 tournament, in Brazil, saw fewer – 22 goals in 11 games, an average of two. Both competitions were a far cry from the prolific 1927 event in Peru, where 37 goals across six games averaged out at 6.17.

SEEING RED

Brazil may have the worst FIFA World Cup disciplinary record, but neighbours Uruguay assume that unenviable position in the Copa America. Uruguayan players have been sent off 31 times, followed by Peru on 24 dismissals, Argentina (23), Brazil and Venezuela (20) apiece, Chile (17), Bolivia and Paraguay (13 each), Colombia, Ecuador and Mexico (nine each), and Costa Rica, Honduras and Japan (one apiece). Only the United States have, so far, made their way through Copa America participations with 11 men on the field throughout. Despite their overall record, however, Uruguay were given the Fair Play Award for the 2011 competition. Venezuela's Tomas Rincon, by contrast, suffered double disgrace – given not one but two straight red cards in matches that tournament.

MARKARIAN MAKES HIS MARK

The 2011 Copa America was not only a Uruguayan success story for the eventual champions, but also third-placed Peru's Uruguayan coach **Sergio Markarian**. Uruguay's winning manager Oscar Washington Tabarez had Markarian as his club coach at Bella Vista in the 1970s. Markarian could also claim some credit for Paraguay's runners-up finish, having been a successful and influential coach in that country during the 1980s, 1990s and early 21st century.

PICTURE CREDITS

The publishers would like to thank the following sources for their kind permission to reproduce the pictures in this book. The page numbers for each of the photographs are listed below, giving the page on which they appear in the book and any location indicator (C-centre, T-top, B-bottom, L-left, R-right).

Action Images: /Matthew Childs: 133BR

Getty Images: 15TL; /2010 Qatar 2022: 40R; /AFP: 17BR, 25L, 38BR, 93C, 134R, 148B, 157TL, 157BL, 167B, 194BR, 199R, 206BL, 208L; /Luis Acosta/AFP: 56BR, 156B; /Nelson Almeida/AFP: 41L; /Anadolu Agency: 32BL, 109BL, 168-169; /Odd Andersen/AFP: 22TR, 39L, 71R, 111C; /Rodrigo Arangua/AFP: 12TL, 152R; /The Asashi Shimbun: 30C; /Anthony Au-Yeung/LatinContent: 10TL; /Brian Bahr: 188BR; /Steve Bardens: 78L; / Dennis Barnard/Fox Photos: 145TL; /Scott Barbour: 170BL; /Lars Baron: 8-9, 98BL, 145B, 173BL; /Juan Barreto/AFP: 154T; /Farouk Batiche/AFP: 15B; /Robyn Beck/AFP: 35TR; /Sandra Behne/Bongarts: 174BL; / Fethi Belaid/AFP: 161BR; /Bentley Archive/Popperfoto: 23BR, 116C, 117BL; /Martin Bernetti/AFP: 150TR, 155BR; /Gunnar Berning/Bongarts: 31BL; /John Berry: 129BR; /Bongarts: 21BL, 74L, 118BR; /Shaun Botterill: 32C, 34BR, 43TR, 44TR, 58T, 99BL, 166TR, 196BR; /Gabriel Bouys/AFP: 71TL, 80B, 126L; /Chris Brunskill Ltd: 161C, 20TR, 24BR, 54BL; /Clive Brunskill: 151R; /Simon Bruty: 154BR; /Rodrigo Buendia/AFP: 141BL; / Eric Cabanis/AFP: 12R; /Jose Cabezas/AFP: 10TR; /Giuseppe Cacace/AFP: 41B, 51BR, 73T; /David Cannon: 56L, 77R, 88BR, 93BR, 112BR, 144TR, 183TR; /Nico Casamassima/AFP: 38BL; /Mario Castillo/Jam Media/ LatinContent: 186BR; /Jean Catuffe: 7BC, 16TR, 26BL, 165B; /Central Press: 115BL; /Central Press/Hulton Archive: 100BR; /Andre Chaco/FotoArena/LatinContent: 37BL; /Graham Chadwick: 112TR; /Yasuyoshi Chiba/AFP: 70TL; /Chung Sung-Jun: 15TR; /Robert Cianflone: 119T, 121L, 187BR; /Michal Cizek/AFP: 105BC; /Timothy A Clary/AFP: 191BR; /Thomas Coex/AFP: 19R; /Fabrice Coffrini/AFP: 10BR, 30BL, 34BL, 99R; /Chris Cole: 32TR, 147BR; /Phil Cole: 95BR, 124C, 162TL, 186BL; /Vinicius Costa: 160TR; /Kevin C Cox: 6R; /Stephane de Sakutin/AFP: 43L; /Carl de Souza/AFP: 27TR; /Adrian Dennis/AFP: 31TR, 196TR; /Philippe Desmazes/AFP: 42TR; / Dimitar Dilkoff/AFP: 90BL, 106L; /Kevork Djansezian: 189C; /Denis Doyle: 81BR, 84L; /Stephen Dunn: 164BR; /Paul Ellis/AFP: 65C; /Elsa: 46-47, 114L, 155L, 184-85; /Darren England: 12BL, 12BR; /Francisco Estrada/ LatinContent: 176BR; /Evening Standard: 172; /Franck Fife/AFP: 59BR, 61TR, 61BL, 163TR, 200TR; /Julian Finney: 87TR, 100L, 154L; /Stu Forster: 37TR, 53TL, 94C, 111BL, 130BL, 131BL, 143TL; /Stuart Franklin: 28TL, 39TR, 99T; /Romeo Gacad/AFP: 96C; /Daniel Garcia/AFP: 204BR; /Lluis Gene/AFP: 75TR; /Paul Gilham: 6BR, 81TR, 85TL, 166C; /Georges Gobet/AFP: 97BR; /Sergio Goya/AFP: 204C; /Otto Greule Jr: 188TR; /Laurence Griffiths: 18T, 24L, 67TL, 80R, 94L, 114TR, 140TR, 173R, 183L, 189TR; /Alex Grimm: 6-7C, 85BR, 107TR; /Jeff Gross: 174TR, 190BR; /Gianluigi Guercia/AFP: 44BL, 69R; /Jack Guez/AFP: 14BR; /Valery Hache/AFP: 31C, 160C, 198BL; /Matthias Hangst: 143B; /Ronny Hartmann/AFP: 126TR; /Alexander Hassenstein/Bongarts: 60TR, 67R, 174L; /Haynes Archive/Popperfoto: 14TR, 101BR, 205BL; /Richard Heathcote: 165R; /Scott Heavey: 54L, 131T; /Alexander Heimann/Bongarts: 191BL; /Marcelo Hernandez/LatinContent: 151TL; /Patrick Hertzog/AFP: 57BR, 60R, 79BR, 128TR; /Mike Hewitt: 6TR, 103BR, 106B, 149BL; /Antonia Hille: 136C; /Boris Horvat/ AFP: 76BL, 197T; /Hulton Archive: 22BL, 30BR, 101TR; /isifa: 121BR; /Karim Jaafar/AFP: 167L, 170C, 175TR, 176L, 179BR; /Amin Mohammad Jamali: 3, 7TL, 85BL; /Jose Jordan/AFP: 84BR; /Jasper Juinen: 52C, 82C, 83TL, 196L; /Gorm Kallestad/AFP: 104BL; /Keystone: 56TR, 100BL, 115BR; /Keystone/Hulton Archive: 69BL, 83BL; /Saeed Khan/AFP: 10BL; /Ian Kington/AFP: 54TR; /Ross Kinnaird: 26TR; /Pedro Kirilos/LatinContent: 43R; /Toshifumi Kitamura/AFP: 13C, 88T; /Joe Klamar/AFP: 95L, 105TR; /Mark Kolbe: 171TL; /Patrick Kovarik/AFP: 135C; /Kirill Kudryavtsev/AFP: 43B, 114B; /LatinContent: 202-203; /David Leah: 29TL; /David Leah/ Mexsport: 186TR; /Christopher Lee: 120TR, 121TR, 123C; /Bryn Lennon: 110TR; /Francisco Leong/AFP: 62TR, 115C; /Matthew Lewis: 25B, 106TR; /Alex Livesey: 11TR, 23R, 76BR, 92TR, 96TR, 103TR, 115TL, 123TL, 130C, 149R, 177BR, 201TR; /Juan Mabromata/AFP: 89TL; /John MacDougall/AFP: 113BR; /Ian MacNicol: 7BL, 22TR; /Pierre-Philippe Marcou/AFP: 24TR, 82TL, 164TL; /Francois-Xavier Marit/AFP: 35TL, 48-49; /Clive Mason: 19BL, 64L, 87BR, 92BL, 95TR, 125C, 127BL, 165TL; /Jamie McDonald: 45, 76T, 94BR, 100TR, 110C, 122TR, 180TL, 187C; /Chris McGrath: 141TR; /Miguel Medina/AFP: 57TR; /Buda Mendes: 7, 138-139; /Buda Mendes/ LatinContent: 153TR, 207TR; /Philippe Merle/AFP: 157R; /Damien Meyer/AFP: 192-193; /Douglas Miller/Keystone: 50BL; /Filippo Monteforte/AFP: 132C; /Dean Mouhtaropoulos: 21TR, 171TR; /Peter Muhly/AFP: 110BR, 134BL; /Marwan Naamani/AFP: 180BR; /Jonathan Nackstrand/AFP: 199L; /Hoang Dinh Nam/AFP: 178BL, 188C; /Mark Nolan: 171BR; /Jeff Pachoud/AFP: 195C; /Valerio Pennicino: 69TL; /Doug Pensinger: 52BR; /Ryan Pierse: 28B, 132BL, 182TR, 190L; /Jan Pitman/Bongarts: 36TR; /Hrvoje Polan/AFP: 90C, 92C; /Joern Pollex: 62BL, 66R, 97TL, 163C; /Popperfoto: 13BR, 21BR, 23L, 28C, 51C, 58BL, 64BR, 66BL, 67B, 72BR, 91BR, 102BL, 112L, 122C, 148L, 151BL, 175L, 178R, 179T, 181B, 189BL, 194BL, 198TR, 200B, 207BL, 208BR; /Anne-Christine Poujoulat/AFP: 109BR; /Mike Powell: 40L; /Savo Prelevic/AFP: 137B; /Craig Prentis: 187TR; /Adam Pretty: 147TR; /Gary M Prior: 148TR; /Ben Radford: 29BR, 149C, 173T; /Roslan Rahman/AFP: 181TR; /Aizar Raldes/AFP: 156TL; /Michael Regan: 50TR, 55TR, 128B, 131BR; /Rafa Rivas/AFP: 83R; /Miguel Rojo/AFP: 142TL, 157TR, 209TL; /Rolls Press/Popperfoto: 53B, 71B, 146TR; /Clive Rose: 17TR, 22TL, 33BL, 34TL, 36BL, 52TL, 117C, 119BL, 129BL, 144BL, 152BL; /Martin Rose: 59C, 63TR; /Martin Rose/Bongarts: 127TR, 132BR; /STR/AFP: 137TR, 177TR; /Jewel Samad/AFP: 109TR; /Mark Sandten/Bongarts: 39BR, 162BL; /Issouf Sanogo/AFP: 163BL, 167TR; /Genia Savilov/AFP: 107L; /Roberto Schmidt/AFP: 18BL; /Antonio Scorza/AFP: 153BL; /Lefty Shivambu/ Gallo Images: 166L; /Torsten Silz/AFP: 25TR; /Janek Skarzynski/AFP: 201BL; /Javier Soriano/AFP: 17L, 158-159, 197BR; /Jamie Squire: 160BR, 161TL; /Michael Steele: 34TR, 91T, 122BL; /Srdjan Stevanovic: 119R; / Patrik Stollarz/AFP: 7C, 38TR, 64TR, 135BL; /Stringer/AFP: 127BR; /Graham Stuart/AFP: 116TR; /Henri Szwarc/Bongarts: 195BL; /Bob Thomas: 36C, 42B, 44BR, 65R, 68TR, 70BL, 70BR, 86TR, 97R, 102TR, 103C, 103BL, 107BR, 108TR, 110BL, 150BL, 116L, 130TR, 130BR, 142TR, 143C, 146BL, 153BR, 161TL, 175BR; /Bob Thomas/Popperfoto: 11B, 38TC, 66TL, 84TR, 136BL, 145TR; /Mark Thompson: 104TR; /John Thys/AFP: 88BL, 89R, 135R; /Omar Torres/AFP: 176TR, 209BR; /Pedro Ugarte/AFP: 27B; /VI Images: 75TL, 78B, 79T; /Robert van den Brugge/AFP: 86BL; /Claudio Villa: 73BL, 136BR; /Claudio Villa/Grazia Neri: 72TR; /Nigel Waldon: 105BL; /Ian Walton: 77BL, 82B, 190TR

Press Association Images: 118TR, 142R, 206BR; /ABACA Press: 19TL; /AP: 20BL; /Matthew Ashton: 147C, 171C, 182BL, 191TR; /Barry Coombs: 98TR; /Malcolm Croft: 13TL; /DPA: 16BL, 60L, 65TL, 75B, 170TR; /Sean Dempsey: 63BR; /Paulo Duarte/AP: 108L, 108C; /Denis Farrell/AP: 40B; /Dominic Favre/AP: 124BR; /Gouhier-Hahn-Orban/ABACA: 124TR; /Jae C Hong/AP: 183B; /Intime Sports/AP: 98C; /Ross Kinnaird: 207C; /Tony Marshall: 21TL, 72L, 77TL, 126B, 146TL, 205TR; /Cathal McNaughton: 50C; /Phil O'Brien: 68BL; /Natacha Pisarenko/AP: 208C; /Nick Potts: 57BL; /Duncan Raban: 144BR; /Peter Robinson: 33TR, 63L, 73BR, 74TR, 102C, 116BR, 118L, 120BL, 129TR, 140L; /S&G and Barratts: 30TR, 51T, 53TR, 55B, 108BR, 111BR; /SMG: 117TR; /Ariel Schalit/AP: 162R; /Murad Sezer/AP: 61C; /Sven Simon: 146BR; /Neal Simpson: 89BL, 91BL, 113TR, 125BR, 206T; /Topham Picturepoint: 123BL, 134TL, 140B; /John Walton: 133TR, 143TR; /Witters: 35B

Every effort has been made to acknowledge correctly and contact the source and/or copyright holder of each picture and Imagine Publishing apologises for any unintentional errors or omissions that will be corrected in future editions of this book.